P9-BJK-873

58 16

Mexican-American Folklore

Mexican-American Folklore

Legends, Songs, Festivals, Proverbs, Crafts, Tales of Saints, of Revolutionaries, and More

Compiled and edited by

John O. West

This volume is a part of
The American Folklore Series
W.K. McNeil, General Editor

August House / Little Rock
PUBLISHERS

Published by August House, Inc.,
P.O. Box 3223, Little Rock, Arkansas, 72203,
501-663-7300.

Printed in the United States of America

10 9 8 7 6 5 4 3 2 1

LIBRARY OF CONGRESS CATALOGING-IN-PUBLICATION DATA

West, John O.
Mexican-American folklore.
(The American folklore series)
Includes index.
1. Mexican Americans—Folklore.
I. Title. II. Series.
GR111.M49W47 1988 398'.08968073 88-3367
ISBN 0-87483-060-5 (alk. paper)
ISBN 0-87484-059-1 (pbk.:alk. paper)
First Edition, 1988

Cover illustration by José Cisneros
Production artwork by Ira L. Hocut
Typography by Diversified Graphics, Little Rock, Arkansas
Design direction by Ted Parkhurst
Project direction by Hope Coulter

This book is printed on archival-quality paper which meets the guidelines for performance and durability of the Committee on Production Guidelines for Book Longevity of the Council on Library Resources.

AUGUST HOUSE, INC. PUBLISHERS LITTLE ROCK

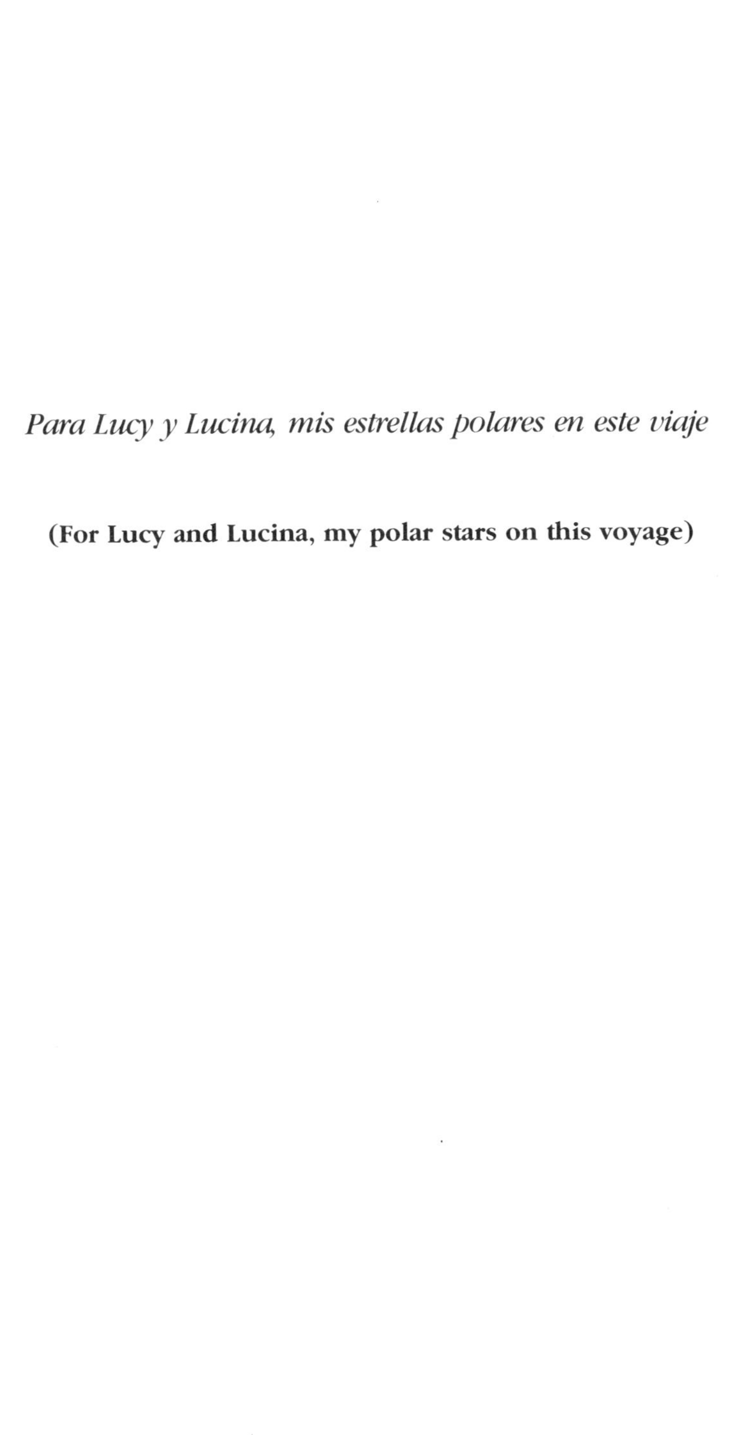

Para Lucy y Lucina, mis estrellas polares en este viaje

(For Lucy and Lucina, my polar stars on this voyage)

Contents

Introduction

THE FOLKLORE OF few ethnic groups in the United States has been so frequently collected as that of the Mexican-American. Most of the significant collections and studies have dealt with the Southwest, and such an emphasis is understandable because the greatest concentration of Mexican-Americans is in that region—California, Texas, and Arizona being the three leading population centers. Yet in a sense the publications distort our view of the culture by suggesting, if only by implication, that there are no substantive Mexican-American traditions outside this five-state area. There are a few authors, however, who have concentrated on other parts of the United States.

Those who have looked outside the Southwest for Mexican-American lore have concentrated on Florida, another state that in recent years has come to be a center of Hispanic-American population. At least some of this work resulted from efforts to change an existing situation regarding folklore scholarship. Traditionally folklorists in both Latin and North America have been more knowledgeable about the development of their field in Europe than in their own hemisphere. Beginning in the late 1930s, some scholars attempted to make folklorists more aware of the work of colleagues in North and South America. Noteworthy among these personalities was Ralph Steele Boggs, a widely respected authority on Pan American and Spanish folklore. In an attempt to build bridges between the two Americas, Boggs initiated the publication in 1937 of an annual bibliography published in *Southern Folklore Quarterly,* which continued through 1972. During the first twenty-two years Boggs himself compiled these bibliographies, emphasizing Latin American and Mexican-American items as did his successors Américo Paredes and Merle Simmons.

Boggs, of course, did much more than just compile bibliographies of publications dealing with Mexican-American folklore. His importance extended far beyond that to include lecturing, writing, and teaching. Beginning in 1929 at the University of North Carolina and continuing later at the University of Miami, Boggs was for years prominent as a professor with a special interest in all aspects of Hispanic-American folklore, a role that has not entirely diminished even though he has been retired now for several years. It was primarily due to his influence that a series of articles on Spanish folklore in

Tampa was written and published in *Southern Folklore Quarterly.*[1] He was also largely responsible for the founding of *Folklore Americas,* a journal he edited from 1941 to 1965, and for the initiation of a number of joint publications involving Latin American and North American scholars. Some of these projects involved Mexican-American traditions.

None of the other people writing on non-Southwest Mexican-American folklore achieved the fame or influence of Boggs, but they did touch upon some important areas of research. Carlota Garfías treated Chicano traditions in New York City.[2] Norman D. Humphrey discussed dietary and health practices of Mexican-Americans in Detroit, a topic that has received relatively little attention from folklorists.[3] Interestingly, most of the research centered on city dwellers rather than rural residents, in other words just the opposite of most American folklore study during the first half of the twentieth century. Finally, the publications are primarily collections, arranged mainly by genre, rather than theoretical works. This situation is understandable because hypothesizing is not very useful until basic collecting has been done.

The difference in quantity between publications on non-Southwestern and Southwestern Mexican-American lore is dramatically illustrated by bibliographies. Except for general compilations like Charles Haywood's *A Bibliography of North American Folklore and Folksong* there are no bibliographies devoted to the non-Southwestern material. On the other hand, there are several devoted to Southwestern items, of which the two most extensive are Marjorie F. Tully and Juan B. Rael's *An Annotated Bibliography of Spanish Folklore in New Mexico and Southern Colorado* (1950) and Michael Heisley's *An Annotated Bibliography of Chicano Folklore from the Southwestern United States* (1977). In addition, there are several more specialized bibliographies, such as Merle Simmons's *A Bibliography of the Romance and Related Forms in Spanish America,* (1963) and there is even Joseph A. Clark Moreno's "A Bibliography of Bibliographies Relating to Studies of Mexican-Americans."[4] Then there are general articles such as Américo Paredes's "El Folklore de los Grupos de Origen Mexicano en Estados Unidos," which categorizes Mexican-Americans by regional groups and discusses various types of folklore unique to this group.[5] All of these publications are based primarily, in most cases solely, on Southwestern items.

Publications on Southwestern Mexican-American folklore date from a relatively early age in the history of American folklore studies and cover a wide range of genres. These works treat folk narrative, folk music, folk speech, customs and beliefs, traditional drama, folk games and play, architecture, foodways, clothing, and folk art. In other words, just about the entire spectrum of folklore as currently understood is covered in these writings but, obviously, some genres have received greater attention than others. Games and those topics coming under the heading of what folklorists call material culture (architecture, for example) have had less consideration than narratives, music, customs, beliefs, and speech. Much the same can be said about American folklore studies generally, for historically traditions such as folk music and narratives are the first to appeal to collectors.

One of the premier personalities in the study of Mexican-American lore is Aurelio Macedonio Espinosa, a native of Colorado who became known as a pioneer in the study of New Mexico's folklore. From 1902 to 1910 he was associated with the University of New Mexico in Albuquerque; the remainder of his academic career was spent at Stanford University. Espinosa's total of over 100 books, articles, and monographs covered many genres, but his main contributions were in the areas of dialect studies and folk narratives. His 1909 dissertation from the University of Chicago, "Studies in New Mexican Spanish," was a pioneering study tracing the development of various strains of Spanish as spoken by New Mexicans. Published in 1909 when originally written, this book was updated and a widely acclaimed Spanish version issued in 1946. One reviewer proclaimed that Espinosa's examination of the Spanish dialect of New Mexico was the most detailed investigation of any regional variety of Spanish.[6] This volume, in its 1909 form, was the basic source of information on Mexican-American speech used by H.L. Mencken for *The American Language* (1918).

Espinosa considered folklore an integral part of a culture and publicized New Mexico's folklore as part of his campaign to promote the teaching of Spanish language and literature. Thus, in one of his earliest publications, *The Spanish Language in New Mexico and Southern Colorado* (1911), he included a chapter on "New Mexican Spanish Folklore" that contained the texts of some *versos* and proverbs as well as lists of titles of folktales and other forms of oral tradition. A year earlier, in 1910, he started a series of articles on "New Mexican Spanish Folklore" that appeared over a period of six years. Many of these collections dealt with folk narratives; one was even concerned with anecdotes, a type of narrative not commonly published by folklorists of the time.[7] The initial entry in this series dealt with what Espinosa called myths, although nowadays folklorists would call most of these narratives legends for the simple reason that many of these accounts of witches, dwarves, the Devil, and monsters are set in historic times. Three succeeding issues contained folk narratives while others of the eleven articles treated proverbs, riddles, and various other genres. Espinosa later published an article on Spanish language folktales from California and a 1951 essay in the *Journal of American Folklore* on the same topic. In the latter he attempted to delineate the characteristic groups and types of folktales, collected from Spanish-speaking Americans, that reflect a "civilization that is basically and fundamentally Spanish."[8]

Espinosa's major statement about Mexican-American folk narrative, and all other aspects of what he referred to as folk literature, did not appear until nearly three decades after his death. In the late 1930s he completed a manuscript about Mexican-American folklore that remained unpublished at the time of his death in 1958. It finally appeared in 1985, as edited by his son, J. Manuel Espinosa, under the title *The Folklore of Spain in the American Southwest: Traditional Spanish Folk Literature in Northern New Mexico and Southern Colorado.* The book, whose orientation is evident from the title, distills Aurelio's views on Mexican-American oral traditions. Two chapters devoted to folk narratives put forth Espinosa's argument that while the Spanish language folktales influenced the traditions of New Mexican Indians, the influence did not go in the other direction. In this way Mexican-American folk narrative traditions differ from those of Mexico.

Espinosa's interest in folk narrative was continued by his son, J. Manuel Espinosa. Not as prolific a writer as Aurelio, the younger Espinosa did produce one major work on folk narrative. His *Spanish Folk-tales from New Mexico* (1937) appeared as Volume 30 in the Memoir Series of the American Folklore Society. This collection of 114 narratives recorded by Espinosa in the summer of 1931 from Spanish-speaking inhabitants of the Rio Grande region of northern New Mexico was, for its time, a model of how a folktale collection should be presented. It included accurately rendered texts with English summaries and brief notes about the individual narrators. Although theoretically the younger Espinosa generally agreed with his father's ideas about Mexican-American folklore, that is implied rather than explicitly stated in the book.

A more prolific writer of J. Manuel Espinosa's generation was Juan B. Rael, who like Aurelio Espinosa was a professor at Stanford University. His academic affiliation was not the only thing Rael shared with the elder Espinosa. Rael also did important work in several areas of Mexican-American folklore including bibliography, folksong, folk drama, and folk speech. His first love, however, was folk narrative; his 1937 Ph.D. dissertation "A Study of the Phonology and Morphology of New Mexican Spanish Based on a Collection of 410 Folk Tales" combined his interests in folk tales and speech.[9] Later that same year Rael published his first article on folk narrative, a study of thirty-three versions of the international tale type "Theft of butter (honey) by playing godfather," which is Type 15 in Aarne-Thompson's *Types of the Folktale.*[10] Two years later, in 1939, Rael published the first of a two-part collection he compiled while doing fieldwork in Colorado and New Mexico in 1930. Under the title "Cuentos Españoles de Colorado y de Nuevo Méjico" a total of 111 folktale texts are given, the first article being devoted to narratives thought to be of European origin, the second to indigenous items.[11] Rael concluded his folk narrative work with a two-volume collection, also titled *Cuentos Españoles de Colorado y de Nuevo Méjico* (1940). This book included some of the items in the *Journal of American Folklore* articles and other texts recorded by Rael. Unfortunately, although, Rael takes some pains to trace the histories of the stories, he tells readers very little about the narrators.

Arthur L. Campa, another significant scholar who worked in many genres of

Mexican-American folklore, is primarily remembered for his contributions to the study of folk narrative and folksong. Born in Mexico to American missionary parents, he grew up in West Texas where his family moved in 1914 after his father was killed by Pancho Villa. In 1930 he submitted an M.A. thesis on "New Mexico Spanish Folk-Tales" to the University of New Mexico and ten years later, in 1940, received the Ph.D. from Columbia University with a dissertation on "Spanish Folksongs in New Mexico." Then he spent twenty-six years as Chairman of the Department of Modern Languages and Literature at the University of Denver. Although Campa worked in the areas of folk speech, customs, foodways, and folk drama, and finished up his career with the important survey volume *Hispanic Culture in the Southwest* (1978), his main interests were revealed by his M.A. thesis and Ph.D. dissertation. His major contribution to Mexican-American folk narrative studies was *Treasure of the Sangre de Cristos: Tales and Traditions of the Spanish Southwest* (1963), a general study dealing with legends of lost treasures, mines, and pioneer life. In his preface Campa speaks at some length about traditional tale tellers he encountered and their method of presenting narratives. Considering such mention one might expect faithful renderings of oral tales, but Campa's book instead offers greatly rewritten accounts derived from the material he collected. Thus, *Treasure of the Sangre de Cristos* adequately presents several themes commonly found in Mexican-American folk narratives but is wholly inadequate as an example of their style of presentation.

Anthropologist Helen Zunser also merits mention here for one publication, the lengthy article "A New Mexican Village," that appeared in the *Journal of American Folklore*. This essay is important because it is one of the first to place Mexican-American traditions in context. Zunser provides an ethnographic account of the town of Hot Springs in northeastern New Mexico. Among the topics covered are customs, beliefs about courtship and marriage, children's games, religious holidays, and, of course, narratives. Among the latter are some widely known tales, several of which are localized versions of stories reported by the Grimm brothers. Zunser also commented on what she considered a curious attitude:

> Our friends called themselves Spanish Americans, but called their language Mexican. There was deep antagonism in their attitude towards the people and country of "Old Mexico" and they resented being called Mexicans. "Bad country, old Mexico. Too many bandits. Kill all the time, have long knives. Like to fight." . . . They always spoke of temperamental differences, as if the Mexicans were much more violent than they were. Yet we knew of individual cases where Old and New Mexicans had been friends, and we were told that their language differences were slight.[12]

Writers and collectors associated with the Texas Folklore Society have also made great contributions to the collection and study of Mexican-American folk narrative. Founded in 1909 by John Avery Lomax and Leonidas Warren Payne, Jr., the society is the second oldest active folklore organization in the United States. Its first publication appeared in 1916, and in 1923 the society began issuing its annual book to members. During a period of forty-eight years J. Frank Dobie, Mody C. Boatright, and William M. Hudson produced over thirty volumes. In 1971 the society's office was moved from the University of Texas to the Stephen F. Austin State University campus in Nacogdoches; since that time Francis E. Abernethy has been the secretary-editor. Most of the annual volumes pay some attention to Mexican-American traditions and a few, such as *Puro Mexicano* (1935), are primarily concerned with them. In addition, Dobie published a number of books on his own that deal in varying degrees with Mexican-American folk narrative. *Coronado's Children: Tales of Lost Mines and Buried Treasures of the Southwest* (1930) is typical. This volume contains both Anglo and Mexican-American lore in literary retellings.

Some students of Mexican-American folk narrative got their start as a result of federally funded projects during the Depression of the 1930s. Among the most important of these personalities is Lorin W. Brown, Jr., who recorded a vast amount of material from 1936 to 1941 while a member of the New Mexico Federal Writers' Project. Given the task of collecting Hispanic folklife in northern New Mexico, Brown concentrated on interviewing elderly residents of isolated communities such as Cordova and Truchas. This type of collecting is today often sneeringly dismissed as the gathering of survivals but in the 1930s it was not passé, and, regardless of what one thinks of the motives behind the fieldwork, it cannot honestly be denied that Brown gathered much useful data. Unfortunately, most of the material he recorded remained in manuscript form until shortly before his death in 1978. Then in the last months of his life Brown went through the items collected in the 1930s with the intent of publishing the best texts. This project was brought to completion by Charles L. Briggs and Marta Weigle, being issued as *Hispanic Folklife of New Mexico (1978).*

Brown's book includes several genres of folklore but is especially rich in folk narratives. Enormously increasing its value are numerous notes that often give extensive background on informants and the circumstances of the collection. Moreover, the method of presentation is intended to set materials in context rather than give them as seemingly superorganic texts separated from people and communities. Briggs and Weigle explain how they arranged material in order to bring the folk and their lore together: "These texts have been organized to give an orderly, readable overview of Hispanic history and village life in the region. They are woven together with brief, interspersed editorial remarks. Occasional further editorial matter is bracketed within the reprinted material. Otherwise, all manuscripts appear substantially as Brown submitted them."[13]

One other posthumous publication based on Brown's collection merits mention here. Between 1937 and 1939 he recorded a number of legends from Guadalupe Martínez of Cordova, an old woman who tended the village chapel. Between June 1938 and July 1939 Bright Lynn, a student at New Mexico Normal University (now New Mexico Highlands), collected an extensive body of legends and magic tales from Guadalupe Bara de Gallegos of Las Vegas. Texts recorded by the two collectors were combined to produce *Two Guadalupes: Hispanic Legends and Magic Tales from Northern New Mexico* (1987). This book compares the narratives of the upper-class Gallegos with those told by Martínez, a member of the village working class. Considerable biographical detail is given about both women and texts are presented as recorded. The net result is a volume that reveals a great deal about the way folk narrative functions in the lives of two Mexican-American women. With approximately one-third of its total pages devoted to a discussion of the backgrounds of the two narrators it is safe to say that *Two Guadalupes* is as much concerned with the informants as their texts. That feature virtually makes it unique among American folk narrative publications.

Elaine K. Miller's *Mexican Folk Narrative from the Los Angeles Area* (1973) is another collection that is in several respects exemplary. Eighty-two narratives from twenty-seven informants are given under six headings, each section prefaced by scholarly commentary. While Miller's focus is clearly textual she does not ignore the narrators. She includes a section of informant biographies and tells much about the 1966-67 fieldwork during which she collected the texts. Tales are presented in the colloquial Spanish in which Miller recorded them; English summaries and comparative notes are provided. It is also noteworthy that this material is identified as Mexican rather than Hispanic, as is the case with most previous collections.

Perhaps less well-known but equally significant are *Hispanic Folktales from New Mexico* (1977) and *Hispanic Legends from New Mexico* (1980), selections taken from the extensive files accumulated by Ralph De Loy Jameson at New Mexico Highlands University. Jameson spent much of his career as a teacher and writer in Europe and China, later working for the Library of Congress and the National Red Cross before coming to the Las Vegas school for the last twelve years of his life. The 900 texts in the two books provided an extensive sampling of oral narratives in and around Las Vegas. The legend volume is of special interest because it is the largest compilation of such narratives among Mexican-Americans yet published. A lengthy introduction by Stanley L. Robe, a renowned scholar of Hispanic folk narrative, discusses the major themes found in the collection. Three aspects of traditional belief are of major concern to Jameson's informants—witchcraft, ghostly apparitions, and the presence of the Devil in physical form. Robe also provides comparative notes, making this in a purely textual sense an ideal collection. It shares one flaw with most narrative compilations, namely that it reveals little about the informants and their sources for the tales. Thus, the reader is left without much idea of how the narrators shaped their texts. In other words, one learns about the more mechanical aspects of the tradition but not much about the human aspects.

An equally voluminous body of material has been unearthed on Mexican-American musical traditions, so much in fact that, as in the discussion of folk narrative publications, it is possible to mention here only some of the most significant. One of the most colorful figures involved in the recording of this tradition was also one of the first students of Mexican-American folklore. Charles F. Lummis was a Massachusetts native who first gained fame in 1884 for a five-month walk from Cincinnati to Los Angeles, a feat he recounted in *A Tramp across the Continent* (1892). This was just the sort of flamboyant adventure for which Lummis became known, but it was important in his career because it brought him to the Southwest for the first time. Lummis almost immediately thought of the area as his own special province.

> . . . Once I had reached Spanish America and the hearts of its people, I realized that this was where I belonged.
>
> Though my conscience was Puritan, my whole imagination and sympathy and feeling were Latin. That is, essentially Spanish. Apparently they always had been, for now that I had gotten away from the repressive influence of my birthplace I began to see that the generous and bubbling boyish impulses which had been considerably frosted in New England were, after all, my birthright.[14]

It is hardly necessary to say that Lummis spent the remainder of his life in the Southwest.

A man given to colorful dress and colorful, and often unconventional, prose, Lummis relished being a character. He also found folksongs of Spanish origin especially appealing, noting that they had "a peculiar fascination, a naiveté, and yet a vividness and life, a richness of melody with a certain resilience and willfulness which give it a preeminent appeal. It has more music in it, more Rhythm, more Grace. It is more simpatica. It not only joys my hearing and tickles my pulses but cuddles my heart more happily than the songs of any of the score of other nationalities to which I have given friendly ear."[15] He soon came to believe that these songs were the musical record of a vanishing way of life in the Southwest, an idea that spurred him on to record these numbers before they were lost. So, for a reason common in the history of folklore collecting, Lummis gathered nearly 600 songs in the years from 1888 to 1928. A sampling of fourteen pieces appeared in *Spanish Songs of Old California* (1923), a book that has remained in print until the present.

Lummis's brief selection of fourteen songs was in some respects ahead of its time. For example, it included musical transcriptions, a feature relatively uncommon in folksong collections of the day. Such transcriptions were required because the book was issued as part of the American Folk-Song Series published by G. Schirmer. Actually, Arthur Farwell's piano accompaniments were not in keeping with the spirit of the material, but at the time no better musical settings of songs like these were generally available. Lummis's collection also provided both Spanish lyrics and English translations but, like other collections of that day, revealed little about the individuals who sang these songs.

Although some contemporaries, such as John G. Bourke in "Notes on the Language and Folk-Usage of the Rio Grande Valley," made brief comments on musical traditions, Lummis had no rivals in the recording of Mexican-American songs until Eleanor Hague started gathering her collection. A member of a well-to-do Stockbridge, Massachusetts, family, Hague spent some time in the first two decades of the twentieth century collecting Spanish language music materials, primarily in California. Beginning in 1911 she published many of the items she collected in a series of articles in the *Journal of American Folklore,* concluding her work on this topic with *Early Spanish California Folksongs* (1922), a book aimed at a popular audience.[16] More significant from a scholarly standpoint is *Spanish-American Folk-Songs* (1917), issued as Volume 10 in the Memoir Series of the American Folklore Society. This collection of ninety-five songs with Spanish and English lyrics and melody lines was recorded from eighteen informants, including the wife of writer Dane Coolidge and a priest named O'Sullivan. Songs were taken down from the singing of Mexican-Americans, South Americans, and Cubans. Hague emphasized that the songs she presented were widely traveled but, surprisingly, did this not by means of comparative notes but by generalizations such as "very familiar in Spain and Spanish America."[17] Totally predictable, though, was Hague's reason for recording songs. Indeed, her motivation as explained in the following passage is very similar to that which until recently inspired most collectors of folksongs and other oral traditions:

> Unfortunately, these songs are fast dying out: for, as a rule, the younger generation is more apt to indulge in rag-time than in the songs of its parents. This tendency is prevalent to a greater extent here than in Mexico, but, sad to say, it is increasing in both countries. In the last ten years even, many of the old singers have died; and, as a rule, their songs have died with them, unrecorded, and untransmitted by word of mouth.[18]

John D. Robb, longtime faculty member of the University of New Mexico, spent more years than anyone since Charles Lummis recording Mexican-American folk music. Unlike most collectors of traditional music, Robb had an excellent background in classical music. He studied musical composition under Darius Milhaud; other teachers included Roy Harris, Nadia Boulanger, and Paul Hindemith. A prolific composer who wrote the musical play that became *The Fantastiks,* Robb spent nearly forty years collecting folk music in New Mexico, starting in 1942 and concluding with the publication of *Hispanic Folk Music of New Mexico and the Southwest: A Self-Portrait of a People* (1980). Over 700 songs with musical transcriptions are included along with comparative information. Several photos of singers and, in many cases, lengthy biographical comments as well as descriptions of collecting situations are given. All of this material combined produced the most comprehensive and important collection of Hispanic-American folk music yet published.

Américo Paredes is responsible for two classic works on Mexican-American folksong, including the best study of a single song. A native of Brownsville, Texas, Paredes got his Ph.D. at the University of Texas with a dissertation that later became *"With His Pistol in His Hand": A Border Ballad and Its Hero* (1958). This is a study of "El Corrido de Gregorio Cortez," which tells the story of Gregorio Cortez Lira (1875-1916). A ranchhand of Mexican parentage, he became a hero to the borderfolk in 1901 as a result of a misunderstanding in which a Texas sheriff was killed. Cortez was eventually captured and sentenced to prison, and died within three years of his release. In legend and corrido he still lives, and Paredes deftly traces his apotheosis as folk hero in both. An absorbing study, *"With His Pistol in His Hand"* remains one of the best examinations of a narrative folksong and its protagonist.

Eighteen years later Paredes produced a second important book, this one more in the vein of Robb's survey publication. *A Texas-Mexican Cancionero: Folksongs of the Lower Border* (1976) is among the first folksong volumes to emphasize Mexican rather than Spanish heritage. This collection of sixty-six songs was compiled with both scholarly and general audiences in mind. Designed as a songbook and a representative collection of folksongs from the Texas-Mexico border, the book gives "examples of the main forms and the principal themes of Texas-Mexican folksong."[19] Broken down into five sections, each prefaced by lengthy, informative essays, the volume contains historical information about each song and some consideration of its meaning to those who keep the tradition alive. Moreover, Paredes provides considerable detail about the manner of performing. The total reveals a scholar with an impressive command of border folksong.

Two other works on Mexican-American folksong merit mention here. Dan William Dickey's *The Kennedy Corridos: A Study of the Ballads of a Mexican American Hero* (1978) is important as a study of the changes commercial recording, urbanization, and immigration have brought to the corrido tradition. Furthermore, the book provides ample evidence that Mexican-American narrative folksong is still vital and evolving. Manuel Pena's *The Texas-Mexican Conjunto: History of a Working Class Music* (1985) is a highly theoretical attempt "to describe *conjunto*'s [a type of traditional accordion music that developed around 1930] stylistic evolution and to analyze the link between this evolution and the fundamental changes Texas-Mexican society entered into as a result of World War II."[20] Pena gives a chronological account of the music's development, beginning with its late-nineteenth century precursors and going through the 1970s, placing strong emphasis on the role of record companies and key performers. The author's Marxist views often obstruct his history. For example, despite his awareness of the media and its potential for influencing tradition, he often sees musical developments arising largely from class and ethnic consciousness when reality seems more complex. Nevertheless, Pena's book is the best account to date of this particular form of Mexican-American music.

Folk speech is an area of research that is only now beginning to receive much attention. Actually, at an early date several writers commented on the subject, but even so the quantity of publications is not overwhelming. When one confines the count to significant works the total is even smaller. Many early collections, such as Bourke's article previously mentioned, were merely attempts to catalogue survivals. More valuable from a modern standpoint are two articles by Rosan Jordan and Sylvia Grider. In "Language Loyalty and Folklore Studies: The Mexican-American," Jordan investigates the relationships between the use of language and a sense of ethnic identity and acculturation.[21] She uses several humorous anecdotes to illustrate the tension wrought by conflicting cultural pressures among Mexican-Americans. This is a fine example of an essay in which the author goes beyond merely presenting data and attempts to tell what the material means.

Grider's "*Con Safos:* Mexican-Americans, Names, and Graffiti" is a survey of the uses and meanings of the untranslatable term *con safos* in graffiti found in urban Mexican-American communities.[22] Unlike most graffiti that has been studied, con safos is not "dirty," humorous, or erotic; it is used by Mexican-Americans to protect their written names. Grider includes sketches from Dallas, Texas, showing how the phrase is used, breaking the material into a three-part classification system consisting of simple con safos, enclosed names, and combined motifs. Most articles on folk language would stop there but Grider goes further, adding the comments and beliefs of the people who use the term. By so doing she makes this one of the more worthwhile articles on folk speech in any American ethnic group.

Important collections of Mexican-American riddles have been published by Arthur L. Campa, Aurelio M. Espinosa, and Aurora Lucero-White Lea, among others. There have been several articles and brief collections of proverbs but the most prolific scholar of this genre of Mexican-American lore is Shirley Lease Arora. Author of numerous articles on paremiology, including a series of essays on Spanish language proverbial comparisons and exaggerations, Arora considers the imagery, structure, formulas, and usage of sayings recorded primarily in the Los Angeles area.[23] Most of her articles include detailed annotations and much bibliographic information.

Studies of American custom, belief, and ritual generally focus on exotic or unusual traditions of this type. This statement is also true of examinations of these genres among Mexican-Americans. This trend undoubtedly accounts for the inordinately large number of publications on Los Hermanos Penitentes, or Brothers of Our Father Jesus. This lay religious organization related to the Roman Catholic Church is found primarily in northern New Mexico and southern Colorado, men of Hispanic descent making up virtually its entire membership. Penitente Lenten processions involving cross-bearing and self-flagellation combined with the Brotherhood's well-known secrecy have made this group appealing in a sensationalistic way. These features were definitely the main reason such early authors as Charles F. Lummis were interested in the order. Lummis photographed their Easter rites during the time he lived with the Penitentes in the early 1890s.

Lummis was only one of dozens of writers of varying skills who manifested interest in the Penitentes. Marta Weigle's *Brothers of Light, Brothers of Blood: The Penitentes of the Southwest* (1976) is the recent, and most comprehensive, look at the brotherhood. Through a variety of documents Weigle traces the history and development of the Penitentes and discusses their contributions to Southwestern life. Rather than just a bizarre bunch of fanatics as they have often been pictured, Weigle effectively argues that the Brothers played an important role on the frontier. Through various acts of charity, supervision of wakes, funerals, and religious observances, the Penitentes were a strong force insuring community survival and spiritual life in a large portion of the Southwest. Lucid writing and an excellent synthesis of disparate materials make Weigle's book important not only for folklorists but for scholars interested in religious history and Southwestern culture as well.

Among those scholars of Mexican-American custom and belief who have not dwelled on the Penitentes, Arthur J. Rubel and Marc Simmons deserve special mention. In a series of articles and a book, *Across the Tracks: Mexican-Americans in a Texas City* (1966), Rubel examines social relations and customs of Mexican-Americans in South Texas.[24] Among Rubel's special interests are traditional concepts of health and disease and the ways in which these beliefs contribute to the maintenance of a community's social system. Unlike those scholars who merely list items of folklore, Rubel attempts to determine their socio-cultural function. In *Witchcraft in the Southwest: Spanish and Indian Supernaturalism on the Rio Grande* (1974), Simmons provides an illuminating discussion of the beliefs and nature of witchcraft in Texas, New Mexico, and Colorado. Specifically, he treats the way in which "Hispanic and Indian cultures intermingle and cope with the aggressive intrusion of 'Anglos,'" using witchcraft and supernatural beliefs as the focal point of investigation.[25] Simmons's account of how the beliefs fit into contrasting world views makes for absorbing reading.

In the United States folk drama is usually thought of as a minor field of research mainly because that tradition is thought to be dead or lacking vitality in most of America. Scholars of Mexican-American lore do not share this attitude; in fact studies of this ethnic group's folk drama are almost as numerous as those on narrative and music traditions. Much of this attention has centered on *Los Pastores* (The Shepherds), a play blending ritual, piety, theatrics, music, song, dance, and pageantry. Basically a version of the Christmas story in which the antics of the shepherds and the Devil are in the forefront, *Los Pastores* first attracted the attention of observers from outside the Southwest in 1889. In that year Honora de Busk saw the play at San Rafael, New Mexico. Two years later, in 1891, John G. Bourke witnessed *Los Pastores* at Rio Grande City, Texas. In 1907 their texts, along with Bourke's photographs, appeared as Volume 9 of the American Folklore Society's Memoir Series. In 1921 Corinne Wright obtained an M.A. at the University of Southern California with a thesis on the play, and beginning in 1927 Mary Austin published four popular articles about the drama. After this a number of scholars engaged in serious work on the subject.[26]

In the early 1930s Arthur L. Campa produced three significant publications on the subject of religious folk drama.[27] Aurora Lucero-White Lea, a member of a prominent Las Vegas, New Mexico, family who eventually became known as a folklore authority, first attracted attention for her translations of folk dramas. In 1940 she published two versions of *Las Pastores* and later, in the survey *Literary Folklore of the Hispanic Southwest* (1953), published several plays as well as other types of folklore. John E. Englekirk traced the history of the plays and the scholarship about them in several articles containing much comparative data.[28] Finally, in a brief article in *Western Folklore* Stanley L. Robe discussed the relationships of *Los Pastores* to other folk dramas in the Hispanic tradition.[29]

While most work has focused on *Los Pastores,* some other plays have received attention. One such is *Los Comanches,* a traditional play concerning the struggle between the Indians and Spanish colonists. This drama has been the subject of monographs by Arthur L. Campa and Aurelio M. Espinosa.[30] Thomas M. Pearce is among those who have studied *The Moors and the Christians,* a miracle play from which episodes are often borrowed for performances of *Los Pastores.*[31]

Folk games have generally been slighted when compared with the treatment given other genres of Mexican-American folklore. There are, of course, popular collections like *Mother Goose on the Rio Grande* (1944) but scholarly accounts are rare. Aurelio M. Espinosa published two valuable articles in the *Journal of American Folklore* and the WPA produced two booklets, but these works certainly do not exhaust the available material and they are descriptive rather than analytic.[32] Of a different order is a 1975 article by Inez Cardozo-Freeman in which she analyzes games and songs collected from women of

Mexican ancestry living in Mexico and the United States. Cardozo-Freeman concludes that some of the games Mexican women play as children and recall as adults are reflections of their own personal attitudes and life situations. This material portrays "an adult life that is distressing—a life of invasion, betrayal, abandonment, and forced seclusion."[33] Thus, the author demonstrates that seemingly trivial matter often lends great insight to cultural analysis.

Traditional architecture is another aspect of folklore research that has received little attention except in nostalgic popular accounts. Such volumes as Manuel Gamio's *Mexican Immigration to the United States: A Study of Human Migration and Adjustment* (1930) do devote some pages to housing but the subject is of only passing concern to these authors. Rare, indeed, are publications like Richard E. Ahlborn's *The Penitente Moradas of Abiquiu* (1968), which is a study of two houselike buildings known as *moradas* used by the Penitentes. Ahlborn's commentary considers the ways in which the buildings are utilized by the community and the importance of folk art such as altars, crosses, crucifixes, and statues in this context. His narrative is supplemented by a number of photographs.

Although the first article on American traditional foodways published in the *Journal of American Folklore* was on Mexican-American cookery, there has been little written on the subject since. John G. Bourke's "Folk Foods of the Rio Grande Valley and of Northern Mexico" (1895) was for years one of the only articles on American traditional foods written from a folklore viewpoint. Bourke described many dishes calling attention to regional variation and historical origins of various cooking practices. Modern readers may find many of his comments, which are largely based on evolutionary thinking, ethnocentric and condescending towards inhabitants of the region, but they were not at odds with scholarly approaches of the 1980s. Moreover, Bourke saw collections such as his as ultimately beneficial to the people from whom he collected data. Knowing existing practices of the Mexican-Americans made it possible for their more enlightened neighbors to aid them in their "struggle upward and onward in the path of civilization."[34] Subsequent works on Hispanic foodways are mostly brief papers such as those by Alice M. Crook and Ruth Dodson.[35] Two important essays, one by Alicia González and the second by Judy Perkin and Stephanie F. McCann, appeared in books published in the 1980s.[36]

Works on traditional clothing are also small in number. Volumes like Margaret G. Mackey and Louise P. Sooy's *Early California Costumes 1769-1847* (1932) discuss the clothing of California's colonizers of Hispanic descent but are inadequate from a folklore standpoint. Outdated though it is, John Bourke's 1986 article "Notes on the Language and Folk-Usage of the Rio Grande Valley" is still the best publication dealing with traditional Mexican-American clothing, and it is only partially concerned with the topic.[37]

One aspect of Mexican-American material culture that has received considerable scholarly attention is folk art. Most of the publications deal with *santos* or sacred images. The late Elizabeth Boyd, who usually signed herself E. Boyd, alone wrote over twenty articles, monographs, and books on the subject. Her major statement is found in *Saints and Saint Makers of New Mexico* (1946). José E. Espinosa's *Saints in the Valley: Christian Sacred Images in the History, Life, and Folk Art of Spanish New Mexico* (1960; revised 1967), a meticulous study of sacred images in New Mexico from 1598 to the present, brings together all the documentable facts about the tradition and also contains much illustrative material, a detailed bibliography and catalogue, and an analysis of the style of individual *santeros* (makers of the santos). A more recent valuable study is Charles L. Brigg's *The Wood Carvers of Cordova, New Mexico: Social Dimensions of an Artistic "Revival"* (1980), which focuses on the influence of one santo carver, José Dolores Lopez, and his influence. Briggs gives great attention to the business of tradition, noting how demands of the marketplace have influenced the development of the carver's art in the twentieth century.

This bibliographic essay has, of necessity, mentioned only a few of the most significant publications in various areas of Mexican-American folklore. Hopefully, it has sufficiently noted the major areas of past research and those aspects of tradition that still await their magnum opus. With luck, perhaps the current volume will inspire someone to undertake the work necessary to fill in the gaps of our knowledge concerning Mexican-American folk tradition.

W.K. McNEIL
Ozark Folk Center
Mountain View, Arkansas

Notes

[1]Many of these articles were authored by Boggs, but O.H. Hauptmann and others also contributed essays. There were seven articles covering folktales, legends, beliefs, witchcraft, and other types of oral tradition that appeared in *Southern Folklore Quarterly* between 1937 and 1939.

[2]Carlota Garfías, "Mexican Folklore Collected in New York City," *Journal of American Folklore* 51 (1938): 83-91.

[3]Norman D. Humphrey, "Some Dietary and Health Practices of Detroit Mexicans," *Journal of American Folklore* 58 (1945): 255-58.

[4]Joseph A. Clark Moreno, "A Bibliography of Bibliographies Relating to Studies of Mexican-Americans," *El Grito* 2 (1971-72): 47-59. Four hundred and fifty-seven bibliographies are listed.

[5]The Paredes article appears in *Folklore Americano* 14 (1966): 146-63.

[6]Amado Alonso, quoted in Aurelio M. Espinosa and J. Manuel Espinosa, *The Folklore of Spain in the American Southwest: Traditional Spanish Folk Literature in Northern New Mexico and Southern Colorado* (Norman: University of Oklahoma Press, 1985), p. 18.

[7]The first article appeared in 1910 and the eleventh and last in 1916. Numbers 1, 3, 7, and 8 were devoted to folk narrative.

[8]Aurelio M. Espinosa. "Spanish and Spanish-American Folk Tales," *Journal of American Folklore* 64 (1951): 151-62. The quote is from p. 51.

[9]His degree was from Radcliffe College.

[10]Antti Aarne and Stith Thompson's *The Types of the Folktale* is the standard tale type index. The two men did not collaborate on this work; rather, Thompson updated Aarne's previous publication.

[11]The second article appeared in 1942. The book was issued two years earlier.

[12]Helen Zunser, "A New Mexican Village," *Journal of American Folklore* 48 (1935); 125-78. The text quoted here is on p. 141.

[13]Lorin W. Brown, Charles L. Briggs and Marta Weigle, *Hispano Folklife of New Mexico: The Lorin W. Brown Federal Writers' Manuscripts* (Albuquerque: University of New Mexico Press, 1978), xii.

[14]Turbese Lummis Fiske and Keith Lummis, *Charles F. Lummis: The Man and His West* (Norman, Oklahoma: University of Oklahoma Press, 1975), p. 16.

[15]Ibid., pp. 45-46.

[16]Articles on songs appeared in 1911 and 1914; two articles on dance music in 1915.

[17]Eleanor Hague, *Spanish-American Folk-Songs* (Lancaster, Pennsylvania and New York: The American Folk-Lore Society, 1917), p. 85.

[18]Ibid., p. 24.

[19]Américo Paredes, *A Texas-Mexican Cancionero: Folksongs of the Lower Border* (Urbana: University of Illinois Press, 1976), xiii.

[20]Manuel Pena, *The Texas-Mexican Conjunto: History of a Working-Class Music* (Austin: University of Texas Press, 1985), p. 1.

[21]Jordan's article appeared in *Western Folklore* 31 (1972): 77-86.

[22]Grider's article appeared in the *Journal of American Folklore* 88 (1975): 132-42.

[23]Arora's articles include "Some Spanish Proverbial Comparisons from California," *Western Folklore* 20 (1961): 229-37; "Spanish Proverbial Exaggerations from California," *Western Folklore* 27 (1968): 229-53; "Como la Carabina de Ambrosio," *Proverbium* 15 (1970): 428-430; "More Spanish Proverbial Exaggerations from California," *Western Folklore* 30 (1971): 105-18; and "Proverbial Exaggerations in English and Spanish," *Proverbium* 18 (1972): 675-83.

[24]Rubel's articles include "Concepts of Disease in Mexican-American Culture," *American Anthropologist* 62 (1960): 795-814; "The Epidemiology of a Folk Illness: Susto in Hispanic America," *Ethnology* 3 (1964): 268-83; "The Mexican-American Palomilla," *Anthropological Linguistics* 7 (1965): 92-97; and "Prognosticative Calendar Systems," *American Anthropologist* 78 (1965) 107-10.

[25]Marc Simmons, *Witchcraft in the Southwest: Spanish and Indian Supernaturalism on the Rio Grande* (Lincoln: University of Nebraska Press, 1980), xii.

[26]Austin's articles are "Native Drama in Our Southwest," *Nation* 124 (1927): 437-40; "Native Drama in New Mexico," *Theater Arts Monthly* 13 (1929): 564-67; "Folk Plays of the Southwest," *Theater Arts Monthly* 17 (1933): 599-610; "Spanish Manuscripts in the Southwest," *Southwest Review* 19 (1934): 402-9.

[27]These publications are "Religious Spanish Folk-Drama in New Mexico," *New Mexico Quarterly* 1 (1931): 3-13; *Spanish Religious Folktheater in the Southwest (First Cycle),* The University of New Mexico Bulletin, Language Series 5 (1934): 5-71; and

Spanish Religious Folktheater in the Southwest (Second Cycle), The University of New Mexico Bulletin, Language Series 5 (1934): 5-157.

[28]These articles include "Notes on the Repertoire of the New Mexican Spanish Folk-theater," *Southern Folklore Quarterly* 4 (1940): 227-37; "The Source and Dating of New Mexican Spanish Folk Plays," *Western Folklore* 16 (1957): 232-55 [this was in a special issue devoted to *Los Pastores*]; and "The Passion Play in New Mexico," *Western Folklore* 25 (1966): 17-33, 105-21.

[29]"The Relationship of *Los Pastores* to Other Spanish-American Folk Drama," *Western Folklore* 16 (1957): 281-89 [this article was in a special issue devoted to *Los Pastores*].

[30]Aurelio M. Espinosa, *Los Comanches: A Spanish Heroic Play of the Year Seventeen Hundred and Eighty.* The University of New Mexico Bulletin, Language Series 1 (1907): 1-46; Arthur L. Campa, *Los Comanches: A New Mexican Folk Drama.* The University of New Mexico Bulletin 7 (1942): 5-42.

[31]T.M. Pearce, "Los Moros y los Cristianos: Early American Play," *New Mexico Folklore Record* 2 (1947-1948): 58-65.

[32]Espinosa's articles are "New Mexican Spanish Folklore: X. Children's Games," *Journal of American Folklore* 29 (1916): 505-19 and "New Mexican Spanish Folklore: XI. Nursery Rhymes and Children's Songs," *Journal of American Folklore* 29 (1916): 519-535. The WPA booklets are *Spanish American Singing Games* (1940) and *The Spanish-American Song and Game Book* (1942).

[33]Inez Cardozo-Freeman, "Games Mexican Girls Play," *Journal of American Folklore* 88 (1975): 12-24. The quoted portion appears on p. 12.

[34]John G. Bourke, "The Folk-Foods of the Rio Grande Valley and of Northern Mexico," *Journal of American Folklore* 8 (1895): 41-71. The quoted portion appears on p. 41.

[35]Crook's essay, "Old Time New Mexican Usages," appeared in J. Frank Dobie, ed., *Puro Mexicano* (1935), pp. 184-89, the twelfth volume of the Publications of the Texas Folklore Society. Dodson's paper, "Tortilla Making," is found in J. Frank Dobie, Mody C. Boatright, and Harry H. Ransom, eds., *In the Shadow of History* (1939), pp. 137-41. This was the fifteenth volume of the Publications of the Texas Folklore Society.

[36]González's article, "'Guess How Doughnuts Are Made': Verbal and Nonverbal Aspects of the Panadero and His Stereotype," appears in Richard Bauman and Roger D. Abrahams, eds., *"And Other Neighborly Names": Social Process and Cultural Image in Texas Folklore* (Austin: University of Texas Press, 1981), pp. 104-22. The Perkin and McCann article, "Food for Ethnic Americans: Is the Government Trying to Turn the Melting Pot into a One-Dish Dinner?", is contained in Linda Keller Brown and Kay Mussell, eds., *Ethnic and Regional Foodways in the United States: The Performance of Group Identity* (Knoxville: University of Tennessee Press, 1984), pp. 243-47.

[37]John G. Bourke, "Notes on the Languages and Folk-Usage of the Rio Grande Valley," *Journal of American Folklore* 9 (1896): 81-116. Despite its title, which suggests an essay on folk speech, the paper is concerned with cultural survivals such as customs, furniture, food, proverbs, and, of course, dress.

CHAPTER ONE

The World of the Mexican-Americans

MEXICAN-AMERICAN FOLKLORE in its earliest form, Hispanic-American folklore, first came into being soon after Columbus discovered the New World. Indeed, it was then that the first influences of European culture began to touch this new continent. There are, of course, oft-repeated and well-verified claims concerning Viking voyagers who crossed the North Atlantic, explored Vinland, and established settlements—albeit short-lived ones—on the North American continent. But they came and went, leaving only an occasional rune to note their visit. It was the Spanish conquistadores and *padres* who followed Columbus over four centuries ago who were the first Europeans really to leave their marks on the New World—especially the area now called the Spanish Southwest, an area where Spanish is still commonly spoken, and where Spanish/Mexican folkways still shape the lives of countless Americans. There were, of course, other people here before the Spaniards came—the many different groups of people we lump together as Indians. They came from afar too, anthropologists tell us, crossing the land bridge from Siberia to Alaska and then working their way south. And it was the intermingling and interaction of these two cultures—native American and Spanish—that produced something both old and new: Hispanic culture and folklore. Then in the nineteenth century when another set of outsiders, English-speaking explorers and settlers from the eastern seaboard and the southern United States, came to the area, still another element of culture entered the mixture. Even so, the Spanish-Indian (or Mexican-Indian) culture continues to be dominant in the Spanish Southwest, ranging from the Mississippi River westward to California, but also lingering in cultural islands throughout the United States. Small or large groups of Spanish-speaking (or Hispanic cultured) people in New York, St. Louis, and other metropolitan areas continue, in a somewhat reduced way, to follow the beliefs and customs of Hispanic America. In the Southwest, of course—Texas, New Mexico, Arizona, Colorado, and California—the large percentage of people of Mexican origin maintain what might be called a purer strain of the old ways—the ways of the Indian-Spanish mixture that has shaped life for many thousands of people for more than four centuries.

It was here, in the Spanish Southwest, decades before colonists came to the eastern seaboard (except for St. Augustine), that the first settlements were made by Europeans —established and lost to Pueblo revolt and then re-established.[1] It was here, along the Rio Grande, that the first drama was performed in what is now the continental United States.[2] Here, on April 30, 1598, the first Thanksgiving was celebrated, when Don Juan de Oñate's group of soldiers, friars, and settlers gave thanks to God for their survival after the horrendous crossing of the Chihuahuan desert of northern Mexico.[3] And it was here that Hispanic folkways first took root and flourished.

Interestingly enough, northern New Mexico, where Spanish settlers and Pueblo Indians had their earliest and most enduring contacts, has maintained what might most accurately be called Spanish-American culture, rather than Mexican-American. A student survey undertaken in the summer of 1985 suggests some of the differences that are involved in this regional/cultural separation. Elizabeth Aeby, raised in the small Spanish village of Española, New Mexico, had been exposed to "Spanish customs there and had always taken them as a part of life." When she moved to El Paso, Texas, in 1982, she experienced what could almost be called culture shock. "The Hispanics of El Paso are proud to be Mexican," she noted, "but the Hispanics of Española will fight to the death anyone claiming that they are anything but Spanish." One young man she interviewed recalled a rattlesnake hunt undertaken when an uncle returned to the Albuquerque, New Mexico, area; the skin of one of the victims was saved to decorate a belt, and the meat of the snake was eaten, ceremonially, to celebrate the return—as the youth recalled his family having done under similar circumstances when he was quite young. The ceremonial nature of this use of the rattlesnake perhaps reflects the Pueblo veneration for the snake; family members say the custom was brought to the Albuquerque area from Socorro, New Mexico, where early Spanish settlers lived near a Pueblo settlement and padres converted many of the Indians to Christianity. By contrast, Mexican-Americans interviewed in the El Paso area view rattlesnakes as having curative powers, not just ceremonial uses: they cut them into one-inch pieces which are salted away. After six months the salt from the process is added to food to prolong the eater's life. Other people roast and eat the middle portion of the snake's body, or dry it and grind it up to sprinkle on food—both methods to cure eczema, while the skin is dried and ground to a powder and sprinkled on food, to increase circulation; the powder is also applied to boils in the form of a poultice.

The custom of hanging baby shoes on the rear-view mirror of a car, a harmless custom in the El Paso area to announce the birth of a baby or to show off having a baby in the family, is taboo in the Española area—it portends the death of the baby in a car wreck. As a sort of parallel marking what may be called an obsession with death in car wrecks, I have viewed a number of crosses—painted on roadside rock walls, or made of wood and driven into the right-of-way—marking the scene of death of people in accidents, a custom Miss Aeby also commented on. The custom of marking death scenes is not common farther south. Even acceptable social behavior differs between the two areas, in Miss Aeby's observation. When an El Paso Mexican passes in front of seated persons in a theater, he faces the front of the auditorium; in Española, he would face the people he was passing in front of, considering it bad manners "to stick his butt in somebody's face!" While this survey was brief and limited in scope, it does suggest that there are indeed basic cultural differences between the Hispanic-Americans of northern New Mexico and Colorado and the Mexican-Americans of the American Southwest in general.[4] What is more impressive is that folklorist Richard Dorson expressed the same views concerning the two areas of culture, Hispanic and Mexican, noting that

> particularly in the isolated plateau country north of Santa Fe have language and traditions retained their ancient forms. The center of the state, cushioned in the Rio Grande river basin, has passed more noticeably under "Anglo" influence. . . . South in the Mesilla Valley [near El Paso, Texas] the proximity with Mexico has kept fresh and fluid the Spanish tongue and the Mexican civilization.[5]

As Mark Simmons, Southwest folklorist and historian, points out in *People of the Sun,*

> the Southwest is the home of not one, but two different cultures whose roots lead back to Spain. The oldest is the Spanish or Hispano culture of northern New Mexico and southern Colorado. The second, and more recent, is the Mexican-American, or Border culture, concentrated along the boundary from Brownsville to Tijuana. . . . The Hispano has its own distinct psychology, grounded in the land of his forefathers (the upper Rio Grande Valley) and in the ancient customs and folkways brought long ago from Spain. . . . Colonial New Mexicans [loyal to King and Church], though they were separated from the mother country by half a continent and an ocean, carried on, in virtual isolation century after century, the familiar pattern of Hispanic daily life.[6]

Mexican immigrants into the United States, on the other hand, are closer to home—Mother Mexico—than the Hispanos. With the revolution that made Mexico a nation in 1821 Spanish loyalties were violently rejected. Yet when Mexicans migrate to the United States, they tend to maintain cultural ties with Mexico. In addition, successive waves of immigration—legal or not—have the effect of bringing in fresh transfusions of *Mexicanidad*—Mexicanness—into the lives of third- and fourth-generation citizens of their adopted country, reinforcing the tendency to maintain their Mexican cultural values.

Even so, it is not accurate to say that Mexican-American folk and folklore are entirely different from the so-called Anglo culture surrounding them. In fact, one of the most fascinating characteristics of folklore is that it teaches—demonstrates clearly—how basically alike we humans all are, regardless of our differences in language or skin color or religion. Most cultures, after all, have their wise sayings, their home remedies, their stories that account for customs and beliefs and practices. These are precisely the essential elements that validate so many of our cultural characteristics. And to the student of folklore it is often comforting to note how similar we all are, how often there are exact parallels to be found in the folkways of several cultures. How often we do the same things for different reasons, or seek to achieve the same results through different means! For example, *El perro que ladra no muerde* may sound strange, perhaps, to the English speaker, but it is an exact translation of the familiar English saying "A barking dog never bites." Other proverbs in Spanish preserve concepts found in other languages in only slightly differing form. To be *entre la espada y la pared* (between the sword and the wall) is very similar to being "between the devil and the deep blue sea" or, as we say in Texas, "between a rock and a hard place." And from classical antiquity comes the saying about being "between Scylla and Charybdis"—that is, between the rock and the whirlpool that Homer (and other notorious spreaders of folklore) said were monsters causing the destruction of Greek and Roman ships in ancient times.

Still, in spite of the many similarities, the universal themes and forms of folklore, there continue to be features that are especially characteristic of a single culture or folk group. It is in these areas that the exploration of Mexican-American folklore is particularly exciting and significant. And it is in the Spanish Southwest that the search for such elements of culture is especially rewarding.

By its very nature, folklore assumes a number of readily definable forms, regardless of national or ethnic characteristics. Folklore may be verbal, partly verbal, or nonverbal; it may be discerned as habits of speech or naming, found in proverbs and riddles, rhymes and folksongs, and prose narrative forms (both sacred and secular). Folk recreation leads to games and dances, while folk beliefs produce customary practices, motivate ceremonial dances and dramas, and shape daily life. The desire to create and decorate produces folk customs, foods, arts, and crafts; the basic need for shelter produces, even among the most unlettered folk, an architecture that is both practical and artistic. Thus it is with Mexican-American folklore: the people and their varied heritage assume forms and shapes that are at once part of the world at large and a distinctive reflection of their own special culture.

Much of the material to be found in this book comes from the fieldwork of folklore students at the University of Texas at El Paso collected over the past twenty-plus years. These resources are filed in the University of Texas at El Paso Folklore Archive. Fellow laborers in the folklore vineyard have provided other material — especially Lurline Coltharp, Mark Glazer, Joe S. Graham, Kenneth I. Periman, Karina Ramirez, Stanley Robe, Marc Simmons, Julia Kumor, and the late Haldeen Braddy—while the printed volumes of the Texas Folklore Society have added geographical breadth. And without the linguistic and moral support of my wife, Lucy Fischer West, and her mother Lucina Lara Rey de Fischer, who are both

bilingual, I would often have been lost in the maze of Spanish idiom. Structurally, the plan of the book follows the organization of Jan Harold Brunvand in his widely used text *The Study of American Folklore,* now in its third edition.

CHAPTER TWO

Folk Speech and Naming

DWELLERS IN THE Spanish Southwest who do not hold themselves aloof from the variety of cultures around them inevitably acquire a unique language —especially the "Spanglish" that has grown out of cultural blending. Witness the American cowboy, whose work vocabulary is derived from that of the *vaquero* (literally "cowman," but in the mispronunciation of the Texan, "buckaroo"). *La reata* became "lariat," *chaparreras* was shortened to "chaps" (but pronounced with a harder *ch* sound than in Spanish). And when the cowboy got a bit too wild, he might wind up in the "hoosegow," a word derived from the Spanish *juzgado* —literally "judged."[1] Of course, with English being the dominant language, many Spanish speakers similarly mis-heard or mispronounced a host of unfamiliar words. Some years ago, walking past a bar on the main tourist street in Juárez, Chihuahua (across the Rio Grande from El Paso, Texas), I noticed a sign on the door advertising two qualities of Scotch: "Scotch—50 cents; Enikain, 75 cents." A bit of experimenting with the pronunciation of this drink revealed that the bar owner was offering the brand most often called for when the customer asked for Scotch—"Any kind"—and selling it at a premium.

Not all the linguistic curiosities of the Southwest involve such errors. People of Mexican-American or "Anglo" origin often choose to play with the two languages—as in the whimsical form of "I'll be seeing you," which comes out *Ay, te watcho,* and parking lot attendants sometimes call themselves *watchy-carros,* while their clients are *parkiando sus carros.* Many English words thus acquire currency in Spanglish—*estuche* is a station wagon, *pee-cup* a deliberate but recognizable alteration of the English "pickup." In the classroom, English words sometimes acquire Spanglish pronunciations, with the sign of the infinitive in Spanish, *-ar, -er,* or *-ir,* being tacked onto the English word without much change in pronunciation. Thus *testiar* would be pronounced *test-ee-arr,* and so on. Witness the following list from an El Pasoan of Mexican ancestry:

testiar	to test
flunquiar	to flunk
pasar	to pass
espeliar	to spell
taipiar	to type
feiliar	to fail.

From the football field come *rachar* (to rush), *tecoliar* (to tackle), and *famboliar* (to fumble); baseball yields *pichar, cachar,* and *betiar* for three of the players, and *estraiquiar* (to strike).[2]

Teenagers of my acquaintance in greeting others often ask, *"¿Qué ondas?"* (literally, "What do you wave?" but coming across as "What's going on?"), playing on the similarity in sound between *andar* (to go or walk) and *ondear* (to wave or flow).[3] Throughout my own years on the border, I have quite naturally acquired a host of Spanish words that flavor my conversation, ranging from the *adiós* (goodbye) heard everywhere to *¿como le va?* (how goes it?), and other terms less generally adopted by Anglos. Twenty-five years ago, while watching a touch football game in Austin, Texas, with a group of my dormitory mates, many of them Spanish-speaking, I hollered out spontaneously, *"¡Córrele!"*—urging the ball-carrier to run. My buddies laughed at how "Mexican" I was—but I honestly hadn't been aware of having shifted languages. On the same wavelength, to eavesdrop on conversations between bilingual natives of the border area is a marvelous experience, as they shift freely from one language to the other and back again —sometimes without being conscious of doing so, according to my conversations with them.

Richard Bradford's novel *Red Sky at Morning,* while its fictional Sagrado Corazon location in middle New Mexico is beyond the geographical limits of this work, includes an excellent example of this mixed language. Baltimorean Frank Arnold can't manage Spanish, but in working with his Hispanic man of all work he develops a facility with the local dialect. They are painting the house, and he asks, *"¿Qué pasó con el paint?"* (What happened to the paint?). His helper replies, *"Yo lo* diluted *con* turpentine," and all concerned have communicated.[4]

The word *gringo* perhaps reflects this same sort of wordplay. Theories abound as to the word's origin—including the fanciful notion that Texas colonists singing "Green Grow the Lilacs" thus named themselves.[5] In early times in Texas, when rivalry was strong between Texan and Mexican, derogatory labels were often heard: gringo for Americans, and "greaser" for Mexicans. But for one Mexican-American to call another *agringado* is a term of contempt, meaning he is getting too "yankeefied." Another such term is *Tió Tomás*—Uncle Tom—for one who serves the dominant culture at the expense of his own, like the "Oreo" label applied to subservient Blacks (recalling the cookie, black outside, white inside).[6] Today, a person of non-Mexican origin—of whatever race or skin color—is called an Anglo. A small-town high school in West Texas with a winning football team was recently marveled over, with admirers always pointing out that there were only three Anglos on the team, and one of them was Black![7]

Mexican-Americans' names for themselves vary considerably from area to area. In some towns, where the inhabitants have lived there for several generations, people call themselves Mexicans. Others use the term "Latin" or "Hispanic," even away from New Mexico, and political activism since the 1960s has made popular the term "Chicano"—although many non-activists find the term objectionable.[8] And long before the Chicano movement, LULAC (League of United Latin American Citizens) and PASO (Political Association of Spanish-speaking Organizations) dealt somewhat satisfactorily with the awkwardness of ethnic labels. Yet these labels exist; Mexican-Americans use the common term *cholo* to describe people of low class in their culture—perhaps just as Anglos in Texas look down their noses at "stompers" or "shit-kickers" in the Anglo element. Among these cholos, also frequently called by older terms *tirilones* or *pachucos,* a third language has come to be—in essence a secret language used to exclude the outsider and females as well.

This language, called *caló* by insiders and linguists alike, uses some of the same characteristics that produce Spanglish—deliberate reshaping of English words or Spanish words. While it is not a universal language, nor truly a dialect, it does reach into the comprehension of many middle-class Mexican-Americans and it has spread far from its presumed place of origin—South El Paso—to Tucson, Arizona, Los Angeles, California (*Los* and *Califa* in caló), as well as San Antonio, Texas.[9] There are even reports that the "Valley girl talk" of the West Coast has similarities to caló, while others see connections to pidgin spoken in Hawaii, which certainly has a kinship with the concept of a private language.[10]

Caló is often thought of as the argot or slang of drug-users, dropouts, or those who have spent a few *abriles* (literally "Aprils," but meaning years) in the *corre* (correctional institution, which has apparently aided the geographical spread of the "language"). But teenagers, in particular, living in disadvantaged areas enjoy the specialness of their own "language." A listing of a sample of the sub-language, truly a folk (i.e., group) phenomenon, should give some of its flavor:

Caló	**Standard Spanish**	**English Translation**
pedo	fart	trouble
buscar pedo	to look for a fart	looking for trouble
bote	boat	jail
huevos	eggs	guts—"balls"
pelarse	get a short haircut	to go, or escape
calmar	to be calm	to wait for someone
agarrar	to grab	to be caught by the police
de aquella	of that	very nice
clavar	to nail	to stab, steal, or hide things
sancheando	(no equivalent)	to go from male lover to lover
mueble	furniture	a "stacked" or well-built woman[11]

There are, of course, thousands of caló expressions, and it is an ever-changing mode of communication. Youngsters who want to appear *macho* (tough, manly) often use caló to add to their stature, pretending to be something they are not. To most Anglos, the term *tirilón* is usually unknown; *pachuco* is a label left over from the 1940s and 1950s, a long-haired man with a jangle chain and narrow cuffed (peg-topped) trousers and a surly disposition—often a member of a street gang. Today, the term *cholo* covers that same basic ground and more: cholo usually means any person of Mexican descent, on a par with older terms like "pepper-bellies," "chili-pickers," and, of course, "greasers." Mexican-Americans label Anglos, too—as *güero* (literally, blond), for one example, though its feminine form, *güera,* is used by bilinguals all along the border to mean "Blondie," not simply Anglo.[12] The wife of a man I worked for as a teenager was always referred to (outside her hearing) as "the" güera—not using the Spanish prefix *la* as might be expected; and a blond buddy of my grammar school days was always called Güero (we pronounced it "Weddo")—most folks probably thinking it was his given name.

On an everyday level, the diminutives or nicknames of people with Spanish given names reflect Mexican traditions. *Chuy* is common for *Jesús,* and *Lalo* for *Eduardo* (Edward). *María* (Mary, traditionally among the most common names for girls) produced *Chepa, Chulia, Maida,* and a host of other familiar forms. As an Anglo growing up in the El Paso area half a century ago, I learned these names as standard, not realizing that they were diminutives. We always called Chuy Chuy—and I didn't know for many years what his given name really was. Of course true diminutives (like Johnny for John) are also used, the suffix *-ito* for boys and *-ita* for girls producing *Juanito* for *Juan* and *Adelita* for *Adela.* Reversed comments appear in common conversation—*viejo* (old man) is often applied as a greeting to a young man, while *joven* (young man) may greet an older person. *Maestro* (master, teacher, or expert) is used to greet an older person whom one respects—or even whimsically to one who is younger or ordinarily of lower status. My mother, who taught in elementary school in a Mexican neighborhood in El Paso in the 1930s, used to tell about the student missing from school. Tattletales in the class would confide that the student was "playing the fox"—skipping school. The word for fox, *zorro,* means also "sly" or "sneaky"; there's no Spanish verb *zorrear,* but *hacerse la zorra*—to play the fox—covers the idea adequately.[13]

Just as the cowboy acquired the terminology of his trade from a misunderstanding or mispronunciation of Spanish, much humor grows out of the Anglo who misuses Spanish words, or the Spanish speaker who gets mixed up in the linguistic aspects of cultural clash. In fact, both groups share such jokes in an easy recognition of the friendly rivalry involved. One such story involves two "wetbacks"—a gently derogatory term meaning illegal aliens—who had been picking fruit in the lower Rio Grande Valley. They had heard a lot about Florida, and decided they would hitchhike over to see it for themselves. As car after car whizzed by without stopping, they edged farther and farther out onto the highway. Finally one car, swerving to avoid them, almost ran into the ditch on the other side of the road.

"Another carro don't stop!" said one of the wetbacks (who had begun practicing his English).

"No le hace (that doesn't matter)," said the other. "We on the right road. The driver said something about 'sunny beaches'!"[14]

Another wetback, encountered down the Rio Grande from El Paso by a *migra*—a shortened form of the term "immigration officer"—who had a limited knowledge of Spanish (although like most Anglos in such stories he was quite sure of himself and his ability to communicate).

"¿Donde nácio?" he asked, thinking he was asking, "Where were you born?" The wetback, hearing, "Where's (Ig)nacio," because of the misplaced accent, pointed to the brush and answered, *"Atrás del mesquite"* (behind the mesquite bush). *(Nació* means "was born").

"¿Tener papeles?" asked the migra, thinking he was asking if he had papers —i.e., was legally in the United States.

The wetback, hearing, "Does he have papers?" figured the officer understood why Ignacio was behind the bushes and was sympathetic with what he was doing there, and answered *"No señor. Con piedras tiene"* (No sir, he'll have to make do with rocks). And even if the hearer is not fully bilingual, translation results in a roar of laughter.[15]

José González, another Mexican visitor to the United States, took in his first baseball game, and decided that these *norte americanos* (North Americans) were truly friendly and considerate people. He had just arrived when they all stood up and began singing, "José, can you see?"[16]

A *bracero* (laborer), carrying a violin, and his buddy, carrying a guitar, got on a city bus in El Paso and started to take seats. The driver called out to them, "Token."

The guitar man asked what he said, and the driver repeated, "Token."

The violinist said, *"O, quiere que toquemos"* (Oh, he wants us to play). *(Toquen* is the command form of *tocar,* to play).

So they tuned up and started playing—and were thrown off the bus.[17]

On the other side of the "taco curtain" between the culture groups, there's the one about the Anglo who went on vacation to Mexico City. (No knowledgeable Spanish speaker adds the word "City," since "México" says it all! The country is simply referred to as *la república*—the republic). He enjoyed his stay so much, including practicing his Spanish, that he almost missed his flight home. Running through the airport carrying his bags, he called out, *"¡Escusado! Escusado!"*—thinking he was saying, "Excuse me! Excuse me!" People got out of his way all right. He was really saying, "Bathroom! Bathroom!"[18]

Another American (a common term that ignores the fact that America includes a number of countries in the Western Hemisphere) was traveling in Mexico and was admiring the beautiful buildings. To his question "Who owns that?" he got the standard response *"¿Qué dice?"* meaning, "What did you say?" He decided, "This fellow Kay Deesey must be a very rich man! He seems to own everything in Mexico!"[19]

Another tale, which shows that national or ethnic bias is not always required for a Mexican-American joke, just misunderstanding, tells of the famous Mexican general Jesús Quevedo. He was traveling on a train in Mexico and felt the urge to go to the bathroom—but the train was not equipped with such facilities. The general noticed that the train was coming to a tunnel, so he thought he'd open the window, extend his backside, and relieve himself outside.

Just as he was finishing his business, the train came out of the tunnel and a woman saw his exposed rear. She cried out, *"¡Jesús, que veo!"* (Jesús, what do I see?) (An internal *d* sound, as in *Quevedo,* is almost swallowed, making the pun more easily understood to a Spanish speaker.)

The general shook his head. "That's what happens when one is so well known," he said.[20]

And to top things off completely, a person who gives up on a project or job, or quits, or even dies, is said to *colgar los tenis* (to hang up his tennis shoes)—a graphic picture for modern times in a bilingual society.[21]

This richness—this intermixture of English and Spanish, coupled with a good-humored attitude towards oneself and one's linguistic/cultural predicament—is an integral part of the Mexican-American's world.

CHAPTER THREE

Proverbs

AS SUGGESTED IN Chapter One, virtually every culture group has its proverbs, its bits of wisdom, its short traditional guides to conduct. The Book of Proverbs in the Bible is an excellent example of this characteristic of a culture: general truths and observations on how to behave abound, along with standards for evaluating other human beings. Witness the many descriptions of the good woman to be found there: "A gracious woman retaineth honor" (11:16); "A virtuous woman is a crown to her husband" (12:4); "Who can find a virtuous woman, for her price is above rubies" (31:10). But there are explicit warnings as well: "Every wise woman buildeth her house: but the foolish plucketh it down with her own hands" (14:1); and "Give not thy strength unto women" (31:3).[1]

Proverbs—wherever found—fit the description "the wisdom of many, the wit of one."[2] In Mexican-American lore they are plentiful. Under the labels *refránes* (refrains) or *dichos* (sayings), but never *proverbios,* they "constitute a philosophy of life."[3] The majority of the dichos to be found in the Mexican border area are true proverbs, existing in relatively fixed forms, in complete sentences, and often exhibit the characteristics of poetry—rhythm, rhyme, and alliteration. Proverbial comparisons are less common, and according to Archer Taylor and my students' experience, "Spanish Wellerisms are practically unknown."[4] Nonetheless, student collectors ranging from Los Angeles and Mountain View, California, to Tucson, Arizona, found an even half-dozen.[5] Of course, with the intermixture of cultures in the Southwest, English Wellerisms do exist—wise or punning sayings attributed to an appropriate (or inappropriate) speaker—like "'I see,' said the blind man, as he picked up his hammer and saw."[6]

Most common among Mexican-American dichos are words of wisdom or advice. One El Paso woman, who fled the Mexican Revolution with her family half a century ago, told an interviewer, "People with little education depend on proverbs to make their point. . . . The proverbs give a very concise explanation of different situations in life."[7] Yet another informant pointed out that

> without proper circumstances, a proverb wouldn't make sense. It needs the circumstances, otherwise it's just a remark. I went to the store and bought something just because it was shiny and pretty, and it turned out to be a 'lemon.' And my mother told me, *"Recuérdate, no todo lo que brilla es oro"* [Remember, not all that shines is gold]. My husband likes to go to the races, and he says, "Look, with two dollars I can win twenty!"

> And I tell him, *"Más vale un pájaro en mano que cien volando"* [A bird in the hand is worth more than a hundred flying]. Proverbs should be used to help people, but nobody takes advantage of them. They think they're just words. But afterwards they remember the wisdom they failed to follow.[8]

The range of subjects for proverbs is almost without end, although comparisons, analogies, and hidden significances often deal with the most common items of life—household details, domesticated animals, foods, everyday activities—in short, the "facts of life" as experience teaches them to us. Witness *Al que he nacido para tamal, del cielo le caen las hojas* (For him destined to be a *tamal,* corn shucks [for wrapping the *tamal*] fall from Heaven).[9] This *que será, será* philosophy sounds fatalistic, but it reflects an admission that one's fate is inescapable. Likewise, *Suerte y mortaja del cielo bajan* says that life and death come down from Heaven.[10] Yet *El que siembre vientos recoje tempestades* (He who sows winds will reap tempests),[11] or more simply, *Lo que siembra se recoje* (One reaps what one sows).[12] The opposition involved in these four dichos is virtually identical with that of the English proverbs "Look before you leap" and "He who hesitates is lost." In short, you can't win for losing, as we say in Texas. There seems to be a saying to cover—or confuse—almost any of life's concerns. The richness of proverbial wisdom is exemplified by the following list taken from El Paso-centered student collections, with comparisons showing their currency in New Mexico, Arizona, California, and other parts of Texas:

Dios no da alas a los alacránes porque volando picarían (God doesn't give wings to scorpions, for they would sting while in flight).[13]

Para gato viejo, ratón tierno (For an old cat, a tender mouse). Said of an old man courting a young woman.[14]

Al nopal lo van a ver solo cuando tiene tunas (One goes to see the *nopal* cactus only when it bears fruit).[15]

El que adelante no mira, atrás se queda (He who doesn't look ahead stays behind).[16]

De tal palo, tal astilla (From such a stick, such a splinter. A chip off the old block).[17]

Lo mío, mío y lo tuyo de entreambos (What is mine is mine; what's yours is ours).[18]

Cada uno sabe dónde le aprieta el zapato (Each one knows where the shoe pinches him),[19] which is comparable to *El buey solo bien se lame* (Only the ox can lick himself well).[20]

Mona en seda pero mona queda (A monkey [dressed] in silk is still a monkey).[21]

Despacio se va lejos (Slowly one goes far),[22] comparable to *Grano a grano llena el buche la gallina* (Grain by grain the hen fills her crop).[23]

Más vale llegar a tiempo que ser invitado (It is better to arrive on time than to be invited).[24]

La carga hace andar al macho (The load makes the mule go; cf. "Money makes the mare go").[25]

No niega la cruz de su parroquia (He doesn't deny the cross of his parish; or, You can take the boy out of the country but you can't take the country out of the boy).[26]

En la tierra de los ciegos el tuerto es rey (In the land of the blind the one-eyed man is king).[27]

No todos que silban son arrieros (Not all who whistle are muleteers; or, All that glitters is not gold).[28]

El árbol que crece torcido nunca se endereza (The tree that grows crooked can never straighten out; or, As the twig is bent, so is the tree inclined).[29]

Food, dear as it is to us all, has its own series of dichos expressing repeatedly how easily we are satisfied. "Belly full, heart easy" is central to most of these sayings, including the exact translation, *Panza llena, corazón contento,*[30] or *Barriga llena, corazón contento.*[31]

Con buena hambre no hay mal pan (With real hunger, there's no bad bread).[32]

El que hambre tiene en el pan piensa (He who is hungry thinks [only] of bread).[33]

Las penas con pan son buenas (Misfortunes with bread are good).[34]

Las penas son menos con pan (Misfortunes are less with bread).[35]

Donde no hay harina todo es muina [*mohina*] (Where there's no flour, all is discord).[36]

¿A quien le da pan que llore? (Who will cry if he's given bread)?[37]

But one mustn't cast pearls—or bread—before swine: *El que da pan a perro ajeno pierde el pan y pierde el perro* (He who gives bread to a strange dog loses the bread and the dog).[38]

And *Vuelta la burra al maiz* (There goes the burro to the corn again; or, Here we go again),[39] recalls the retort *Cada loco con su tema* (Every crazy person has his "thing" [a one-track mind]).[40]

Love and marriage, like bread, are common themes for dichos—and sometimes they are hopeful: *Amor, pesetas, y tiempo para gastarlos con una prieta* (Love, money, and the time to spend [or enjoy] them with a brunette) was one of the favorite sayings of my father-in-law;[41] others sometimes put it *Poco dinero, mucho trabajo, y mucho amor* (A little money, plenty of work, and plenty of love).[42] And remember, *Amor, dinèro, y cuidado nunca puede ser disimulado* (Love, money, and caring cannot be feigned).[43] However, another dicho says that

El amor para que dure ha de ser disimulado (For love to last, it *must* be disguised).[44]

Dos para quererse, deben parecerse (Two, to love each other, must be alike).[45] But when love does come, *Cuando dos se quieren bien, con uno que coma basta* (When two really love each other, it's enough if one can eat).[46]

On the pessimistic side, however, *Amor con celos causa desvelos* (Love with jealousy keeps one awake).[47]

Amor de lejos es amor de pendejos (Love from afar is love for fools).[48]

Para amores que se alejen, busca amores que se acerquen ([To replace] loves that leave, look for loves that come toward you).[49]

And parents who meddle in their children's lives are warned, *¿Las quieres enamoradas? Que se sienten despreciadas* (If you want them to fall in love, make them feel scorned).[50]

And a final bit of advice: *No compres caballo de muchas fieras ni te cases con muchacha de muchos novios* (Don't buy a wild horse, nor marry a girl with many boyfriends).[51]

Proverbs on the subject of women—one of the parties involved in love—are only sometimes as positive as those to be found in the Book of Proverbs, although a few sound as if they might have come from that source:

El tesoro de la mujer es la virtud (The treasure of a woman is her virtue).[52]

La mujer honesta nunca debe creerse sola (The honest woman should never believe herself alone).[53]

But a viewpoint that suggests the attitude of the so-called male chauvinist is present in *La mujer, en sus quehaceres, para eso son las mujeres* (Woman at her housework—that's what women are for).[54] In fact, in sheer numbers, dichos seem to bear out a negative picture of womankind. The fair sex comes across as tricky, vain, greedy, and given to manipulating men:

Las viuda rica con un ojo llora y con el otro sonríe (The rich widow cries with one eye and smiles with the other).[55]

Cuántas veces, sollozando, se esta riendo una mujer (How many times, while sighing, is a woman laughing).[56]

Las mujeres ríen cuando pueden y lloran cuando quieren (Women laugh when they can and cry when they want to).[57]

La que de amarillo se viste a su hermosura se confía (The woman who dresses in yellow trusts her beauty).[58]

La vergüenza en la mujer se conoce en el vestido (Shame in a woman is known by her dress).[59]

Mujer que viste en seda, en su casa se queda (The woman who dresses in silk stays at home).[60]

Attention to appearance among women is appropriate, according to one dicho: *La comida y la mujer, por los ojos han de entrar* (Food and woman must go in [be appreciated?] through the eyes).[61] Similarly, the woman to whom you give what she asks you for, is the woman who will give you what you ask her for—*Mujer a quien le das lo que te pide, mujer que te dará lo que le pidas.*[62]

But where the Book of Proverbs simply says that a good woman is rare, Mexican-American dichos are less optimistic: *Entre cien hombres he encontrado uno bueno, entre cien mujeres, ninguna* (Among 100 men I have found one good one; among 100 women, not one),[63] and *Es más fácil encontrar un cuervo blanco que una mujer buena* (It is easier to find a white crow than a good woman).[64]

With such a gloomy attitude, it is a wonder that men have anything at all to do with women, but there's a rule to guide one: In picking a wife, *Gallo, caballo, y mujer por su raza has de escoger* (Rooster, horse, and woman should be chosen by breed).[65] How a man handles a woman is important, too: *Al caballo con la rienda, y a la mujer con la espuela* ([Manage] the horse with the reins, the woman with the spur).[66] In addition, *El que presta a la mujer para bailar o el caballo para torear, no tiene que reclamar* (He who lends his wife to dance, or his horse to bullfight, has no complaint to make).[67]

But all is not lost. As puzzling as women are, *No hay bonita sin pero, ni fea sin gracia* (There's not a pretty girl without fault, nor an ugly one without charm).[68] In the long run, *Con amor y aguardiente, nada se siente* (With love and liquor, you don't feel anything).[69] And, in a spirit worthy of Benjamin Franklin, a dicho assures us that youth in women isn't everything: *Gallina vieja hace buen caldo* (An old hen makes a good stew)—which has been translated metaphorically as "Old maids make good lovers."[70]

Human relations of a broader range find observations galore in dichos; money is a recurring theme, usually with the same sort of pessimism found in the sayings about women:

Más da el duro que el desnudo (The miser gives more than the naked one).[71]

Paga el que quiere y no el que tiene (The person who wants, pays—not he who has [the money].[72]

Págame lo que me debes; de lo que te debo, cuenta tenemos (Pay me what you owe me; what I owe you, we'll keep track of).[73]

Primero es la amistad que el dinero (Friendship before money).[74] And a comparative view exists in *Al amigo sin razon; al enemigo ni con ella* ([Give] to the friend with no cause; to the enemy—not even with one).[75]

Muy pocos amigos tiene el que no tiene que dar (Very few friends has he with nothing to give).[76]

Dinero mal prestado, en la loma de un venado (Money loaned unwisely [is like putting it] on the back of a deer).[77] Yet if the borrower is too well known—*Dan más donde no conocen* (They give more where you aren't known).[78]

El dinero se paga, pero el favor, no (Money is repaid, but a favor is not).[79]

La miseria ahuyenta amigos y el dinero los atrae (Misery gets rid of friends, and money attracts them).[80] After all is said and done, according to the dicho, *El mejor amigo es un peso* (The best friend is the peso [money]).[81]

Even with that wry view to give us pause, there are several sayings among the Mexican-Americans on the value of friendship. *En la cárcel y en la cama se conoce quien es tu amigo* (In jail or in bed, you know who is your friend).[82] This adage is close to the English saying "A friend in need in a friend indeed," also to be found in exact Spanish translation: *Amigo en adversidad, amigo re realidad.*[83] And friendship has its compensations: *Dos agujas no se pican* (Two needles don't prick one another),[84] and *Los lobos no se muerden* (Wolves don't bite each other; there is honor among thieves).[85]

Similarly, "A man is known by the company he keeps" has its parallel in *Dime con quién andas y te diré quién eres* (Tell me whom you walk with [who your friends are] and I'll tell you who you are).[86] Using a name obviously chosen for the sake of rhyme, *A donde va Vicente va toda la gente* (Wherever Vincent goes, everybody goes)[87] has some of the flavor of the comment "Fools' names and fools' faces are always seen in public places." Another dicho warns, *Vale más solo que mal acompañado* (Better alone than in bad company),[88] since *El que mal anda mal acaba*—loosely translated as "He who takes the wrong path comes to a bad end").[89]

Dichos, with all their wisdom, even have sayings about their own validity. *Los adagios de los viejos son evangelios chiquitos* (The adages of old people are little gospels).[90] Even so, experiencc is thc best teacher. *No hay consejos como los que el tiempo da* (There are no counsels like those that time gives).[91] The range of these counsels is truly without limit, with every area of life having a dicho to guide one. From such a wide variety, a dozen plus a few will serve as examples:

Más pronto cae un hablador que un cojo (A braggart falls more quickly than a cripple).[92]

No hay rosas sin espinas (There are no roses without thorns).[93]

El muerto a la sepultura, el vivo a la travesura (The dead to the grave, the living to mischief).[94]

Cuando la gente está joven le dan su carne al diablo; cuando llegan a viejos le dan sus huesos a Dios (When people are young, they give their flesh to the devil; when they become old, they give their bones to God).[95]

Cuando no llueve, llovisna (When it doesn't rain, it sprinkles. Cf. "When it rains, it pours").[96]

Del dicho al hecho hay mucho trecho (From the word to the deed is a long way).[97]

Después de la calma viene la tormenta (After the calm comes the storm).[98]

No hay mal que por bien no venga (There's no ill that good doesn't [or can't] come from; cf. "It's an ill wind that blows nobody good").[99]

El que tiene mas saliva traga más pinole (He who has more saliva can swallow more *pinole*—loosely, He who has, gets; or, The one who has abilities gets farther. Pinole is a ground powder made from parched corn, sugar, and cinnamon. It can be made into a delicious drink, or it can be eaten dry, by sticking a saliva-wet finger—or even the tongue itself—into the container. A dry mouth or tongue, obviously, wouldn't be much use in eating pinole).[100]

El sordo no oye pero compone (What the deaf man doesn't hear, he makes up).[101]

Perro que ladra no muerde (The dog that barks doesn't bite).[102]

La zorra nunca se ve su cola (The skunk never sees his own tail; cf. "The fox smells his own tail first").[103]

Dios habla por el que calla (God speaks for him who is silent).[104]

Tanto va el cántaro al agua, hasta que allí queda (The pitcher that goes to the well [too] often, stays there).[105]

Están más frescas las tardes que las mañanas (The evenings are cooler than the mornings—or perhaps, Old age is calmer than youth).[106]

El lobo pierde los dientes más no las mientes (The wolf loses his teeth, not his nature).[107]

Entre menos burros, más olotes (Among fewer burros, more corncobs).[108]

En casa del 'horcado, no se habla de cabresto (In the house of a hanged man, one doesn't speak of rope).[109]

But of all the wisdom to be found in Mexican-American dichos, the most undebatable is *En boca cerrada no entran moscas* (A closed mouth catches no flies).[110]

Dichos, refránes—whatever the label, Mexican-American proverbs run the gamut of proverbs in any culture. As demonstrated, women, love, money, friendship, and an unending assortment of bits of wisdom are shared by the folk of the United States-Mexican boundary and the area lying alongside it. If the existence of a folk group were doubted when considering this culture area, the richness of proverbs alone would remove any questions. Shared lore is the prime proof of such a folk group,[111] and in this category alone there is an overwhelming body of material confirming this matter.

CHAPTER FOUR

Riddles

RIDDLING IS A worldwide game that almost everyone has played at one time or another—sometimes without realizing it's a game. Huck Finn, visiting the feuding Grangerford family on his way down the Mississippi, ran into a riddler in the form of Buck Grangerford. When Buck asked Huck where Moses was when the candle went out, Huck was stumped. "Which candle?" he asked —and he was still in the dark, like Moses, when Buck told him the answer. Huck's retort was prompt: "Well, if you knowed where he was, what did you ask me for?"[1] One wonders if literal-minded Huck ever learned how to riddle.

The basic idea of the riddle, as Jan Brunvand describes it, is asking traditional questions with unexpected but traditional answers, "verbal puzzles that demonstrate the cleverness of the questioner and challenge the wit of the audience."[2] Youngsters growing up soon learn to play the game; in some cultures, riddling has been reported as the serious occupation of adults as well, perhaps like the cocktail party games of modern America, where people play for hours with puzzling brain-teasers. Among Mexican-Americans, the *adivinanza* (riddle) passes away many an otherwise tiresome hour, along with puzzles called *rompecabezas* (head-breakers). Yet over the past quarter of a century, my folklore students have never become interested enough to search out and collect riddles in this part of the Southwest. I might speculate that riddles are seen by my university students as too "childish" for serious study—yet collectors from the southernmost tip of Texas to upper New Mexico and on out to California have found delight in the venture. Especially when one attempts to evaluate and categorize riddles, following the beginnings of Archer Taylor and other folklorists, the challenge becomes truly a serious undertaking, well worth one's time and interest.

One of the problems with adivinanzas, riddles, brain-teasers, puzzles, or whatever name one finds to be common in a folk group, is that "inside" knowledge is often one of the major blocks to figuring out the answer. Witness the following:

My mother went over to your mother's house
to borrow a wim babble, wam babble,
a hind body, fore body,
whirl-a kin nibble.[3]

Since very few people today have a personal knowledge of the once-common spinning wheel, its parts and the sounds it makes, it is almost impossible for anyone to figure this puzzle out. And when the "inside" knowledge involves another language, the problem can become much more complex. Thus the adivinanza, asked by one facile in the Spanish language of someone who is not, is uncommonly complicated—beyond the already puzzling nature of riddling. Even if the person being questioned has some command of the denotative meanings of Spanish words, the following adivinanza involves an unexpected twist:

En un cuarto muy obscuro	In a very dark room,
Estaba un vivo y un muerto	Was a live man and a dead man,
El muerto le dijo al vivo	The dead man said to the live man,
¿Duras?	Do you survive?
Y el vivo le dijo	And the live man said,
Nó.	No.[4]

The answer to this conundrum (a riddle containing its own answer within the wording) plays with the two replies in Spanish: *Duras* + *no* = *durazno* (peach); but nobody without a wild imagination plus native ability in Spanish would figure out that was the proper response, any more than a person with a modern urban background would have guessed "a spinning wheel" to the previous one.

Although my own students at the University of Texas at El Paso have thus far been completely inactive in the area of riddle collecting, those of Mark Glazer at Pan American University in the lower Rio Grande valley have collected quite a respectable assortment. And, fortunately, those riddles have been made available to the world of folklore scholarship through *Flour from Another Sack,* a rich book of Mexican-American lore which takes its name from a dicho —*Harina del otro costal,* a saying which implies that a person or a concern is beyond one's control or jurisdiction.[5] Dr. Glazer and his publishers have granted permission for me to reprint a representative sampling from the riddles published in that book, for comparison with adivinanzas found elsewhere in the Spanish Southwest.

The riddles to be found in Glazer's collection follow essentially the classification established by Archer Taylor.[6]

True Riddles

A. Comparisons to a living creature:

Anda y no tiene pies, habla y no tiene boca y adivina lo que es? (It travels but has no feet; it talks but has no mouth and guess what it is?) *La carta* (A letter).[7]

A pesar que tengo patas yo no me puedo mover; llevo encima la comida y no me la puedo comer (Although I have feet I can't move myself; I carry the meal on my top and can't eat it). *La mesa* (A table).[8]

¿Qué es aquéllo que colgado en la pared da sin tener manos y anda sin tener pies? (What is it which hangs on the wall, gives without hands, and walks without feet?) *El reloj* (A clock).[9]

B. Comparisons to an animal:

Paso por la casa. Voy a la cocina. Meneándo la cola como una gallina (I pass through the house. I pass through the kitchen. Wagging my tail like a chicken). *La escoba* (A broom).[10]

Vuela sin alas, silba bin boca y no se ve ni se toca. ¿Qué es? (It flies without wings, whistles without a mouth, and you can't see or touch it. What is it?) *El viento* (The wind).[11]

C. Comparisons to several animals:

Unas vacas pintas y otras blancas, las blancas se echan y pintas se levantan (Some pinto [spotted] cows and some white ones. The white ones lie down and the pinto ones get up.) *Las tortillas y frijoles* (Tortillas and pinto beans).[12]

Tengo un par de caballitos que cuando los amarro se van y cuando los suelto aquí están (I have a pair of ponies that when I tie them they leave, and when I let them loose, they stay). *Los zapatos* (Shoes).[13]

D. Comparisons to a person:

Soy enemigo del sol y en mí brillan muchos soles, y a pesar de tantas luces, me illuminan con faroles (I am enemy of the sun and in me many suns [stars] shine; in spite of the many lights they illuminate me with lanterns). *La noche* (The night).[14]

Una vieja flaca y la escurre la manteca (A skinny old lady and all her lard is draining out). *Una vela* (A candle).[15]

E. Comparisons to several persons:

Son hermanos muy unidos, donde quieren van juntitos (They are brothers very united; wherever they go they go together.) *Los dedos* (The fingers).[16]

Veinticuatro hermanas nobles, buenas, puras. Unas mueren claras, otras obscuras (Twenty-four noble sisters, good and pure. Some die in the day and some at night). *Las horas* (The hours).[17]

F. Comparisons to plants:

Un árbol de doce ramas, cada con su nombre, adivina si eres hombre. (A tree with twelve branches, each with its name; guess it if you're a man.) *Los meses* (The months).[18]

G. Comparisons to things:

Mi padre tenía un dinero que no podía contar (My father had money he couldn't count). *Las estrellas* (The stars).[19]

Cartas van y cartas vienen y en el aire se detienen (Letters go and come and in the air they are kept back). *Las nubes* (The clouds).[20]

H. Enumerations of comparisons:

Redondo como una manzana y como un sartén plano; la figura de mujer y la figura de hombre (Round as an apple and flat as a pan, with the shape of a woman and the shape of a man). *Un centavo* (A penny).[21]

Chiquito como un ratón, cuida su casa como león. (As small as a rat, it guards your house like a lion). *El candado* (A padlock).[22]

I. Enumeration in terms of form or function:

Sombrero sobre sombrero de rico pano. El que adivine esta adivinanza tiene término de un año (Hat upon hat, hat of rich cloth. Who guesses this riddle wins his goal in a year). *Una cebolla* (An onion).[23]

J. Enumeration in terms of color:

Blanco ha sido mi vestido, y amarillo mi corazón (White is my dress, and yellow is my heart). *Un huevo* (An egg).[24]

K. Enumeration in terms of acts:

Sube el cerro y baja y siempre está en el mismo lugar (It goes up the hill and comes down the hill always in the same place). *El camino* (The road).[25]

Trabaja y trabaja todo el día, pero no gana ningún centavo (He works and works all day but he doesn't earn a single cent.) *Una hormiga* (An ant).[26]

¿Qué cosa nunca puedes alcanzar, y siempre anda contigo? (What thing can you never reach, but it is always with you?) *Tu sombra* (Your shadow).[27]

Conundrums—Riddles with Answers Contained Within

Tres cazadores cazando. Tres palomas van volando. Cada uno mató la suya y dos se fueron volando (Three hunters hunting, three doves flying. Everyone shot his and two went flying.) *El que mató la paloma se llama Cada uno* (The one who shot his dove was named "Everyone").[28]

En el monte está un catre, y en el catre está un rey. ¿Qué es? (In the mountain in a cot, and on the cot is a king. What is it?) *Monterrey* (The city, Monterrey).[29]

¿Oro no es, plata no es, adivíname lo qué es? (It isn't gold, it isn't silver; guess what it is.) *Platano* (A banana).[30]

Riddle Problems

Estos eran cuatro gatos, cada gato en su rincón, cada gato veía tres gatos, adivine cuántos gatos son (There were four cats, each cat in its corner; each cat saw three cats. Tell me how many cats there were). *Cuatro gatos* (Four cats).[31]

Riddling Questions

En qué se parece el café al autobús? (How are coffee and a bus alike?) *En los asientos* (In the grounds [seats]).[32]

¿De qué color era el caballo blanco de Napoleón? (What color was Napoleon's white horse?) *Blanco* (White).[33]

¿Cuales son las cuatro letras que hacen a una niña mujer? (What are the four letters that make a girl a woman?) *Edad* (Age).[34]

¿Cuantas estrellas hay en el cielo? (How many stars are there in the sky?) *Cincuenta—o, sin cuenta* (Fifty—or countless).[35]

A Neck Riddle

Éste era un rey que tenía preso a un padre de familia. Y el rey no quería darle libertad. Vino el hijo para hablar con el rey, porque quería que le diera libertad a su padre. El rey le dijo que si le traía una adivinanza que él no pudiera adivinar, entonces le daría libertad a su padre. El muchacho se fué y como a los tres años regresó a visitar al rey, y traía su adivinanza preparada:

Vengo en lo que no es nacido
De riendas traigo a la madre
Adivíname buen rey
O dadme libre a mi padre.

There was once a king who had imprisoned a family man. The king didn't want to free him. The man's son came to talk with the king because he wanted his father set free. The king told the son that if he brought him a riddle he couldn't guess, then he would set his father free. The son went away and after about three years returned to visit the king, and he brought his prepared riddle:

I come on what was not born
I have the mother for reins
Answer me good king
Or set my father free.

The answer, briefly told, is that the son had killed a mare about to foal; he took the colt, raised it, and then rode it to the king, using reins made of the dead mare's hide.[36]

Pretended Obscene Riddles

¿Qué le mete el hombre a la mujer cuando se casa? (What does a man put on [or, in] a woman when he marries her?) *El anillo* (A ring).[37]

Riddling Wellerisms

As rare as Wellerisms are in Spanish (according to Archer Taylor), Américo Paredes reported a riddling game involving the Wellerism pattern—like, "What did the wallpaper say to the wall? 'Don't move, I've got you covered.'" Representative of a type popular in Mexico and the Spanish-speaking Southwest during the 1930s and 1940s, the *¿Qué le dijo?* reported by Paredes is

¿Qué le dijo el brasero al soplador? (What did the brazier say to the bellows?)

Con la estufa que han traido no soplamos ya niguno de los dos. (Now that they have brought in a stove, neither of us can do much blowing [i.e., neither of us is worth much]).[38]

Student collectors of folklore in the lower Rio Grande valley also reported the riddling Wellerism type:

¿Qué le dijo el piojo al calvo? (What did the louse say to the bald man?) *No te agaches por que me caigo* (Don't bend over or I'll fall off).[39]

¿Qué le dijo la luna al sol? (What did the moon say to the sun?) *Tan grande y no te dejan que salgas de noche* (You're so big, and [yet] they don't let you go out at night).[40]

In this short segment have been represented a full display of Taylor's categories of true riddles, as well as assorted conundrums, riddle problems, riddling questions, a neck riddle, riddling Wellerisms, and a pretended obscene riddle. Such an assortment of riddles, collected from a variety of geographical locations, further demonstrates the liveliness of Mexican-American folklore.

CHAPTER FIVE

Rhymes and Folk Poetry

FROM THE CRADLE upwards, children respond to the characteristics of poetry —rhythm, rhyme, and words that do interesting things. The simplest detail of life can acquire these characteristics—like the youngster running into the house singing, "I'm going upstairs to potty, I'm going upstairs to potty," to the widespread tune of

Johnny's got a girl- friend!

A tale that has a bit of poetry seizes the child's imagination forcefully. I remember reciting once to my five-year-old daughter an item I had just learned in freshman German: *Spieglein, Spieglein an der Wand, wer ist die Schönste im ganzen Land?* and I was delighted that she immediately knew the English equivalent of what I was saying—"Mirror, mirror on the wall, who is the fairest of them all?"

If a poetic pattern such as that can bridge the gap from one language to another, one must accept the importance of poetry to the young. And throughout the folklore of the world's cultures, verses linger on in minds no longer young. In every culture, I would wager, mothers amuse their little ones with rhymes and musical words; the Mexican-American mother is certainly no exception. Visualize, if you will, the mother, singing to the baby she's bouncing on her foot,

Caballito, caballito	Little pony, little pony
no me tumba, no me tumba	do not throw me, do not throw me
a galope y a galope	galloping, galloping
recio, recio, recio	watch us go—
¡Qué viva Antonio!	Long live Antonio![1]

And what mother has not amused a child by counting toes or fingers with a rhyme? This one goes with the toes:

Éste era un pollito;
éste lo pescó,
éste lo mató,
éste lo guisó,
éste lo comió.

Here we have a little pullet;
this one caught it,
this one killed it,
this one cooked it,
this one ate it.[2]

A variant from Santa Barbara, California, used for counting fingers, starting with the little one, is remarkably similar:

Éste mató un pollito.
Éste puso el agua a calentar.
Éste lo peló.
Éste lo guisó.
Y éste se lo comió.

This one killed a little chick.
This one put the water to heat.
This one plucked it.
This one cooked it.
And this one ate it up![3]

And that explains why the thumb is so fat! Another, again counting off the fingers beginning with the littlest one, goes

Niño chiquito y bonito,
el señor de los anillos,
el largo y flaco,
y mira lejos,
y el cuadrilongo.

ONE is a boy, pretty and small;
TWO is the man of the rings;
THREE is a soldier, slender and tall;
FOUR can point at things;
and FIVE is strong as a wall.[4]

A Fort Hancock, Texas, mother of five used this counting rhyme which she got from her mother:

Niño chiquito
Señor de anillos
Tonto y loco
Lambe casuelas
Mata piojos

Little child
Ringman
Dumb and crazy
Lickpot
Killer of lice.

The thumb was called "killer of lice" because lice picked out of the hair were mashed with the thumb.[5] From Tucson, Arizona, comes a rhythmical game one plays with a child who is beginning to sit up:

Reque, reque, requesón,
pide pan y no le dan.
Pide queso y le dan un hueso
pa que se rasque el pescuezo.

Reque, reque, cottage cheese,
ask for bread and they don't give it to you.
Ask for cheese and they give you a bone
so you can scratch your neck.

With the first three lines, the child's hands are held and moved back and forth;

on the fourth line the child is allowed to fall backwards on the pillow, while he is tickled on the neck.[6]

To put a child to sleep, says Frank Aguilar of Tucson, the following rhyme is repeated monotonously. It doesn't have much tune, he says:

Lulú que lulú	Lulu, what a lulu
que San Camaleón,	that Saint Chameleon,
debajo de un hueco	under a hole
salió un ratón.	a mouse came out.
Mátalo, mátalo	Kill it, kill it
de un guantón.	with a big glove.
Éste niño quiere	This child wants
que le cante yo.	me to sing to him.
Cántele su mamá	His mama can sing to him
que ella lo parió.	since she gave him birth.[7]

What child could grow up properly without learning hand coordination, as is done with "Pat-a-cake" or a similar rhythmical verse? Since many a Mexican-American child has seen someone in the family making tortillas, patting out the cornmeal dough in alternating directions (by turning the hands back and forth), the following from the lower Rio Grande comes quite naturally:

Tortillitas, tortillitas	Little tortillas, little tortillas
tortillitas para papá	little tortillas for Pa-pa,
tortillitas para mamá;	little tortillas for Ma-ma;
tortillitas de salvado	little tortillas made of bran
para papá cuando está enojado	when Pa-pa is a worried man;
tortillitas de manteca	little tortillas brown and snappy
para mamá que está contenta.	for Ma-ma when she is happy.[8]

Although folk games will be considered more fully later, rhymes are integral parts of many children's pastimes—especially counting out, to see who will be "it." The Mexican-American child's world is no exception. The following, which defies translation, is one example; as the rhyme is chanted, fists of the children, in a circle, are touched:

Pín, marín, de Don Pinqüé,
cácara, mácara, Pipiri fué.

On the word *fué,* the fist is withdrawn from the circle and the chant goes on, till only one fist—belonging to "it"—is left.[9]

An El Paso variant of the previous item is longer, and one suspects that is possibly the "right" version—if there were such a thing in the world of folklore:

De tin marín, de dopingüéy	De tin marín, de dopingüéy
cúcara, mácara, títere fué	cúcara, mácara, the puppet's it
Yo no fuí, fué teté	I'm not it, it's teté
Pégale, pégale, ella fué	Hit her, hit her, it's her.[10]

Even the attempted translation, done by a bilingual native with a college degree, makes no real sense—but the children apparently love the nonsense words just as English-speaking children enjoy the equally nonsensical "Eeny, meeny, minie moe" of their own selection process.

In Tucson, the same system is used, but by pointing to each child:

Pín pín sarabín.
Yoqui yoqui pasaré
por los lagos de San Juan.

Basically nonsense words, except for "will pass by the lakes of Saint John," the verse eliminates the person being pointed at on the words *San Juan*. The old familiar counting-out rhyme "Engine, engine number nine, coming down Chicago line..." has been collected on El Paso playgrounds by María Elena Hernández, and the verse is sufficiently familiar that a football player in Canutillo, Texas, in 1963 who wore jersey number nine was generally called "Engine, engine" by his classmates, who were much more at home in Spanish than in English.[11]

Jumping rope is another widespread pastime involving verses to keep a rhythm, and in many places along the Mexican border, a sort of cultural confusion takes place. Richard Southern, a student in my first folklore class, provided the material for the following note about the school playgrounds of South El Paso:

> . . . If one listens with even half an ear, he can hear the most marvelous confusions, linguistically speaking. None of these are as interesting, in my experience, as what happens to standard jump-rope rhymes. One, the familiar "Ice cream soda, Delaware Punch,/Tell the initials of your honey bunch. . ." comes out thus...
>
> Ice cream soda, lemon pop,
> Tell me the licious of your sweet hot. [sic]
>
> [The alphabet proceeds, to the initial of the jumper's current flame, Henry.]
>
> Henry, Henry, do you love Dolores?
> Yes, no, may-be so,
> *La besó en el cho*
> Yes, no, may-be so,
> *La besó en el cho.*

The recurring line translates "He kissed her in the movie"—but the Spanish words for movie, *cine* or *película,* neither scan nor rhyme. Every youngster knows what a "cho" is, and gives a common Spanish sound to the beginning consonant of the word "show."[12]

Another student collector, who recalls from her own childhood that they almost never jumped rope to Spanish verses, recalled an interesting variation of the above, with a variety of possible lines:

Ice cream soda
Made the stars
Tell me the 'nicials
Of your sweetheart.
A, B, C,. . . (miss)
Carlos, Carlos, will you marry ——?
Yes, no, *la besó* (he kissed her)
Yes, no, *la cacheteó* (he slapped her)
Yes, no, *la pegó* (he hit her)
Yes, no, *se la llevó* (he took her with him).[13]

Even without such a mixture of language, however, cross-cultural blending produces some interesting variations. The following item from South El Paso illustrates such a point:

Hallo, boys, how about a date?
I'll meesha at the corner of [sic] half past eight.
I can do the Kootchie Kootchie,
I can do the splits
I can hold myself for just a little bit.
First comes love,
Then comes marriage,
Next comes Sylvia
With a baby on her hand.

Obviously, the usual version has Sylvia with a baby carriage, to carry out the rhyme—but South El Paso Sylvias generally don't have such fancy aids to child-rearing. Thus the playground variation follows the jumper's experience of seeing Mamá or Aunt carrying a baby "on her hand."[14]

One collection from South El Paso includes two jump-rope rhymes in Spanish, one sixteen lines long. The other reflects a common practice, that of counting—boxes of powder to fix a girl's face, or doctors to help the girl who kissed a snake, etc.[15] It goes thus:

Tán, tán.	Knock, knock.
¿Quién es?	Who is it?

El cartero.
¿Cuántas cartas trae?
Uno, dos, tres...

The mailman.
How many letters has he?
One, two, three. . .[16]

Children in every culture doubtless enjoy playing jokes or making fun of one another. Mexican-American children have a goodly assortment of taunting rhymes. The following examples are probably typical. For a crybaby, one says

¿Señora Santa Ana
Porque llora el niño?
Por una manzana
Qué se le ha perdido.

Mrs. Santa Ana,
Why is the baby crying?
For an apple
That he has lost.

And as occasions arise,

¡Mentiroso,
Cara de baboso!

Liar
Face of a fool (literally, slobberer)!

¡Chino, chino, japonés,
Come caca y no me des!

Chinaman, Chinaman, Japanese,
Eats shit and doesn't give me any!

Pelón, pelontete,
Cabeza de cohete,
Que vende tamales,
De a cinco, de a siete.

Baldy, bald head
Head like a rocket,
Who sells tamales
By fives and sixes.[17]

Almost any person's name can lend itself to a rhyming insult, inventive as children are:

¡Juana la marrana se cayó en el soquetel;
Vino Pancho Villa, y ni él pudo levantar!
(Janie, the pig, fell in the mud; along came Pancho Villa [the famous bandit and guerrilla fighter] and even he couldn't pick her up!)[18]

¡Arturo, pan duro,
Yo te curo
Con un palo duro!

Arthur, hard bread,
I'll cure you
With a hard stick![19]

And then there is an all-purpose rhyme, ready for the name to be filled in:

¡—— paleta,
Cara de peseta!

—— lollipop,
Face like a twenty-five cent piece![20]

Of course nonsense words can be used for taunting as well:

¡Pilorillo, Camotillo, *Tienes cara de zorrillo!*	Pilorillo, little sweet potato, You have a face like a skunk![21]

And for the local dumbbell, there's the ubiquitous

¡A-E-I-O-U, *El burro sabe mas que tú!*	AH-AY-EE-OH-OO, (phonetically) The donkey knows more than you![22]

And a general-purpose taunt of the same order,

Ola que viene, ola que va *¿Hola baboso, cómo te va?*	Wave that comes, wave that goes, Hello stupid, how's it going?[23]

In northern New Mexico, says Charles Aranda, the practice of taunting went far beyond childhood:

> *Chiquillados* [mischievous pranks] were very short verses recited by a man either to humor or impress a woman he wanted to dance with. If the woman accepted the verse, she would get up and dance. The chiquillados, which rhyme like some dichos and proverbs, sound better in Spanish,. . .[and] in the process of translation. . .they may lose their charm.

A selection of his chiquillados follows, together with his translations, but lacking any indication of his sources or the times these rhymes were popular:

Anoche fuí a tu casa, *tres golpes le dí al candado,* *tú no sirves para amores,* *tienes el sueño pesado.*	Last night I went to your house I knocked three times— you aren't good for love because you sleep too heavily.
Aunque tu padre me diera *los bueyes y la carreta* *no me he de casar contigo,* *ojos de borrega prieta.*	Even if your father would give me the oxen and the cart, I would never marry you, eyes of a black sheep.
De ésta flor *y de ésta rosa,* *señora, usted es coja.*	From this flower and this rose, Madam, you are lame.

(This is a play on words. The poor woman thought she had been given her choice. *Usted es coja* = You are lame; *Usted escoja* = You choose.)[24]

While this custom—perhaps from northern New Mexico—involves little rhymes, a similar practice occurs in other parts of the Spanish Southwest as well. Around El Paso it is called *echando flores* (throwing flowers) or *piropos* (compliments, or flirtatious remarks). One informant told my student collector that "definitely there is a difference in the *flor* [flower, compliment] in Santa Fe [New Mexico] and what is used here [in El Paso]"—but she gave no particulars.[25] Perhaps the difference between the Santa Fe area and farther south is that playful insults are the rule in New Mexico (judging by Aranda's collection), while the compliments along the Mexican border are frankly positive, although they are seldom in rhyme. There were guidelines for such flowery comments: Never compliment a girl walking with her father or older brother.[26] However, when she's walking with her mother, a double dose of flattery is possible—"Look at those lovely sisters!"[27] Doubtless, if the neighborhood area is Spanish-speaking, the flores are in Spanish, but all that my students collected were basically in English—and pleasant, not vulgar: "What beautiful eyes you have. What beautiful flowers!"[28] or "I like the one in green"—which causes the girls to look around to see who's wearing green, and often no one is!),[29] or the simple and eloquent *Máma-cita!*—which translates directly as "Little mother," but says so much more —like, "Wow, baby, you're something else!"[30]

In Mexico, where the custom of complimenting goes both ways between the sexes (a girl might say, *¡Ay, qué guapo!* "My, how handsome!" as easily as a boy might utter his approval), rhymes are sometimes used, but they seem to be set patterns learned by the *echador*—the "thrower" of compliments—so he (or she) will have a good comment handy when the time arises. My Chihuahua-raised mother-in-law, Lucina Lara Rey de Fischer, recently told me of a paperback book of such sample compliments, written, appropriately, by a Señor Flores, which she saw in a bookstore to help the *pueblo*—the common people—to appear as sophisticated as the upper classes. And in Spain, she says, there's even another word —*requiebro,* also meaning "flattering comment," to cover the practice. Generally, rather than the practiced rhyme, the flatterer uses a spontaneous comment —like "What great legs you have!"[31] Others are as simple as "You're still green; I'll wait till you ripen,"[32] or "May I accompany you, you beautiful creature?"—to which the young lady might well respond, "You certainly may not!"[33] Even with such potential put-downs, the Mexican-American practice of complimenting young ladies is here to stay, and even expected by the young ladies, who see it as the young man's duty to let a female know how he feels, even if he can't come up with a rhyme. One informant, raised in Italy, continues to enjoy the attention of men at the age of 72, especially the notorious Italian pinching and patting; she suggested that American women are most likely to visit areas in Italy where the young men are well-known for such attentions![34]

A more innocent diversion, hand-clapping, is another frequently found folk pastime involving rhymes. One such game involves several children, arranged in a circle facing each other; the play follows as the motions in the rhyme indicate, for as long as the participants can hold out:

Por arriba, por abajo	Upwards, downwards
Por el lado, por el otro.	To one side, to the other.[35]

Three other hand-clapping rhymes, collected with only directions that they had "accompanying clapping or appropriate movements," offer quite a variety:

Abajo del puente, dale Pepito	Under the bridge Pepito comes out
Tocando su guitarra	Playing his guitar.
¿Verdad que toca bien?	Doesn't he play well?
Ti-lin-tin-tin.	(strumming an imaginary guitar)
¿Verdad que toca mal?	Doesn't he play badly?
Ton-lon-ton-ton.	(strumming clumsily)
Éste juego se acaba a las tres	This game ends on three—
¡Uno-dos-tres!	One, two, three![36]

A rather macabre subject is gaily chanted in the following:

Don Martín, tirilín, tirilín,	Mr. Martin, tirilín, tirilín,
Se le murió, torolón, torolón,	He had die, torolón, torolón,
Su chiquitín, tirilín, tirilín	His little child, tirilín, tirilín
De sarampión, torolón, torolón.	Of measles.[37]

(Possibly, as in the previous game, the sounds indicate well- or poorly-played musical instruments, or it may simply be repetition or imitation of the ending sounds *-in* and *-on).*

And then there's a question-and-answer rhyme of considerable humor:

Chango, gorila,	Monkey, gorilla,
¿Quién te hizo el pelo?	Who gave you your haircut?
¡Ramon!	Ramon!
¿Cuánto costo?	How much did it cost?
¡Toston!	Half a dollar!
¿Cómo te quedo?	How did it suit you (or, leave you)?
¡Chueco!	Lopsided![38]

"Rain, rain, go away"—how often that chant has been sent heavenward by children who want the skies to clear up so they can play out of doors. It's even possible that a few mothers have recited it fervently under their breaths, tired of having the youngsters in their hair. Mexican-American children have their equivalent rhymes—but with the opposite purpose, to bring rain. Perhaps, in the frequently arid portions of the Spanish Southwest, it is logical even for children to chant

Que llueva, que llueva,	Let it rain, let it rain,
La virgen de la cueva,	Virgin of the cave,
Los pajaritos cantan,	The little birds sing,
La luna se levanta.	The moon is rising.
Que sí, que nó,	Yes, no
Que caiga un chaparrón,	Let a downpour fall
Que sí, que nó	Yes, no
Le canta el labrador.	Sings the laborer (or, plowman).[39]

It is interesting to note that the official textbook for the primary grade in Mexico teaches the identical version of the rhyme, under the heading *"La Lluvia"* (The Rain), differing only in exclamation marks at the end of the first line and wherever commas appear in the last four lines.[40]

The only other rain-related rhyme I have discovered is simply descriptive:

Cuando Juana se tapa el rebozo	When Juana wears her misty shawl
y Pedro el sombrero	and Pedro his sombrero tall,
se güisa aguacero.	full well we know that rain will fall.

The source comments, "Pedro is the Saddle Mountain above Monterrey, Mexico, and Juana is a neighboring peak. The same rhyme is used for their peaks in Mexico."[41] But none of my student collectors has recorded this one.

The *piñata* is built upon a clay pot, covered with papier mâché to form an animal or other shape, and topped with strips of fringed colored tissue paper. Filled with candy, it is suspended above the head of a blindfolded child, usually at a party, while the child swings wildly with a stick. The adults in charge of the party pull the rope, keeping the piñata above the reach of the stick, to the accompaniment of laughter from the surrounding children at the wild misses of the determined stick wielder. The group often chants

Dále, dále, dále,	Hit it, hit it, hit it,
no pierdes el tino,	Don't lose your aim,
porque si lo pierdes,	For if you lose it,
pierdes el camino.	You lose your way.

Finally the piñata is lowered within the child's reach and broken, and the goodies cascade downward to the waiting group.[42]

Another popular game dependent upon a rhyme is the following, found often in the Mexican border area. It resembles "London Bridge" in its actions, with two children holding hands to make a bridge while the line of other children passes through:

Víbora, víbora, de la mar,	Snake, snake, of the sea

Por aquí pueden pasar.	Can pass through here.
La de adelante corre mucho,	The one in front runs hard
Y la de atras se quedará.	And the one behind is left.

On the word *atrás* (behind) the person under the bridge is captured. Then:

Que pase el Rey que ha de pasar	Let the King pass, who should pass,
Y la hija del conde se va a quedar.	And the Count's daughter remains.

She is captured. Then:

La casita se quebró:	The little house is broken;
La mandaron componer	They ordered it fixed
Con azúcar y café.	With sugar and coffee.[43]

From this point on, the game takes many forms; often the captured one has to choose whether he or she is to be a *sandía* (watermelon) or *melón* (cantaloupe)—then a tug-of-war begins between the two groups of melons, headed by the two who formed the bridge.[44] To illustrate the variety involved in this rhyme game, the Mexican primary textbook presents a much longer version—seventeen lines—with a fuller assortment of fruits and flowers named, but no apparent choosing of sides as in the border versions.[45]

Nonsense rhymes abound in the Mexican-American culture:

Luna, luna, dame una tuna	Moon, moon, give me a prickly pear;
la que me diste	The one you gave me
se cayó a la laguna.	Fell into the lake.[46]

And there are even tongue-twisters:

El arzobispo de Constantinopla se quiere desconstantinoplizar.
El que lo desconstantinoplice será un gran desaconstantinoplizador.
The Archbishop of Constantinople wants to be de-constantinopled;
whoever de-constantinoples him will be a great de-constaninopler.[47]

Some years ago I was delighted when a student from El Paso, knowing of my interest in the Mexican bandit Pancho Villa, shared an old rhyme with me:

¡Pancho Villa	Pancho Villa
mato su tía	killed his aunt
con una pistola	with a pistol
que no servía!	that didn't work.[48]

A few years later, another student collected the same rhyme—and then topped it with more Villa nonsense of the pattern:

¡Pancho Villa	Pancho Villa
mato su tía	killed his aunt
con un zapato	with a shoe
que no servía!	that didn't work![49]
Pancho Villa	Pancho Villa
planchó su tía	ironed his aunt
con una tortilla.	with a tortilla.
¡Pancho Villa	Pancho Villa
'plastó la tortilla	mashed the tortilla
con mantequilla!	with butter![50]

Street vendors with their cries are found in many cultures, and rhyme and rhythm often decorate them. Jan Brunvand has an interesting group from the South,[51] but they are found throughout the Spanish Southwest as well. As a child, traveling eastward through Texas from El Paso, I could hardly wait till we reached the little railroad town of Del Rio, where the train crews changed and during twenty or so minutes the *tamalero* (tamale seller) sang out, "Tamales, hot tamales," over and over. Those tamales, anticipated for endless miles of clacking wheels, were the finest feast a kid over hooked a lip over. John G. Bourke, who reported on Mexican foods from San Antonio to Mexico City, reported similar simple cries of street vendors[52]—but nothing he tells can surpass those of the narrow streets of Juárez, Chihuahua. Almost anything is for sale: from the 1960s I recall *Naranjas, naranjas, seis por un peso* (Oranges, oranges, six for a peso [the peso was worth considerably more then than in the '80s]), or *Elotes, e-e-e-lo-o-otes* (Corn on the cob). But the classic of them all was the fellow who had a break in his quavering voice. Each Saturday he came down *Calle* (Street) *Gabino Barrera* selling *menudo* (a kind of watery soup cooked with beef tripe and *pozole,* hominy-like corn), singing out *Menudo, calientito el men-u-u-do-o,* his voice dropping in pitch and almost deserting him on the last syllable. He sold lots of menudo (which is a traditional hangover cure among many imbibing Southwesterners), but the chant with its awkward rhythm and grating musical qualities was —and is—far more wonderful to me. *There* was a folk rhyme!

CHAPTER SIX

Prose Narratives

A FORM OF folklore that crosses all age and sex boundaries is the prose narrative—vast in its spread from serious religion-based legends to whimsical anecdotes, from tales only a few sentences long to wandering accounts that could run to small book-length, given the skill of a good yarn-spinner. Modern times have come to the Mexican-American culture of the Southwest, with dependence upon television soap operas (called *novelas* in Spanish), and the near disappearance of the extended family that once kept the old ways alive by keeping close contact between—and among—the generations. Once old *tías* (aunts) or *abuelos* (grandfathers) were close at hand to have a hand and a voice in bringing up the children. Many a family had an assortment of rooms, apartment-like, arranged around a central patio where little ones played, and older ones sat in the cool mornings or evenings, taking time just to be, to savor the juices of life. With such an arrangement, according to the Mexican folk description of family perfections, *junto pero no revueltos* (together but not mixed up), folklore had a better chance at living, or at least the prose narrative did.

Now the schools in Mexico try to keep things alive, and textbooks teach the stories of national heroes, like Miguel Hidalgo y Costilla and José María Moreles, or fables to guide the conduct of the young, like *La zorra y la cigüeña* (The fox and the crane) or *Las manos que no querían trabajar* (The hands that didn't want to work)—in adaptations that read well, yet seem to lack the spontaneity and flavor of a real-life sharing experience.[1] Even so, the prose narrative is alive and well in most of its forms among the Mexican-Americans, kept going by folks' continuing desire to share a "good one," or to pass on an accounting of why something is so or how a geographical feature came to be. And even knowing that some of the retold narratives are as "made-up" as Parson Weems's story of George Washington and the cherry tree or some of the Paul Bunyan tales, the human animal is gregarious and geared to sharing ideas and experience.

One major exception to the presence of living narratives among the Mexican-Americans, as among North Americans,[2] is in the area of myth. While myth is seldom found in oral tradition, teachers still retell stories of Aztec times to their pupils, and various methods of preserving them in print are used. For example, one of my treasures is a 1962 calendar distributed by the National Lottery of Mexico, picturing accounts of *Momentos culminantes de la medicina en México* (Outstanding moments in Mexican medicine)—contributions of the Aztecs to

Surrounded by votive candles and native plants, the rock bearing the image of the Virgin of Guadalupe can be compared with a chromo (colored print) of her picture as she appeared, according to legend, on Tepeyác Hill, formerly sacred to an Aztec goddess, Tonantzín.

the medical knowledge of Spanish conquerors—as well as bringing to common knowledge facts about how advanced medically the Aztecs were. One of the events deals with an Aztec herbal doctor tending a head wound Conquistador Hernán Cortés had suffered during the *Noche triste*—the "sad night" in 1520 when the Spaniards were nearly annihilated by the Mexican natives. Such education, although it lacks the fluidity and variability one associates with folklore, does stimulate respect for the culture, which is certainly one of the end results of the sharing of folklore. And knowledgeable teachers in the United States also build self-esteem among their Mexican-American students by using similar materials.

Another subject for calendar art—found almost everywhere, in homes, meat markets, *molinos* (mills where corn is ground for use in tortillas, tamales, and the like), and on both sides of the United States-Mexico border—is Aztec legendry. Stalwart warriors stand guard over sleeping Aztec princesses, both dressed scantily but in plumed and colorful costume; others have the warrior fighting off wild animals; any number of other situations reflect the mystique of the bygone era that existed in a sort of Garden of Eden yesteryear before the coming of the Spaniards. The anti-Spanish feelings described in Chapter One are at the root of

A stained-glass window in a church in northern Mexico, part of a set, reveals the final act in the drama of the appearance of the Virgin of Guadalupe to Juan Diego. She had sent him to tell Bishop Zumárraga, on the right, that she wanted a chapel built on Tepeyác hill in her honor; the bishop, demanding a sign, was sent one—the center picture, which miraculously appeared on Juan's cape where he had wrapped roses he gathered at the Virgin's command to show to the bishop. This picture is reproduced virtually everywhere in Spanish America, in paintings, murals, and *grutas.*

this veneration of *la raza* (literally "the race," the Aztecs, but with far richer connotations of pride). Even though the Aztec mythology as oral prose narrative has passed away, its influence shapes the Mexican—and the Mexican-American—mind.

Religious Legends

In a culture that is strongly Catholic, where the Virgin Mary and the saints are asked daily by thousands to intercede for them with their problems, it is certainly understandable that religious legends and personal experience stories would grow up to accompany the "official" saints legends. Jan Brunvand notes the existence of the approved, non-varying stories that shape the faith of adherents to organized religion everywhere, but he also speaks of the folk variations on such themes that qualify as living folklore. Such is certainly the case with the Virgin of

Guadalupe, patroness of Mexico and of the Western Hemisphere. The official miracle relates how a lady appeared to a lowly Indian, Juan Diego, in December 1531 on a hill outside Mexico City—a hill sacred to the worship of Tonantzín, an Indian "Mother of Heaven" cult figure. The lady told Juan that she wanted a chapel built on that spot, and sent him to inform the bishop. As might be expected, Bishop Zumárraga doubted that the Virgin would use such a lowly messenger and asked for a sign. When Juan returned to the hill, the lady received the bishop's reply and told the Indian to take his *tilma* (cape) and gather up the roses that had appeared on the rocky hillside—in cold December—and carry them to the bishop. When the load of roses tumbled out on the floor before the bishop, the tilma's rough surface contained a picture of the Virgin—and the sign was received as genuine.[3]

This picture of the Virgin of Guadalupe hangs in millions of homes, adorns hundreds of churches, and is enshrined in the hearts of countless believers—often supported by reproductions on advertising calendars like those that continue the Aztec traditions. Scientific studies have been made in recent years to confirm the authenticity of the story (as has been done with the Shroud of Turin, said to have wrapped Jesus' body). One such study was undertaken to determine if Juan Diego's image was preserved in the eye of the Virgin in the picture.[4] But as someone has pointed out, it is not the church that makes saints—it is the beliefs of the people. And among many Mexican-Americans, as with their relatives in Mexico, such studies are pointless: it was the Virgin Mary who appeared to Juan Diego, and countless pilgrimages to her shrine have been made, sometimes to ask for help but more often to express gratitude—to pay a *manda* (promise) for having received the requested help. *Casos verídicos* (true accounts) are related of how the Virgin or a particular saint has cured a serious ailment or brought fruit to a childless marriage.

One of the stories dearest to my heart involves a family that lives in El Porvenir, a village of three thousand souls some fifty miles downriver from El Paso on the Mexican side. Several years ago I was collecting, via color slides, the *grutas* (home religious shrines) that are so common to the Spanish Southwest. Repeatedly I was told of the miraculous rock to be seen in El Porvenir—one of my informants being the sheriff of El Paso County, a devout Catholic. I went to the village, soon was directed to the house, and was welcomed as the family had welcomed literally thousands of believers—pilgrims, almost—to what had become a modest shrine. Eagerly the wife, Señora Ruvalcaba, told me how many years ago her husband, then a boy of ten, had been hunting in the *Sierra de Guadalupe*—a cluster of mountains in northern Chihuahua named for the Virgin. He had picked up a curiously shaped rock, about the size of a football, that had a huge crack running through it. Something told him, she said, to pull the rock open; inside he discovered a geode-like formation of black and white crystals bearing a strong resemblance to the Virgin of Guadalupe, and in the image also of Juan Diego, kneeling before her, showing even the folds in his white

Decorated for the Christmas season, the religious relic with the image of the Virgin of Guadalupe draws hundreds of friends and worshipers to the humble home of the Ruvalcaba family in northern Chihuahua—including many Mexican-Americans from across the border in the United States.

peasant trousers behind the knee. The images were very close to the way calendar art often depicts the scene. The rock was taken home and kept safe, and the local head of the *aduana* (customs) force provided an elegant case for it of dark, walnut-like wood. The rock—relic, call it what you will—has become a community treasure for El Porvenir. The boy, now a grandfather, is quite humble that he was chosen to discover this wonder.

The miraculous image has left the humble home only once: the local mayor asked to be allowed to borrow it for a while, as is the custom; saints' figures are even borrowed from local churches overnight in many communities.[5] After a week, the husband and wife had the same dream. A luminous cloud shape had appeared in the corner of the bedroom, where the rock was usually kept, and *la Virgen* told them that she wanted to come home. At daybreak they went to get her, and she hasn't left the house since. But thousands of people have come to the house to see her, to pray for assistance before the image, and to leave small gifts or *milagros*. These literally are "miracles," little silver- or gold-covered arms, legs, or other representations of body parts or even animals, about an inch and a quarter high, symbolizing the subject of the Virgin's healing power—or, sometimes, I am told, helping the Virgin to see what needs Her help. (These symbols have the technical name *ex votos,* and demonstrate the concept of public acknowledgement of the generosity of the Virgin or the saint involved.)

On the evening of December 11 each year, the small house is crowded with people. The family and neighbors have brought together holiday foods —tamales, *piloncillo* (cones of compressed brown sugar), *capirotada* (a sweet concoction of brown sugar and bread)—and soft drinks (some of it bought with coins left before the Virgin's image throughout the year), and a rich assortment of decorations around the shrine, which has been brought out to the *sala* (living room) for the event. Then a quiet evening of fellowship begins. People from as far away as Los Angeles, Veracruz, and Mexico City have come to the celebration, Señora Ruvalcaba told me. At midnight, when it is December 12, begins the Feast Day of Our Lady of Guadalupe (the traditional day on which the miracle of the picture occurred). The whole town is welcome, and they linger until dawn, leaving with the feeling that they have been blessed, the Señora said. There have been no miracles, as such, but in a era cursed by the sins of the flesh, the family has been spared: *"No viciosos, no borrachos, no divorciados"* (No drug addicts, no drunks, no divorces), she told me.[6]

Mexican-Americans on both sides of the border seem to feel a personal closeness with their *santos* (saints) and *La Guadalupana* (the Virgin of Guadalupe). One little lady in Cordova, New Mexico, who was honored with the job of cleaning the church and keeping the santos neat and clean, talked to the statues as if they were children—or at least, close friends:

> She would tell San Antonio, as she gave the child in his arms a loving pat on the cheek, "Be careful with that child; do not let him fall, good Saint Antonio." She would promise the Virgin a new dress because the one she wore had a spot of melted wax from the taper that stood by it . . . Then she shook an admonitory finger in the face of Santa Ines [she's in charge of finding lost things], and said, *"¡Mira!* (Look!) I will not make you that new dress if you do not help my nephew Manuel find his burro so his family will not lack wood."[7]

Indeed, I have often heard accounts of San Antonio's having the baby Jesus taken from him as punishment, or a santo being stood on its head for the same reason, when a favor has been requested but apparently ignored by the saint. However, I have never heard of the Virgin's statue being treated that way.

The Santo Niño de Atocha, a manifestation of the child Jesus, is held in very high regard, and legends attribute unusual activities to the statue in a chapel adjoining the Sanctuary of Chimayó in New Mexico. The little church has a *pozo* (literally, "well," but actually a little hole in the ground) which yields yellowish earth said to have miraculous properties, especially for healing cripples. A room adjoining the pozo is hung with hundreds of leg braces, pairs of crutches, and other equipment for the lame—and the healing is attributed to the dirt, which is believed to replenish itself. People come from far away to the little New Mexico village for the cure, and they always visit the small chapel where the statue sits, richly dressed in its traditional costume. Local stories abound that the statue walks about in the valley each night helping people, and wears out a pair of shoes a week.[8]

Another legend which attracts tourists as well as the faithful is about the Miraculous Staircase in the Loretto Chapel in Santa Fe. As the story goes, the nuns who sang in the choir loft in the chapel had difficulty climbing up the ladder to do their devotions. Prayers were answered when a journeying carpenter appeared, and providing his own wood, built a self-supporting spiral staircase for the nuns—and then disappeared. Naturally it was assumed that the carpenter was Saint Joseph, plying his old trade—and as the story goes, the wood was unidentifiable, nor were there any scraps left over. Researchers have actually identified the carpenter as a man from Germany who returned there for family reasons—but the legend goes on, and provides financial support for the Sisters of Loretto.[9]

Less commercial, but no less sincerely believed on a local basis, are the legends concerning the statue of San Miguel (Saint Michael) that adorns the mission of La Purísima (Our Lady of the Immaculate Conception) in Socorro, Texas, twenty miles down the valley from El Paso. Many years ago (as many good stories begin), a wooden *carreta* (cart) was hauling the statue from a prosperous church down in Old Mexico to a struggling mission or chapel in New Mexico. (It was the custom for churches replacing their old statues to send them to less fortunate congregations.) When the carreta neared the present site of La Purísima, its wheels sank in the sand and could not be budged—even when additional teams of oxen were hitched to the cart. Finally the attendants realized that a miracle was at work: San Miguel wanted to stay there! So a *ramada* (brush shelter) was built for the statue, and the carreta was immediately freed from its sandy trap. Later the statue was moved into the church, where it receives devotion from the parishioners.[10]

Some years later, according to local legend, an Indian attack threatened the little settlement of Socorro, and the statue of San Miguel, sword and all, disappeared from its pedestal. Several days later it was back, sword nicked and garments tattered—as if the santo had been in battle. And the Indians never attacked.[11]

Some years back, when I was doing a slide presentation on home shrines, a member of the audience told a story involving a statue of the Virgin Mary that was left behind, according to the account, when the Pueblo revolt drove out the Spaniards and Christianized Indians from the Santa Fe area of northern New Mexico. When the reconquest brought the Spaniards back, the statue—shot full of arrows—was found behind the altar in the mission where it had been left. The explanation I was given was that this particular representation of the Virgin had her standing on top of a writhing serpent—symbol of life to the Pueblos—and

Inside this adobe mission, La Purísima, built to replace an earlier building washed away by the flooding Rio Grande, is the statue of San Miguel (Saint Michael), about which legends abound. The mission was founded in 1680; this building was erected in the 1840s in Socorro, Texas, where New Mexican Pueblos and Spanish settlers fled after an Indian revolt in northern New Mexico.

therefore she was a very unwelcome image for them, a threat to their way of life. New Mexico's most celebrated statue of the Virgin, called *La Conquistadora* (The Conqueress), was taken south in 1680 with the refugees and returned in triumph with Governor Diego José de Vargas in his reconquest of the territory in 1693.[12]

Near the town of Silver City, New Mexico, a curious rock formation has given rise to a host of related tales. It is in the shape of a nun kneeling in prayer—and there are those who say that even the folds of her habit are visible in the rock, which is about one hundred feet high. The Grant County Chamber of Commerce has a leaflet which tells one version of the legend associated with the formation, and the story "had been immortalized in poetry," according to one collector. But the legends are varied. In several of the stories, the characters are given names—Raquel Mendoza de Alarcón and Captain Don Fernando Alarcón (but the name Juan Diego is often used as well, recalling the story of Our Lady of Guadalupe.) Sometimes it is simply a story of a girl who is led astray by a dashing soldier, against her parents' wishes, and is turned to stone as punishment. But the most prevalent story—and the most romantic in many ways—is the following: Long ago, a convent was set up at Silver City to convert the Indians. There were priests and nuns, and soldiers to guard them. One day a young soldier was brought in, severely wounded in a battle with the Indians. A young nun who was assigned to care for him fell in love with him, despite her vows of chastity, and was terribly torn between love and her promises of service to God. She went away from the convent, out to a hill nearby, and prayed to the Virgin Mary for help in her dilemma. To preserve her from sin, the Virgin turned her to stone, and there she stays, the Kneeling Nun.[13]

If one believes in the power and presence of saints, it follows that one will believe in the power and presence of the Devil. They are like the two sides of a coin—and, truly, were it not for *El Diablo,* we would not need the help of the santos, no? At any rate, Satan is omnipresent in the Spanish Southwest, waiting to trap unwary souls, punishing sinners, and even converting the wayward. Obedience legends involving the Devil abound, with strikingly graphic legends taught by the elders to the thoughtless youth of their acquaintance.

One of the most widespread of such tales involves the disobedient daughter who slips out and goes to a dance, in spite of her mother's wish that she stay home and look after her little brothers and sisters. When she arrives at the dance, a handsome stranger dressed in black seeks her out, and dances every dance with her. He talks sweetly, and she begins to have visions of wedding ceremonies and to hear wedding bells in her mind. Toward midnight, in the midst of a whirling dance, the handsome stranger snags his trouser leg on a nail, and a child, sleeping on the floor under a table, wakes in time to see that the stranger has a foot like a rooster. *"¡Mira—pata de gallo!"* (Look—a rooster foot!) cries the child. The lights go out and there is a terrible scream; when the lights are restored, there's the girl, lying half out the door, her lovely face clawed to shreds. It had been the Devil! So, girls, you'd better obey your mamá, or El Diablo may get you. And those dance halls—that's where he waits for you.[14]

A similar story is told of a very disobedient girl—she even fought with her mother over going to a dance, and threw a pair of scissors, sending her mother to the hospital with a serious wound. The mother said, "If she goes out that door [to the dance] the ground is going to open up and eat her," and that's what happened. But the mother relented, and hired all sorts of men, with tractors, to try to dig the girl out—"but they n-e-e-e-ver found her."[15]

A related story, which involves others tempted by the Devil, recounts how a good-looking, well-dressed man came into a bar in Roswell, New Mexico. He had lots of money, and shared it with everyone. While the bar owner was enjoying the rush of business, two men in the bar decided they would rob this rich man. The men followed the man to the Hondo River, where he disappeared—but something jumped out and clawed them, and they ran back to the bar all bleeding. The next day, a woman who had spent a lot of time with the rich man went back to the bar to get the money she had left for safe-keeping with the owner—but it was gone, as was all the money the man had spent. The bar owner had to close his bar, because no one would come in to drink any more. They knew it was the Devil who had been there![16]

Supernatural Legends

Witches, of course, are the Devil's helpers. Just as in the Anglo traditions, they fly about at night, doing mischief, and frequently are associated with cats. A New Mexico *abuela* (grandmother) used to keep the children entertained—and keep them cautious about strange women who might be witches—by telling stories around the fire (after the children had brought in enough firewood, well before dark; they didn't want to be out in the night). One involves a boy who used to play cards with two sisters, but they always sent him home at dark. Two evil-looking cats hissed at him if he came around after sundown, and he generally stayed away. But next day, when the sisters were playing cards, they always knew all the news of the village, and the boy wondered how they found things out. One night his curiosity was strong, and the two cats were not in sight, so he went to the sisters' house. A fire burned in the fireplace, and on the hearth were two pairs of human eyes—left there, apparently, to stay warm. The eyes made the boy feel sick so he scooped them up with a spoon and threw them into the fire, where they popped and sputtered; afraid, he tried to get them out of the fire, but they were hard and black, like walnuts. Just then the cats came in—without eyes—and tried to get him, so he ran away. Next day when he went to play cards with the sisters, they avoided the light, stumbling over tables and chairs. He could finally see that they had round cat eyes. After that they didn't play cards with the boy anymore, but at night they went out, as usual, and the boy kept his doors and windows locked tight![17]

Another witch tale involves both cat's eyes and the form of an owl—recalling the name *La Lechuza* (literally barn owl, but to the folk an evil night influence: a witch!). The witch in this story bewitched her *yerno* (son-in-law), who was a doctor, by burning some of his hair with some owl feathers. He went around acting crazy, pointing at things no one else could see, until finally a psychiatrist who had heard about him came to see if he could help. Asking around, he found that each night since the man had become sick, an owl had flown over the house at dusk. The psychiatrist, who apparently knew his business, announced that the man had been bewitched, and that he suspected the owl. A little detective work revealed that the mother-in-law was to blame, and once when she was out doing her mischief—with cat's eyes instead of her own—the witch's familiar, a male owl, for some reason destroyed the eyes she had left behind. When the witch was punished and her belongings destroyed, the doctor returned to normal.[18]

The legend of the ghostly woman who wanders along canals and rivers crying for her missing children, called in Spanish *La Llorona* (the Weeping Woman), is found in many cultures and regions, but her Hispanic roots make her perhaps the most widely known ghost in the Spanish Southwest. Her New World history goes back to the time of Hernán Cortés, and links her with *La Malinche,* the mistress of the conquistador, who aided the conquest of Mexico as a translator for the Spanish. As tradition has it, after having borne a child to Cortés, La Malinche was replaced by a high-born Spanish wife. Her proud Aztec blood plus her jealousy (according to the folk) drove her to acts of vengeance against the intruders from across the seas. Sometimes it is simply "a Spanish nobleman" and a peasant girl. But the Cortés variant is especially savored by militant Chicanos who have adapted it to focus resentment against the non-Mexican elements in their culture. As Ralph Montelongo expresses the matter, "The Mexicans consider her a traitor and her name is a symbol for all that is bad in women."[19]

The more usual story, however, is much less a symbol of cultural resentment than a simple one of love betrayed. Some years ago, they say, a young *hidalgo* (a "somebody") fell in love with a lowly girl, usually named María, and over a period of time she bore him two or three children. She had a *casita* (a little house) where the young man visited and brought his friends, and in almost every way they shared a happy life together, except that their union was not blessed by the church. His parents, of course, knew nothing of the arrangement, and certainly would not have allowed him to marry beneath his station. Still, they were getting on in years, and urged him to marry a suitable lady and give them grandchildren.

Finally he gave in, and sadly he told María that he must marry another. But he would not desert her, he promised—he would take care of her and the children, and visit them as often as he could. Enraged, she drove him away, and when the wedding took place she stood veiled in her shawl at the back of the church. Once the ceremony was over, she went home, and in a crazed state killed the children and threw them into a nearby body of water and then drowned herself.

But when her soul applied for admission to Heaven, El Señor (the Lord) refused her entry. "Where are your children?" He asked her. Ashamed, she confessed she did not know. "Go and bring them here," the Lord said. "You cannot rest until they are found."

And ever since, La Llorona wanders alongside streams at night, weeping and crying for her children—*"¡Ay, mis hijos!"* (Oh, my children)—and according to some, she has been known to take revenge on men she comes across in her journey—since a man was the cause of all her troubles. She usually dresses in black, and her face is sometimes that of a horse, but more often horribly blank, and her long fingernails gleam like polished tin in the moonlight.[20]

One story tells of a pair of *compadres* (good buddies) who after drinking too much tequila ran across a mysterious lady as they staggered home. The thought of a conquest thrilled them, and they followed her along a canal to El Paso. Somehow they couldn't gain on her, so they called her to wait. She obliged, and as they neared her she turned toward them. When she raised her clawlike hands at them, nails reflecting the moon's rays, they ran, pell mell, to escape the horror, and people say they never touched tequila again![21]

La Llorona's wailing is often heard in the night, and once in the 1970s, people in Canutillo, on the Rio Grande near El Paso, were so terrified by hearing her that they gathered together in a neighbor's home for comfort—and while their own homes were deserted, someone robbed them. Functionally, the story of the Weeping Woman is an obedience legend: it is told to youngsters as a "true" story of what might get you if you're out after dark. But the most frequent use of the story is aimed at romantic teenaged girls, to warn them against falling for a young man who may have nice clothes and money, but who is too far above them to consider marriage.[22]

A variant of the story, set in the Philippines, was told after World War II. A young woman captured by the occupying Japanese soldiers was used for their pleasure for the entire time of the occupation. She had several children as a consequence, and when the war was over she wanted to return to her village—but there existed the evidence of her shame: the children. She killed them, and then, in remorse, went mad, and wandered about searching everywhere, crying for her hijos.[23]

Related by name and actions, there is also the story of *El Llorón,* La Llorona's male counterpart. Although it is told of Durango, Mexico, it resembles stories I have heard told about other areas within the United States. As the story goes, a rich miner back about 1812 feared that revolutionary activities would cause him to lose his fortune of money and silver bars, so he took a *peón* (workman) out in the dead of night to bury the treasure. The peón's wife, fearing the miner's intentions, wrapped up her baby against the chill night air and went to see the wife of the *patrón* (boss) to get her to intercede in the matter. The miner's wife wrapped up her own baby and, leaving the worker's wife in the house, went to see that no harm came to the man. The miner, having just killed the workman and thrown his body in the hole, saw the figures approach and assumed that it was the peón's wife and that his crime was about to be discovered. He killed his wife and baby, and their bodies went into the hole as well, which he covered up before returning home. There, to his shock, he saw the worried wife of the worker, rocking her baby—and he realized what he had done. He hanged himself, and every year, on the anniversary of the event, his ghost is heard weeping, crying for his lost wife and child.[24]

The stories of La Llorona are essentially ghost stories, and ghosts are generally the product of fear—fear of the unknown. Since death is one of the great mysteries, including the question of where people "go" after death, many a tale has been conjured up to account for the unaccountable. Ghosts, or spirits, are the souls of dead individuals—human or animal—that continue to have a separate existence.[25] Jan Brunvand says that

> the term ghost stories suggests blood-curdling scare tales about white-sheeted or invisible spooks who are out to destroy humankind. But most ghosts in American legends are lifelike in appearance, and come back from the dead only to set right an error or finish a task. A better term for these creatures is *revenants,* or returners—those who return from the world of the dead, usually only temporarily. Their reasons for coming back are numerous, and harmless to anyone with a clear conscience. Only a few spirits return for revenge, and they always have justification; more commonly they return for such a purpose as to reveal hidden treasure, to ask that a crooked limb in the coffin be straightened, or to reveal the cause of death.[26]

Ghost stories told by Mexican-Americans have been collected in all these categories, including the revenge motif of many of the La Llorona stories.

Take, for example, the ghost that comes back with pure motives, to set something straight. The effect can still be unnerving, as in the case of José and María. She died, leaving poor José alone and lonely. After a while, his neighbor, Donaciana, took pity on him. She brought him food and flowers, and began looking after him regularly. After a while, José fell in love with her, and they were married. One night, when Donaciana had gone to spend the night with her sister in a neighboring village, José slept outside under the cottonwood trees on a cot, because it was very hot. About midnight he awoke suddenly with something cold pressing his feet. In the dim light of the moon he saw that it was the ghost of María, holding his feet with her cold hands. With a terrified yell he ran into the house and barred the door. After a sleepless night he went to see the priest, who reassured him. María was a kindly soul, the priest told him, who would not harm him. He must ask her, if she came back, what she wanted. The following night was hot and José again slept outside. And again, about midnight, María woke him with her cold hands. Remembering the priest's words, José said, "María, what do you wish of me?"

She answered, "José, I am glad that you are happy with Donaciana, but I cannot rest. I owe the grocer, Xavier, *seis pesos,* and I cannot rest until it is paid. Give him the money, José, so I can rest peacefully." José was Xavier's first customer next day; he paid the six pesos and María never returned to trouble José's life with Donaciana.[27]

Another ghost with a foot-grabbing habit appeared several times to a man named Colomo in Clint, Texas. The covers would be pulled off him, and cold hands would grab his feet. A friend told him to ask the ghost what he wanted, so the next time it happened, he said, *"A su servicio. ¿En que le puedo servir?"* (At your service. How may I serve you?) The ghost told him that there was buried treasure in the house, and told him how to find it—but warned that if the treasure caused argument, it would disappear. The next night, Señor Colomo and his friend dug up the box of treasure, but they began to argue about the division of the loot. The friend wanted it split fifty-fifty, and Señor Colomo wanted three-fourths of it. When the box was opened, the treasure had turned to white rocks! The ghost still pulls the covers off people who sleep in the house—but not the descendants of Señor Colomo. And if they have the nerve to speak to the ghost—and don't argue—they may get the treasure.[28]

A haunted house in Chamberino, New Mexico, has a number of spooky stories associated with it. One is that when new tenants moved into the house, each night about 1:00 a.m. a young boy woke up the household screaming, "The man is going to get me!" His description of "the man" was identical to that of another boy about the same age who had lived in the house previously—and had the same experiences, and at the same time of night. Mexican workers avoid the house, and ghostly noises, rattling chains, and cars that won't start are part of the reports, as are doors that open themselves, lights that turn themselves on, and mists that appear, frightening horses. Elsie Hayden, who collected the stories, was given several accounts of the causes for ghostly activity. One of the explanations follows:

> The house was built with an adjoining chapel. Like all old Spanish houses, its walls are thick. The ones in the chapel are approximately four feet thick. One day when the threat of an Indian attack became a reality, the men joined forces to fight the Indians, leaving behind only the women [including some nuns] and old men. When they left, the walls of the chapel had not been completed. Yet when they returned, the walls were completed and everyone had disappeared. It is believed that the nuns are buried in an upright position in the thick walls of the chapel. Since they were deprived of a proper Christian burial, their spirits haunt the place. As of today, no one has yet torn down the walls to verify the story.

Buried treasure, a skeleton found in a secret chamber (perhaps that of a young man who quarreled with the owner of the house—and then disappeared), and ghosts trying to warn of a coming disaster are some of the other local explanations.[29]

One ghost, who appears in a border village on the Mexican side, like La Llorona has no face—but she is helpful. She finds a *borracho* (a drunk) and leads him—perhaps lures is a better word—to the local bull ring. When he sees her face, he passes out and she vanishes, leaving him to sleep off his intoxication. It is said that this is the lady's regular practice, taking borracho after borracho to the bull ring to sober up.[30]

A revenant story told in the Philippines by a Spanish-speaking jitney driver is of a missionary, "about 100 years ago," who went out to civilize the natives and didn't come back. His wife went looking for him but found only his head. She went mad, and carried the head all about, looking for his body. Now she haunts the island coconut groves, still looking, because she can't rest until she finds it. The jitney driver saw her and nearly ran off the road—"but he was just as drunk as the rest of us," says the collector.[31]

A "jump story" that recalls Mark Twain's "Who's Got My Golden Arm" was told in San Antonio, Texas, some thirty or so years ago. It involves a little boy who was sent to the meat market for some *tripas* (tripe, animal intestines), but he spent all the money on candy. Afraid to go home, he was wandering around when he passed by the cemetery—and an open coffin. Thinking quickly, while no one was around, he took out his pocket knife and opened the corpse's stomach and helped himself. Finding some butcher paper, he wrapped the tripas up and took them home to mama. He didn't eat, which puzzled his mother, but when she urged him to he finally ate a bit of the tripas. That night the boy heard digging noises—like the corpse digging himself out of the ground. Then footsteps came closer and closer, and menacing sounds came to him: "I'm out of the grave, I'm getting closer, you can see my bones, I want my tripas"—and the voice kept getting closer and louder. Finally, with "My tripas! My tripas!" the teller grabs the listener's stomach.[32]

Of all the Mexican-American ghost stories I have ever heard, my favorite is one collected over fifty years ago by Dr. C.L. Sonnichsen, veteran historian and collector of folklore. I love to end my recitations on El Paso ghosts with this account:

The Amorous Ghost

Near the church San Elizario is an old, rambling adobe house of many rooms. It was once a mansion, the property of a famous local character named Mauro Lujan. Years ago this house was the scene of many a gathering of plotting politicians. During the Salt War of 1877, the bloodiest affair in Valley history, Don Mauro's house is said to have been headquarters for the leaders of the mob.

Since the old man's death, it has gone to ruin. No whitewash has touched its walls for years, and no one has bothered to repair the places where the adobe has crumbled. Still, Don Mauro must love it, for he has often been seen wandering from room to room saying his rosary.

Many people have lived in his house. To one pair of tenants, María de Ramírez and her husband Alejo, he revealed the location of a pot of money with which they were to have masses said for his soul. They, however, were unfaithful to the trust. They took the money across the river into Mexico, where they set themselves up in the grocery business. They did not prosper, however, and María soon died, as one would expect.

Then an elderly pair named Maciel moved in, to whom Don Mauro was only a name. Antonio worked until late at night, leaving Bonifacia to go to bed by herself. At last the old lady went to her friend Doña Tomasa Girón and told her a strange tale.

"Every night," she said, "I go to bed by myself, because my husband is working and comes home late. And every night the ghost of an old man with a long, white beard gets in bed with me. When my husband comes home and wishes to go to sleep, he has to say, *'Con su permiso'* (with your permission), before the old man will let him get in bed."

"Hm," said Doña Tomasa, "does he get out of bed when your husband get in?"

"Oh, no! He just moves over."

"It sounds like Don Mauro," remarked Doña Tomasa, thoughtfully, as her mind traveled back over Don Mauro's record. "He used to be very fond of the ladies," she added—*"era muy enamorado."*

"Y todavía es," said Bonifacia de Maciel, looking very wise. *"Y todavía es. Me hace cariños"* (He still is; he caresses me).[33]

And just for the record, a census of the valley for 1841 lists one Mauro Lujan, then two years old, living in San Elizario, so he at least did exist once.[34]

Urban Belief Tales

The distance between ghost stories and urban belief tales is sometimes very short. The key word is *belief*—and frequently weird stories are devoutly believed by the teller, as are some ghost stories. For example, a revenant who returns to the place of death, or to a place frequented in life, rests in the never-never land between the two areas.

Many such stories have been collected from Mexican-American informants over the years, in a number of places in the Spanish Southwest. The following story, told to a young boy by his grandmother, is one of the "standard" vanishing hitchhiker tales:

> One evening, a boy named Antonio went to a dance. There he met a girl named Marta. He danced all evening with her. When the dance was over, he offered to walk her home. The night was cold so he lent her his jacket. When they reached her house, she left him at the gate. The house was surrounded by several trees and it was very dark. He was not certain,

but he thought he saw her enter the house.

The following morning he went again to the house to get the jacket he had given the girl. When he asked the girl's mother about her, the mother replied, "My daughter has been dead for ten years."

"But I danced with her last night!" the boy gasped.

The woman invited him inside. "I'll show you a picture of my daughter," she told him.

After he had seen the picture he was even more certain. "That's the same girl I danced with last night," he insisted.

"Come, I'll take you to the cemetery—to see where my daughter is buried," the girl's mother suggested.

When the two arrived at the cemetery, they made their way towards the girl's tomb. When it came into sight, the first thing the boy saw was his jacket, draped over the stone.[35]

A Juárez taxi driver, they say, got a call late one night to take a lady to a church, from an address in the rich section of the city. She was dressed all in black and had a thick veil over her face. They went to several churches without finding one open, so she asked him to return the next day for his fare, and he agreed, but when he came back, the house looked abandoned. He asked a neighbor about the lady, describing her—and was told she had been dead for several years.[36]

Another story, told of someone identified simply as the Bishop of Durango, Mexico, when he was a young priest, circulates in the El Paso area. Collected some twenty years ago by one of my students, it lingers in my mind partly because I enjoy telling it, even though I have lost the source. As I remember it, late at night, three men came knocking at the door of this priest. He was told that a young woman lay dying, and that she was calling for a priest. They had stopped by out of kindness, but couldn't accompany him to the house, although they gave him good directions. He dressed hurriedly, got his bag of priestly equipment, and soon found himself at the house, at the end of a long, winding road. No one came to meet him as he stepped up on the porch, so he opened the door and went in. There was a dim light, 'way down at the end of the hall, and he made his way there. Inside he found the girl on a bed, twisting and crying out for a priest. He calmed her down, heard her confession, gave her absolution, and administered the last rites—although he tried to cheer her up, and promised to come back to see her the next morning. But when morning came and he retraced his steps, he couldn't believe his eyes. The yard was full of weeds, the house was almost falling down, and when he stepped up on the porch he nearly fell through the rotten boards. When he pushed the door it fell with a clatter, and he walked inside a house that looked as if it had been deserted for years. At the end of the hall he found the room—and a rusty bed with bare springs, but no one lying upon it. There was no sign that he had been there just the night before. Puzzled, he went to a neighboring house and asked for information about their neighbors, but nobody knew a thing—until a tottering old grandmother came into the room. She told him of a girl who had died in that house, calling in vain for a priest—fifty years before. Even as I type this story, goose bumps are running all over me.

Three stories—that actually involved hitchhikers, or at least people being picked up along a road—were told to one of my student collectors. One concerned a taciturn Indian ("He didn't said nothing!"). One was of a lady dressed in black who got on a bus near Clint, Texas, and never got off. And one was even more intriguing than most:

> One day when my father and cousins were going over to the ranch, there was a lady hitchhiking. Over there by the canal. And my father picked her up and told her [sic] where was she going. And she told my father she was going where he was going. And so they took her to the ranch and my father was talking to her. . .and then my father went outside with her and my cousin too. Then my grandmother called my father and my cousin because it was ready [time] to go to bed. Then my father came out to tell the lady that they were going to sleep and he went outside and there was nothing. And [when] he got closer there was only a doll.[37]

The same collector got three versions of the well-known Kentucky Fried Rat story from sixth-graders; one has details that suggest that the art of story-telling is alive and well among some young Mexican-Americans; in this case the point of view—at least part of the time—is that of the rat:

> There was this rat that went in [to Kentucky Fried Chicken] and it was sleeping there and there was a bag of flour and when they threw the flour around, the rat was passing by and it [the flour] fell on the rat and the rat fell down. And they were mixing all the stuff up with all the spices and they were putting them in the boiling water and when they put him [the rat] in and they boiled him and when he came out he really looked like a piece of chicken. So this lady came by to buy this bucket of chicken and she got the rat and she took it to her house and they were eating it. And the lady, she got the rat and she didn't know it was a rat, and she ate it and she died.[38]

Personal Legends

Legends attached to persons are frequently found in Mexican-American lore. Heroes who uphold the traditions of the Mexican culture are especially popular; Gregorio Cortez of South Texas, Pancho Villa of northern Chihuahua, and Joaquín Murieta of the California mines are particularly widely known.

Cortez was recently the subject of a feature film, following in subject matter (although not in spirit) the work of Américo Paredes, *"With His Pistol in His Hand."* Cortez was a South Texas rancher falsely accused of having stolen a horse, who was forced into a shooting confrontation with a deputy sheriff and then undertook a fabulous ride evading the law. After all, it was the least a man could do, when confronted by irresponsible forces, when he had "his pistol in his hand' —the means to resist.

Gregorio Cortez, besides his manly self-confidence (essentially downplayed or even lost in the movie), was a victim of a system that surrounds today's Mexican-American far too often. Paredes presents the situation beautifully when he contrasts the motto of the famed Texas Rangers, "Shoot first and ask questions afterward," with the Mexican translation thereof, "Shoot first, and then see what you're shooting at."[39] Gregorio got into trouble because, as is often the case, the law enforcement officer didn't have command of the Spanish language—but thought he did. When he asked Gregorio about having sold a *caballo* (a horse), the "suspect" replied he had not sold a caballo, which was true: he had sold a *yegua* (a mare). The deputy thought he knew better, and that Cortez was lying —so the shooting began, and the *rinche* (an offensive word, that rhymes with a nasty one) wound up dead and Cortez became a fugitive. Cortez has several characteristics of a Christ figure—he is falsely accused, betrayed by a fellow countryman, and tried very unjustly (he was quickly tried for stealing the horse on which he made his fabulous ride, so he could be referred to legally in court as a convicted horse thief, which was even worse than being a Mexican!), and he died (tradition says he was poisoned) despite his innocence. The fact that the appeals courts eventually found him innocent and the deputy as being out of line, and that they turned Cortez loose, is really beside the point to Chicano activists. He died, in a sense, for the sins of his culture—being Mexican in a Texan world.[40] Gregorio Cortez was the victim of the system, much as today's teenaged glue-sniffer or petty criminal is sometimes assumed to be guilty until proven innocent. Often in South El Paso, for example, such a petty offender will be arrested by a force of three or more patrol cars of officers, giving rise to the contemptuous comment *"Tantos perros con un pobre hueso"* (so many dogs, with one poor little bone); the "perros" comment is not lost on the officers, who know at least that much Spanish.[41]

Joaquín Murieta, a Latin working peacefully in the California mines, was forced into outlawry, according to tradition, by Anglo miners who had raped and/or killed his beautiful wife. He formed a sort of vigilante gang, and raided successfully the miners and others of the usurping race that had taken over Spanish California because of the Gold Rush—and Mexico's inability to defend the territory.[42] Although the whole story may well be a fabrication, it has gone into legend much as the story of Gregorio Cortez has done—as if the times needed a legend to strengthen a worthy cause. And it is significant that details of the Murieta story abound in cruelty and bloody deeds—which are presumably typical (to Anglos) of the stereotypical Mexican, but only appropriate to members of a beleaguered race. What else is a man—who is really a man—to do?[43]

Most prominent of all the outlaw heroes dear to Mexican-American hearts is Doroteo Arango—better known to the world as Francisco (Pancho) Villa. Like Joaquín Murieta, Pancho was forced into lawlessness by an act of an establishment figure: the son of a *bacendado* (the owner of the hacienda, or ranch) took advantage of Villa's innocent younger sister, and Pancho retaliated in fashion familiar to followers of Murieta.[44] A man who said he knew Villa personally told a collector that the man known as Pancho Villa was a simple farmer. "When Villa was only thirteen years old, a rich land-owner raped his sister. Villa killed this man and became a hunted man from that day. He had no choice but to become an outlaw."[45]

Villa has two faces—that of the monster who killed anyone who opposed him and even killed for fun; and the revolutionary leader and hero-guardian of *los de abajo* (the underdogs), who hated the government and its heartless mercenaries (or anyone who fell into the category of being disliked or distrusted by Villa).

The ugly fact is told—almost with pride—of how Pancho never let anyone put anything over on him. Stories are plentiful about how Villa punished people for opposing him and his men in their search for young women. One young man told how Villa would ride into a town and order all the inhabitants to come out. He would pick out all the prettiest girls and take them with him. He would also pick out the strongest-looking men or leaders of the village. He would order these men castrated or have their ears cut off. By doing this he would discourage anyone from following him to get the girls back.[46]

Many people tried to kill Pancho Villa. Once a woman offered him flowers as he rode through town, a common custom, but she had a gun hidden in the bouquet as she approached him, a baby in her arms. One of Villa's officers saw the trick and knocked the flowers from her hand. Villa ordered her—and the baby—to be burned.[47] In a similar story, Villa was told that a woman from the town of Jiménez was going to kill him, but she was not identified. Then in a Herod-like action, he had ninety-nine women from the town area killed, so he wouldn't miss the guilty one.[48]

A Chihuahua grandmother passed on a secondhand story of fathers in northern Chihuahua who hid their daughters when there was a rumor that Villa was coming. The original teller of the story said she was walking down a village street and Villa saw her, telling her, "I'll come back for you tonight." She ran home and told her father, who said they would be prepared. When Villa returned, the fathers were ready—but Villa won the ensuing skirmish. He entered the house, took the girl out, and then set the house on fire, burning the parents inside.[49]

But Villa and his men didn't always win. Once his soldiers came to a farm where a woman awaited her husband's return; with her were a teenaged daughter, a younger son, and a baby. When the troops asked for food, the woman sent the daughter—presumably to get food from a shed—to go hide. When the daughter didn't return, the mother sent the boy to look for the daughter (and to hide). Finally, the mother went herself—but she forgot the baby. When the soldiers realized they were being tricked, they threatened to kill the baby if the daughter wasn't sent out. The woman told them to do what they were going to do —since she knew they would anyway. The soldier holding the baby dashed it against the door, killing it instantly, but the woman still refused to open the door. Finally they began digging under the door to the shed, and one of the men started to crawl inside. The mother grabbed an ax and cut his head off—and the siege stopped. Never did they admit having been defeated by a mother with her children.[50]

But Pancho Villa has another face as well. He exacted contributions from prosperous people to educate young boys[51] and looked after Mormon missionaries in Mexico because Mormons had helped his wounded men after a battle,[52] and one of his reasons for fighting the government—and especially foreigners—was the exploitation of the poor. This aspect of his motivation helped give him a Robin Hood reputation. One fourteen-year-old Mexican-American, who recently became a resident of the United States, was quite clear about his views concerning Villa:

> I consider Pancho Villa to be a brave man because he did many things for us. Long ago, when people from other countries discovered that Mexico was a rich country, they came and took over our land. They started businesses and employed men to work for them. They knew that these men were not educated so they paid them 25 cents [per day]. When Villa found out about the barbaric things that these foreigners were doing with his people, he got a group of friends who agreed to follow him and they started a revolution against the evil men, as well as the evil Mexican men in the government. As the leader of a troop he would fight against the government soldiers. He robbed the rich and gave their money to the poor people.[53]

Yet when I was touring northern Chihuahua about 1967, I ran into a boy of about the same age waiting on his burro for the soft drink truck to come down the road near Parral, where Villa was gunned down. I asked him what he knew of Pancho Villa, and I'll never forget his reply: "He must have been a bad man, because he was a revolutionary." This from a boy standing only a few yards from a hacienda taken over by the revolution and its lands distributed to the poor—like his own family. *Sic transit gloria mundae!*

But General Villa lives on, in stories and legends about how great a military man he was despite his lack of education, his whimsy, his fate. One story concerns an Englishman named Benton who came storming into Villa's headquarters, demanding the return of some stolen cattle. When he acted too belligerent, a Villa guard shot him down. Later, an advisor told Villa that international law was going to cause him trouble, since this man was an Englishman—so Villa had the corpse dug up, propped up in an impromptu courtroom, tried, and convicted—and shot again.[54]

In another story, Villa, who loved publicity, told a newspaper reporter that he was going to raid and destroy a town the next day. When the reporter told him that the final game of the World Series would be taking the headlines that day, Villa delayed the attack for one day.[55]

Old Pancho was really sneaky, they say. Once he rode into town just ahead of some federal troops when a funeral was going on. Pancho got into the coffin that was being carried to the *camposanto* (holy ground, graveyard), and when the troops started to open the coffin to examine the corpse, they were told that the dead man had died of leprosy![56]

But Pancho Villa was not all bad. He was very religious, always saying his prayers in the morning and again at night before he went to bed. Although he married several times—he never took a woman to bed without "marrying" her—he always did it "legally." He even captured a priest named Esquivel (who, unfortunately, had been defrocked, but as Pancho said, "Once a priest, always a priest") and had him perform ceremonies whenever needed.[57] In my childhood in El Paso, there was a saying that Pancho Villa couldn't throw a rock in Juárez for fear of hitting one of his children—but I knew even then that was an exaggeration.

Even in death, Villa's prominence attracted attention. According to innumerable accounts, Villa's head was wanted by unnamed American universities, who wanted to examine the brain to find out how he could be so smart with no education. In 1926, his body was disinterred in the *panteón* (graveyard) in Parral, and the head was actually cut off and spirited away, possibly to the Del Norte Hotel in El Paso. A *jardinero* (gardener, or grounds-keeper) at the panteón added to the legend when he solemnly told me, "When they cut off the head of *mi general,* blood went all over the ground." [Villa had died three years earlier, in 1923!] "How did he have so much blood left?" I asked. *"Era muy macho, señor"* (He was quite a man, mister).[58]

Like Joaquín Murieta and Gregorio Cortez, Pancho Villa continues to be a legend to Mexican-Americans far removed in space and time from the times in which each flourished. The statement of Villa's best-known biographer, Haldeen Braddy, also holds true for the Spanish Southwest: "As long as tales are told in Mexico, Pancho Villa will live on."[59]

Another revolutionary leader, Emiliano Zapata, was to the south of Mexico what Villa was to the north. The only tale about Zapata that I have heard along the Texas-Mexican border, however, tells of Zapata's sorrow at the loss of his beautiful stallion in a battle for a small town. He would not eat nor sleep for quite a while. Then in a battle for another small town, the commander, a Spanish colonel, was killed and his horse was given to a good priest. The priest introduced Zapata to the horse, a handsome black stallion. The horse responded immediately to Zapata, and the new master liked the horse, giving him the name *Relámpago* (Lightning). The horse and the man were inseparable, even dying together in an ambush—and now they ride the rim of the valley of Mexico, on guard against evil forces that would mistreat the poor Indians Zapata fought for in the revolution.[60]

Treasure Tales

But the legend of Pancho Villa lives on in another way too—the matter of buried treasure. Dozens of stories tell of his capturing federal payrolls, the savings of merchants, the gold of ranchers like Don Luis Terrazas—and of his burying it in out-of-the-way places, usually with a ghost or two to guard it, ghosts of his men who dug the hole and then were shot and pitched into it, since, as with pirates, *Los muertos no hablan* (Dead men tell no tales).[61]

One story tells of Villa having robbed a U.S. Army pay wagon of a large number of silver coins. Pursued by soldiers, he realized that he'd never reach the border with all that weight, so he buried it "in the vicinity of Anthony or Canutillo, and then escaped into Mexico." The money has never been found. Another load of silver—this time for the purchase of ammunition and weapons—was taken by Villa to Juárez, where he expected to meet Americans with the goods. But the U.S. Army had confiscated the guns and imprisoned the men. To avoid having to take all that silver back to Chihuahua, he buried it near Zaragosa in a large hole between two large trees —along with the two men who dug the hole. In a variation on the last tale, it was on the U.S. side of the Rio Grande, opposite Zaragosa, and specific directions for its location are given:

> There was a large cottonwood tree on the edge of the field which was shaped in the form of a "Y." If a sighting is taken through the "Y" toward Mt. Franklin, and the tallest peak of Mt. Franklin can be seen centered in the "Y," then 30 feet toward that peak is the spot where the silver is buried.[62]

In addition to the tales of Villa's caches, treasure tales are found throughout the Spanish Southwest, a natural outgrowth of the search for gold—the Seven Cities of Cibola, and Eldorado, and other stories—that lured the Spaniards into the territory in the first place. J. Frank Dobie collected many such tales over the years and published two books of them—scores of them involving Mexican informants or searchers for lost mines and buried treasures.[63] But treasure tales continue to circulate orally, as the collections of my students and reports in the Publications of the Texas Folklore Society bear witness. One story involves mysterious happenings and only a hope that treasure is involved, but it is well worth repeating:

> There was this man that worked with me on a sheep ranch [near Carlsbad, New Mexico]. One day when he was out, a wind storm came up. It

was blowing so hard, he went into a cave for shelter. Well, he saw some beautiful stalagmites and stalactites in this cave. He broke some off to take back to his children. Just then, a half man-half horse came running out at him. He backed all the way out of that cave. He jumped on his horse and rushed back to the ranch, still holding those stalagmites. He told us at the ranch what had happened to him in the cave. . . . Let me tell you, there had been no wind storms all that day. But where did he get those stalagmites? We believe that there is a treasure in that cave. Also that half man-half horse was in the cave to guard that treasure.[64]

One often wonders how details about hidden treasure can be so specific, and told with such conviction, by folks who can't find it. The following is an example of such detailed reporting:

On the right side of Highway 80 just before you reach Smeltertown [in El Paso] there is a large black hill made up of slag from the smelter. Approximately one mile to the east of this hill there is a rough mound-shaped hill with many loose stones on it. There is a small hole, perhaps one foot in diameter and covered with a stone, on the hill in which is hidden [sic] several bags of gold. The gold was hidden by a Mexican bandit who was being pursued in connection with the murder of an old prospector in Chihuahua. He was killed after hiding the gold, and no one ever found it.[65]

The questions raised by this story are manifold, obviously, and there are no "signs" to help the hunter—such as mysterious lights. One lady from Clint, Texas, told of walking out one night with her mother and a friend when they saw

this bluish and red light—just came up from nowhere. The little old woman drew our attention to it. She said, "Oh, look—there's money buried there." She had barely mentioned money when the light went away. If you see a treasure light, you must never mention a treasure. You will never find it.[66]

Another sign, as an old Mexican field hand found out, is a headless horseman. The old man followed him across a field to where he disappeared, dug there, and found hidden treasure![67]

But of all the treasure tales my students have collected, the most popular—at least in the El Paso area—is the Lost Padre Mine, which isn't a mine at all, but a cache. As is natural with folklore, the stories vary widely, but the most common version deals with a threatened Indian attack on the Guadalupe Mission, in what was originally called *El paso del norte* (the Pass of the North), but is now known as Juárez. The padres took all their valuables—gold and silver chalices and candlesticks—and carried them across the Rio Grande and buried them in a hole on Mount Franklin. Then they covered the treasure with many loads of red earth from the river, and for no explained reason, never came back to get it. Directions for finding it? Go to the bell tower of the mission at sunrise on Easter morn, and look toward the mountain. The sun's rays will illuminate the mouth of the cave. Another version of the story connects the Padre Mine with the Pueblo Revolt of 1680. When the padres reached the Pass of the North, fearing further Indian attacks, they buried the treasures (including ten burro-loads of emeralds!) in the cave and covered it with river dirt, as in the other stories. And the view from the Mission of Guadalupe is still part of the story.[68]

But there is one small problem, these days: the cathedral in Juárez is built between the bell tower and the mountain, so no one can see the cave even from the right place on magical Easter morning. I know, because I climbed the bell tower to see for myself. Of course, with buried treasure, there is always "one small problem"—lost landmarks, landslides that obliterate any clues that might help. In the case of the Padre Mine (in some stories, the Lost Padre really is a mine, operated by the priests in Guadalupe Mission) there are ghosts guarding the site—especially that of an Indian chief named Cheetwah, whose profile can be seen atop a peak across the Rio Grande in Mexico.[69]

Animal Tales and Fables

One of the most interesting inhabitants of the Spanish Southwest is Señor Coyote, the yellowish dog-like animal who carries a lot of infamy on his back. He is to the Southwesterner what Loki is to the Scandinavians, or other tricksters in their own cultures. The coyote (pronounced *ki-yote, ki-yotey,* or *co-yo-tay* by native Anglos, Easterners, and Spanish-speakers, in that order) is usually into some mischief, but he is often too stupid to succeed in his devilishness. Take, for example, the following Tar Baby-like story:

'Mana Zorra (Sister Fox) and 'Mano Coyote (Brother, or Br'er, Coyote)

Sis Fox had been stealing a chicken every night from a rancher, who finally hit on the idea of using a wax man as a dummy to scare the villain away. As in the Tar Baby story, Ole Sis Fox responded with anger when the figure didn't answer back nor get out of the way, so she wound up stuck tight to the wax man—when who should come along but Br'er Coyote. Sis Fox fooled him with a wild tale:

> This Christian [person] and I have come to blows over a chicken. I have a contract with the ranchero which provides me a hen a night, but this

> little fellow can't read and had made up his mind to interfere. Hold him for me, 'Mano Coyote, and I will get a hen for both of us.

So simple Br'er Coyote held the wax man, and only slowly realized he'd been tricked. Next morning, the *caporal* (overseer) found the coyote, and complained that the coyote had tried to steal a hen, when the caporal would have given him one out of friendship, just for asking. But then he promised to give the coyote another chance. Having put him in a shed with a broken window, he cautioned the coyote not to try to escape till the caporal gave the word, or the dogs would get him. Again the gullible coyote fell for the trick: when the caporal gave him the signal to jump out the window to freedom, Coyote fell into a tub of scalding water that the caporal had placed beneath the window.

Hairless and lacking several toenails, 'Mano Coyote was bent on revenge when he found the fox, who pretended to be watching a huge cheese in a *laguna* (pond), which was, of course, the reflection of the moon. She promised to bring him a fat hen if he'd watch the cheese and not let it get away—and he fell for the trick again. When the "cheese," after several hours, began slipping under the bank of the pond, he jumped in to save it—and got chilled to the bone. Going after Sis Fox with fire in his eye, he discovered her sleeping on her back in a low cave—but she said she was helping the caporal by holding the world up with her feet while he went for help. Meanwhile, she was starving to death. This time the coyote tricked himself, offering to hold the world up while she went for a hen. Of course she didn't come back, and he was even madder this time.

When he found Sis Fox she was watching a hornets' nest—which she claimed was a class of boys she was being paid by a schoolteacher to keep an eye on. Again food was mentioned, and the coyote volunteered to watch the "boys" while she went for a couple of chickens. When the "boys" stopped their humming (it was a "blab school," apparently, where they said their lessons aloud) 'Mano Coyote shook them up—and had to run for the laguna to escape their stings.

At last finding 'Mana Zorra in a canebrake, Br'er Coyote was determined to kill and eat her in repayment for all the tricks—but there was one trick left: she said a wedding party was coming that way, and they could take part in all the eating and drinking. Coyote was to watch, while the fox went to look for the wedding party. When Coyote heard fireworks, he would know the celebrants were coming. But Sis Fox slipped around the canebrake and set it on fire. When the burning cane started popping, the coyote jumped for joy, finding out too late that he was dancing at his own funeral.[70]

In another story, however, Señor Coyote shows the wisdom of Harun Al Rashid, Caliph of Baghdad:

Señor Coyote Acts as Judge

A rattlesnake had a huge boulder fall on him while he was napping, and when Mr. Rabbit came along, the snake begged to be freed. The rabbit pushed the rock off the snake, who then announced his intention of eating his benefactor. About that time, Señor Coyote came up, and the rabbit appealed to him for justice. The snake claimed that he had crawled under the rock to rest, but the rabbit was trying to crush him by moving the rock, and so deserved to be eaten. Brother Coyote pretended that the scene had to be reenacted so he could judge fairly —and when the snake was safely under the rock, and squirming in pain, the coyote rendered his verdict: "*Pues* (well then), that is the way you will stay," said Señor Coyote. "Now you have your reward for trying to eat Mr. Rabbit after he had treated you with kindness."[71]

A mouse named Ratoncito Pérez and an ant are the central characters in another animal tale that charms children.

Ratoncito Pérez

The ant found a *real* (an old Spanish coin worth about six and a quarter cents—half a bit) and decided to dress herself up, buying a dress, some boots, and a ribbon for her hair. Then she went shopping for a mate. Everyone thought she was beautiful and proposed to her. But the cat mewed too frighteningly, and the dog barked too roughly as well. A bull and a lamb fared no better, but Ratoncito Perez's little voice, saying "Ee, ee, ee," was just her style, so they married and lived happily together for a long while. One day the ant left Ratoncito in charge of cooking the soup, and the mouse fell in it and drowned, leaving the poor ant inconsolable. "Even to this day she grieves and mourns for Ratoncito Pérez and his sweet voice."[72]

From the Sangre de Cristo mountains of New Mexico comes the story of a parrot who was too smart for his own good:

One day a parrot was home alone when two *leñeros* (wood vendors) came by singing their wares. Since the parrot had heard the master buy wood many times, he knew how to say, "*¡Sí, compro leña!*" and the vendors dumped two burroloads of firewood by the woodpile. When nobody came to the door to pay them, they decided to come back later. The master was angry when they asked for pay, but the mistress figured out that the parrot was the guilty one, and scolded him so fiercely that he took refuge in the cellar. While all this was going on, the cat climbed up on the table and stole the piece of meat the master had bought—and the mistress caught him and threw him into the cellar. When the parrot saw the cat thrown into the cellar, he asked, "What happened? Did you buy firewood too?"[73]

Bilingual Animals

Another parrot—a bilingual one—was for sale in a pet store. A *gringa* (female Anglo) walked in and asked, "How much is this parrot?" The owner said, "Oh, ma'am, this is a very expensive parrot, because he speaks both Spanish and English." "Oh really, can you get him to speak in both languages?" "Oh, yes. Look: if you pull his left leg, he speaks English." And he pulled the parrot's leg and the parrot said, "Good morning!" "And if you pull his right leg like this, he speaks Spanish." And the parrot said, *"¡Buenos dias!"* And the gringa asked, "What happens if you pull both of his legs, will he speak Tex-Mex?" And the parrot said, "No, I'd fall on my ass, you stupid *gringa.*"

José Limón, the folklorist who collected this gem, suggested that the Mexican-American who speaks Tex-Mex (as Spanglish is called in the Brownsville, Texas, area) will "fall on his ass" socially.[74]

The value of speaking two languages is explicit in another animal tale:

This cat was chasing a mouse, which ran into its hole. The cat mewed outside the hole, but the mouse stayed safely inside. The cat said, "Bow wow, bow wow," and the mouse, thinking the cat was gone, came out—and the cat ate him. As the cat was cleaning his whiskers, he said, "It's nice to be bilingual."[75]

The Burro and the Wise Men

Some weathermen once asked a New Mexican lady named Angélica if they could set up their instruments outside her home so they could study the stars. She warned them that it was going to rain, and they had better put their instruments inside the house. In their superior wisdom they decided to stay outside, while the burro Miguelito shook his head, seeming to agree with Angélica. Soon the wind got up, and a downpour began, and the scientists grabbed their equipment and ran for the house, where they spent the night. Next morning, after paying for their breakfast, they asked Angélica how she had known it was going to rain. She looked at Miguelito and said, "Yesterday afternoon my burro went running and jumping all around the yard. That always tells me that it will rain very soon." Then she asked if they were going to study the stars anymore. One of the wise men said, "What's the use of our studying the stars when a burro knows more about the weather than we do?"[76]

The Man, the Burro, and the Dog

It seems that God was parceling out years. To man he gave sixty, adding that there would be both good and bad years, but the good ones would outnumber the bad ones. The man thought that he was being short-changed, but he held his peace. God gave the burro thirty years, but warned that the bad ones would outnumber the good—so the burro asked that he be relieved of ten of those years, since they were going to be so hard. The man asked for, and got, the ten years the burro gave up. Likewise the dog was offered twenty years, more bad than good, and he said he'd be content with ten—and the man begged for the extra ten. "And that is why man lives the life of a donkey from sixty to seventy, and also why he lives the life of a lowly dog from his seventieth year on!"[77]

The Man Who Knew the Language of Animals

There was a shepherd boy who went out to seek his fortune. He saved a snake from a forest fire, and in return received the ability to understand the language of animals—but he was warned not to tell anyone of his gift, or he would die. Among the conversations he overheard was that of two crows who told of hidden treasure left by some bandits. He found the treasure, and took it home a little at a time, and invested in land and livestock. Finally he married a lovely lady. After a while they were riding out to check on his livestock, he on a fast horse and his pregnant wife following behind. He heard the fast horse complain at being held back by the slower one, and the wife's mare (who was also pregnant) said that there were four of her and her rider, while there were only two of the man and his horse.

The man broke out laughing at this reply, and the wife was puzzled at to what he was laughing about, but he couldn't tell, recalling that he would die. But the wife kept on begging, and finally said, "If you don't tell me, I'll know you don't love me." He loved his wife very much, and decided that he would have to tell her. His dog, who somehow knew the whole business, was sad, and berated the rooster for being happy. "Don't you know that we will soon be in mourning?" And he told the rooster what was going on. The rooster offered the opinion that the man wasn't much of a man if he couldn't manage one wife; the rooster bossed fifteen of them and did very well.

The man overheard all this, and went in to see his wife. Taking off his trousers, he told her to put them on. She hesitated, saying that he was the husband, and she was the wife. He replied, "Well, if you want to rule the house and know all that's on my mind, I will gladly wear your dress and you can wear my pants. But if you think I am a good husband, then trust me and allow me to have some privacy." She saw the point, "and they lived happily together many years thereafter."[78]

Other Fable-Like Stories

A story with fable qualities that has been reported to me from several places is well told from a New Mexico source:

Doña Sebastiana

A poor woodcutter who stole one of his wife's setting hens to have an unaccustomed feast all by himself was approached by a stranger as the hen, being cooked in a remote area, was dripping juicily, ready to be devoured. The stranger asked for food, and the woodcutter asked who he was. When the stranger said he was the Lord, the woodcutter refused him, on the grounds that He favored the rich and neglected the poor. Then a woman approached, and identified Herself as the Virgin Mary; again the man claimed unfair treatment of the poor, and refused to share his food. Then Doña Sebastiana, Death herself, appeared and told him who she was. He invited her to share his bounty, since Death treats all people equally!

And one version of the story continues further:

Death gave the woodcutter the power to cure sick people, to be a *curandero*. But she warned that if he ever saw her standing at the head of the sick person's bed, he should not cure the ill one, no matter what pay or promises he was offered. For many years he healed the sick and became famous. Then one day he was called to the bedside of the richest man in the whole area, and he was offered a great deal of money—so he disobeyed Doña Sebastiana, whom he saw standing at the head of the rich man's bed. He wrestled her away from the head of the bed and dragged her to the foot, and then healed the man.

She met him on the road home and forced him to come with her, into a dark room where two candles were burning, a short one about to go out and the other one standing tall and burning brightly. "You have made a grave mistake," she told the man. "Once you were like the tall candle and the sick man was like the short candle. But now you are the short candle and the man you cured is the tall one." Just then the flame went out on the small candle, "and the curandero's soul was added to Doña Sebastiana's cart as it slowly made its way into eternity."[79]

The Boy and the Grandfather

There once was a man who had a wife, a small son, and an aged father living together in one house. But the wife grew irritated with the old man—he was always in the way, she said, and she insisted that he be moved to a small room out of the house. There he was often forgotten, even going without food sometimes. One cold day he asked his little grandson to find him a blanket, because he was cold, and the boy could find only an old rug. He ran with it to his father, asking that it be cut in half.

He explained that he wanted to take half to his grandfather, who was cold. The father told him to take the whole rug, but the boy said, "I want you to cut it in half so I can save the other half for you when you are as old as my grandfather. Then I will have it for you so you will not be cold." The father saw the light, moved his father into a warm room, and took loving care of him from then on.[80]

Compadres Tales

A whole series of tales with fable overtones exists among Mexican-Americans involving two compadres—usually one rich and one poor. The rich one often has a wife who begrudges even a tortilla to the poor one, with a wide array of results. In one tale, the poor buddy loved meat, but his friend's wife never served him any, no matter how often he brought the subject up. Finally one day she got some very tough meat and invited him to eat. He accepted with delight, but couldn't manage to chew the meat, finally giving it back to her.[81]

In another story, the poor compadre arrived just as the *comadre* (his friend's wife) returned from the *tienda* (store) with a quarter-kilo of cheese. She hid it under a *metate* (grinding-stone for corn, to make tortillas) just in time—she thought.

As the friend entered, he said, "Ah, Comadre! You wouldn't believe what I was just thinking. Just now my comadre would have warm tortillas with cheese. Just see what food I was going to get."

"Ah, my compadre," she replied, "always with your *antojos* (whims, hasty judgments). No, compadre, I have not made supper."

The compadre then told her he had had a bad fall and twisted his leg—"I gave such a fall like from here to where the cheese is!"[82]

Riley Aiken, who collected "A Pack Load of Mexican Tales," has several compadre stories, some of them ten or more printed pages long. One presents a *pobre* (poor) compadre who decided to get even with his *rico* (rich) friend who never gave him anything but "Buenos días." Borrowing money to buy a pen and some paper, and catching two wild jackrabbits, he began his plot. He was writing a letter (when his wife told him she saw the rich friend coming) and tied it to one rabbit, telling the rich man he was sending a letter to a friend in the city—and the rabbit saved both time and money. When the rabbit was released, he took off like a flash, and the rich man was so impressed that he wanted to see the results of the rabbit's trip.

Next day as the rich man came up, the poor one pretended to be removing a reply from the other rabbit (which he had chased around the room so the rabbit was panting). The rich man had to have the rabbit, took him over the poor man's pretended protests, and told him to come to the house to collect a thousand dollars.

The rico's wife was delighted with the purchase, and decided to send some jewels to a friend in the city, and tied them with some letter onto the rabbit. In the presence of the pobre they turned him loose—and he ran like the wind. When three days passed with no reply, the rico feared he had been tricked, and swore revenge. But the pobre was a step ahead. He prepared a beef bladder filled with blood and hid it under his wife's dress. Meanwhile, he had close at hand an unusual-looking flower she had picked at his command.

When the rico arrived and started arguing, the wife (as prearranged) told her husband not to fuss with his compadre. He pretended anger, and stabbed her in the bladder, with blood gushing forth as she fell "dead" before them. The rico was appalled, but the pobre calmly waved the flower beneath his wife's nose and she arose, completely cured. The rico had to have the magic and gave the pobre twenty-five thousand dollars for it. When the rico's wife cautioned him for dealing with the man who had tricked him before, he stabbed her in anger, then waved the flower in her face—but she was dead *de veras* (for real)!

When the irate rico arrived at the pobre's house, there he was, laid out beneath a sheet, with candles at his head and feet. The wailing wife said he had died "Of too—too—toothache," but the rico still wanted revenge. He dumped his friend into a sack and was taking him to the ocean, to throw him in. He told two *arrieros* (burro drivers) to load the sack onto their burro and wait while he saddled his horse. While he was gone, the pobre spoke to the arrieros and complained that he was being taken against his will to marry a rich girl, even though he was already married. One of the drivers offered to take his place, and climbed into the sack. The rico dismissed the other driver (he had promised not to tell about the exchange) and took the sack to the ocean, threw it in, and returned home.

When the rico passed by his compadre's house, there was his friend sitting out front—with the sack of jewels he had found in the thicket where they had fallen off the messenger rabbit. The pobre said he hadn't been dumped far enough out to sea, that the sea people had given him the jewels (with which the sea floor was covered). As usual, the rico was greedy enough to want to be thrown into the sea. The pobre said no, something might go wrong and that he would get the blame. But the rico put his hacienda in trust for the pobre and was dumped into the sea. The pobre is now a rico, and "held in high esteem by the people of his town for his many innocent little pranks."[83]

Charge This to the Cap

Again, there were two compadres, one rico and one pobre. And one day the poor one decided to appeal to his friend for help, but got laughed at. The rico told him to take his shabby cap, full of holes, and sell it as a curiosity. The humiliated pobre went home sorrowing. Three years later, having earned a little money, he developed a plan. He replaced the despised cap with a gray one with a blue band and then went to a watchmaker and bought a cheap watch; he told the watchmaker to keep it until he returned and pretend that it was more expensive; and then, when the customer said, *"Debo de gorra"* (Charge it to the cap), to hand it over. He went to another store and bought a cheap string of pearls, leaving the same instructions, and paid for two meals in the same manner at the inn. Then he went to spring the trap on his hard-hearted rich friend.

The rico noticed the new cap, and the pobre said it was useful—then invited the rich man to go shopping with him. At each stop he "charged it to the cap," to the amazement of the rich man. Finally, after much persuasion, the poor man sold his new hat to the rich one for thirty thousand dollars. The rico ran home to tell his wife, and she asked for the diamond necklace she had been wanting. But when the pair got to the jewelry store, "Debo de gorra" didn't work—and when the rico insisted on taking the necklace without paying, the clerk called the police —and now the rico is in a madhouse, where he keeps insisting, "It worked; I saw it with my own eyes. It is a magic cap I tell you. . . . All one has to say is, 'Debo de gorra.'" The formerly poor compadre, of course, lives in luxury.[84]

Ordinary Folktales

The "ordinary" folktale is sometimes called a "fairy tale," after the type collected by the brothers Grimm in Germany and a number of the Perrault stories from France. Essentially, they have things happening in patterns—there are often three brothers, or three princesses needing husbands or rescuing, or three tasks to be performed; royalty is often present, as are devils, witches, and enchanted objects, and the whole story takes place in a sort of magical never-never land. Witness this New Mexico tale:

The Three Brothers

An old couple had three sons, and when the oldest wanted to go and seek his fortune, the couple gave him their blessing, telling him to remember his parents and to be kind to old people. On the road he met a woman who asked him for water, but he pretended he had none. She told him to go to the city and he would find her son, who would help him. Following her directions, he found the son, who sent him to deliver a letter; a dog would accompany the first brother, and wherever the dog stopped would be safe to stay. They passed a city where everyone was partying, but the dog didn't stop so they went on. Finally they came to a river of blood across their route, and the messenger was afraid to cross, so he returned to the man who sent him, who offered him his thanks ("God bless you for your kindness") or a bagful of gold. He took the gold, went to the dazzling city, and soon forgot his parents.

When the second son asked permission to go seek his fortune, the parents hesitated, saying that the eldest son had forgotten them, not having sent home a nickel—but he promised not to do likewise, and they gave him their blessing. He met the same woman on the road, refused to share food and water with her, and was sent to find her son. The same errand, with the dog as guide, was accepted by the second son, and he too was repulsed by the river of blood, chose the bag of money as his brother had done, and went to the beautiful city where he, too, forgot his parents.

The third son finally overcame his parents' objections and set out on his own journey. He shared his water and food with the woman he met, and insisted that she take the remainder as well, pointing out that his parents had taught him to be kind to those in need. She took the gift and disappeared, and as the son walked on, he found that his pack had gotten heavy; it had been filled with food and water, and he wondered if the woman was a witch or a saint. He, too, came to the house of the woman's son, got the same job, and followed the same route with the dog as his guide. He passed the beautiful city, though he was tempted to stop and look for his two brothers, and came to the river of blood. Remembering that his parents had blessed him, he waded across the river safely. Next he came to a river of swords, and again his parents' blessing carried him through. Then he came to a pair of mountains that seemed to be fighting each other, the earth shaking and boulders flying. He passed this obstacle as well, and came to a huge flock of fat sheep grazing where there was no grass. He tried to drive them to where the grass was lush, but they refused to go. The dog disappeared during the sheep effort, and so the boy sat down to wait for the dog's return. They continued their journey, coming to thin sheep grazing in rich grass—another marvel which he resolved to ask his master about when his job was done. The dog led him to another wonderful city, to a house where he found the woman he had met on the road, and he delivered the letter. Then he fell asleep until the woman woke him up.

When he arose, she told him he had slept a hundred years, and the mirror showed him older and bearded. He was worried about his parents, but the woman said they were just as he had left them. He hurried back to his master, eager to go see about his parents, but met no obstacles on the return. The master offered him a simple "God bless you for your kindness" or a bag of gold, as he had done with the older brothers. The third son said, "God's blessing is more valuable than money." Pleased with the response, the master offered to grant a favor, but first the boy wanted to ask some questions. He found out that the beautiful city was Hell; the river of blood was Jesus' blood, shed for sinners; the swords were the swords that wounded our Lord; the mountains battling were two compadres who fought with each other instead of living in peace; the fat sheep were the poor people of the world who believe there is a God; the thin sheep in the rich pasture were those who denied the existence of God. The beautiful city at the end of the road was Heaven, and the woman was the master's mother; finally the third son figured out that his master was Jesus, and the favor he asked was that he and his family would be taken to Heaven. The master, however, refused to let the brothers go to heaven: "Because they were bad sons, and did not take care of their parents, they deserve to spend eternity in the fires of hell."[85]

The Three Counsels

Once there was a boy who ran away from home. He had three bad habits: he would not stick to a purpose, he was always inquiring into other people's business, and he would not control his temper. He had hardly gone any distance when he left the highway for a trail, ran into an old man and asked his business, and lost his temper when the man did not reply.

Finally, the *viejito* (little old man) spoke, saying that he was a peddler of advice and for a peso he would tell the boy some. The boy had only three pesos, but he gave one to the old man and was told, "Don't leave a highway for a trail." The boy was angry at such advice, so the viejo said for another peso he would give him more. The second advice was, "Don't ask about things that don't concern you." Again, the boy was angry, but finally parted with his last peso, only to hear, "Don't lose your temper." And the old man vanished.

The boy went on his way, his pockets empty, and a stranger galloped up on a black horse, advising him to take a shortcut on his road to the city; the boy, however, couldn't stick to a purpose, so he ignored the path. He came to a ranch house, and a bandit seated in front of the house invited him to dinner. When a man's head was served him, he decided that he'd better not ask questions. When the bandit couldn't get any inquiries about the head, he took the boy to see his keepsakes—skeletons of men who were too inquisitive about the head they were served. Since the boy had not been nosy, he was given three mules and a horse, each mule having two bags of gold tied on its back.

As he went down the road with his riches, he came to another bandit who demanded to know what was in the sacks. Instead of losing his temper, the boy said simply that he preferred not to tell. "Speak or I shall kill you," said the bandit. The boy said, "If you feel that is best, then follow your conscience." The bandit, pleased with the boy's wisdom, let him pass.

Soon the boy had gone into business in the city and was doing well, marrying a wealthy girl. But best of all was the fact that she, too, "did not leave the main road for a path, asked no questions about things that did not pertain to her, and always kept her temper."[86]

John of Calais

A wealthy man had two sons—one adopted—and the adopted son was jealous of the other, who was named John. The two boys went out to seek their fortune and came across a corpse with a collection box on his stomach. John found out that the man had debts to be paid before they could bury the man, so he paid the debts, paid for the funeral, and gave money to the widow—over the protests of the other son, who said John was wasting his money. The two boys put out to sea, and soon came across pirates who had captured two girls and wanted to sell them. John paid all his remaining money for the two, again over his brother's objections. One of the girls, Constancia, was a king's daughter, and John soon fell in love with her and they were married when they reached land. The other girl, Isabel, who was a viceroy's daughter, was angry because the princess had married beneath her station. Meanwhile, the adopted son had written home about John's wasting his money, and soon the father wrote saying he never wanted to see John again.

John, Constancia, and Isabel returned to John's home town, but they did not go see his parents. John did not know anything about the parents of the two girls he had rescued from the pirates, and they made him promise not to ask. After a year, Constancia had a baby, and John had built a ship. Constancia asked that a picture be taken of her, Isabel, and the baby and placed on the front of the ship as a figurehead, and that he sail with them to Lisboa.

When the ship arrived, people recognized the king's daughter's picture on the front of the ship, and told the king, who came to see for himself. After he fainted and had been revived, he told John who Constancia really was, and John told the king the whole story. A rival for Constancia's love, John of Lisboa, sailed with the whole bunch to Calais and then sailed back toward Lisboa. When a storm arose, John of Calais went topside to manage the ship and his rival pushed him overboard. Constancia suspected foul play, since she didn't like John of Lisboa anyway.

Meanwhile, back at the island where John of Calais had floated with the aid of a tree trunk, he had nothing but weeds to eat. After a year of this existence, John was bearded and ragged, watching daily for a passing ship. Then after a year, a short fat man showed up, saying he had just come from the city. "What's the news?" John asked, and was astounded to hear that the king's daughter was about to marry John of Lisboa, since Constancia's husband had been dead for a year. John of Calais said he would give anything if only he could get there and stop the wedding—and the fat man offered to take him, in exchange for half of everything John had. At the fat man's request, John closed his eyes and was immediately outside the king's palace at Lisboa. Isabel was passing by, and did not recognize John in his rags, but he held up his hand and she saw Constancia's ring on his finger, and ran to tell her friend the news.

Soon John of Calais was bathed and shaved and reunited with his family—and John of Lisboa was burned to death on the celebration bonfire he had planned for his wedding. Then the little fat man showed up to collect, and insisted on half of everything—including the child. John offered the whole child, but the man refused. He even insisted that John help him slice the child down the middle! John agreed at last to hold the child while the fat man did the cutting. Then the fat man revealed himself: he was the corpse John had pity on, and he came to thank John. So the fat man disappeared, and probably John of Calais and Constancia and the baby and Isabel all lived happily ever after—but the story doesn't mention that.[87]

Mexican-American folktales include a host of other marvels—wonderful snakes, Faust-like stories, and on and on. But of them all, the worldwide story of John the Bear, forerunner of Beowulf, seems the most interesting to me, perhaps for personal reasons. The first master's thesis I ever directed was that of Robert A. Barakat, who collected and analyzed a fascinating group of the Juan Oso stories from the El Paso/Juárez area in 1964. The story is popular throughout the Spanish Southwest, having been collected in many variants, and by many folklorists. As Barakat has analyzed the story, which is basically Aarne-Thompson Type 301, it has the following recurring divisions:

I. The hero's supernatural origin
II. The hero's descent into the lower world
III. The stolen maidens
IV. The rescue of the maidens
V. The betrayal of the hero by his treacherous companions
VI. The recognition of the hero after he presents tokens

Those familiar with the story of Beowulf will recall the presence of only divisions I, II, and V, a matter explained by the fact that the Anglo-Saxon epic was formed of a wide variety of additional folk and historical materials.[88] But Beowulf has been translated as *bee-wolf,* i.e., *bear*—an interpretation that strengthens the associations with the various bear stories. The bear in European stories is called "Juan, John, Jean or Giovanni, and in most cases Oso, bear, Ours (or Oursin), and Orso."[89] Barakat's first tale (which he collected in Spanish and translated) is closest to Type 301:

John of the Bear (Juan del Oso)

Once upon a time there was a king. This king had a very pretty daughter who enjoyed taking walks in the garden. On one of those occasions, a bear captured her and carried her away to a cavern where he lived—in his lair.

The princess remained in this strange dwelling many, many days—to her it seemed years. The autumn season seemed sad to her and the winter cold. Poor little princess! But spring arrived, and when the trees and bushes started to become green again, she gave birth to a beautiful child. She deliberated much upon a name for her son and decided to give him the name of Juan del Oso (John of the Bear). . . . They were prisoners, for a great rock served as the door to the cavern.

. . . Twelve long years went by. The child, John of the Bear, was now twelve years of age. He, by virtue of conversations with his mother, knew that outside of the cavern the world was big and full of marvels. He wished to go out; his mother had told him there was a blue canopy and that many lights called stars and planets adorned the heavens. . . . She also told him that he was a member of the nobility, and that his grandfather was a king.

John of the Bear suggested to his mother that they leave their cavern-prison, that he would remove the stone *con la ayuda de Dios* (with the help of God), and this happened. Mother and son spied on the bear, and when it left the cavern, John of the Bear ran to the door and removed it, that is, the great rock that served as a door. John of the Bear was very strong, extraordinarily strong.

When the rock fell, although the bear was by this time very distant, he heard it and returned to the cavern. He found it deserted, and with a bear's instinct, he started in pursuit of them. John of the Bear told his mother: "I shall wait for the bear and I shall kill it; you walk ahead, Mother." And so it happened. John of the Bear cut, or rather uprooted, a pine and armed in that manner, waited for the bear to arrive and then killed him. The princess and her son were now free.

[When they arrived at the king's palace he was overjoyed and they had a fiesta. Soon John of the Bear was enrolled in school; the schoolmaster was told to take special care of him, since he was nervous and excitable. One day the students were taken swimming, and when John of the Bear disrobed, he was man from the waist up, but a bear below the waist. The children taunted him, and in anger he struck one of them and killed him. The teacher dismissed John from school, and the grandfather had to supply a tutor, but John learned everything a prince should know, very rapidly. Then he decided to see the world, and his grandfather had a weapon made, so big that it took eight men to deliver it, but John could swing it around his head easily. Then he set out, meeting in turn Little Big Ears, who could even hear plants grow; Little Big Runner, who was four times faster than the wind; Mountain Mover; and Pine-Twister. He promised them good pay and they went on together.]

While on the trip they ran out of money. They kept walking and found a cave. John said: "We shall take lodgings here, because it is necessary to steal for we are out of money." [But a Negro came and beat the travelers and told them to go away, then he went into a hole. They followed him into a tunnel and there found him feeding five women.] They were five princesses, and when the Negro [who was actually a black devil] came out of the subterranean room, John entered and spoke with the first one, and asked what she was doing there. The princess told him that she was one of five sisters, princesses, whom the black devil had kidnapped and she proposed to give him her royal crown if he would take her away from there. And she gave it to him. [The other princesses made the same offer, and John had them pulled up to the top of the ground with a rope, one after another. Then when he pulled on the rope as a signal to pull him up, the rock it was tied to fell, leaving him underground—and facing the black devil. John swung his weapon at the devil and knocked him out, also cutting off his ear.]

. . . When the devil had recuperated from the blow, he said to John: "Give me my little ear." John told him: "No, not until you get me out of here." And the black devil told him: "Shut your eyes." And he got out of the pit. When John found himself out of the cave, he told the black devil: "Here is your little ear."

The black devil, in gratitude, told John: "I am going to give you a little gourd; when you find yourself in some predicament, just tell it: 'Little gourd by dint of the virtue that you possess and what God had given you, I want you to...' (and here one asks for whatever is desired)." [As John walked along, he met two little old men who told him of a fiesta that was taking place. The five princesses had been returned by four men. Was he going to the fiesta? He said he was a prince, but too poor. Then when he was alone, he asked the little gourd for a good horse and prince's attire. Then he went toward the palace. On the way he passed the little old men, asking alms, and gave them a lot of money. At the fiesta, an announcement was made that the one who had the crowns of the princesses and returned them intact would marry one of the princesses. John sent the little old men to say that replica crowns were on the way, and the king's response was that if the crowns were not exactly like the lost ones, the old men would die. John slept calmly, but the old men cried about their plight till they fell asleep.]

John got up and cleaned the crowns and placed them on a pole and returned to sleep. The next day he was awakened by the bugles of the royal guard. The little old men went up and showed the crowns to the king. The princesses exclaimed: "Truly, they are intact!"

John of the Bear was married to the youngest princess. And that's how it happened.[90]

The story of Juan Oso has been reported literally hundreds of times, in a variety of forms and degrees of completeness. One version has three brothers setting out, one after another, to rescue three enchanted princesses from the bottom of a well. By the help of the ear that the youngest brother cut off a Negro at the bottom of the well, he finds out that the princesses are guarded by a bear. The Negro tells the youngest brother how to rescue the first, on the promise that his ear will be returned—but the brother keeps the ear, rescuing in turn the other two princesses, getting the princesses out, and then being transported to the palace in disguise, where the two wicked brothers are getting all the credit for having rescued the princesses—two of whom they were to marry. Aided by the Negro, the youngest brother passes the tests that prove he rescued the princesses, and he asks for forgiveness for his brothers and for the hand of the youngest princess. And presumably the Negro finally got his ear back.[91]

Another tale displays many of the Juan Oso story's motifs, and although it was collected down in the state of Chihuahua, it demonstrates the spread and variety of the story. It is the tale of *Catorce* (Fourteen), a man who ate fourteen of everything—indeed he lived by fourteens. He was a terrific worker, but one of his meals would wipe out his employer's provisions—and livestock as well. His prowess earned him fame, until a king sent for him to kill a seven-headed serpent that was destroying cattle and people in the kingdom. Catorce wasn't interested in the prize—the hand of the king's daughter—since food was his only interest. But Catorce went to the *sierra* (mountain), killed the serpent by cutting off its seven heads; then he removed the fangs and pocketed them, skinned the serpent, and stretched it over some trees to make a shelter. When someone else claimed the reward, bringing in the seven heads Catorce had left behind, Catorce went to the fiesta, and asked if the serpent heads had fangs—and produced them when the time came. He didn't want to marry a princess who came up only to his knee, but he had to obey the king. "So Catorce married. He killed other serpents and had to marry other princesses, and he had his rations every fourteen days as long as he lived."[92]

Many other ordinary folktales are told along the Mexican border and throughout the Spanish Southwest. To conclude the section, the following story should serve well:

The Son of **Tata Juan Pescador** *(Daddy John the Fisherman)*

Once a fisherman (Tata John), his wife, and son Juanito, were visited by a beautiful blonde woman, pretty as a princess, riding in a carriage pulled by six white horses. She asked to take Juanito with her, and finally the parents let him go, after she said that she was a fairy and that they would never regret giving Juanito to her. She left with them a magic vase: all one had to do was say, *"Compónte, jarrito"* (fill up, vase) and it would be full of money. Juanito was bathed and dressed like a prince and they set out, driving across the desert. Juanito fell asleep (after being told not to), and when he awoke he was ragged and dirty and alone on the desert. He had heard that when one is uncertain as to where he should go, he should throw his *huarache* (sandal) in the air and follow the direction the toe points, so he did and wound up walking north.

Soon he came to an ant, an eagle, and a lion fighting over the carcass of a dead cow. At their request, Juanito made an equitable division of the cow—head to the ant, loins to the eagle, and the rest to the lion. In payment the lion gave him a hair and the ant a leg, but the eagle flew away. Juanito was puzzled, and asked what he should do with his trophies; he was told that he could call on the animals for help whenever he was in trouble. He was to hold the hair between thumb and forefinger and say, *"Dios y mi buen león"* (God and my good lion), or hold the ant leg likewise and say *"Dios y mi buena hormiga"* (God and my good ant), and they would appear and do his bidding. His first command was to the lion to take him to the town of Canela (where the fairy had come from). As they were about to go, the eagle reappeared and told them to wait until they had food.

A beef was driven into camp, the ant bit its foot, and the lion killed it. After they had eaten, the remainder was turned into jerky and bagged. The eagle told the boy to climb on its back, carrying the meat, and every time the eagle said, *"Carne"* (meat), to give it a piece. After seven such feedings, the meat was gone and they arrived at a lagoon, where a monster lived. The ant and eagle were called up. The monster was finally defeated, and when he was cut open a snake came out of his body. When the snake was killed, a dove flew out of its body. Inside the dove was an egg, and when the egg was broken on the head of the guard outside the castle where the fairy lived, he found that his father had extracted so much money from the magic vase that he was now governor, and had also become terribly vain—and when the son tried to see him, the son was thrown into a cell: he had no son! Finally there was a revelation and joyful reunion, the son went back to the castle to live, and his parents continued to be rich.[93]

Tricksters, Jokes, and Joke Cycles

Jokes and anecdotes are very popular among Mexican-Americans. Witness the story of the *mojado* (wetback) collected in a restaurant in Austin, Texas, with the teller switching languages as the story demanded:

> Well this mojado had just held up a bank and was running away with the money with a *rinche* (Texas Ranger) after him. When the mojado went around the corner, he put the money in a garbage can. Then the Texas Ranger caught him and wanted to know where the money was, but he couldn't speak Spanish and the mojado couldn't speak English. Then the rinche called a Mexican-American who was passing by and told him to ask the "Meskin" about the money. "He wants to know what you did with the money." The mojado answered, "I put the money in a garbage can." The rinche says, "What did he say? What did he say?" And the Chicano says, "He says you are a chicken sonofabitch and you're not man enough to kill him!"[94]

Another joke revolving around language confusion involved a South Texan who tried to buy a horse from a paisano, who kept saying, "I no sell. The horse he don't look too good." The Anglo finally prevailed, bought the horse, and returned next day complaining that the horse was blind. The paisano said, "Señor, I told you he don't look too good."[95]

Other jokes deal with the worldwide character called by folklorists the numskull—often named *Juan Tonto* (Foolish John), although sometimes the Tonto is called Pablo, and he is coupled with *Juan Hábil* (Skillful John). And, as in the folklore of other cultures, the foolish one often comes out ahead. One of my favorites over the years, always told with a thick accent and demonstrations of Pablo's actions, has Juan Hábil taking a siesta in the shade when Pablo comes by, and he's holding something in his cupped hands. "Whatchu got there, Pablo?" asks Juan.

"I got a honney sockle," says Pablo, after he looks to see what it is.

"Whatchu gon do weeth it?"

"I gon down the road to gat me some honney."

"Pablo, you crazy. You don gat honney from a honney sockle! You gat honney from a bee!" But Pablo goes on down the road, and pretty soon he comes back carrying a bucket of honey. Juan scratches his head; he can't understand this. The next day, Juan is taking his siesta when Pablo comes by, and he's got something in his hands. "Whatchu got there today, Pablo?"

"I got a botter fly," says Pablo, after he takes a peek to see.

"Whatchu gon do weeth it?"

"I gon down the road to gat me some botter."

"Pablo, you crazy. You don gat botter from a botter fly! You gat milk from the cow and you churn it and make the botter." But Pablo goes on down the road, and pretty soon he comes back carrying a pound of butter. Juan scratches his head; he can't understand this.

The next day, Juan is taking his siesta when Pablo comes along, and he's got something in his hands. "Whatchu got there today, Pablo?"

After Pablo takes a careful peek he says, "I got a horse fly."

Juan gets up, saying, "Wait, I get my hat, I go weeth you!"[96]

In another story, reminiscent of the Bremen Town Musicians, there are two Juans—Juan Tonto and Juan Hábil, who lived with their grandmother. One day Juan Hábil left Juan Tonto in charge of the grandmother, with instructions to give her a bath. But Tonto had the water boiling before he put the old lady in, so she was scalded to death. He took her out, dressed her, and put a cigarette in her mouth, just as Juan Hábil rode up. Tonto insisted she couldn't be dead, since she was smoking. The two brothers left home, and Hábil sent Tonto back to get the door *(puerta)* as a memento, but Tonto brought a *puerco* (pig). When they came to a wood after dark, and heard strange voices, those of some bandits. The two climbed into a tree to spend the night—but Tonto had to relieve himself. Finally he could hold himself back no more, and let go right over the bandits, who thought the sky was falling and ran away, leaving their loot.

With the loot, Juan Hábil bought a mansion, one room of which was covered with mirrors. Juan Tonto had never seen a mirror, so when he wandered in, he was delighted. He laughed, and all the images copied him; everything he did, the images did the same. Finally he became tired of the copycats, but could not make them go away—so he took a rock and broke all the mirrors. Juan Hábil also had a chicken farm, and the Tonto was enchanted with the idea of hatching chicks—so he gathered a bunch of eggs and sat on them himself. When Juan Hábil finally got him off the crushed eggs, he found not *pollitos* (baby chicks) but big fat worms that had come to eat the eggs.

Juan Tonto's final stupidity brought his end. Looking into a well, he saw a beautiful big cheese—the moon's reflection, of course, as in countless other stories. He jumped in to get the cheese for his brother and was drowned. So Juan

Hábil was left to mourn, but he had all that money to comfort himself with.[97]

The stories associated with Pedro de Urdemales, who has kinships with a wide variety of liars such as Baron Munchausen, and a history going back to Spain, are more like joke cycles than anything else, although the ordinary folktale with its impossible tasks and contests appears from time to time. Witness the time Pedro tricked everybody he came into contact with:

Pedro de Urdemales

Pedro cut the tails off a herd of hogs (belonging to somebody else, of course) and stuck them, cut end down, into the mud of a swamp. When a stranger rode up, Pedro began weeping for his hogs that were being swallowed up by the mud of the swamp. The man figured Pedro was too stupid to know how to pull the hogs out of the mud and agreed to buy them for one thousand dollars. Pedro was quick, and he left before the trick was discovered. Soon Pedro was down on his luck again, and he figured out a new scheme to fool someone with. He bought a pot and some beans, dug a small furnace in which he laid a fire, and set the pot of beans to boiling on top of the hidden furnace. As the beans became done and floated to the top of the pot, Pedro speared them with a long cactus thorn and ate them. A traveler came by and was astounded to see a pot boiling without a fire. Hearing from Pedro that it was a magic pot, the man bought it for one thousand dollars, but Pedro said the pot might be angry if it found out it had been sold, so the new owner should wait until Pedro was out of sight before assuming command of the pot. Pedro left, and bored holes in some of the gold coins he had received; he tied them to a mesquite bush as if they were growing there. He was in the process of "gathering his crop" when two men came by and offered to buy the marvelous bush. They would not take a refusal, so Pedro finally sold them the bush for the present crop plus one thousand dollars. He gathered his crop and left, and it was the following year before the men realized they had bought an ordinary mesquite. Of course, in all these stories, the ones who got taken were tricksters themselves, trying to get something marvelous for a small price, so we don't feel too sorry for them.

Finally Pedro came near meeting his match. A giant was approaching him, and Pedro, who saw the giant first, was fearful for his life. Thinking quickly, he took off his huarache and threw it up into the air. The giant saw the sandal fall, and asked Pedro what was going on. The lie that came forth was that Pedro had thrown a man into the air three days before, and the man's sandal was the first evidence seen since. The giant was impressed, but he challenged Pedro to a contest of three events. The first was for each to drive his fist through a tree. Pedro asked for a day to get ready, and removed the bark carefully and cut a hole through the tree and replaced the bark. Next day, aiming carefully, he easily drove his fist deep into the tree and the giant admitted he was beaten. The next contest was to see who could throw a rock farther, and Pedro threw a quail he had up his sleeve, so he won again. The next contest was set when the giant said, "Tomorrow we wrestle." This time Pedro prepared by ripping his clothes and tearing up the ground as if a battle had just taken place. When the giant appeared he was impressed; Pedro told him he had thrown a man into the air—a man much larger than the giant—and he hadn't fallen to earth yet. Again the giant gave up, and insisted on taking Pedro home to spend the night. There a trap was set to crush Pedro while he slept, but Pedro managed to turn the tables on the giant, who was crushed instead.

As Pedro was leaving, he met the man who had bought the hog tails, whose revenge was to put Pedro in a barrel, with the intention of drowning him. While the man and his servants were eating, prior to drowning Pedro, the captive rocked the barrel back and forth till it fell over and rolled down a hill, where a sheepherder found it. Pedro was being forced to marry a king's daughter against his will, he told the sheepherder. [Sound familiar?] The shepherd quickly agreed to give Pedro his herd of sheep, in exchange for taking Pedro's place, and the barrel was rolled back up the hill to where it had been left. Pedro gathered up his sheep and drove them away. The sheepherder and the barrel were thrown into the river, where it went, *"Gori, gori, gori,"* as it sank. Several days later, the man who thought he had drowned Pedro found him with the sheep. Pedro told him that each "gori" had been a sheep, and the underwater people had freed him, sending him on his way with the magnificent flock of sheep. The man let Pedro go, and after selling the sheep, Pedro went into the service of the king, who after a time had enough of Pedro's tricks and ordered him hung—but Pedro was given the right to choose the tree on which he was to hang, so he chose a sunflower plant![98]

Don Cacahuate

Another trickster in the Mexican-American tradition is Don Cacahuate (Mr. Peanut), who sometimes wins and sometimes loses but is always doing something stupid. Once he was fulfilling a promise to take his wife for a train ride, and as a freight train passed through, he grabbed hold and was dragged several yards before he turned it loose. "Why didn't you get on?" he asked his wife. "I was slowing it down for you."[99]

UT El Paso student Norma Morales observed that in the *barrio* (Mexican-American neighborhood), Don Cacahuate stories were told within a circle of friends, taking the place of movies and television that the people couldn't afford. The stories frequently involve culture conflicts between Mexican-Americans and Anglos—often playing upon Don Cacahuate's ignorance of the other group. As an example, she told of a time Don Cacahuate went to the railroad station to wait for a train—but he didn't know what a train looked like. A man replied, "A train is black and big with smoke puffing on top." Don Cacahuate stood near the tracks, waiting, and he saw a hobo come along. He was a Negro, and very tall, and he was smoking a pipe. So without hesitation, Don Cacahuate climbed on the hobo's back and left the station.[100]

Perhaps it is because of the first part of Don Cacahuate's name (*caca* means feces, and he is often called "Don Caca") that so many episodes in the story cycle concern defecation. For example, one day Don Caca was walking with his wife, and all of a sudden he had to go to the restroom. They were walking through a park, and he saw some shrubs and decided to go there—but his wife told him to climb a tree. So he took off his hat and placed it, upside-down, under the tree. But every time he would "do his necessities," he would miss the hat. Two nuns were passing by and smelled the odor. They looked up at Don Cacahuate and told him he was uncouth. He replied that he wasn't uncouth—his aim was just bad![101]

In another tale, Don Cacahuate steals some green corn growing beside the road as he travels to Los Angeles. The corn gives him diarrhea, and he has the urge, proceeding to "go" in the middle of the street. When the policeman who was directing traffic, and who knew a little Spanish, told him, *"¡Es delito!"* (That's a crime!), he replied, "No es delito; es de elote!" (It's not a crime; it's from corn on the cob).[102]

Don Cacahuate and his wife were once down in their luck. There was nothing at all in the house to eat or drink. In desperation over their plight, he told his wife to get him a cup of coffee. *"¿Como?"* (How?) she asked. *"Con crema y azúcar. Tu sabes come me gusta el café"* (With cream and sugar; you know how I like my coffee).[103]

Other tricksters worthy of mention include those who traffic in illegal merchandise. The story is told in South El Paso of a couple who sold marijuana cigarettes, and while the woman was cooking beans one day, the narcotics people from the El Paso Police Department showed up following a tip. She dumped the weed into the pot of beans, and the police found nothing but a lady eating beans. When her husband showed up, having heard by the barrio grapevine that the cops had been there, she was very happy. "Where did you hide the stuff?" he asked. "It's all right, man. Everything's in the pot, man," she replied.[104]

Another woman, who was suspected of smuggling whiskey from Juárez into El Paso, was always taking a bath in a tin tub in the back yard when the Border Patrol showed up. So one day they waited until she was away from home, and found that the tub she bathed in covered a cache of bottles of whisky. That was why she was so clean![105]

A nameless trickster was one of a pair of brothers who had made a *manda* (promise) to climb Mount Cristo Rey, with beans in their shoes, to a religious monument west of El Paso, in payment for a granted request. The elder brother groaned and complained all the way up and down the mountain, but the younger brother climbed with no sign of discomfort. Finally the elder brother could stand it no longer, and asked the other why it was he was not in pain. "Hermano, I promised the Christ I would climb up and down His mountain with beans in my shoes, but I did not say that the beans wouldn't be cooked first!"[106]

A nameless woodcutter (who must be kin to Juan Tonto) from Haciendita, Texas, made his living cutting and hauling wood with a little cart and four burros. He would drive to the place where he was going to cut the wood, and turn the burros loose to graze while he worked. One morning he mounted one burro and rode out to bring in the others—but he could find only three. He hunted all day, mounted on the burro, but he could never find the one he thought was missing. Finally he gave up, and decided to see how far he could get with only three burros to pull the cart. Having hitched up the three, he turned around and saw the other one. *"Pues qué hombre tan bruto"* (What a stupid man), says the story-teller. "He was mounted on the burro and looking for him!"[107]

A traveling anecdote that I have heard in several versions is often localized in a Catholic girls' school in El Paso. Sister Marie called up the Sergeant of the Day at Fort Bliss nearby, asking him if he could provide one hundred men to escort her girls at a dance that weekend—but she specified that she definitely did not want anyone of the Jewish faith. The night of the dance, a handsome Black lieutenant stepped off one of the buses carrying the men and asked for Sister Marie. One hundred Negro soldiers came forth behind him, and Sister Marie was overwhelmed. "There must be some mistake!" she blurted. "No, Ma'am," the lieutenant said. "Sergeant Rosenheimer never makes mistakes."[108] Twenty-five years ago in Austin, I heard the same story, but it was Mexicans the lady didn't want and Sergeant Rosales who never made mistakes.

And then there are the international rivalry jokes. Repeatedly there is a contest of wits or braggadocio between a Mexican and men of other nationalities, and the Mexican always wins by his cleverness, or another culture is put down:

Once a Russian, an Anglo, a Frenchman, and a Mexican were arguing over which was the cleanest. For a test, they put a skunk in a room and entered one at a time to see who could stand the most. The Frenchman went into the room and lasted only thirty seconds; the Russian lasted a minute, and the Mexican two minutes. Then entered the Anglo, who was a little filthier, and the skunk came out snorting from the smell.[109]

A group of men from different countries were showing off the qualities of the weapons typical to their homelands. The Argentine took his *bolo* and threw it at the feet of a galloping horse, tying it up. A gringo took a fine pistol and killed a fly in mid-air. Then the Mexican took his *machete* (big brush-chopping knife) and flung it at a flying *moyote* (mosquito), which kept on flying. The other men made fun of the Mexican, but the Mexican calmly answered them, *"Sí, siguió volando, pero no volverá a ser padre"* (Yes, he kept flying, but he'll never again be a father).[110]

And in another confrontation between nations, a Russian, an American, and a Mexican were describing the superiority of their countries' attainments. The Russian said, "We have the most powerful airplane in the world. It can fly all the way into outer space." The others told him not to exaggerate, so he said, "O.K. then, two inches lower."

The gringo, not wanting to be left behind, said his country had the most powerful submarine in the world, one that could dive to the deepest part of the ocean—"O.K. then, two inches lower."

Then the Mexican took his turn. "In my country," he said, "women give birth through the navel." The Russian and the American said this was impossible. So the Mexican said, "O.K. then, two inches lower."[111]

In a sort of reverse battle for superiority, a story is told of Mexico's having built the world's biggest ship—but they built it of adobe, and it melted and sank—a genuine numskull joke.[112]

Because of his efforts at resolving difficulties between the United States and Mexico, and because of his positive attitudes toward Mexican-Americans, President John F. Kennedy's memory is held in high regard in the Southwest. In this context a final anecdote is offered:

When Kennedy got to heaven after being assassinated in Dallas, they told him that General Santa Ana, president of Mexico during the Texas Revolution, wanted to meet him. After they met, Santa Ana said, "Now you know why I sold Texas to them?"[113]

Tall Tales

Although Stanley Robe reports that tales involving lies and exaggerations are not common in Hispanic areas, his collections and indexes of folktales do include a few, as do the Publications of the Texas Folklore Society. Student collections at the University of Texas at El Paso tend to bear Robe's stand out, with almost none of the genre having been collected there in the past twenty-four years. Lies, of course, do exist—witness the Don Cacahuate tales, and the lying contests just reported. But the tall tale is alive; in fact, Robe may be correct in suggesting that collectors have not considered the material as valuable as legends and ordinary folktales.[114]

Perhaps our friend Don Cacahuate is as good a place to start as any. He is not only a trickster, he appears in a number of tales, including the following sample:

Don Cacahuate once doubted the paternity of his three sons, since his wife was excessively friendly. So he devised a test. He took his sons riding out into the mountains. When they came to a canyon, he looked far across it and asked if the boys saw a doe on the other side. Two said no, but the third said, "There is a doe and a fawn."

"How do you see a doe and a fawn when we don't even see a doe?" one of the brothers asked.

"I didn't say I saw them. I heard the fawn sucking its mother." So Don Cacahuate knew that at least one of the boys was his true son.

Another time Don Caca was rolling a cigarette but had no matches. His horse, Palo Verde, heard him cursing his luck. Just as lightning flashed from a thundercloud overhead, Palo Verde sprang up and Cacahuate lit his cigarette on the lightning's flash.

Once Palo Verde was really showing off with his fancy singlefooting on a cobblestone street, making the sound *Za-ca-TE-cas, Za-ca-TE-cas*—but he did it so forcefully that he broke in two. (Sometimes it is a lightning bolt that cuts the horse in two.) Then Don Cacahuate heard only *Za-ca, Za-ca, Za-ca, Za-ca.* He looked back, and saw the rear half of the horse; he waited for the rear end to catch up and then they went on, *Za-ca-TE-cas, Za-ca-TE-cas* as before.

Don Cacahuate went hunting one day, taking a *morral* (feedbag) of peaches along for food. He came upon a deer and began loading his gun, but discovered he had no shot—so he rammed in a seed from a peach he had just eaten, and fired at the deer's head. The buck fell, but before Cacahuate reached him he jumped up and ran away. Three years later Don Cacahuate was hunting again in the same area and came upon a peach tree loaded with ripe fruit. He climbed up to gather some, and suddenly the tree began running through the meadow! It was growing in the head of the deer he had shot with the peach seed. So he climbed down, stabbed the deer to death, and dined that night on venison and peach preserves.[115]

Pedro de Urdemales also is involved in tall tales. In a longer tale than the one reported earlier in this chapter, Pedro survives death by claiming he is being forced to marry against his will, sells the pigs' tails, stuffs gold coins up a burro's rear (selling him to a gullible man when the burro "deposits" the coins), and then takes some coins to tie to a tree which he sells. As a result of all these unbelievable events, he becomes a compadre to Dios, overcomes Death, and winds up in heaven. Since such a rascal is not fit for heaven, he is turned into stone, but is content because he still has his eyes to see all the wonders about him.[116]

In a series of lies by one man that are confirmed indirectly by another, a common folktale type (suggested in Don Cacahuate's paternity test), a man comes to a remote village with instructions to his traveling companion (whom he pretends not to know) to back up his lies. The first "news" told is that the river downstream is on fire, but the villagers do not believe the story. When the second traveler arrives, he says he doesn't know about the fire, but he saw carts full of fish boiled and baked by hot water in the river. For this wonderful news the two are feasted for several days.

Next the first traveler meets an old man and tells him of a huge bird that lives in the mountains; when it flies, it darkens the sky so the chickens go to roost, thinking it is night. The old man is disgusted by such a liar, but the second traveler comes up with a story about an egg that has been found in the mountains, an egg so huge that it had to be moved by several man and boys with levers.

The next lie concerned a deer that the first traveler had shot in the head and the hind foot with the same bullet—but the second liar was equal to the challenge. He said the deer had been scratching his head with his hind foot when he was shot.[117]

In a similar situation collected in New Mexico, the first liar says there was a baby with seven heads in the next village, a claim which is confirmed by the second liar, who said that he didn't see the baby, but he saw a little shirt with seven collars hanging out on a clothesline.[118]

From widely separated sources come three tales with a similar theme: in two stories, a man loses some livestock, either mules or horses, and after much searching, finds them inside a huge pumpkin; they eat some of the outside, and then eat their way in, where they stay. In the third, the pumpkin is so huge that a sheepherder beds down a thousand sheep inside it.[119]

Another tale from New Mexico relates that a man was swallowed by a buffalo drinking water from a stream while the man was bathing. As the buffalo grazed, the man would reach out and grab some weeds, with which he would build a fire to roast the buffalo meat he cut off the buffalo's insides. Finally the animal died (from internal combustion?) and the man cut his way out.[120]

But such a tall tale is mild compared to one with a similar theme with which I will close this chapter. The story is told by Don Gregorio Jáquez, "a teller of tales, and liar of infinite parts," who insisted upon "absolute gravity and unconditional acceptance of his tales." The circumstantial details with which he tells his story make it nearly impossible to shorten without losing the flavor:

> . . . I was on my way to this fiesta; I had a good horse, the one I called the Wasp. He was only a colt still—I had finished the first stages of breaking him in, and was riding him with the *bozal* [a woven horsehair noseband, instead of a bridle], but he was already trained to lead like a kitten and to stand like an oak.
>
> . . . Late in the afternoon I saw something in the road behind me that simulated a whirlwind and which was coming in my direction with great speed. I observed it carefully, and in the end I said to myself, "Gregorio, amigo, that is no whirlwind that you see; it is a troop of Apaches that have winded you and are running you down."
>
> [The race began, and the Wasp did his best, but the Indians kept gain-

ing.] I swerved the little Wasp out of the path, and we plunged into the mesquite, which at this place was exceedingly tall and thick, with that whole troop of accursed Indians pounding after.

I looked everywhere for a place to hide, but there was nothing, and the savages almost had me by the hair; but just at the last moment, when there seemed to be no chance left, the holy saints, to whom I had been industriously commending myself, furnished me with a refuge.

For it happened that I ran almost full tilt into a bull—a big black ten-year-old, with white feet and a big blaze, lying under a mesquite right in my path. He had just finished chewing his cud, and was yawning widely after swallowing it when I checked the Wasp to keep from crashing into him; and seeing that cavern gaping in front of me, I said, "Gregorio, the saints have sent you this refuge; this is the reward of your prayers and of a life spent in the pursuit of truthfulness and virtue." And without the loss of a moment, I cast myself off the Wasp and dived in, not even waiting to turn my spurs [as a gentlemanly vaquero would do on entering a dwelling, to keep from scratching the furniture, etc.].

[Realizing that only a sheepherder, the most stupid creature on earth to a vaquero, would be dumb enough to starve in the midst of such plenty, Gregorio scratched up a fire and was soon broiling a fat steak cut from the bull's insides. He lived thus for three days; then, figuring that the Apaches had gone, he decided to leave his host.]

When I had dived in, I had, by rare presence of mind, kept a tight hold on the Wasp's halter rope, and this proved to be a great aid to me in climbing out; and I further helped myself by irritating the bull's throat with my spurs, so that, partly by hand-over-hand work on the rope and partly by the impulse of the bull's coughs, I managed to drag myself up and out. It was noon when I emerged, and there, at the end of the rope which I still held in my hand, was the Wasp, all sleek and rested and ready to mount.

[Riding to town, he found a fiesta was going on, and he took part in it all, including a bullfight which was scheduled—but when he faced the bull, he recognized his recent host. He called out to the mayor,] "Señor Alcalde, you cannot fight this bull, he is unfit to perform in any ring. He is an incomplete bull—his entire insides are missing; and it would be a discredit to this fiesta to use him...If you do not believe my word, open him, then, and let your own eyes tell you that I know what I am talking about."

[When the bull was killed and opened up], there was nothing inside, nothing—just the hide stretched over the ribs, and where the stomach should have been, there was a pile of dead ashes where I had made fires and done my cooking.

When the people saw this they were dumbfounded, and. . .I was compelled to linger for over a week in the town after the fair was over, eating and drinking of the best, the guest of the entire pueblo, and the events of the fair were quite forgotten in the excitement which was aroused by the story of my unique escape from the Apaches.[121]

Baron Munchausen is probably sitting around heaven—or Parnassus, or Valhalla, wherever the good liars go—quite glumly, since he has obviously been outclassed by Don Gregorio Jáquez!

José Cisneros

CHAPTER SEVEN

Ballads and Folksongs

FOLK MUSIC, ACCORDING to Donald Robb, is music bearing the stamp not of the individuality of a single composer, "but rather of the thoughts and emotions of a people united by such ties as language, religion, nationality, and residence. . .[and it] embodies traditional elements of the folklore of the people, or at any rate, their attitudes toward life."[1] The process of folk transmission, depending as it has always done upon the ear and the memory, often produces curiosities far from the original forms (if they could be determined), but also polishes and reshapes materials into a new beauty and simplicity. Ballad scholar William J. Entwistle called this process of improvement "fortunate forgetfulness,"[2] a term that Don Robb would certainly approve of. The richness of folk music and the process which reshapes it are deeply ingrained in the culture of the Spanish Southwest.

Folksongs and ballads among Hispanic Americans often have roots going all the way back to Spain, at least in New Mexico and Colorado. Aurelio M. Espinosa pointed out in the 1930s that "a large number of the old Spanish ballads, especially of the novelesque type, are still recited and sung wherever Spanish is spoken, . . .[even among] the Pueblo Indians of New Mexico who speak Spanish recite and sing old Spanish ballads today." Amazingly, the exploits of El Cid, the eleventh-century Spanish hero in the battles against the Moors, "were still remembered in one of the most distant corners of the Hispanic world, Santa Fe, New Mexico."[3]

The case is different among Mexican-Americans, as discussed earlier. Along the Rio Grande and the rest of the border between the United States and Mexico, Mexico has replaced Spain as the homeland and as the major influence on balladry. The *vaqueros* (cowboys) of South Texas were particularly strong in carrying on the singing traditions of Mexico. Just as Anglo-Americans continue to sing ballads about Jesse James and Billy the Kid, outlaw heroes are enduring subjects for Mexican-American singers. Still sung are the ballads of Heraclio Bernal, Juan Cortina, Pablo González, and especially Gregorio Cortez, whose fame as a defender of his rights was spread by Américo Paredes in his powerful book *"With His Pistol in His Hand": A Border Ballad and Its Hero.*[4] And as many collectors have demonstrated, a full assortment of other kinds of folksongs and ballads lives in the Southwest.

But the several types of folksongs are complex, and a full discussion of them would require of the reader a considerable amount of technical knowledge—plus the ability to sift out an enormous amount of material to arrive at some semblance of concord among the many writers on the subject. Norman "Brownie" McNeil, who has sung Mexican songs for a wide variety of audiences, including presidents and kings, expresses the situation well:

> There is in Latin-America, strangely enough, no general agreement on what to call a ballad. In Mexico the word used most commonly to designate a ballad is *corrido,* but several terms have been encountered by the author in his peregrinations, all used to designate the same thing. In Mexico, some people erroneously borrow the Spanish term *romance.* Besides this and the word *corrido,* many singers call the ballad any one of the following: *tragedias* (tragedies), *versos* (verses), *ejemplos* (examples), *coplas* (couplets), and *mañanitas* (morning songs). *Versos* and *tragedias* are used more in South Texas than even the term *corrido.* Some persons in South Texas and the border region failed to respond at all when asked about *corridos,* but understood immediately the term *versos.* A *mañanita* is really a song of lyric character sung usually as a serenade in the early morning hours, but in Mexico it is sometimes used to refer to a ballad.[5]

Singing style among Mexican-Americans is often unusual, at least to Anglos. An early collector of folksongs in Spanish observed that

> the American of Nordic extraction who hails from the haunts of "civilization" is likely to be somewhat startled and even somewhat irritated by his first contact with Spanish as sung in New Mexico, for the conventional style for male voice is high falsetto, produced rather largely through the nose; yet this is one situation where familiarity breeds not contempt, but enjoyment, and the man who cursed the song yesterday finds himself with his ear cocked for more and yet more until he is ready to swear that the conventional styles of singing to which he has been brought up have no charm at all when compared with this.[6]

The presentation in print of folk music material—especially in Spanish—involves several problems. A folksong without the music is "just" a piece of folk poetry, and even printing the music is useful only to those who can read and perform it. (I do not let my students collect folk music unless they can write the music down—which rules out most of them.) Writing over sixty years ago, the same folklorist said that

> singing a Spanish song learned in any other way than by ear is always rather decidedly a puzzle. At some points words must be cramped and telescoped to fit the music, at others they must be stretched, and at still others grace notes must be introduced to carry the plethora of words,

> and only an inspiration or a general acquaintance with the native method can distinguish which place from t'other.[7]

Even a record included with this book would merely be a curiosity, although a lively one, for most readers. Thus, as the early publishers of ballads were forced to do, I must be satisfied with presenting the texts of representative pieces and their translations, without music in most cases, realizing that the text without the performance is only part of the picture. And since other resources can be used by the interested reader to puzzle out the several technical types of folksongs among Mexican-Americans, I will follow essentially the categories employed by Dr. Paredes in his *Texas-Mexican Cancionero.*[8]

Old Songs from Colonial Days

"La Ciudad de Jauja" (The City of Jauja) is very similar to the American song "The Big Rock Candy Mountain," with its dreams of plenty to be had for the taking. Wishful thinking—and bitter irony—it might have been, especially to the dispossessed during the Depression when sung by folks whose next meal was an elusive hope:

Desde esa ciudad de Jauja me mandan solicitar
que me vaya para alla un tesoro a disfrutar.

¿Qué dices, amigo? vamos a ver si dicen verdad,
si es verdad de lo que dicen nos quedaremos allá.

Las iglesias son de azúcar, de caramelo los frailes,
de melcocha los monaguillos y de miel los colaterales.

Válgame la Cruz de Queso en sus penas de tortilla!
Vuelan los patos asados con su pimienta y su sal.

Levántate, amigo, y vamos a ver si dicen verdad,
si es verdad de lo que dicen nos quedaremos allá.

Arroyos que corren leche, jarros y cazos de atole,
Hay barrancas de panochas, hay azúcar con pinole.

Hay árboles de tortillas y labores de empanadas,
eso de tamales turcos, las calles estan regadas.

Ese Guadalupe Guerra tenía unas chivas muy finas,
y se las cambió a Julián por unos sacos de harina.

Levántate, amigo, y vamos, vámonos sin vacilar
donde agarran a patadas al que quiera trabajar.

They have sent from that city of Jauja, asking for me;
they want me to go over there, so I may enjoy a treasure.

What do you say, friend? Let us go see if they're speaking the truth;
if all that they say is true, we will remain there.

The churches are made of sugar, the friars of caramel,
the acolytes of molasses candy, and the altars of honey.

May the Cross of Cheese protect me, on its tortilla rocks!
The roasted ducks fly about garnished with pepper and salt.

Get up, my friend, let us go see if they're speaking the truth;
if all they say is true, we will remain there.

There are creeks that flow with milk, pots and kettles of atole;
there are mounds of brown sugar, there is sugar with pinole.

There are trees bearing tortillas and fields with crops of turnovers,
and as for Turkish tamales, the streets are covered with them.

That Guadalupe Guerra used to have some very fine goats,
and he traded them to Julian for some sacks of flour.

Get up, my friend, let us go, let us go without delay
where they kick hell out of you if you try to work.[9]

Of a much more serious subject is the song "Delgadina," which employs the incest theme present in some of the versions of "Cinderella"—the father king demanding that his daughter become his mistress, and when she refuses, having her locked up with only coarse food and salty water for her sustenance. She prays to the Virgin, and as the song ends,

La cama de Delgadina de ángeles está rodeada,
la cama del rey su padre de diablos está apretada.

Delgadina está en el cielo dándole cuenta al Creador
y su padre in los infiernos con el Demonio Mayor.

Ya con ésta me despido a la sombra de una lima,
aquí se acaba cantando la historia de Delgadina.

Delgadina's bed is surrounded by angels;
the bed of the king her father is crowded with demons.

Delgadina is in Heaven being judged by God;
her father is in Hell, with the Chief Devil.

Now with this I say farewell, under the shade of a lime tree;
here is the end of the singing of the story of Delgadina.[10]

Songs of Border Conflict

Along the English-Scottish border for many decades and on many other boundaries, songs of conflict have often given a measure of emotional relief to people. The border between the United States and Mexico is certainly one involving cultural clashes and misunderstandings, and as with the underdog culture in other rivalries, life there has produced an impressive body of songs as a result. When the Texas Revolution ended, Texans insisted on claiming the Rio Grande as their southern boundary; when the conclusion of the Mexican War made that boundary a fact, a vast number of Spanish-speaking people were separated artificially from their kin and their associates—much as the Berlin Wall has done in recent history in another part of the world. On the north bank of the river, the Anglo was usually in control, even when he was not in the majority, and this situation continues to some degree even today. Away from urban centers of population, people can visit one another freely across the border, without encountering official restraints. Not long ago in the Big Bend area of Texas, for example, I was offered a twenty-five-cent ride across the Rio Grande in a tiny rowboat called a *chalupa* (a shallop, but also a bowl-shaped tortilla filled with ground meat and other food)—and I was assured that everyone crossed that way, without interference. For once, apparently, the Border Patrol realized that such crossing was innocent and without international or criminal significance. Near El Paso and other large population areas, fear of smuggling or illegal entry keeps the age-old resentments alive among many Mexican-Americans. Thus it is understandable if they sing the old songs—as they do—of men and situations not entirely different from their own day.

It is in this context that the hero songs flourish. Heraclio Bernal, who was a successful gadfly to the regime of Porfirio Díaz during the 1880s, for example, was—and to some degree still is—the Mexican-Americans' "Beowulf, their Cid, their St. George, and their Robin Hood all in one." The song in his honor, "Corrido de Heraclio Bernal," reflects these heroic qualities, even in translation:

Town of Sinaloa, State of Michoacán,
is where they took out the order to arrest Bernal.

The Squadron of the North from the Military College went out,
to ride through the mountains to arrest Bernal.

Heraclio Bernal said that he was a man and didn't back down,
that he, mounted on his horse, gave pardon only to God [i.e., wouldn't "take anything" off anyone else].

Heraclio said at the Pericos Hacienda
that he did not rob the poor, only the very rich.

A family in the mountains found itself in dire need;
he gave them seven hundred pesos so that they might alleviate their troubles.

How handsome was Bernal on his dark horse,
in the midst of the *Acordada* [troop of rural police] with a nice big cigar.
[Tradition says he disguised himself and joined the Acordada for their group portrait, with a cigar to set himself apart.]

. . . .
And in Mazatlán they killed him by treachery and from behind,
because that don Crispín García was good at selling someone out.

Oh, you rich (people) of the coast, you will no longer die of fright;
now they have killed Bernal, and you can sleep with ease.

Fly, fly little dove, light on that walnut tree;
now the roads are empty, now they have killed Bernal.[11]

The "Tragedia de Remigio Treviño," recited in Rio Grande City, Texas, in 1928, has been called "the earliest Mexican ballad composed on Texan soil," and its story grows out of the anti-Anglo feeling of the lower border area. Treviño crossed the Rio Grande, intent on killing or expelling all the "invading" Anglos, but he was captured on one raid, and hanged. The night before his execution he composed the following song, in the best tradition of the "prisoner's last good night" so familiar to ballad lovers:

El año del '63	The year of '63
fue desgraciado pa' mí	was unfortunate for me;
yo la cárcel conocí	I got to know the jail,
engrillado de los pies.	shackled by my feet.

Muertos me acumulan dies [sic]	I killed a total of ten.
Pronto me llevan a la horca	Soon they'll take me to the gallows;
el dinero no ha valido.	money [a bribe?] was useless.
Yo, Remigio era me nombre,	I, Remigio was my given name,
Treviño, mi apelativo.	Treviño, my surname.

And the final verse completes the farewell:

Adios madre y hermanos,	Goodbye, mother and brothers,
adios todos mis amigos;	goodbye, all my friends;
den un doble de campanas	give a tolling of the bells
que de por Dios se lo pido	which for God's sake I ask you,
pues ya me voy al olvido	for I'm going to oblivion,
me quito de padecer.	my suffering ended.
Yo, Remigio era me nombre,	I, Remigio was my name,
Treviño, me apelativo.	Treviño, my surname.[12]

Despite such anti-American feelings as those of Treviño, Mexican singers were capable of seeing similarities between Mexican and American struggles for freedom. Two songs sung in San Ignacio, Texas, for the first time in 1867 were still being sung there in 1954, extolling the bravery and dedication of Ulysses S. Grant and Ignacio Zaragosa; when the songs were composed, Grant was secretary of war and about to become president, while Zaragosa was the victor over the French at the Battle of Puebla. In geography and culture they differed considerably, but the flame of freedom was seen burning within them both—and the French "La Marseillaise" was echoed in both tunes as well![13]

The same spirit of freedom was exhibited in song when activity against Porfiro Díaz, in the early stages of the Mexican Revolution, boosted the composition of the corrido, a situation which affected the people of the lower Rio Grande area. Their natural sympathies, of course, were not stopped by the international border, and Texas served for years as either a staging area for anti-Díaz raids or as a refuge of rebels being hotly pursued by government forces.[14] When the revolution was in full swing, and General of the North Francisco "Pancho" Villa's ragged army was carrying the fight with vigor, the soldiers and their female *soldaderas* marched and sang "La Cucaracha"—which has become one of the most remembered songs of those times, symbolic of the underdogs who overthrew the ricos who ran the country under Díaz. Who but underdogs would sing of a lowly cockroach with such ardor? Most familiar of all is the refrain,

La cucaracha, la cucaracha,	The cockroach, the cockroach
Ya no puede caminar,	Isn't able to travel,
Porque no tiene,	Because she hasn't
Porque le falta	Because she lacks,
Marihuana que fumar.	Marijuana to smoke.

The verses of "La Cucaracha" are almost endless, with all sorts of situations being described, not all related to the war by any means. Witness the following:

Cuando uno quiere a una	When a fellow loves a maiden,
Y ésta una no lo quiere,	And that maiden doesn't love him,
Es lo mismo que si un calvo	It's the same as when a bald man
En la calle encuentr' un peine.	Finds a comb upon the highway.

And another:

Mi vecina de enfrente	My neighbor across the road
Se llamaba Doña Clara	Used to be called Doña Clara,
Y si no habia muerto,	And if she hasn't died,
Es probable se llamará.	She's still called that.

But the war has its place too:

Una cosa me da risa—	One thing makes me laugh—
Pancho Villa sin camisa.	Pancho Villa without a shirt.
Ya se van los Carranzistas	Now the Carranzistas are leaving
Porque vienen los Villistas.	Because the Villistas are coming.

Incidentally, one of the fascinating details of the song involves the word *cucaracha,* which means not only "cockroach," but "dried-up old maid"—and the rival leader, Venustiano Carranza as well![15]

The soldadera, who accompanied her fighting man, cooked and washed for him, bore his children, and picked up his rifle and fought if he fell in battle, was memorialized in the song "Adelita," still sung today by Mexican-Americans and their Anglo brothers as well. Although the theme is understandably the love of a man for a woman, the war and its uncertainties enter the picture also:

Adelita se llama la ingrata,	Adelita's the name of the ingrate
La qu'era dueña de todo mi placer.	Who was mistress of all my pleasure.
Nunca piensas que llegue a olvidarla	Never think I could come to forget her,
Ni cambiarla por otra mujer.	Nor change her for another woman.

Si Adelita quisiera ser me esposa,	If Adelita wanted to be my wife,
Si Adelita fuera mi mujer,	If Adelita were my woman,
Le compraría un vestido de seda	I'd buy her a dress of silk,
Y llevaría a pasear el cuartel.	And take her walking in the barracks.

Ya me llama el clarín de campaña,	Now the trumpet calls me to battle,
Como soldado valiente a pelear,	To fight like a valiant soldier,

Correrá por las calles la sangre, *Pero olvidarte jamás me verán.*	In the streets the blood will run, But I'll never be seen forgetting you.
Si acaso yo muero en campaña *Y mi cadáver en la tierra va a quedar,* *Adelita, por Dios te lo ruego* *Que por mi muerte tú vayas a llorar.*	If perhaps I should die in the battle, And my body be left on the field, Adelita, for God's sake I pray you For my death to weep.

But since life is short and women are fickle, the soldier promises

Si Adelita se fuere con otro, *La seguiría la huella sin cesar,* *En areoplanos y buques de guerra,* *Y por tierra hast' un tren militar.*	If Adelita were to run off with another, I'll follow her track unceasingly— In airplanes and ships of war, And on land even with a military train.[16]

Songs for Special Occasions

As Américo Paredes points out, life in the Southwest includes far more than war and cultural rivalry: the many festivals and activities of life are celebrated with songs for special occasions.[17] Among these is the song "Las Mañanitas," sung for birthdays and other special "family" days. A common use of the song is to wake people up—sweetly, of course—on *Día de las Madres* (Mothers' Day) and the like with a *gallo* (literally, rooster, but suggesting the function the rooster fulfills in crowing at dawn). On such a morning, a group of young men will gather beneath the window of the mother of one of the group; they will sing the song, and then go on to the home of another and repeat the action. One version of the song is "Las Mañanitas de San Juan," sung in the 1920s by vaqueros as they saddled their horses on misty mornings on the ranches of south Texas:

Qué bonitas mañanitas, *como que quiera llover;* *parecen las mañanitas* *en qué te empece a querer.*	What beautiful mornings, as if it might rain; they are just like mornings when I began to love you.
Despierta, mi bien, despierta, *mira que ya amaneció;* *ya los pajaritos cantan,* *la luna ya se metió.*	Awake, my beloved, awake, see, it is already dawn; the birds are already singing, the moon has already gone down.[18]

A popular version around El Paso, serving both as gallo and the Mexican equivalent of "Happy Birthday to You," employs the word "mañanitas" as a name for the song rather than translating it as "little mornings"; it goes

Estas son las mañanitas,	These are the morning songs
que cantaba el Rey David	which King David used to sing
a las muchachas bonitas;	to all the pretty girls;
se la cantamos aquí.	we sing them here to you.[19]

And a New Mexico variant seems to be a sort of greeting, and does not use the term "mañanitas," but has the standard refrain except for using *mi amor* (my love) instead of *mi bien:*

En el marco de esta puerta	On the threshold of this door
el pie derecho pondré,	I will place my right foot,
y a los señores caseros	and to the hosts
los buenos días les daré.	I bid them good morning.[20]

At Christmastime, when the travels of the Holy Family from house to house looking for shelter are reenacted in a traditional event called *las posadas* (the inn, or the lodging), a little song is sung by the travelers and answered by the people who won't let them in:

Muy buenas noches, aldeanos dichosos,
posada les piden estos dos esposos.
A very good evening, fortunate villagers,
this husband and wife ask you for lodging.

Response: *Seran bandoleros o querrán robar.*
You may be highwaymen, wishing to rob us.

Robarte pretendo pero el corazón,
por eso en tu choza pedí un rincón.
I do want to steal, but only your hearts,
that is why I have asked for a corner of your hut.

Response: *Vayan mas delante, está una pastoría*
Que allí dan posada de noche y de día.
Go farther down the road, there's a place where shepherds stay;
there they give lodging by night and by day.

Then at some point, by prearrangement, the hosts of a house will sing a welcome:

Vengan, vengan, vengan, Jesús y María
y su amado esposo en su compañia.
Abran esas puertas, rómpanse esos velos,
que viene a posar el Rey de los Cielos.
Come, come, come Jesus and Mary
and her beloved husband in their company.
Let those doors be opened, let those veils be rent;
the King of Heaven comes to take lodging here.[21]

The Christmas season, extending from December 25 to January 6 (Epiphany or "Old Christmas"), has traditionally had another group of strolling singers —young boys who go from house to house singing carols. Invited inside, they are given food and drink and gifts *(aguinaldos)*. One song they sing asks for gifts —recalling the Mummers who similarly go "begging" in the British Isles and in Philadelphia:

Los Aguinaldos

De los aguinaldos si nos han de dar,
que la noche es corta y tenemos que andar.

Desde Puente Piedra venimos andando,
al Niño Chiquito venimos buscando.

¿Quién cortó el cogollo de la verde caña?
El Niño Chiquito, Príncipe de España.

¿Quién cortó el cogollo del verde limón?
El Niño Chiquito, rosita en botón.

De los aguinaldos si nos han de dar,
que las noche es corta y tenemos que andar.

Will you give us some New Year's gifts, for the night is short and we have far to go?
All the way from Puente Piedra we have come walking; we have come looking for the Little Christ Child.
Who cut off the top of the green sugarcane? The Little Christ Child, the Prince of Spain.
Who cut the tender shoots off the green lemon tree? The Little Christ Child, a rose in the bud.
Will you give us some New Year's gifts, for the night is short and we have far to go?[22]

And a lullaby—present in every culture—is part of Mexican-American life as well. It is sung unaccompanied, except for "the creaking of cradle or rocking chair." Best known throughout the Spanish-speaking world is "Señora Santa Ana":

¿Señora Santa Ana, porqué llora el niño?
Por una manzana que se ha perdido.

Iremos al huerto, contaremos dos,
una para el niño y otra para Dios.

Manzanita de oro, si yo te encontrara
se la diera al niño para que callara.

Santa Margarita, carita de luna,
méceme este niño que tengo en la cuna.

Duérmase me niño, duérmase mi sol,
duermase, pedazo de mi corazón.

And then comes a delightfully down-to-earth passage,

María lavaba, San José tendía
eran los pañales que el niño tenía.

Lady Saint Anne, why is my baby crying?
Because of an apple that he lost.

We will go to the orchard to pick two,
one for my baby and the other for God.

Little golden apple, if I could only find you,
I would give you to my baby, so he would hush.

Saint Margaret, little moon-face,
rock for me this baby that I have in the cradle.

Go to sleep my baby, go to sleep my sunshine,
go to sleep, little piece of my heart.

The Virgin Mary was washing, Saint Joseph was hanging out to dry,
these were the diapers that the baby had.[23]

Romantic and Comic Songs

Folk music and folk singers provide a great deal of enjoyment—as well as a great deal of variety—for life among the Mexican-Americans. Love songs, of course, are universal, and as the soap operas well prove, people are attracted by troubles and tragedies. The even tenor of life of those happily in love or happily married is not exciting. It is unrequited love, or love that misses its timing, that catches our attention. Of such is the popular account of Rosita Alvírez,

> the little flirt who died at the hands of Hipolito, whom she rudely insulted. If one can use the localization of a majority of the versions as evidence, Rosita lived and died in Saltillo, Coahuila, around 1900. . . . In this ballad, Rosita is at a dance, to which (it is important to note) she has gone against the wishes of her mother.

Hipolito asks her to dance, since she is the prettiest one there, but she rudely refuses him. He whips out a pistol and shoots her three times, after which she advises a friend to be polite and not to insult the men. Her mother, crying over her dying daughter, tells her, "I told you so!" The song is so popular that comic verses have attached themselves to it:

La casa era colorada y estaba recién pintada;
con la sangre de Rosita le dieron otra pasada.
La noche que la mataron Rosita andaba de suerte;
de tres tiros que le dieron, nomas uno era de muerte.

The house in which Rosita was killed had just been painted red;
so they gave it a second coat with Rosita's blood.
The night she was killed was Rosita's lucky night.
They shot her three times, but only one of the shots was fatal.[24]

Dances are popular social occasions among Mexican-Americans, despite the warnings given girls through the medium of obedience legends like "The Devil at the Dance" and songs like "Rosita Alvírez." In New Mexico dances are enlivened by singers who mount on chairs and sing songs about dancing couples, made up on the spot, like coplas; the songs follow the music being danced to, and they continue until the singer is bribed to stop.[25] Among the songs that might be sung and danced to is the lament to the *payo* (rustic):

Coplas del Payo

Estaba un payo sentado en las trancas de un corral
y el mayordomo le dijo: No estés triste Nicolás.

Si quieres que no esté triste lo que pida me has de dar;
y el mayordomo le dijo: Va pidiendo Nicolás.

Necesito treinta duros porque me quiero casar
y el mayordomo le dijo: Ni un real tengo Nicolás.

Necesito de mi Chata porque me quiero casar
y el mayordomo le dijo: Tiene dueño Nicolás.

El payo desesperado al barranco se iba echar,
y el mayordomo le dijo: De cabeza Nicolás.

A rustic was seated on the rail fence of a corral
and the overseer said, "Don't be gloomy, Nicolás."

"If you object to my sadness you must give what I ask."
And the overseer said, "Begin asking, Nicolás."

"I need thirty dollars because I want to get married."
And the overseer said, "I don't have a cent, Nicolás."

"I need [the love of] my Chata because I want to get married."
And the overseer said, "She already has a master, Nicolás."

The desperate rustic was about to jump off a cliff,
and the overseer said, "Go head first, Nicolás."[26]

Vaqueros on long cattle drives, says Frank Dobie, sang only love songs. Separated for months from their sweethearts—or any women, until they got to Dodge or Ellsworth or whatever trail end they came to—it was only natural for their songs to be sad, like "El Abandonado," of which the following verses are representative:

Me abandonastes, mujer, porque soy muy pobre
Y la desgracia es ser hombre apasionado.
Pues ¿qué he de hacer, si yo soy el abandonado?
Pues, qué he de hacer, será por el amor de Dios.

Tres vicios tengo, los tres tengo adoptados;
El ser borracho, jugador, y enamorado.
Pues ¿qué he de hacer, si soy el abandonado?
Pues, qué he de hacer, será por el amor de Dios.

Pero ando ingrato si con mi amor no quedo;
Tal vez otro hombre con su amor so habra jugado.
Pues ¿qué he de hacer si soy el abandonado?
Pues, qué he hacer, será por el amor de Dios.

You abandon me, woman, because I am very poor; the misfortune is to be a man of passionate devotion. Then, what am I to do if I am the abandoned one? Well, whatever I am to do will be by the will of God.

Three vices I have, the three I have adopted: drunkenness, gambling and love. Then what am I to do. . . .

But I go cast down if with my love I cannot remain. Perhaps another man has toyed with her love. Then what am I to do. . . .[27]

Anglos and Mexican-Americans alike respond to the tune of "El Rancho Grande," and although the Anglo pronunciation tends to be less than skilled, enthusiasm is undiminished when, around a campfire or in a church group, the song is raised. Presumably composed in Mexico around 1925, it became an immediate favorite on Texas ranches. Although a romantic element is present, so is the love of a good horse:

Allá en el rancho grande, *allá donde vivía* *había una rancherita* *que alegre me decía*	Down there at the big ranch, down there where I lived, there was a little ranch maid who gaily said to me,
Te voy hacer tus calzones *como los que usa el ranchero* *te los comienzo de lana* *y los acabo de cuero.*	"I'm going to make you some trousers like those worn by the rancher. I shall begin them with wool, and finish them with leather."
El gusto de los rancheros *es tener un buen caballo* *ensillarlo por la tarde* *y darle vuelta al potrero.*	The greatest joy of the ranchers is to have a good horse, to saddle him in the afternoon and take a turn around the ranch.[28]

A song that recalls the cumulative tales and folksongs of other cultures is "Dos Reales" (Two Bits, or Two Dollars), also known as "La Polla" (The Hen):

Por unos dos reales que tenga *compro una polla:* *y tengo mi polla*	If I have a couple of dollars I'm buying a hen: Then I have my hen

que pone su huevo,	Who lays her egg,
y siempre me queda	And I still have
mi mismo dinero.	The same money.
Con otros dos reales que tenga	If I have another couple of dollars
compro una vaca,	I'm buying a cow:
y tengo mi vaca	Then I have my cow
que tiene becerra,	Who has a calf,
y tengo mi polla	And I have my hen
que pone su huevo,	Who lays her egg,
y siempre me queda	And I still have
mi mismo dinero.	The same money.

The song goes on, with the purchase of a house, a butler, a garden, a mine, and a miner—and he still had the same money![29]

A child's counting song, "Los Diez Perritos," tells how "I" had ten puppies, and one by one something happened to them, a familiar situation. One was buried in the snow, one swallowed a biscuit, one was taken away by the King, and so on:

Y de uno que tenía	And the one I had left
me lo mató con una pedrada.	Was stoned to death.
No me queda mas que nada,	Then I had nothing,
nada, nada, nada, nada.	Nothing, nothing, nothing, nothing.
Y de nada que tenía	And of (the) nothing I had left
se lo lleva un embustero.	A liar took it away.
No me queda mas que cero,	Then I had only zero,
cero, cero, cero, cero.	Zero, zero, zero, zero.[30]

Another song involves what some would consider a waste of money, instead of the investing involved in the previous song. It is "El Crudo" (the hung-over one):

Al pie de un verde nopal yo me acosté,
al ruido de unas guitarras yo me dormí,
al grito de unos borrachos yo desperté,
¡que crudo estoy! Quiero curarme y no hay con que.

Pero ¡ay, Dios mio! quítame esta cruda,
porque esta cruda me va a matar.
La Virgen de Guadalupe me ha de salvar,
¡qué crudo estoy!
la cantinera no quiere fiar.

I lay down at the foot of a green cactus;
I fell asleep to the sound of some guitars;
I woke to the yelling of some drunks.
What a hangover! I'd like to cure it, but I lack the wherewithal.

But, oh my Lord! Take this hangover away,
for this hangover is going to kill me.
The Virgin of Guadalupe must save me.
What a hangover! The barmaid won't give me credit.[31]

*The **Pocho** Appears*

The sorrows of alcoholic indulgence are not the only ones that shape Mexican-American folksongs. Contact with—and perhaps the corruption of—the Anglo has produced quite a few songs over the years. The *pocho* is a Mexican who has become *agringado*—too yankeefied—and often lives to regret deserting his own culture. He might sing of how wonderful home—Mexico—is, or he might brag on the opportunities of the United States, but he is an in-between person, not accepted by his own people because he has become something of a traitor, and still a "greasy Mexican" to the Anglos he tries to imitate and gain acceptance from, even if he has served in the American Army during wartime.[32] Little wonder, then that he should sing of his adopted land yet long for home, as in the following:

Bonita Esta Tierra

Bonita esta tierra, no puedo negar,
el oro y la plata se miran brillar
el oro y la plata se miran brillar,
bonita esta tierra, no puedo negar.

Bonitas muchachas que bajan al real,
a gastar dinero de este mineral,
a gastar dinero de este mineral,
bonitas muchachas que bajan al real.

Yo dejé mis padres por irme a pasear,
por ir a Toluca y a la Capital,
por ir a Toluca y a la Capital,
yo dejé mis padres por irme a pasear.

Yo deje a mi patria por irme a pelear,
por cruzar las olas, por cruzar la mar,
por cruzar las olas, por cruzar la mar,
yo deje a mi patria por irme a pelear.

Qué amarga es la vida de un pobre cautivo
que está en una tumba y se encuentra vivo,
que está en una tumba y se encuentra vivo,
qué amarga es la vida de un pobre cautivo.

Quisiera de un vuelo cruzar esa sierra,
salir de esta cárcel y estar en me tierra,
salir de esta cárcel y estar en me tierra,
quisiera de un vuelo cruzar esa sierra.

Beautiful is this land, I cannot deny it;
gold and silver may be seen shining everywhere.

Beautiful are the girls who come to the camp
to spend the money from these mines.

I left my parents to go and travel,
to go to Toluca and to Mexico City.

I left my country to go and fight,
to cross the waves, to cross the sea.

How bitter is the life of a poor prisoner,
who is entombed and is yet [finds himself] alive.

I'd like to cross these mountains in one long flight,
to be out of this jail and to be in my land.[33]

But the plight of today's expatriate Mexican is only a new form of a situation with a long history. In much the same way, vaqueros on long trail drives sang laments and lovesongs because of homesickness—and their treatment at the hands of trail bosses and labor contractors. Witness "El Corrido de Kansas," where the vaquero's hard life was far from his hoped-for adventure:

Cuando salimos pá' Kansas	When we left for Kansas
Con una grande partida,	With a large party,
Nos decía el caporal:	The foreman said to us:
No cuento ni con me vida.	"I don't count on even my own life."

[Mil]quinientos novillos eran *Pero todos muy livianos,* *No los podiamos reparar* *Siendo treinta mexicanos.*	There were fifteen-hundred steers And they were all very wild, We could not keep them herded Being only thirty Mexicans.
Cuando llegamos a Kansas *Un torito se pelo,* *Fue a tajarle un mozo joven* *Y el caballo se voltéo.*	When we arrived in Kansas A young steer took off, A young boy went to cut him off And his horse fell down.

When the group returned to Texas (after a gap in the singer's memory),

La madre de un adventurero *Le preguntó al caporal:* *Oiga, deme razón de mi hijo* *Que no lo he visto llegar.*	The mother of a driver Asks the foreman: "Listen, give me news of my son, As I have not seen him arrive."
Señora, le voy a decir *Pero no se vaya a llorar,* *A su hijo lo mato un novillo* *En la puerta de un corral.*	"Lady, I will tell you But don't go and cry, A steer killed your son On the gate of a corral."[34]

Other encounters with Yankees appear in song, as in "El Contrabando del Paso," in which smugglers are apprehended and taken to jail from El Paso to Kansas—a state well-known from cattle driving days, but also the location of a federal penitentiary at Leavenworth. In a manner suggesting the advice to friends given in a prisoner's "last goodnight" on the gallows, the song tells the hearers that the money from smuggling is good, "But what I don't like is that they take me prisoner." The singer then urges his friends not to listen to tempters and to stay away from *el charco seco* (the dry marsh) where smuggling takes place, because there, it's every man for himself, and friendships and promises are forgotten.[35]

The tradition—much resembling the broadside tradition of the Middle Ages—of reporting the news, especially that of violence and crime, lives on in Spanish-speaking cultures. The corrido form, which Brownie McNeil describes as "a running account of a story the singer has to tell," straightforward and non-emotional,[36] was recently used to tell the story of eighteen "wetbacks" who were trapped in a Santa Fe Railroad boxcar near Sierra Blanca, Texas, in the summer of 1987. In early September, a student handed me a broadside entitled "Corrido a Sierra Blanca," which she assumed has music to it, since she knew such corridos are sung. Authorship is claimed by Felipe Martinez Sandoval, who recounts how a *coyote* (slang term for an agent for illegals, but also one that suggests the trickster in many Mexican tales) took the money of the illegals:

A cada indocumentado *cobra dólares cuatrocientos* *que con trabajo han juntado* *con algunos sufrimientos.*	To each undocumented one It cost four hundred dollars, Which they had gathered together With some suffering.
Los dieciocho [sic] *aspirantes* *los encerraron por fuera,* *al rato no era como antes* *no lo pensaron siquiera.*	The eighteen hopeful ones Were closed up from the outside; In a while, everything changed; They didn't think what would follow.
. . . .	
Cuando abrieron el vagón *ya muertos los encontraron* *pobres en esta ocasión* *ni a sus destinos llegaron.*	When they opened the boxcar They found them already dead, Poor ones on this occasion Didn't even reach their destination.
. . . .	
A sus casa los llevaron *pero ya no fue en vagón* *por que en un avión llegaron.* *Los recuerdo en la ocasión.*	To their homes they were taken But not in boxcars this time, Because they arrived in an airplane. I pay tribute to them on this occasion.[37]

Only one of the men survived the ordeal, and one irony of the event is that apparently it was not an Anglo but a fellow Mexican, the "coyote," who sealed the men in the boxcar, to prevent their being caught by immigration officials. But the bad feeling that ensued—blame upon the railroad, the immigration officials, and the whole world of Yankeedom—affected Mexican-Americans adversely, since men from their culture and old homeland were dead because of their aspirations. Whether the song will enter the folk imagination and be transmitted orally down the years is an open question, but it is clear that folk processes and traditions are still alive and well along the border, and Mexican-Americans can be assumed to be part of that continuation.[38]

CHAPTER EIGHT

Beliefs and Superstitions

THE TWO WORDS "belief" and "superstition" mean approximately the same thing—faith in something that cannot be proven in a scientific laboratory, something incapable of being confirmed logically. Yet the first term is a moderate one, often associated with religious faith, while the second carries the sense of "what some other fool believes." Folklorists going out to collect beliefs have learned that the term "superstition" has a negative connotation, while people on many cultural or educational levels admit to holding a variety of beliefs as natural consequences of faith.

People of all degrees of economic, social, or educational development believe fervently in cause-and-effect relationships that outsiders—uninvolved with the truth or falseness of the matter—would label as ignorant or even downright stupid. Yet there are many beliefs arising out of observation that, while they may not be easily confirmed by hard-nosed scientists, are nonetheless more often true than not. For example, consider the old belief, held true worldwide, that a red sky in the morning predicts stormy conditions, while a reddish sunset foretells calm: "Red sky at morning, sailors take warning; red sky at night, sailors delight." Weathermen may discourse learnedly about particulate matter in the atmosphere that causes this or that—but the bottom line is, simply, that centuries of observation have told people, "This is true," and that's all there is to it! Similarly, folk remedies have found their place in cultural beliefs and practices simply because they work—or because they appear to work, which is perhaps as comforting as any other remedy might be. My mother, who grew up on a Mississippi farm, acquired many cures for the ailments that affect us all. Whenever she called the doctor to report that one of us children was sick, the doctor would ask her, "Well, Bertha, what have you already given him?" He knew that she always tried all the resources that she had learned from her mother and grandmother before she called him. And, like a dutiful son, I always try a mustard plaster for a chest cold, or a piece of bacon fat to draw out a splinter or thorn, and on and on. Foolish beliefs? Success says otherwise—loudly! And such is the case with beliefs in the Mexican-American culture. Faith, observation, folk wisdom—these are the launching platform for much that is easily tossed aside as "mere" folklore, believed by what some regard as ignorant peasants.

Assuredly, many beliefs do deserve the negative term superstition. Why should putting sliced potatoes—or halves of a split bean—on the temples relieve a headache? And what good would it do to put boiled tomatoes in one's shoes to cure a cold? These remedies appear to be as nonsensical as burying a dirty dishrag at a crossroad at midnight under a full moon to get rid of a wart, as many Southerners are said to do. But the fact is, such beliefs exist, and are followed—or at least reported—as folk practices of many people.

Some beliefs, such as obedience legends, are certainly beyond verification. But those who believe in the reality of Satan, for example, would certainly believe that stories of the devil at the dance could, and perhaps even *did,* happen. And the circumstantial details in such legends—"This happened at the Red Mill Camp. . ." or "Once at the Black Cat Cafe in Juárez. . .," or "I didn't know this girl, but my grandmother did, and she told me that. . ."—make the belief as positively "true" as any fact capable of scientific proof. Not wanting to appear judgmental, or to cast doubt on anyone's favorite notion, I will resist the temptation to divide this chapter into the categories of beliefs and superstitions, realizing that such a division would appear to be loaded with bias.

Medical Beliefs and Remedies

Folk remedies in another culture often seem strange to outsiders, while they are part and parcel of the culture in which they flourish. Such is the case with folk medicine among Mexican-Americans. Joe Graham, who grew up in the Big Bend area, points out that despite the great strides in scientific medicine in this country, folk medicine is still a viable force in West Texas. A part of the reason is that Mexican-Americans there have until recently constituted a separate culture. Despite the physical closeness between Anglos and Mexican-Americans, cultural traits have been slow to merge, and Anglo remedies and their scientific medicine are no more likely to blend with Mexican cures than any other aspect of culture. In the whole border region between El Paso and Del Rio—a stretch of over 400 miles—there is not a single licensed Mexican-American doctor, despite the fact that over half the population is Spanish-speaking. Of course, the Aztec ancestors of the Mexican heritage had a working medical system when the Spaniards came to the New World, a system which continued to be practiced in the Spanish Southwest even after the Anglos came.[1] In a way, scientific Anglo medicine doesn't work with Mexican-Americans because the ailments are often different in the two cultures, in urban and rural areas alike. Cures in this area of illness are usually carried out by a folk healer—a *curandero*—who has the *don* (the gift) of being able to heal, often after recourse to medical doctors has been fruitless.

A study in the *Journal of the American Medical Association* confirms this view. A group of seventy-five Mexican-American housewives in a housing project in Dallas were interviewed: ninety-seven percent of them knew about the five common folk ailments being studied, and eighty-five percent had appropriate folk cures for the illnesses: *mal ojo* (often translated as evil eye), *empacho* (surfeit), *susto* (magical fright), *caída de la mollera* (fallen fontanel), and *mal puesto* (hex, or sorcery). In an interesting sidelight to this study, one of the subjects who was herself a curandera called it quits early one day: her doctor had advised her to get more rest![2]

Mal ojo is perhaps more accurately translated as "sickness from looking," since the evil intent involved in "giving the evil eye" is not usually present. Looking admiringly at a child without touching him to take away any bad potential can send him into a listless condition. When our young blond son went shopping with us in Juárez some years ago, he was the object of many admiring glances and expressions—and the admirers would walk all the way across the street to touch him; they didn't want to give him the ojo! *Barriendo* (sweeping) the child with a whole egg begins one cure; then the egg is broken into a saucer and placed under the child's bed overnight. If the illness is indeed "ojo," an eye will have formed on the yellow of the egg. Then the envious one, or the one who looked too admiringly at the child, must pass three mouthfuls of water to the sick one. Another diagnosis involves heating a certain stone; the face of the one who gave the ojo will appear on the stone, and the above cure is carried out. Ojo can be fatal if not treated, according to many informants.[3]

Empacho can come about in a number of ways: eating too much *asadero* cheese can bring it on, or too much raw food can stick to the stomach lining, causing loss of appetite, diarrhea, vomiting, and stomachache. Cures range from rubbing the stomach or back, or pulling up a fold of the skin on the back and then releasing it, three times, or until a telltale "pop" reveals that the food has been dislodged. Then a tea of *estafiate* (larkspur) or *manzanilla* (chamomile) will serve as a purgative, or even a tea made from the ashes of the food that caused the illness.[4]

Fallen fontanel is seen in a sunken "soft spot" on the top of an infant's head. It is caused, according to some, by the child's having been dropped, or more commonly by its having the mother's breast or the nipple of the bottle pulled too abruptly out of its mouth. One remedy is to insert a finger into the child's mouth and push his soft palate up and back; another is to hold the baby over a pan of water with his hair barely touching it; a poultice of water and soap shavings applied to the soft spot is also believed to work—and all three can be tried in the same case.[5] A handbook prepared for social workers and teachers in rural Mexico asserts that the cause of *caida de la mollera* is simply dehydration, and supplies practical measures to be taken. It also warns against the upside-down-over-the-water treatment.[6]

Susto is the result of a traumatic experience, and is more likely to affect children than adults, but it may affect whole groups, such as an entire family who went into a form of shock after the drowning of one of the sons.[7] Susto is usually treated by barriendo—sweeping the patient, who lies on the back, sometimes with arms extended on the form of a cross. The object used in the sweeping may be a broom, an egg, or a bundle of herbs. In addition, the recitation of a *credo* (the Apostles' Creed) accompanies the sweeping.[8] One healer reported that she used to jump over her susto patients during the cure, rather than sweeping, but arthritis had forced her to alter her methods, and now she just sweeps.[9]

Since all these ailments can come about in the natural course of life, they are called *males naturales* (natural ills), and with the exception of mal de ojo, are not caused by other people. But *mal puesto,* which can be a very serious ailment, is imposed upon a person by someone having a willful intent to harm—i.e., deliberate hexing by a *brujo* or *bruja* (witch, male or female). Remedies for mal puesto often involve calling in a curandera to remove the spell. "Black" witches are sometimes called in, if no "white" ones—i.e., curanderas—are handy.[10]

A number of curanderos have become quite famous among Mexican-Americans through the years: Nino Fidencio, Teresita Urrea, and especially Don Pedrito Jaramillo. Fidencio cured the daughter of Mexican President Plutarco Elias Calles, in the process becoming quite famous, although he never left his native village. Quite a cult has arisen in his name with followers called Fidencistas, dressed in white shirts and wearing red handkerchiefs, going into trances and healing in his name.[11] Teresita, also called the Saint of Cabora (a ranch in northern Mexico) and the Mexican Joan of Arc, was expelled from Mexico at the age of nineteen by the dictator Porfirio Díaz, who feared her popularity with the masses.[12]

Don Pedro Jaramillo has truly become a folk saint over the decades since he received the don and devoted the rest of his life to healing others. As Ruth Dodson heard the story, he was working as a lowly sheepherder when an accident laid him low; he was unconscious many days. God then gave him the gift of healing, and "made it known to him that from that time forward he should devote himself to helping suffering humanity."[13]

He lived at Los Olmos (The Elms) Ranch near Falfurrias, Texas, and was widely renowned for his cures—and they were as simple as he was. Water was often a central part of his cures, bathed in or drunk seven days running at dawn, or used in some other down-to-earth fashion. Once a vaquero who had been hit in the eyes by a mesquite limb was told by Don Pedrito to work hard, chopping with an ax from dawn to dusk without rest—and without pay—for nine successive days. The man did as he was told, till Sunday came; he took the day off from work, and he became blind and stayed that way all his life.[14]

Although the Los Olmos Ranch was in a thinly settled part of Texas, Don Pedro reached out to others in a way undreamed of in a era when a house call is unknown. This curandero traveled hundreds of miles on occasions,

> . . . making stops at convenient places where the people flocked to him in great numbers, securing his prescriptions and giving him whatever they chose in money in return.
>
> While Don Pedro was away on these trips, which might include San

> Antonio and Laredo, provision was made at his home to take care of all who might come in his absence—both man and beast.[15]

Don Pedrito was so successful that people came from far away for his services, for which he never charged—to do so risked losing the don! But people repaid him with their prayers and with gifts—sometimes quite unusual ones. The following story is an excellent example of the stories that are handed down about this revered curandero:

The Marvelous Cure of a Shepherd

Mónico Hinguanza was a shepherd who had been sick for some time. He took various home remedies, but they did him no good, and instead of getting better he grew worse.

His friends told him of the cures that Don Pedrito had made, and they advised him to go to the curandero. But as Mónico lived sixty miles from Los Olmos, he thought it too difficult to make such a long trip.

Finally, when he found that he had to get help, he borrowed a horse and set out for Los Olmos Ranch and Don Pedrito. He reached there the second day at dark. It had rained and the creek was swollen; Don Pedrito's hut was near the bank.

When Mónico asked him for a remedy, Don Pedrito got up and took a piece of heavy canvas and a pillow. Telling the shepherd to come with him, he took him to the edge of the creek, where the water made an eddy. He threw the canvas into the eddy, which caught it and extended it in the turn of the water; then he tossed the pillow onto the canvas. The curandero then picked up Mónico and placed him on the canvas, which instead of sinking supported him. All night Mónico remained on this canvas bed, rocked by the movement into a pleasant sleep. In the morning Don Pedrito came and took him out of the water, sound and well.

Mónico was so thankful that he made Don Pedrito, who had never married and had no family, a present of one of his boys, to live with him and serve him in all that he might command.[16]

When Don Pedrito died, he left the ability to prescribe *(recetar)* to a few believers:

> On each of their altars, an essential piece of equipment for every curandero, is a picture of Don Pedrito. It is possible that they may not have an image of the Virgin there, but not to have a picture of Don Pedrito. . ."*¡Ay no!*" one says with pain in her voice, "*¡Es imposible!*" One curandera. . .in South Texas has a special altar for Don Pedrito. She prays first to him and then to the Virgin.[17]

Other curanderos have different gifts, and differences in what they use those gifts for. Doña Graciela, a well-known curandera of San Antonio,

> . . .does a tremendous business in helping people pass their driver's license tests. This she is able to do by quite simple means. When a timid soul comes to her with such a problem, she advises him to go on a certain day to take the test, saying, "Don't be afraid. I will be near to protect you." And so the person goes, filled with confidence. And Doña Graciela *was* near, protecting him. He obtained his license, didn't he? What better proof do you want, *compadre?*[18]

Some healers use the power of concentrated prayer, or the power of positive thinking. Many are knowledgeable about herbs and plants. One curandera is truly a switch-hitter: she gives enemas, hot baths, teas of *hoja de naranjo* (orange leaves) and *barba de chivato* (billy goat's beard), but also prescribes S.S.S., 666, and Hadacol![19]

Hierberos (herb healers) are common among Mexican-Americans. The markets in border towns invariably have a stall or two where there are offered for sale literally hundreds of tiny labeled bags of plastic containing whole or powdered leaves, buds, flowers, or stems of a vast assortment of plants. The hierbero provides diagnosis and directions for using the remedy for what is usually a tiny fee. He likely makes up in number of sales—or treatments—for the small prices he charges. And he is free with advice, too. Many of my folklore students have taken up considerable amounts of time from these people, who often state that they too have the don—and imply that they consequently have the obligation to help people. And large supermarkets also provide such little packages, often packaged and labeled by small-time commercial enterprises, but with no printed claims nor instructions—unless it is how to make tea. Some of the less exotic ingredients—manzanilla, estafiate, and the like—are even put up in boxes of twenty-five teabags!

Thus it is obvious that healing and knowledge of herbs are not just the province of a select few. Any neighborhood where Spanish is the standard language has a *tía* (aunt) or *abuela* (grandmother) who gathers and stores plants for nearly all the ills that flesh is heir to. And these healing elements are amazingly simple: *barbas de maiz* (cornsilks) boiled in water makes a tea that is good for the *riñones* (kidneys); the juice of the pita cactus, dripped into an aching ear, provides immediate relief. Or, for earache, a small cone of paper, stuck into the ear and then lighted, allowing the hot smoke to enter the ear, relieves pain also. These remedies may have little basis in chemical or even physical reactions—but I have heard them praised as true cures that really work —and in the face of such faith, why would one pay out good money to a doctor, and a gringo doctor at that?

A study of the healing herbs of northern New Mexico, done twenty years ago by an outstanding folklore student at UT El Paso, shows that the range of folk cures among Mexican-Americans is almost without limit, going alphabetically from appendicitis to whooping cough—twenty-seven categories, with from one to five remedies each:

> When a family in northern New Mexico has a sick patient, and known remedies have been tried without success, the next step is to call a *médico* (midwife, herb doctor). [The term *curandero* is not common there.] In the area where I was born, which is Mora, New Mexico, the only time people go to a doctor or a hospital is in case of severe accident. Since most of these people wait to contact a doctor until they are severely sick, most likely a high percentage die under the supervision of a doctor. Therefore, the rest have lost confidence in medical doctors.[20]

The situation is not much different down along the United States-Mexico border. My mother-in-law, an educated woman who taught school for over 30 years, has a mental drugstore that covers nearly every common illness, and she is far from unusual. My folklore students, in fact, have so overwhelmed me with Mexican folk medicine over the years that I'll do almost anything to get them off onto another subject for their collecting ventures!

The following brief sample should illustrate the wide range of folk cures and beliefs among the Mexican-Americans of the Southwest.

Trees and Plants

A succulent called aloe vera, cactus-like in appearance, is kept in most Mexican-American households for use in many medical situations—burns, skin irritations, insect bites, athlete's foot, to name only a few. It is even supposed to keep hair from graying and to prevent baldness. The juice, actually a gelatinous substance, is first aid particularly good for burns. And when our son had a horrible case of diaper rash that made his skin as red as a ripe tomato, an application of aloe vera cleared it up within an hour, as his grandmother had predicted.[21]

The *sauco* tree is also a multi-purpose cure-all and preventative: sleeping under the shade of a sauco is extra restful;[22] and having leaves or even branches of the tree under the mattress or even in the bed is beneficial;[23] leaves placed inside the hat keep the wearer cool, and prevent headache;[24] and fever can be reduced by having the patient sleep under a sauco tree.[25]

The Night and Its Evils

El sereno de la noche (night dew) is considered to be very bad—suggesting the "bad air" concept involved in the word "malaria." One informant said that there are bad spirits in the air at night that will make you sick. "You must always cover yourself good when you are outside at night."[26] And the "bad spirits" associated with night dew can enter the body through the clothes or other means.

> It is not wise to leave clothes hanging on the line,. . .or go around with your head and other parts of your body uncovered at night because these spirits will enter you and you will become ill. If a person becomes ill of this there is a drink made from barley and arnica that can be given. . . .[27]

The consequences of not protecting oneself from the dew can be quite serious, according to one informant: "A cousin of mine, not paying attention to her mother, went out into the night dew without covering herself. The air hit her with much force and one whole side of her face became paralyzed."[28]

And the moon, object of veneration and fear in many cultures, has its beliefs among Mexican-Americans. A pregnant woman who goes out during a full moon (or, in some accounts, during an eclipse of the moon) will have her baby born with the features of a wolf or with a harelip, unless she carries a bunch of keys around her waist, over the baby.[29] And if it rains at the start of a new moon, there will be "lots of rain the rest of the month."[30] In fact, the phases of the moon used to have much control over the weather—especially the phases during January, when the *cabañuelas* (weather-predicting period) governs the coming year. An old saying goes, *"Enero y febero loco, marzo otro poco, abril lluvioso hacen a mayo florido y hermoso"* (January and February crazy, March a little more so, rainy April brings a flowering and beautiful May). But the belief is that since the explosion of the atomic bomb, things are all messed up, and the rainy season comes later in the year.[31] Even control of ants is connected to the moon's phases:

> In the summertime when ants are flourishing and bothersome, wait until the time of the full moon to get rid of them. On three successive nights, at midnight, go to the ant bed (the ants will be asleep) then take a stone and pound on the entrance of the ant bed and say three times, "Ants pay the rent, pay the rent, pay the rent." After three days, because they have no money and are ashamed, the ants will move away.[32]

For Mexican-American girls, the predicting of the timing of menstruation is keyed to the moon's phases: If a girl had her period during a half-moon, then her next period would come at the next half-moon. Mothers in the old days did not prepare their daughters for the onset of *la vergüenza* (the shame, or, as with Anglos, the curse). It was customary after the period for a girl to make a *novena* (a nine-day ceremony, usually a ritual of prayers to the Virgin) asking that the period not come again.[33] Not so distantly related is the belief that a woman should not bathe for forty days after bearing a child, or her milk would dry up, and activity in general is traditionally forbidden for the same forty days. Even if a child is to be christened during that period of time, the mother is supposed to stay home.[34]

A Little Bit of Everything

The *flor de la lila* (flower of the vitex tree) is dried and crushed, then put into a little cloth sack. Dampened, it is applied to the site of a boil or a sprain, and is even good for a headache. The ground-up seeds are also useful for a poultice good for headache or toothache.[35]

If you discover an eyelash near your eye, get it and place it between your thumb and someone else's thumb. While you are holding the lash this way, make a wish and it will come true.[36]

If you are fearful, "Take all of your clothing off, then get into bed. Cover yourself with a bed sheet. Have someone sweep you with a broom. In this way, your fears will be swept away."[37]

For stomachache, potatoes [presumably mashed] are wrapped in a towel, sprinkled with vinegar and garlic, and wrapped tightly around the belly button of the patient.[38]

For varicose veins, the patient lies with feet elevated while a plaster of mint puree and wild columbine mixed with starch is massaged into the legs and allowed to set for an hour.[39]

Another headache cure uses a tea made of dried chamiso flowers, and a towel soaked in it is wrapped around the patient's head.[40]

And a cough is cured with equal proportions of whiskey, honey, and lemon juice, to make a cup. Drink it slightly warmed before going to sleep.[41]

Torrents of rain can be stopped by having three women with sharp knives cut crosses in the air in the direction of the rainclouds. This action cuts crosses in the clouds and lets the sun shine through.[42]

Salt—one of the most potent items in the world of folklore—is no stranger to Mexican-American lore. Spilling it requires one to throw some with the right hand over the left shoulder; and allowing the house to run out of salt causes bad luck to come to the family.[43]

Don't walk with one shoe off and one shoe on; if you do, your mother will die a slow and painful death![44]

El que come y canta, loco se levanta (He who eats and sings goes crazy). The informant's mother would always recite this when anyone sang at the table.[45]

And you never take an old broom to a new abode—the implication being that you take your troubles with you if you do.[46]

You should always keep a pail of water by the front door, to capture bad vibrations from visitors as they enter.[47]

Keeping something green in the house—preferably a plant—is a symbol of hope. Of course, if it is an aloe vera plant, it is doubly useful as a veritable medicine cabinet all in one—but if the plant was bought, not given, its curative powers are lost.[48]

If one gets his feet wet, he immediately wets his head as well, to prevent illness.[49] I have also observed this custom in the actions of my own wife and mother-in-law, who claim that otherwise, one gets little blisters on the roof of the mouth!

And then for a finale, there's the *niño de la tierra* (child of the earth), about which beliefs abound. It is a scorpion-like creature, with a face like a baby, hence its name. One story about its origin tells of a La Llorona-type situation in which a poor young girl becomes pregnant by a rich young man—who won't marry her because of her low state. She wanders out into the mountains and when the baby is born dead, she buries it. Later—back at the young man's ranch—a strange plant begins growing, and produces buds with the face of the child he had not wanted to claim. The collector wonders if the cherubs seen on baroque church facades in Mexico, looking like flowers with the faces of children, have given rise to this story.[50]

If beliefs, like salt in food, give flavor to a culture, one must agree that the Mexican-American culture is certainly flavorful!

CHAPTER NINE

Customs and Festivals

"CUSTOM: AN ORDINARY or usual manner of doing or acting; the habitual practice of a community or people; common usage." Thus the *Britannica World Language Dictionary* defines the word. To the folklorist, however, custom means much more. Jan Harold Brunvand says that

> a custom is a traditional practice—a mode of individual behavior or a habit of social life—that is transmitted by word of mouth or imitation, then ingrained by social pressure, common usage, and parental or other authority. When customs are associated with holidays they become calendar customs; and when such events are celebrated annually by a community, they become festivals.[1]

In its section "Manners and Customs," the *International Folklore Bibliography* goes even further, including rites of passage—associated with such important events in the life cycle as birth, coming of age, marriage, and death—as well as calendar customs.[2] A working definition might say simply that custom is what folk do "just because"—because they've "always" done something that way, or because they grew up among folks who did the same. Customs can be logical or illogical, based upon known or unknown causes, but they tend to help set a people—a folk group—apart. And the Mexican-Americans' culture, as has been seen, has a number of folk characteristics that help define them as a people. Their customs are likewise basic to their culture, setting them apart from others. Festivals, which are essentially customs that involve whole communities, are likewise distinctive features of the Mexican-American culture.

Courtship and Marriage

Courting and wedding customs are quite important in many Mexican-American families. Serenades of the young lady by the young man and his friends (he does the same for them) start things off, but nothing is official until a committee of friends calls upon the family of the girl and asks permission for the courtship to proceed. In former times, in fact, the couple was seldom seen together without chaperones, even as the wedding neared, but that is changing. One mother reported that her first daughter had to be accompanied on dates by a younger brother or sister, but association with the Anglo culture had changed the mother's attitude, and later she neither made the younger girls be chaperoned nor limited the number of dates they could have.[3] This change is reflected also in the attitude of another Mexican-American, who feels that life in American cities has caused people to forget many of their customs:

> It's a dog-eat-dog world, and one has to do it to someone else first before they do it to you. . . . The culture has changed because people are no longer concerned with the simplicity of life; they have to keep on trying to beat the Joneses.[4]

Where the "old ways" are still held in high regard, however, invitations to the wedding are delivered personally (never by telephone), and the whole family is included in the invitation, children and all. The groom is expected to pay for all the wedding expenses, but the bridesmaids and groomsmen pay for their own attire, plus other expenses associated with their part of the wedding activities.[5] Even so, there is considerable variation in the degree to which the customs have been followed over the years. In a study made by a student of three generations within her own family, the variation is borne out. The first couple married in 1925. There was a formal *petición de la mano* (asking for the hand), with the groom-to-be, his father, and two well-known men going to the parent and after having a few drinks, formally asking for permission for the daughter to marry; this came after a four-year engagement, although that was a bit longer than customary then. The groom gave the bride 300 pesos (a peso was about a dollar) to buy everything—dress, *lazo* (a rope of wax beads, looped about the couple as they kneel before the priest), headpiece, shoes —and she had enough money left over to buy some sheets and towels. Since they were Catholic, custom and the church demanded that they go separately to confession and to communion, and then to the wedding—a routine that took place over three days. The bride's mother helped "a little" with the wedding banquet, "but it wasn't much, just some beef and chicken." In the ceremony, the lazo was used (to tie the husband down, the informant joked), as was the *arras* (a little box of symbolic gold-colored coins) "so we wouldn't lack money, and rice, so we wouldn't be hungry.") The wedding rings were placed on the right hands of both parties. Because the wedding took place in Mexico, there was a civil ceremony, performed by a judge who came to the house after the church ceremony, and then the whole wedding party ate and drank and danced until seven or eight the next morning. That little bit of beef and chicken apparently went a long, long way![6]

A generation later, in 1952, after a courtship of three years, the petición de la mano involved the groom, his parents, and the groom's boss; awaiting them with drinks were the bride's brother, mother, and aunt. The groom paid for all the bride's finery, while the groomsmen paid for the dance hall, the music, and the drinks. The couple had to go for counseling, and a series of four *amonestaciones* (announcements of intention to marry) had to be published in the church bulletin. The civil ceremony took place a month before the church ceremony—but "nothing happened yet." At the wedding, the lazo, the arras, and the rice were all used, the lazo for unity, the arras for constant income, and the rice to signify lack of hunger. The rings were placed on the couple's right hands during the ceremony; later they were changed to the left hand by the bride and groom.[7]

The most current generation, marrying in 1975, went through simpler procedures—perhaps partly because the groom was Anglo, although Catholic. Instead of asking for the bride's hand (after a courtship of four and a half years), the couple invited their four parents out to dinner at a local restaurant and announced their plans. The groom attended church in a different parish, so permission had to be obtained to marry in his church. Four counseling sessions preceded the wedding, which had to be scheduled well in advance, but no announcements were required. The civil ceremony was dispensed with, although a civil license was acquired. The groom paid for the bride's dress, rings, and bouquet; the bride's family paid for the rest—mariachi singers at the reception, rental of reception and dance halls, and beverages and orchestra at the dance. The priest was "Anglo and military, so he didn't know about the arras and lazo"—so they were simply omitted. Rice was thrown, however.[8]

This streamlining of the customs involved suggests that change is indeed taking place in the rite of passage. One significant detail that remains is suggestive of the charivari found in so many cultures. In all three weddings, the bride and groom were kept busy, with people all around them for many hours, so they could have no privacy—so "nothing happened" until much later. Current custom along the border includes parades of cars, decorated with crepe paper streamers and flowers, going about the streets much of the morning of the wedding day, which is often Saturday. Then, after the church ceremony—noon or later—the newly married couple and their attendants go to a photographer's studio for pictures. Then the cars parade again until time for the reception and dance, by which time the guests are generally in a happy state from the beverages. The dancing does not begin until the couple arrives, and after a couple of ceremonial dances—the couple together, then the groom with his mother and the bride with her father and such—all comers are free to dance with the bride (and sometimes with the groom) for a couple of moments by paying for the privilege with money pinned to the garments of the newlyweds. Defenders of this last detail swear it is an old custom, while detractors say it is borrowed from this culture or that one, and is not a Mexican tradition at all. In any event, the couple gains a fair amount of money in the process.[9]

According to an age-old custom, religious statues in churches are often dressed with real garments—especially when the statues are life-sized. Recently, I was told of a wedding dress that was used to decorate the statue of the Virgin Mary in the Ysleta Mission—in fact, when the church burned in 1907 because a sacristan was trying to smoke out some bats in the building, the Virgin was wearing the dress of Concha Paz Fernández, daughter of one of the most devout families in the church.[10] And in another custom that departs markedly from what Anglo brides do, the Mexican-American bride who is a member of the confraternity *Hijas de María* (Daughters of Mary) will lay her bouquet at the feet of the Virgin's statue, rather than throwing it for someone to catch.[11]

The Mexican-American married woman by enduring custom adds "de" plus her maiden name after her husband's.[12] And it is also customary for all persons to add the mother's name onto the end—perhaps only by initial—thus lengthening the name and preserving the matriarchal part of the heritage as well. On both sides of the Rio Grande I have seen doctors' and lawyers' names carrying at least the initial of the mother's maiden name on office signs, although the spelled-out name is less often seen. A man born in Mexico but who has lived in the United States for over thirty years had this to say about the custom:

> I am Roberto García Beltrán, *a sus ordenes* (at your service)—García for my father, Beltrán for my mother, who would be hurt if I omitted her family name. Perhaps I may do so when she rests in peace, but again, I may not, for García is like Smith among the Yankees, whereas García Beltrán will not be confused with García Romero or García Melgaréjo.[13]

Birth

Another rite of passage, birth, has its distinctive customs among Mexican-Americans as well. The mother-to-be is more sheltered before the birth, and as noted earlier, is expected to stay at home for forty days afterwards. Christening is a big event, and godparents are chosen with great care, since they will be compadres with the natural parents for years to come. The godparents are the centers of attention (along with the newly christened child) at dinners given following the ceremony. Afterwards, the godparents are customarily included in birthdays and all other family activities.[14]

Coming of Age

Coming of age is a big event in many cultures: the bar mitzvah and bat mitzvah for Jewish families, confirmation or "joining the church" for Christians, and coming out or debutante parties for people in general. Among traditional Mexican-American families, the *quinceañera* (celebration of a girl's turning fifteen) is a continuing custom—and one that is being adopted by Anglo families along the border as well. Some years ago when my own daughter turned fifteen, our Mexican maid was shocked that we weren't celebrating—and insisted on bringing a gift and making a little dessert for the girl. I'm convinced, though, that she thought we were all *sinvergüenzas* (shameless ones), lacking any cultural decency at all!

A priest on the border, who encourages families to have a special mass said as a part of the quinceañera celebration, says that Aztecs believed "a woman did not become a human being until she was fifteen."[15] While some families spend almost as much on a quinceañera celebration as on a wedding,[16] it is not just something the wealthy can afford, and church leaders are encouraging families to celebrate more modestly, to emphasize "the true meaning of the quinceañera,"[17] which is to mark the entrance of a young woman not only into adulthood in a social sense, but into adulthood in the church. Planning takes months for a successful event: one girl (whose father, raised in West Virginia, had not grown up with the custom) found *the* dress pictured in *Seventeen,* and ordered it. Eight girlfriends and their escorts made up the girl's "court," while a congregation of about sixty friends and relatives gathered to watch. The girl, escorted by her parents, grandparents, and godparents, filed into La Purísima, the mission church in Socorro, Texas, for prayers that she would grow up virtuous; scriptures read by the godparents; a renewal of her baptismal vows by the girl; and picture-taking galore. After mass, the group went to a dinner, reception, and dance for 300—almost all the trappings of a wedding.[18]

Mourning Customs

That most disturbing rite of passage, death, has strict rules of behavior. Early in this century, formal or personal invitations to a funeral were given (seldom via newspaper announcement), and only men went to the cemetery; mirrors and photographs of the deceased were covered or turned to face the wall, and musical instruments were put out of sight. The women in the family went into deep mourning, never appearing in public except at church, for a full year. The customary strip of black crepe tied to the door was never untied, but simply weathered away.[19]

The Day of the Dead

One of the most interesting of Mexican-American customs—festivals, almost—is *El Día de los Muertos* (Day of the Dead). Along the border among

Texans of Mexican derivation, as well as other parts of the Spanish Southwest, tradition demands that on All Souls' and All Saints' Days, families shall gather in cemeteries to clean and adorn the graves of deceased loved ones. The custom, which has something of a counterpart in community graveyard-cleaning in Anglo areas, goes back to pre-Middle Ages practices established by the Catholic Church in Europe as well as pagan parallels among Druids and others. Families with Mexican roots make a day of the event, taking with them rakes and hoes and water buckets, along with picnic lunches. Prominent also are mounds of flowers in every color imaginable (although Aztec custom specified yellow for adults and white for children). Graves have their weeds cut; mounds are re-molded and sprinkled with water. Names on wooden crosses that have become faint from the Texas sun and wind are re-painted, grave borders (where they exist) are straightened up, and generally everything is made as pleasant to the eye as is humanly possible. Then decorative arrangements of the flowers are placed on the grave—covering the mound, if that is the nature of the grave, or in symmetrical clusters at the four corners of the burial plot. Then the family, seated around the grave, has a picnic meal—no disrespect intended, of course, for it is truly a family gathering, a visit with the members of the family who have "gone on ahead."[20]

A 1974 newspaper advertisement in El Paso, Texas, reveals evidence of an interesting merging of traditions:

All Souls Day
Saturday, November 2

> This year there will be 2 Masses for the dead at Mt. Carmel Cemetery: In Spanish (Saturday), the second English (Sunday). . . .[21]

This notice, in both English and Spanish, shows a modern accommodation to the demands of busy people, rather than strict observance of the age-old customs that made clear distinction between All Saints' Day, November 1, and All Souls' Day, November 2. This celebration of the mass on Sunday, November 3, 1974, was contrary to church practice: the *New Catholic Encyclopedia* says that All Souls' Day cannot be celebrated on a Sunday; if November 2 falls on a Sunday, then November 3 becomes All Souls' Day![22]

The custom of paying tribute to the dead is worldwide, and exists in many cultures—the Druids did it on October 31 each year,[23] Asians do it in connection with the Lunar New Year,[24] and of course Catholics have been doing it for centuries—at least since 373 in the Eastern Church and 731 in the Western Church.[25] Throughout the Middle Ages—especially in Spain—prayers were said for those souls believed to be in purgatory.[26] And, as with the idea of Halloween, there was the belief that

On November 1 and 2, All Saints' and All Souls' Days, devout family members converge on *camposantos* throughout the Spanish Southwest. Here participants bring flowers and tools to clean graves, as well as plastic jugs to carry water to the gravesites.

From babes in arms to grandparents, everybody goes to the *camposanto.*

> souls in purgatory could appear. . .as will-o'-the-wisps, witches, toads, etc., to persons who had wronged them during their life. . . . Many different folkloric and popular customs and practices, especially various forms of food offerings, were associated with All Souls' Day. Among religious traditions, the parish procession to the cemetery, visiting the graves of relatives and friends, and leaving flowers and lights on the graves have remained almost universal.[27]

In the Spanish Southwest, two of these customs—visits to the graves and the bringing of flowers—continue, coupled with a necessary practice in many communities, the cleaning of graves. In another area with Hispanic connections, Puerto Rico, according to one of my students, mourners place lights on graves, even using candles sometimes bought with alms begged for that purpose.[28]

European customs related to All Saints' and All Souls' Days have merged with the practice of the Indians who were here before the Spanish. Flowers, especially white ones for children and yellow for adults, were used by the Aztecs to decorate the graves of their loved ones. That practice continues today, although the color distinctions have been blurred, and plastic wreaths, wrought iron crosses, and paper flowers have joined natural flowers—generally brought from home, at least among the poor.

Half a century ago in Juárez, Chihuahua, as well as in small towns along the border in the United States, family or even neighborhood feasts were common, prepared for the souls of the loved ones who were "coming home" for a visit. Plenty of drink was provided, following the logic that travelers would be thirsty, and sweet foods especially were available for the souls of the children. After midnight the visiting souls were considered to have had their fill, and the living family members could then eat and drink. And it was believed that the "baby souls" had extracted all the sweetness from the delicacies provided for them.[29]

Although such feasts are no longer common, *pan de muertos* (literally, bread of the dead) is found in every bakery at this time. Large, round, flattish loaves of sweet bread—almost like cake—are eaten in memory of the dead. The loaves are topped with the shapes of bones and decorated with purple sugar. The bread is simply eaten as a delicacy only once a year. In other cultures similar bread is eaten—in Germany, *seelen brot* (soul bread), for instance—but there is a belief that eating a loaf (or, sometimes, even a piece) will get a soul out of purgatory.[30] Spun sugar skulls, often with children's names across the foreheads, are given as gifts to friends in Mexican-American communities. In Mexico City and elsewhere—especially in border cities and others with large Mexican populations—poems called *calaveras,* something like comic valentines, are sent to people, especially prominent public figures, poking fun at their foibles or their politics, but ending with the observation that all

Little children learn to take part in the custom by helping their parents. Here a new *corona* (wreath) is headed for the family plot, along with flowers brought from home.

Young boys, hoping to make a little money by helping families with their grave cleaning, fill jugs with water for sprinkling graves and flowers.

Flowers and crepe paper decorate this grave for the Day of the Dead. Resting after their labors, the family is waiting to have lunch at the grave site.

this doesn't matter anyway, since the person under discussion is a *calavera* (skull) and is already dead.[31]

Most colorful of the elements associated with Día de los Muertos is the custom of tending to the graves of loved ones. As noted above, there has been a blending of the two days, but one distinction lives on. All Saints' Day is also called *Día de los Angelitos* (Day of the Little Angels), and on that day the graves of children get special attention. In 1980, when November 1 fell on a Saturday, I was surprised on visiting a Juárez cemetery to note that there was little activity, and that generally only children's graves were being decorated. Everyone I asked told me that this was the children's day; All Souls' Day was for the rest of the people, and that the following day would see the graveyard crowded—and it was so.

After breakfast on the chosen day, and perhaps after a visit to the neighborhood church where a candle is lighted in memory of departed family members, people descend on the graveyards carrying flowers and hoes, rakes, and other tools for the cleaning up of the grave sites. Many graveyards where Mexican-Americans are buried do not have the luxury of perpetual care; similarly, many small town and rural Anglo cemeteries do not, and have regularly scheduled dates, usually Saturdays, when the people turn out to cut weeds, mow the grass, etc.[32] But the special days for Mexican-Americans are far more than just grave-cleaning. In Juárez, where our family goes each year to fulfill our duties to the dead, the custom is seen in a fuller state. It is truly a holiday time: people

Día de los Muertos finds this grave, adorned with the Sacred Heart of Jesus statue, decorated with natural flowers. The grave to the rear has plastic flowers in its urns.

By the end of the two-day tribute to the departed, flowers will fill every vase and adorn every grave stone or mound.

The Day of the Dead (November 2) finds crowds in Mexican and Mexican-American cemeteries, cleaning and decorating family graves and enjoying a picnic-like atmosphere, with taco and sugar cane vendors serving the participants.

bring lunches, paint to decorate crosses and headstones, and new plastic or metal crosses or *coronas* (wreaths), and urchins scurry about carrying plastic jugs of water for the families to sprinkle the graves and water the flowers they have brought, often from their own yards, although flower-sellers do a big business too. Outside the gates of the *camposanto* (holy ground, cemetery), taco vendors and sellers of sugar cane and soft drinks are also present. Inside, after the graves are scraped and re-mounded, weeds pulled and flowers arranged—often in patterns that are quite artistic—the families settle down for a picnic at the family grave site, with no sense of impropriety, even sitting on grave slabs—while at an adjoining grave, a family may be kneeling in prayer.[33] Although this description fits Juárez, in Mexico, many small border towns have essentially the same level and kind of activity going on, even today. In former times along the lower Rio Grande, anniversaries of deaths were celebrated, with personal invitations to friends to come to memorial masses and a feast afterwards, in addition to the grave decoration on All Souls' Day.[34] Graves along the Rio Grande continue to be decorated with shells, especially scallop or conch; the use of shells was also a common custom among non-Mexicans up to the first half of the twentieth century.[35]

Christmas Festivals

The Christmas season traditionally begins on December 12, the feast day of the Virgin of Guadalupe, and does not end until January 6, *El Día de los Reyes Magos* (Day of the Kings or Magi).

As was described in Chapter Six, celebrations in honor of the Virgin of Guadalupe are customary throughout Spanish America. As the "Brown Virgin," she represents an ethnic model for Hispanics; in Mexico, for instance, her banner has led many groups in revolts against entrenched authority, much as Joan of Arc would serve to unite downtrodden Frenchmen. Among the most colorful—and most enduring—of the Christmas customs are the drama-like *posadas,* a series of night journeys when the Holy Family goes from house to house seeking shelter, being turned down repeatedly until finally (by pre-arrangement) one family opens its doors, as described in the chapter on folksongs and ballads.

In New Mexico, *Las Posadas* is reported as taking place on Christmas Eve only, and as a prelude to the performance of *Los Pastores,* the standard Christ mas play, while in Mexico (as along the Texas-Mexico border) it is a novena—a nine-consecutive-night affair, usually ending on Christmas Eve.[36] Some years ago a group of players from UT El Paso (of which I was one) performed annually the Second Shepherd's Play of the Wakefield cycle, beginning in the San Elizario recreation hall, leading the audience—who became temporary shepherds—on a sort of posada-like journey that ended up in the church, beside the altar, where Mary and Joseph and a real live Babe awaited us. One of the shepherds of the play, José Álvarez, following the Wakefield script, gave the Baby Jesus a tennis ball, telling him to "go and play tennis!" While this was not, as performed, a folk activity, it was accepted by the parishioners as true to the spirit of the posada and the whole tradition they were familiar with.[37]

In corroboration of the folk quality of the reenactment, along the Animas River in northern New Mexico, several decades ago, the posadas took place for two weeks before Christmas, according to Honora DeBusk Smith. The pilgrims were guided by three bonfires called *iluminarias* before each house on their route "to Bethlehem." Their song, somewhat different from the Texas version but expressing the same pattern of request and denial, asked,

¿Quién les da posadas	Who will give shelter
a estos peregrinos	to these pilgrims,
Que vienen cansados	who come, tired
de andar los caminos?	from traveling the roads?

And the answer, repeatedly, is *"No será posadas"* (There is ["will be," actually] no shelter.) When an affirmative answer is finally given, the journey ends inside the church.[38] Musicologist Don Robb provides music and words for two verses of a pair of posada songs from New Mexico:

En el nombre del cielo	In the name of Heaven
os pido posada	we ask shelter of thee,
pues no puede andar	because [she] cannot travel,
mi esposa amada.	my beloved wife.

Finally a favorable response to their plea is sung:

Entren santos peregrinos	Enter, holy travelers,
reciban este rincón	receive this corner;
que aunque es pobre la morada	although the chapel is poor,
os la doy de corazón.	I give thee from the heart.[39]

These "iluminarias" are commonly called *luminarias* these days, and are part of a custom common during Spanish colonial days and widely adopted in recent years by Southwestern Anglos. With the advent of paper sacks brought by the traders on the Santa Fe Trail in the 1820s, the custom of bonfires was often converted into using candles set in sand in the bottom of sacks, a variation which is the current form of the custom. People illuminate their homes, churches, driveways, and sidewalks with the sacks for several nights preceding Christmas.[40]

Frances Toor reported that in Mexico, after the pilgrims enter the home that is opened to them, a *piñata* is hung up for children to break, letting candies fall among them, and reports are that this part of the custom continues also in the United States.[41]

Along the border, Christmas gifts are influenced by the Anglos and their culture, but older, more traditional ways had children receiving their gifts on Epiphany (Old Christmas), the sixth of January, the traditional day when the Wise Men brought their gifts to the infant Jesus.[42] Some lucky children get the benefit of both customs—like the Jewish children in predominantly Christian communities (such as El Paso) who wheedle their parents into letting them have a "Hanukkah bush," in imitation of their Christian friends.[43] Mexican-American Christmas feasts feature a wide variety of special holiday dishes, which will be described in the chapter on folk foods, while discussion of the folk play *Los Pastores* will appear in the chapter on folk drama.

Farming and Irrigation Customs

What is probably correctly called a calendar custom, blessing the fields, has been a common practice in many cultures over the centuries, and one aspect of this activity was reported from South Texas by Rosalinda González:

> My mother told me of a quaint custom my grandfather used to observe

A pilgrimage honoring the local patron saint, San Elceario, winds its way around the plaza in San Elizario, Texas, about 1915. Photographs courtesy of Ann Enríquez.

in the cornfields. In the morning, alone or sometimes with my grandmother, he would take a picture of San Isidro to the fields and parade it through the rows of corn. Then he would hang it somewhere while he went about his work. . . . This was usually done when it was too dry and when the corn was in need of water. As he paraded the picture of San Isidro, he would recite a little prayer:

San Isidro, labrador,	San Isidro, farmer,
San Isidro, labrador,	San Isidro, farmer,
Quita el sol y pon el agua.	Take away the sun and bring the rain.

The grandfather's brother-in-law, whose fields were nearby, didn't bother with the custom, figuring that if San Isidro brought rain to one farm, he'd bring it to the whole area![44] In the El Paso valley of the Rio Grande, farmers still have the fields blessed in the spring, with a priest accompanying the statue of San Isidro as he is carried about the fields on May 15 or the Sunday nearest that date.[45] San Lorenzo, patron saint of farmers at Clint, Texas, is honored annually when people celebrate his day, August 10, with a pre-dawn pilgrimage from the town of San Elizario to the Church of San Lorenzo, a three-mile stint. On arrival at the church, the bells ring, Matachines dancers dance, and joy abounds.[46] On September 26 and 27, 1987, a similar fiesta was held in San Elizario, a small valley town named for a saint whose name the Anglos could neither spell nor pronounce —San Elceario. After mass on his feast day, September 17, or the Sunday nearest, the saint's image is carried in procession with priests and parishioners walking, charros in their glistening costumes riding, and farmers standing around firing their shotguns (as they do at special times during the mass), symbolizing their guarding of San Elceario. The procession winds about the town, circling the plaza (which is, incidentally, one of the last surviving examples of Spanish colonial town planning), and then food stalls ranged around the plaza selling boiled corn, gorditas, tacos, and other foods do a rushing business.[47]

Much of the Spanish Southwest, receiving well under ten inches of precipitation each year, relied heavily upon irrigation, as did the Indians before the coming of the Spaniards. Division of water, arrangements for necessary labor to maintain the *acequia madre* (main ditch) and the *sangrías* (lateral ditches, used to lead the water into the fields themselves), and even the governing of the system have come down from earliest times, through the Spanish and Mexican periods, and continue to be standard today—workable folk practices that linger because they have been thoroughly tested by time. Marc Simmons notes that Antonio de Espéjo, who traveled through New Mexico in 1583, wrote in his diary of the Indian cornfields and other crop plots irrigated with a system of dams and ditches.[48] Then the Spaniards improved upon the system, bringing

The fiesta honoring San Elceario continues in 1987, with the saint's banner and his statue being carried around the village plaza, guarded by mounted parishioners dressed in *charro* costume.

methods employed in Morocco and arid parts of Spain and Mexico. Studies also reveal that Canary Islanders had well-developed irrigation systems that were carried into Hispanic America.[49] The Spaniards had done the same thing in the Canaries, improving primitive irrigation systems beginning at least by 1487.[50]

The acequia madre is an especially vital channel, feeding all the lateral ditches, so every year it is cleaned out, in a tradition that has been passed down, father to son, for some 300 years. Each family that has water rights must send a representative to the annual cleaning chore or pay a fine. In Chimayó, New Mexico, a typical remote village, the duty is passed down within the family, each son as he's big enough to handle the job taking his turn at the shovel. A *mayordomo* (steward) is in charge, designating who is to work where. The silt that has accumulated in the ditch must be shoveled out; debris that finds its way into it must be removed; and weeds and grass that slow the flowing of the water must be pulled. All is piled on to the banks, raising them and helping to overcome the gradual wearing away caused by time. The annual ditch-cleaning custom of the Rio Grande Valley of New Mexico is described by one writer as "a kind of rite, renewing cultural and economic ties in many communities."[51]

The *alcalde* (which translates to "mayor," and finds its way into town and village governments) is in charge of distribution of the water, allocating irrigation times to this family or that, depending on the amount of irrigable land to be watered. His is a position of honor, and a man who does the job well keeps it for a lifetime, being elected each year by the water district members.[52] When Elephant Butte Dam was built on the Rio Grande in the 1920s, the existing system of water control was left in place.[53] All down the valley, annual meetings take place of water-users who have traditional and legal rights to irrigation water; they must consider the needs of the year, elect their officials, and assess themselves the fees necessary to carry on the work. The group meeting, with each member having a voice and a vote, closely resembles the traditional democracy of the New England town meeting and other institutions out of the past. In the El Paso Valley, where there are immense tracts of land held by one family, paid crews handle the main canals, but each landholder through whose territory the ditches and laterals pass must be a good neighbor, maintaining his own ditchbanks and seeing that they are watertight. Where I grew up, "down the valley" from El Paso, when there was a break in a ditch, word went out and the whole neighborhood turned out to repair the damage. It was truly a communal effort, since all depended upon each other. Abuse of the system—irrigating when it is someone else's time—is dealt with severely by the elected committee, and fines can be assessed or irrigating privileges can be withheld in serious cases. John Nichols's book *The Milagro Beanfield War* tells humorously if wryly what happens when a landholder loses his right to irrigate—in this case, through governmental shenanigans.[54]

Water rights should be inherent in the land, inseparable from it, but practice is different, with tradition losing out in the process. In San Antonio, Texas, for example, a woman in 1815 directed in her will that her right to one day's irrigation time be sold to pay for her funeral expenses.[55] Similarly, land developers who buy tracts of farm land with water rights have a salable commodity when they convert the land to lots for homes. The matter is like the separate sale or lease of mineral rights; of course the loss or sale of water rights carries with it the loss of responsibility for the conduct of affairs of the water district and a loss of voice in community matters as they relate to the irrigation tradition. I have overheard conversations among old-time Valley residents that suggested loss of prestige—respectability, almost—because of the sale or loss of water rights; it was considered an abdication of community responsibility![56]

Some Mexican-American customs are local in practice, or, in some cases, have died out over the years. In connection with research on irrigation I ran into a variation of the custom associated with the Día de San Juan, June 24. On that day, throughout Hispanic America, people get sprinkled with water. Students sprinkle their teachers and each other; since Saint John the Baptist baptized with water, his day must be remembered by symbolic—and fun-filled—actions. But in northern New Mexico the sangrías—the lateral ditches running out from the acequia madre—are used for bathing in honor of San Juan, in a sort of renewal of the power of the baptismal rite.[57]

A custom unlamented by most people for its passing is one that was once common in New Mexico, and elsewhere in Spanish culture throughout the world—the rooster pull. It would be natural for vaqueros to develop tests of skill executed on horseback; even today riders show off in rodeos and other public performances by snatching a handkerchief or sombrero from the ground as they ride past at a gallop. But the custom reported from the days of Mexican control of New Mexico is less mild—and a lot more bloody. A visitor from the United States back in the 1840s described a rooster pull he watched that was a part of the festivities for the Día de San Juan:

> A common cock or hen is tied by the feet to a swinging limb of a tree so as to be barely within reach of a man on horseback. Or sometimes the fowl is buried alive in a small pit in the ground, leaving only the head above the surface.
>
> In either case the racers, passing at full speed, grapple the head of the bird, which being well greased, generally slips out of their fingers. As soon as someone more dextrous than the rest has succeeded in tearing it loose, he puts spurs to his steed and endeavors to escape with the prize. [If he is caught] the poor chicken is torn into atoms. Should the holder of the trophy be able to outstrip his pursuers, he carries it to the crowd of spectators and presents it to his mistress, who takes it to the fandango as a testimony to the prowess of her lover.

The rooster pull, which goes back into Spanish history, was apparently associated with rainmaking ceremonies in pagan times. "It is no coincidence," says Marc Simmons, "that San Juan's day falls near the beginning of the summer rainy season, both in Spain and New Mexico." Simmons notes that the custom lingered in some villages, especially those of the Pueblos, and in some of them, gifts were thrown from rooftops after the rooster pull, and buckets of water were thrown on the crowd below, simulating rain and hopefully encouraging nature to be bountiful with her rainfall.[58]

The Charreada

Difficult to categorize is a custom or festival or sport called the *charreada*. A Mexican-style rodeo, it involves large numbers of participants as well as spectators of all ages, yet it is not quite a sport. It doubtless began, as the American rodeo did, from workers with cattle showing off their skills. But the American brand has developed into an organized commercial activity with national finals —a World Series of Rodeo. The Mexican variety is popular in much of the Southwest, and there are *charro* organizations and rules to follow, but the feel of the events is those of festival or custom.

Young boys learn to be charros by watching their elders, and by practicing roping and riding tricks; there are prescribed ways of developing those skills, and a boy has to be twelve or older before he can take part publicly. For instance, young Marte Tarriba Villar has been practicing under the watchful eye of his father for three and a half years, and it will be two more years before he can enter a fifteen-and-under *charreada juveníl*. His whole family is involved in the charreada, including his mother. The mental picture one gets of a Spanish lady, riding sidesaddle (of course), erect and proud, is that of the queen of the charreada. There are several events that resemble the parades or grand entry of the American rodeo, especially the parading of the queen, or in some charreadas, the *escaramuza*—a routine of interweaving horses in a fancy pattern by the charras (the lady riders) that suggests the performances of the Spanish Riding School. This event is rare these days, since not many women are training for it.[59]

The charreada takes place in an area shaped much like a frying pan, whose handle, a key-shaped alleyway—the *lienzo*—is used for a variety of feats of skill and strength, and the pan itself—the *plaza*—is used for other *suertes* (the word means "lucks," but "events" in this context). The first competition event, the *cala de caballo* (figuratively, test of the horse), takes place in the plaza: horse and rider, acting as one, come galloping up to the fence, full force, stopping just in time to avoid a smashup. The horse is brought to a stop in three stages, called *rayar* (to stripe, or go in a straight line), where the horse seems to crouch on its haunches, slide forward, and then crouch again. When the horse is at a com-

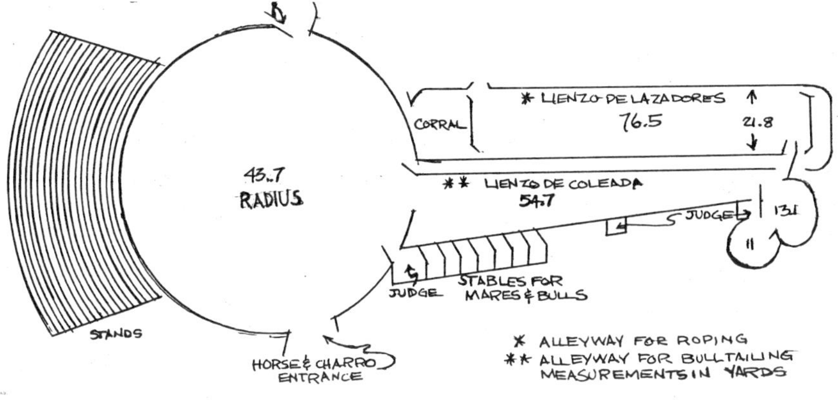

The arena for the Mexican rodeo, *la charreada,* is shaped like a frying pan. Tailing the bull begins in the "handle" to the right of the drawing; roping and fancy riding events take place in the "pan" portion. (Drawing courtesy of ***Sombras del Pasado,*** **Julia Kumor, sponsor.)**

plete stop, it must stand perfectly still and silent; then at a signal from the judges, the rider maneuvers the horse to right and left to a 90-degree angle with the horse's hind legs in a fixed place. Then at another signal, the horse makes a 360-degree turn—hind legs still in the same spot. Next the charro dismounts and remounts, without movement from the horse, and then backs the horse out of the arena in a straight line for at least sixty yards. The slightest wavering, noise, or hesitation on the horse's part results in penalty points. And if the rider loses a stirrup or a sombrero, or even touches his horse's mane, more penalty points may result. If the performance is bad enough, both horse and rider are barred from all other events for that day.[60] In a recent charreada, a horse reared too high in the cala, and the rider fell off—and the crowd gave him a big hand, whether in sympathy or in derision I didn't think I should ask. But he competed later in other suertes, so I guess he wasn't shamed by the fall.

The most popular event, the *coleadero* (the tailing), takes place in the lienzo. Steers or bulls are "tailed" there, in a dust-producing and lively event in which the steer is not left much dignity. As in other part of the charreada, style and ritual are of ultimate importance: as a wild steer is released from a pen at one end of the alleyway, a charro rides alongside, salutes the judges, slaps the steer on the rump three times, and slides his hand along the steer's back until he can grab the tail—and then the fun begins. Once he has hold of the tail, he must wrap it around his boot and then speed up his horse so that the horse is going faster than the steer. This forward motion and speed flip the steer off balance—and the harder he falls, the better the score:

1

2

3

4

5

La coleadera (tailing the bull) is an event of the *charreada* that is hard on the bull's dignity—and his torso. In this sequence, the rider has saluted the judges and slapped the bull on the back before he grabs the bull's tail and wraps it around his boot (scene 1). Speeding up his horse, he pulls the bull off-balance (scene 2) and jerks him over (scene 3). Finally the animal lies flat on his back (scene 4), in a complete triumph for the horse and rider team. The team in scene 5 is not so lucky—and the bull escapes with his dignity unbruised.

> In the coleadero, if the bull lands on its stomach, you would get six points. If the bull does a complete somersault, you could get twelve points. You are allowed 60 meters (65.6 yards) to throw the bull. If you throw it within 30 meters (32.8 yards), you will score higher than if it takes you the entire 60 meters.[61]

At a recent Juárez charreada, celebrating the annual *día del charro* (September 14), I was laughing at the announcer's saying that some rider got no score minus two or more points. I thought he was being cute—but the rider had evidently not only failed to tail his bull, but had failed to do one or more of the required preliminaries before he went after the bull. In another attempt, the announcer said, *"Se agarró por las uñas"* (he grabbed it with his fingernails) when the rider made a clear miss! So announcers do have a sense of humor. There are traditional expressions and signals in the charreada, like *"lienzo no libre"* (the alleyway isn't free) when there's a bull down or running loose, or *"fuera de la competencia"* (out of the contest) when a rider is so far out of the running as to be ruled out to prevent slowing down the proceedings; and the animal is always called a *toro* (bull), even when he's a *novillo* (steer).

The *piales* event is a major roping event, in which a charro is given three tries to rope the "heels" of a running wild mare—but it must be done with style. It is easier on the mare, but it is much more difficult than roping the neck. If the charro does the piales to the satisfaction of the judges, the mariachi band is ordered to play in his honor.[62] Another roping event, the *mangañas* (lassoing), involves a charro standing on the ground while roping the front feet of a running mare after having cast a fancy loop with his rope in the air—and then jumping through it—just for show. But the most dangerous event is the *paso de muerte* (pass of death):

> This is the show-stopper at the charreada. Three mounted charros drive a wild mare and the competitor, mounted bareback, around the ring. The competing charro is required to leap from his horse to the bare back of the wild horse racing beside him. The only thing the charro has to grab ahold of is the horse's mane.[63]

While there are rules galore—concerning dress for charro and charra, kinds of saddles and ornaments for the horses, and so on, the charreada—the whole tradition in fact—is amateur. Although professional charros may be hired to perform at public events, they may not compete. Among their feats are facing a bull with only a sombrero for a weapon, or placing two apples or oranges on the horns of a bull as he charges by.[64] But the amateur charro is deeply rooted in Mexican tradition, and the spread of the custom or sport throughout the American Southwest, while it does not rival the American rodeo or baseball or football, attracts a lot of loyalty. One New Mexico wife told of the devotion to

Fancy roping, a vital part of the *charreada,* is an outgrowth of the daily work with cattle that the contestants—all amateurs—are involved in. This fancy loop is a necessary prelude to the roper's lassoing a galloping mare.

the charreada displayed by her husband and his friends:

> . . . She recalled a time not so long ago when the determined horsemen would go out to a gravel county road and practice by the illumination from the headlights of the trucks and autos roaring past on Interstate 10. [Her husband, after having] put in a full day at the quarry, practiced his horsemanship skills late into the night and drove the 20 miles home. Sometimes dawn would find the driven cowmen still on horseback, trying to hone skills from another era, another world.[65]

Such devotion—and all for the honor and glory of it! Charros do not win prizes other than ribbons or titles, and the proceeds from charreadas go to benefit others. The charro association of Santa Fe, New Mexico, for example, gives a $4,000 college scholarship each year to an applicant from a middle-income family because they are the ones who seem to have the most difficult time finding money to send their children to college.[66]

Other Customs

On December 28, which besides being the Day of the Holy Innocents is the Mexican April Fool's Day, South Texas ranchers used to play tricks on each other, reciting an appropriate verse to the one who was tricked:

Inocente palomita,	Innocent little dove,
Que te dejáste engañar	That let yourself be fooled
Sabiendo que en este día	Knowing that on this day
Nada se debe prestar.	Nothing should be lent.

This verse, written out, was also sent with a silly toy to someone who had requested a loan.[67]

Another custom reported by an early Anglo resident of New Mexico was a formal, printed invitation to attend the hanging of a murderer—an opportunity he declined. A more usual custom that he reported involved a former sheepherder who took off his sombrero when talking with his former *patrón* (boss, or village father figure) as a mark of great respect.[68] In the Mexican-American culture such indications of respect for age or authority are standard; I have often heard of men of importance—a Mexican general during the revolution, for one—who would discard a cigarette and snap to attention when the man's father came into the room. When my mother was an elementary teacher on El Paso's Southside, she said a child who was punished at school for some infraction of the rules caught a real storm at home when the report reached there, since authority was to be respected and obeyed at school as well as at home.[69]

Sometimes customs just seem to happen—like the matter of giving *pilón* (a little something extra). When one pays a bill, say for groceries, it is customary for the merchant to give the customer a little pilón, usually candy for the children, trinkets for the older ones, tobacco for the father, or something decorative for the mother—just a good-will gesture. There's no written law that says pilón is required, but folk custom often involves a quiet boycott of the merchant who fails to do the expected—and he may lose so many good customers that he must change his ways or go out of business![70]

Customs shape a people, indicate the matters they hold to be of value, and give a distinctive quality to their way of life. From the cradle to the grave—and even beyond—the customs of Mexican-Americans provide a cohesiveness of great importance.

CHAPTER TEN

Folk Drama and Dance

FOLK DRAMA IN the Mexican-American tradition goes all the way back to Spain, built upon the traditional battles with the Moors, the battles for Christianity, and the medieval plays based upon Bible stories—especially Nativity scenes—and folk beliefs. It is commonly believed that Saint Francis of Assisi started the whole Nativity drama tradition with a series of scenes in an Italian grotto in 1223. Spanish-based Franciscan friars coming to New Spain used dramatic performances to evangelize the natives—but it was the Jesuits, according to one researcher, who really brought the *pastorela* (the custom of presenting the shepherd's drama) across the ocean. They developed it and encouraged its spread, from their entry into the New World in 1572 until their expulsion in 1767 by Carlos III of Spain.[1] Since both orders accompanied colonists throughout the Spanish settling of the Southwest, either or both could have had a hand in creating the richness of religious drama that remains today in New Mexico. As one authority described the situation in the area,

> we have very complete versions of the several Nativity plays, of the play *Adán y Eva* (Adam and Eve), of the play *Los Tres Reyes* (The Three Kings), of the play *El Niño Perdido* (The Lost Child), as well as of the play *Las Cuatro Apariciones de Nuestra Señora de Guadalupe* (The Four Apparitions of Our Lady of Guadalupe), and a complete and legible version of *Los Moros y Cristianos* (The Moors and Christians).

Although generally most of these plays were never printed, they have survived in manuscript relatively unchanged over the centuries. These manuscripts were apparently copied down by priests from performances in Spain and brought to the New World among the riches of Spain's Golden Age—the same time frame that produced Shakespeare in England having produced Lope de Vega and Pedro Calderón de la Barca.[2]

A play that developed from the historical battle between Juan Bautista de Anza, governor of New Mexico, and the chief of the Comanches, Cuerno Verde (Green Horn), has survived over two centuries from the event in 1779, and is still well known in New Mexico. A religious version of *Los Comanches* is basically dance and pantomime, but a more historical one with the same name also exists, with dialogue, bragging speeches by the leaders of the two forces, dances by the Indians, a charge made by Spaniards shouting their traditional battlecry, "Santiago" (for Saint James), and the defeat and death of the Indian chief.[3]

Los Pastores (The Shepherds)

Many manuscripts of these folk plays have sources in Mexico, and often known authors—frequently amateurs—were involved. Of these dramatic riches, *Los Pastores* is the most widely known; one researcher avows that it is "the only play that is common to the entire American Southwest from California to the lower Texas-Mexican border and from the border to Spanish-speaking pockets scattered over the mid-Rocky Mountain area."[4]

Following the observation that *Los Pastores* is common to the entire Southwest, much of my consideration of folk drama will focus on it as most typical of Mexican-American folk plays. The preservation and publication of one of the *Los Pastores* plays can be credited to Captain John G. Bourke, an American Army officer who served in the Southwest for many years—a man who was truly fascinated by the culture he found where he soldiered. In 1893 he published an article based upon it in the *Journal of American Folklore,* and turned over his copy of the manuscript to the editors for future use. In 1907 it was published, with facing-page translations into English, plus notes and appendixes of related play materials, as Number IX of the Memoirs of the American Folklore Society.[5]

Bourke speculated that the manuscript he acquired on the lower Rio Grande had probably come from the Canary Islands, whence many settlers in northern Mexico and southern Texas had come, but the excitement attending the play was strongly localized, as were costumes and dramatic techniques:

> There are several rather ludicrous incongruities which may be recognized without giving offence to the pious fervor of the actors and actresses, who become intensely wrought up in their parts as the plot unfolds. The Hermit carries, attached to his wrist, a rosary made of wooden spools, and bears in his right hand a large crucifix, although the Savior has not yet been born and his Passion is all yet to be undergone. In every case that I saw or heard of, the rosary was made of these large wooden spools.
>
> Whenever it could be conveniently done, Lucifer was dressed in the uniform of a cavalry officer, but time is working its changes, and at this writing his Satanic Majesty enacts his role in raiment not so pronouncedly martial.
>
> For weeks beforehand the actors selected meet under the supervision of the Head Shepherd (in the present case an intelligent cobbler), and listen attentively and patiently while he reads, line by line and word for word, the part of each. Very few of them can read or write, and none

of them in a manner betokening extensive practice; the dependence for success, therefore, is almost wholly upon eye, ear, and memory, and the rehearsals are repeated again and again, until every man, woman, and child can recite the lines almost mechanically.

> ... Michael and Lucifer rant a little too much to satisfy critical taste.... There are ceaseless repetitions, and promenades and countermarches without end or object, save, perhaps, to allow each artist opportunity for a nasalized enunciation of his verses, in chant or monologue.[6]

In 1899 Honora DeBusk watched rehearsals for *Los Pastores* in San Rafael, New Mexico,

> a New Mexican village a hundred miles west of Albuquerque. The people were accustomed to give the play often at Christmas time, but not every year, as it was too much work. There was no resident priest at San Rafael, so they were obliged to get up the play themselves, without the advice or instruction of anyone in authority. . . . [The whole village attended rehearsals, and] their enjoyment of the final grand performance appeared to be heightened rather than diminished by the fact that they had seen the preparation in all its stages. . . . The men who represented the shepherds were in reality sheep-herders, for sheep-raising is the principal industry of that section. They did not wear their ordinary clothes, but instead, stiffly starched and elaborately ruffled white pantaloons, while the upper part of the body was covered with streamers of gayly colored ribbons, depending from a fantastic head-dress. . . . The Hermit, however, was represented very pleasingly by a venerable looking old man, with long white beard, in ordinary ragged attire. He carried a cross made of corncobs, and when molested by evil spirits would hold up this cross, and they would flee. . . . The stage manager sat on the edge of the platform, and talked over the antics of the shepherds with Michael. Above, a clothes-line was stretched the length of the hall. From it was suspended a smoky kerosene lantern, the Star of Bethlehem, which the stage manager jerked along just in advance of the shepherds, by means of a long wire. . . . When Michael came down from Heaven, a distance of about twenty feet, he descended in a sort of sliding swing, a rope with pulley attachment. There was a painful hitch in the descent, which was finally rectified, so that the angel reached earth without undue loss of dignity.[7]

Richard Dorson reports a version of the shepherd's play, collected in the same area and the same year as Captain Bourke's, entitled *Pastorela.* The text, in English, which is given in *Buying the Wind,*[8] had much of the fun and irreverence to be found in the *Second Shepherd's Play* of the Wakefield cycle in Britain. In both areas it was apparently the antics of the shepherds that caused the priests to push the folk drama out of doors, as is reported in most histories of medieval drama.[9]

The shepherd's play is alive and well along the border today, as it has been for several centuries. In the 1950s there were several troupes—folk or semi-professional—performing in the San Antonio, Texas, area, often in homes or in courtyards. When a composite troupe was put together of players from different groups, some problems arose because they had learned their lines from different traditional scripts![10]

In about 1969, UT El Paso folklore student Nancy Mae Wilkes discovered a traditional group of players who regularly perform *Los Pastores* in Las Cruces, New Mexico, from a manuscript found in California by a Franciscan priest who translated the text into English but left the songs in Spanish. The Franciscan, Father Ralph, was given permission by the keeper of the manuscript of the play, a Doña Emilia, to use it in New Mexico so long as it was presented without charge, and with stress on its sacred nature. When Father Ralph suggested that a local guitar and vocal group get involved with the shepherd's play, they accepted his script and went on to make a local tradition of performing it, preferably in churches, but in other sites when those are the only ones available. For twenty-seven years they have continued the performances, and three or four families are now into their third generation of players. Dan Sosa, the man who plays *el Diablo* (the Devil), is a New Mexico state supreme court justice whose great-grandfather used to play the same part elsewhere in the state. The play is the group's "Christmas gift to the community," and is presented four times each Christmas season.[11]

In most of the presentations of *Los Pastores* reported over the years, the play is traditionally preceded by the drama-like *Las Posadas* discussed in Chapter Nine. As was described there, the audience frequently is involved, following the Holy Family in their search for shelter, and at the final request, where welcome is found, all are invited in for the performance of the play. The version reported by Miss Wilkes actually incorporates a part of the posada into the play itself:

> The New Mexico version begins with Mary and Joseph seeking shelter in a cave near Bethlehem after finding no room in the inns. After the Angel announces the birth of Christ, the shepherds appear singing on their way to the manger. One of the shepherds meets a hermit who tells him about his life of contemplation and informs him that the Messiah has come. Wishing to find out more about the Messiah, the shepherd invites the hermit to the camp. As the hermit arrives at the camp, Gila and her husband Bato are quarreling because supper is not ready. The hermit restores peace. Meanwhile one of the shepherds, Belicio, encounters Lucifer. The shepherd recognizes him and flees. Belicio arrives at the camp, and as he recounts his experiences with Lucifer, one of the shepherds comes in carrying Bartolo on his back. Then Dina enters

and is scolded by Gila for taking so long to fetch the water. Dina explains that she had stopped to listen to some heavenly music. Supper is served and all sit down to eat, except Bartolo, who is too lazy to get up.

While everyone is sleeping after dinner, Lucifer enters with Envy and Pride. Lucifer, fearful of Christ's power, decides to plot against man. He tempts the hermit into kidnapping Gila. The shepherds awake, and catching the hermit, they beat him. Later an angel appears to one of the shepherds, Menalpas, and announces the birth of Christ. After procuring a reward from each shepherd, Menalpas tells them the good news. Only the hermit believes him. While the shepherds return to their sleep, Lucifer encounters the angel Michael. Michael defeats him and Lucifer is vanquished. The shepherds then go to adore Jesus. They leave after singing a lullaby and bidding farewell to the Holy Family.[12]

While the story bears a general resemblance to the Christmas story as recounted in the second chapter of the Gospel of Luke, anyone familiar with the English *Second Shepherd's Play* can see the potential for fun and slapstick humor in the quarreling between Gila and Bato, the berating of Dina, and especially the beating of the hermit.

Other versions of the play follow the same basic story line, with variations especially in the areas lending themselves to comic interpretation—but the seriousness of the event it portrays is never lost sight of, and the conclusion is always on a religious note.

Las Posadas

While the whole combination of posadas, pastores, and piñatas occupies the religious and festive scene in the Southwest from mid-December until January 6, the dramatic elements of the posadas are more common because they are more easily staged. All it takes is a boy and a girl, to represent Joseph and Mary, and a group of parishioners. Since everybody knows the story, and children learn the songs by participating each year, no rehearsal is even needed. Arthur L. Campa reports that in California (where the weather is reportedly always good), there are nine posadas on a succession of nights, but in the villages of New Mexico the people do all the events on one night, Christmas Eve, with the pilgrims going to nine homes, where they are rejected, ending up at the manger, which is set up in the church.[13] On the night of the posada, the congregation is sometimes divided into two groups, one either to accompany the Holy Family or to carry the statues used when no live actors represent them; the other group represents the hard-hearted innkeepers who stay inside the church where they turn the weary pilgrims away. Finally the church—inn—is opened, and the crowd streams in singing and taking part in prayers of celebration. If a piñata party has been arranged, it is usually held in a nearby home. One parish priest noted that

> the piñata I think is just something the Mexican people threw in for the kids because they have piñatas for every occasion. They added the piñata to try to get the kids to come to the celebration and maybe learn something about the true meaning of Christmas.[14]

Modern Social Protest Drama

Twenty centuries after the events portrayed in *Los Pastores,* and using scripts written by known authors, groups similar to these folk groups have used the stage for presenting modern concerns. *El Teatro Campesino* (The Farmworkers' Theater) has dealt repeatedly with the repression and exploitation of *los de abajo* (the underdogs), as Mexican migrant farm workers are often seen by social protestors. Luis Miguel Valdez, central mover in the formation of the Teatro Campesino, is the author of several plays that are close to the spirit of folk tradition, especially in the use of humor to drive a point home.[15]

Another pair of plays, *Soldado Razo* (The Ethnic Soldier) and *Vietnam Campesino* (Vietnam Farmworker), also by Valdez, deal with the "disproportionate number of Chicanos who were losing their lives and draining the barrios of their finest youth" in the Vietnam war.[16] While these plays are not precisely folk in their entirety, the players are often members of the folk group, and amateurs are pressed into service much as they are in true folk dramas like *Los Pastores.*[17]

Los Matachines

A traditional drama/dance, *Los Matachines,* has been widely popular in the Spanish Southwest. Some authorities consider it a drama and others call it a dance—so it seems to provide an effective transition into our next topic. During the 1930s the New Mexico Federal Writers Project collected materials on the performance of *Los Matachines* on Christmas Eve and Christmas morning, preceded by visits from Abuelos and Abuelas—figures of terror for children who are threatened with whippings if they have been bad.

> The Abuelo was the bogeyman of those times. In his grotesque makeup and mask he would make his appearance sometime a week before Christmas. His blood-curdling cry would sound out on the frosty air at dusk as he approached the door of some dwelling. The door would be opened and in he would stride to find a cowering group of children staring at him, bug-eyed and trembling, utterly terrified by this terrible

figure with the long rawhide whip which was a never-absent part of his costume. Cracking his whip, he would roar: *"¿Han sido buenos muchachos estos?"* (Have these children been good?)[18]

Even today in New Mexican villages the old ones appear in a somewhat ritualistic reenactment of what was in the 1940s a regular tradition.[19]

Los Matachines is often called a relative of the Morris dances of England, a sort of sword-dance reenacting the battles between the Christians and the Moors, called in Spain *Danzas de Espadas* (Sword Dances) or simply *Moros y Cristianos* (the word "Morris" is a corruption of "Moorish," according to the *Encyclopaedia Britannica).*

> It is likely that the dance was further dramatized in Mexico by the addition of such characters as *El Monarca,* representing Montezuma, to give it significance to the Aztecs, and that the allegorical characters *El Abuelo* [Grandfather], *El Torito* [Little Bull], and *La Malinche* [translator for and mistress of Cortés] were representatives of the forces of evil against virtue, as in so many of the religious folk plays.[20]

In New Mexico in the 1930s *Los Matachines* was performed on Christmas Eve and Christmas morning, and in Trinidad, Colorado, it was performed until near the turn of the century. Although Colorado is beyond my area of concentration, the description provided by folklorist Honora DeBusk is worth reproducing here—with the observation that she calls it a folk dance. It is significant that the swords are missing from her account:

> Each *matachín* wore long white trousers, elaborately ruffled like the old-fashioned pantalettes. He had a high headdress, from which a myriad long, bright-colored ribbons fluttered, quite covering the upper part of his person. A brilliantly colored silk handkerchief masked the face, hanging loosely and entirely concealing the features. The tall leader, El Monarca, was particularly resplendent. With him danced a young girl as the Princess Malinche, the only girl in the company. She was usually from twelve to fifteen years of age, was dressed all in white, with the long white veil which denotes virginity, and wore neither ribbons nor mask. *El Viejo* (Old Man) and Carrelampio, dressed in gunnysacking, were active clowns. *La Vieja,* also a comic character, often wore the sacking.
>
> . . .El Toro, when I saw him, wore a bull's hide and a mask with horns, and walked on all fours by the expedient of carrying two canes to serve as forefeet. Sometimes he used canes interchangeably as forefeet and horns. He made himself generally obnoxious, diving in and out among the dancers, spoiling their most graceful figures, even upsetting a dancer occasionally and goring at him with the rather inadequate horns. El

> Viejo, enraged, pursued him with the whip but El Toro turned upon him, routing him dismally.

In the midst of all this slapstick comedy, two long lines of dancers performed several numbers, and after some three hours, La Malinche vainly begged the dancers to kill the bull. Finally her father, El Viejo, did kill it, with a toy pistol, and La Malinche mopped up the bull's imaginary blood and showed it to the crowd, who cheered as the bull's body was carried off. "In isolated Spanish-American plazas," says Miss DeBusk, the play "has lost little of its zest and fervor as a holiday celebration in a religious setting."[21]

Folk Dance

A love of dancing has long been an integral part of life for the descendants of the early colonists who peopled the Spanish Southwest. In New Mexico in the old days, according to one folklorist,

> *bailes* [dances] were held in every town or village, in *salas* [living rooms] with whitewashed walls lit by tallow candles. Before 1850 most of the salas had hard-packed clay floors with wheat straw scattered over them to keep the dust down.
>
> At a table at one end of the sala were chairs for the *músicos* [musicians] who played violin and guitar. Often, before the dance, the músicos would ride in a wagon through the town and adjoining villages to express a *convite,* an invitation for everyone to come to the dance.
>
> The large homes of the ricos always had a sala for the bailes celebrating *prendorios* [an archaic word for engagements], *bodas* [weddings], *cumpleaños* [birthdays], and other events to which family and friends were invited. Sometimes in order to be assured of having another dance soon, some couple was *prendado* or *amarrado,* actually tied with a handkerchief, and not untied until someone would promise to redeem them by giving a *baile de desempeño* [dance of redemption].[22]

Rosa Guerrero, El Paso authority on folk dancing and outstanding teacher thereof, recently saw in Santa Fe, New Mexico, an impressive grand promenade that began a dance. In a sort of *marcha* (march), one person, elaborately dressed, entered and began a tour of the sala; another person joined the first, then two more, then four more, and so on, doubling the number each time—until the entire group of dancers was involved, circling the room. Then they separated, in the same fashion, until there was only one promenader left, and then none. "It was truly beautiful—like a dancers' quadrille," she says. She points out that Mexican-American folk dance has varied roots: Emperor Maximilian brought to

Mexico a variety of dances that have developed folk variations—the waltz, schottische, and varsovienne; other cultures have shared their stomping footwork—such as the Egyptians, through Arabic and Jewish migrations—and the rhythms of Africa and the Caribbean have added spice to the dance.[23]

A dance can mark almost any occasion, including the celebration of San Luis Gonzaga's Day, June 21, since he is the patron saint of the dance. Out of New Mexico's past comes an interesting account:

> The saint is seated between the musicians, usually a guitar and a violin player. San Luis's hymn is sung and, after praying the rosary, dancing is the order of the night. Instead of singing couplets in honor of the different dancers, the musicians dedicate their verses to San Luis Gonzago, coupling his name with some one of the dancers on the floor. The individual so honored is expected to give the musicians a coin in acknowledgement of the honor. The dance lasts until daylight, when the saint is joyfully carried back to the church.[24]

Since the event described took place in the remote villages of New Mexico in the 1930s, long before the advent of television and other amusements, one wonders if the tradition still continues. It was a much simpler time then, as it was when a dance was given in Cordova, New Mexico, in honor of a new bell in the church. The bell, cast locally, was christened in much the same way as a baby, and there were a host of activities—horse racing, a feast (to which even the Apaches were invited), and others. Finally the earthen floor of the long hall was spread with straw, and all the dances of the times were performed. "Extempore couplets sung by the guitar player in honor of the bell" were applauded wildly, and the dancers danced a while, returned to the feast, and then went back to the dance, far into the next day.[25]

The traditional dances of the Mexican-Americans in the Southwest are often intermingled with more modern ones today, but they do live on and are an active part of the culture. Especially at wedding celebrations one finds the old dances being performed—*la Indita* (the little Indian), *el vaquero* (the cowboy), *la varsoviana* (the varsovienne), the polka, and many others. Relying heavily upon a "booklet long out of print," as a reprint edition describes it, and realizing that a dance on paper is far from the dance in action, I shall limit my descriptions to four *danzas tipicas* (typical dances).

El galope is literally a gallop. Couples, in a slightly open ballroom position, face the same direction. Man steps forward with left foot; woman with right. Man draws right foot up to left; woman draws left foot up to right. Repeat. This is danced fairly fast.

Then two couples combine. The two men, both facing in the same direction, hold hands high to form an arch, one with the left hand raised, the other with the right raised. With the free hand each man pulls forward the woman, who is standing behind him. The women dance forward and back under the arch; then the men change sides (but still using the same hands) and the women dance forward and back again under the arch. Then all gallop again, and the formations are repeated again and again.[26]

La cuna (the cradle) is a couple dance with aspects of a square dance. Two pairs of dancers form a square, facing in, couple facing couple. Each woman walks forward and takes the left hand of the other man with her own left hand; the men turn backward under the women's left arms. Then each woman takes the right hand of her own partner with her own right hand and makes a quarter-turn left under her partner's arm, finishing facing center again, and the four dancers join hands in close formation, their arms forming a cradle. They dance around to the right, swinging to and fro in imitation of the rocking of a cradle. Then they break formation and polka with their own partners.[27]

El vals de los paños (the waltz of the handkerchiefs) involves two trios, two women to each man. The man stands between the women holding the end of a handkerchief in each hand; the women hold the other ends, and the trio forms a line that faces the other trio. Holding tight to the handkerchiefs, the trios waltz forward toward the center for four measures, then back four measures, and then repeat the movements.

Then, holding arms (and handkerchiefs) high, the woman on the man's left dances through the arch formed by the arms on his right, while the other woman dances around the man toward the left, making a half-circle. The man turns right.

The man makes a half-turn left as the women progress around, completing their circles. The other woman does the dance under the arch formed by the arms of the man and the first woman, winding up with them all in the original position, in line facing the other trio—which has been doing the same movements. Then they repeat the whole routine.[28]

El vals de la escoba (the broom dance) can be danced by any number, so long as there's an extra man to dance with the broom. The dancers line up facing each other, several feet apart, men on one side and women on the other. The man with the broom waltzes between the lines, and suddenly drops the broom and grabs a woman, making away with her. Meanwhile the other men grab for a woman—and somebody comes up short, so he has to dance with the broom. After a while the music stops, the dancers line up again, and the broom dancer repeats the performance, so someone else can have the "honor" of dancing with the broom.[29]

During the Mexican Period, wealthy Californians danced Spanish fandangos, *jotas, contradanzas,* and "all manner of folk dances invented by the Californios."[30] And in an ancient village in Spain, Aurelio Espinosa experienced a festival lasting several days just as in his native New Mexico, with dancing in the streets. One Spanish dance, *danza de corrillo,*

> had a great resemblance to the old New Mexico *vals despacio* [slow

waltz]. Several couples, no definite number, held hands in a circle and walked around slowly in step with the music of the guitar, and at a regular repetition of the monotonous rhythm with quicker tempo the couples broke the circle and danced in pairs, either holding hands or separated. In the New Mexican valse despacio the circles are always of two couples and in the quicker tempo repetition the couples dance holding hands in the traditional manner.[31]

Along the lower Rio Grande, up to the time of the Mexican Revolution, the community dance was a special social event. Girls were closely chaperoned, with parents or maiden aunts handy to keep the proprieties inviolate. The dance would usually begin with a promenade, repeated at intermission time, and although both Mexican and American music was played, "extreme jazz" was not welcome; if the band played jazz, it was toned down considerably. There were often recitations and musical numbers rendered by the young ladies, who were accompanied to the platform where they performed by a committee of at least two people to "stand guard" during the presentation.[32] But, according to Américo Paredes, the community dance was far too often the setting for violence—rivalry between young men for the hand of the same lady, maybe, or some similar conflict of passions. It was anger engendered by a refusal to dance that precipitated the killing of Rosita Alvírez in the true-to-life ballad described earlier—a ballad which stressed the dangers of such affairs, and tried to teach that "nice girls" didn't attend them, even with chaperones.[33]

In modern times the fusion of dance types has produced some interesting mixtures—a situation which reflects, of course, the basic nature of folklore: variation within a framework of tradition. Growing up in Central, New Mexico, after World War II, Ruth Vise recalls this mixture of old and new: the *jarabe tapatío* (often called the Mexican hat dance) was the most often seen and performed folk dance, but at school dances, the scene was marked by a blending of popular, rock, and traditional music and dancing. The dance bands were at home in both Mexican and "American" trends, sliding easily from a norteño love song to a Mexican polka to whatever was currently popular. The dancers, a mixture of Mexican-Americans and non-Hispanics, were expected to know what steps were involved in whatever piece of music was being played. The Mexican polka was especially popular: it was danced side by side rather than face to face, with something of a shuffle to the music, using small steps backward, forward, and sideways. Many of the most popular boys in high school, Vise remembers, could sing equally well in English or Spanish; they were usually handsome and athletic, played guitars, and were often among the groups who serenaded young women on their birthdays and then were invited in for *pozole,* hot chocolate, and other traditional refreshments. They were always on demand as lead singers at the dances—unlike today in such small communities, where other activities have replaced music, and singers at dances tend to be older, professional performers. And although the music of Ritchie Valens was "the MOST," nobody in Ruth Vise's crowd danced the traditional "la bamba."[34]

In the El Paso area, there were community-type dances, often given in public dance halls or gymnasiums by fraternal clubs, high school groups, or social organizations raising funds for some worthy cause. The bands might range from a mariachi group to a *conjunto* (a four- or five-piece ensemble with guitar, bass, violin, and trumpet usually and often a *guitarrón*—a cross between a guitar and a bass fiddle) or even a big band. Sometimes these were billed as *bailes rancheros* —rancher dances—and people came in ranch costume, the women with braided hair and wearing shawls, the men with Levi's or charro trousers and boots, truly colorful occasions. They were given four to six times a year in El Paso, oftener in Juárez, across the river, but "you never hear of them any more," says Margarita Kanavy.[35]

Both Margarita and my wife, Lucy Fischer West, were regular in attendance at the local substitute for the community dance or the bailes rancheros. They attended frequent family-style dances, especially those given by Margarita's father, José Burciago, who as custodian of the local Jewish synagogue was given permission to use the basement gymnasium for dances. Food was provided by Señora Burciaga; music came either from a conjunto or from 78 rm records ("If you had records, you brought them," Margarita recalls). The occasion was quite simple —anybody's birthday, anniversary, christening, or other event—and seldom was there need for invitations: family and close friends just "knew" and whole families showed up, from babes in arms to grandparents. Lucy remembers how the young people, children even, were free to dance in the early evening—*la raspa,* the conga, and a form of *la bamba* done in a sliding step, alternating right, left, right feet, then a hop on the left; then the procedure was reversed. "It really tired us out," she says. Both informants recalled that even if you didn't dance, just watching Señor Burciaga having a good time was entertainment enough. He danced all the women down![36]

These familial dances began with people sitting around chatting, eating, drinking, and listening to the music—and finally, dancing. Adults danced a different sort of la bamba, with no "hop," but a mambo beat—couples with arms about each other's waists, dancing forward and back as they moved about the floor in a circular fashion; then the couples merged into a pair of lines—contra-dance style —with the other dancers, in a rather free form; the grandmothers, of course, muttered about how the dance was done in *their* day, considerably more structured. The polka, the waltz, the two-step all had their place in the program.

How did the little ones learn to dance? "By going and watching and stumbling," Margarita remembers. In such relaxed surroundings two women might dance together, with a pair of children imitating their steps, or an adult would take a child in tow, dancing patiently with the learner until some degree of skill was developed.[37]

One might wax eloquent about how the good old days are gone forever, and nobody knows how to have a good time any more—but when such a nay-sayer goes to a Mexican-American wedding, or a quinceañera, or another traditional celebration, it becomes quite apparent that the culture, complete with traditional dancing, lives on today in the Southwest.

CHAPTER ELEVEN

Folk Games

MEXICAN-AMERICAN FOLK GAMES are a fascinating topic for study, especially those of children—who, after all, are supposed to play games! Brian Sutton-Smith, psychologist-turned-folklorist, says that the basic reason that children play games is to create a game world where they, not adults, are in control. Then they can vary the situation with "wild invention, hilarity, and sometimes complete nonsense." Of course, having accepted the limitations of a set of rules for a game, the child is supposed to be bound by those rules—but even deliberately bending or breaking those rules is part of the fun.[1]

Jan Brunvand notes that for a game (rather than simply a pastime) to exist there must be some form of competition, so somebody can win or lose.[2] Yet some games that children play seem to be for sheer fun. The game of tag, or hide and seek, for example, certainly involves competition, yet nobody keeps score; in fact, from my own recollections, the person who was always able to elude pursuit, or could always hide too well to be found, had less fun than the rest of us, and would eventually let himself be caught. Winning was certainly not everything!

Categories for describing games are generally too vague or too restrictive to be very useful. Brunvand simply breaks them into four groups: action games, games involving objects, mental games—and everything else.[3] Perhaps the Mexican-American children my student researchers have come into contact with are too physically oriented to have much time for mental games—other than riddles and puzzles, already treated in Chapter Four—but the first two categories are well represented in every collection I have noted.

Games of Action

Many games played by Mexican-American children differ little from those played by members of other cultures—*El Chicotito* is simply Crack the Whip; Dogpile is played without the formality of a name; and tug-of-war is sometimes the end of a game in which two "angels" choose children by having them name a color, after which the Good Angel and Bad Angel and their followers engage in a struggle that lacks the cosmic results of the battle between good and evil generally. Sometimes, however, the Bad Angel's side wins, and the children have to come to judgment and pay forfeits, with a formulaic ritual that recalls the "Heavy, heavy hangs over thy head" of my own childhood with its question and response:

Tan, tan.	Rap, rap.
¿Quién es?	Who is it?
El Angel Bueno.	The Good Angel.
¿Que trae el Angel Bueno?	What does the Good Angel bring?
Un preso.	A prisoner.
¿Que delito cometió?	What crime did he commit?
Que lo encontré comiendo queso y no me dió.	I found him eating cheese and he didn't give me any.
Pues la sentencia que le doy es	The sentence that I pronounce
que le den dos buenas nalgadas.	is that he be given two good spanks.[4]

A familiar game with a different name is *Chinchilaqua:*

> This is a game where you get about five boys on two teams. One boy gets to be a pillow. The five boys hold onto each other's waists and bend down. Then team two has to run up, one at a time, and yell "Chinchilaqua!" and jump on their backs. If the team that is bent over can hold up the jumping team, they get a turn at jumping. If they fall, the jumping team gets another turn. Sometimes there isn't a pillow in the game. When you are bent over you have to hold your head down so it won't break. This is a rough game.[5]

If Bill Cosby's friend Fat Albert is on the jumping team, the results are predictable!

Old familiar Blind Man's Buff is played as Blind Chicken ("it" is the chicken), Blindfolded, and Sit on the Pillow—the last being a curious variant in which all but "it" sit in a circle while "it" walks around, then sits on someone and tries to guess the "pillow's" name. In all three, if the person touched or sat upon is guessed, then that person takes the place of "it."[6]

Musical Chairs exists in many variations among Mexican-American children. In *El Gato* (The Cat) a child is put in each corner, and each child has an animal's name. "It" is El Gato, and he goes from corner to corner asking, "Do you have bread and cheese?" The one asked says, "No," and points to another child. As the cat is traveling to the next corner, the children try to exchange corners behind his back. If a child is caught, or the cat gets to the corner that has been left empty, the child who is caught or is without a corner becomes El Gato.[7] In another version, "it" asks, "Who has bread and cheese?" and is answered, "My friend ——." The race for a corner is the same.[8] And there is even one version called *El Juego de las Sillas* (Game of the Chairs), with one fewer chairs available than players. A record is played as the children march around; when it stops, there's a scramble for a seat, with the one without a chair being out. On the next playing of the record, of course, another chair is taken away, and so on.[9] One who has played Going to

Jerusalem might well assume there's nothing new under the sun, regardless of the culture at hand.

Las Escondidas (Hide and Go Seek) and *La Patada del Bote* (Kick the Can), however, have some interesting varieties in the Mexican-American playground. In *Amigos* (Friends), "it" gets help: each person he catches has to help catch the others, until the whole group (except one) is a sort of posse chasing one person —in which case the old saying *¡Tantos perros con un pobre hueso!* (So many dogs with one poor bone!) becomes appropriate. When all have been caught, the first person captured becomes "it."[10] And in Kissing Tag Game, a version that might be expected to be popular with older children, the boys chase the girls. When a boy catches a girl, he kisses her and puts her in jail till all the girls are captured; then the girls chase the boys. One boy—obviously too young to know what was good for him—said disgustedly that he had had to kiss the girl on the leg, since that's where he tagged her![11]

My students have collected at least nine varieties of a game in which the object is to touch or hit someone with a ball. Touch Ball is simply a form of tag, with the tagging being done with a ball.[12] Then there is *La Quemada de Hoyos* (Burning the Holes), in which a ball is rolled toward a series of holes in the ground, one dug by each player. If the ball rolls into one of the holes, the "owner" of the hole has to grab the ball, run to the home base and touch it, and then try to hit one of the other children. Whoever gets hit is the next roller.[13] And the action gets even more violent in some of the other forms. Firing Squad has a group lined up against a wall while a player throws a ball at them. They can dodge, but they can't leave the wall; the first one hit is "it" for the next round.[14]

Other games, far less violent, are also more culturally tied to the Mexican and Spanish roots of the Mexican-American child. *Vibora de la Mar,* described in the chapter on rhymes, has an interesting background. A.L. Campa, New Mexico authority on Hispanic folklore, said that

> this XVIII-century Spanish *Corro de niños* [ring of children] is very popular in Spain and in most of the Hispanic world. Most versions, including the Spanish ones, begin with *"a la vibora, vibora de la mar,"* meaning that they snake through.

The New Mexico version, which is known also along the Mexican border, is one of the best preserved.

A version of this song from Puerto Rico is entitled *La Puerta de Alcalá,* referring to one of the famous gates in Madrid, Spain:

(Las dos niñas:)	(The two girls:)
A la vibora, vibora del amor,	To the snake, snake of love,
De aqui podeís pasar.	Through here you may pass.
(Las otras:)	(The others:)

Por aqui yo pasaré	I'll pass through here
Y una niña dejaré.	And leave one girl behind.
(Las dos:)	(The two:)
¿Y esa niña cual será:	And which girl will it be?
La de alante or la de atrás?*	The front one or the back one?
(Las otras:)	(The others:)
La de alante corre mucho	The one in front runs a lot
La de atrás se quedará.	The one behind will remain.
(Las dos:)	(The two:)
Pasame, si, pasame, ya,	Go by me, yes, go by me, already,
Por la puerta de Alcantará.	Through the gate of Alcantará.[15]

In this game, the child behind is trapped, as in London Bridge, by the arms of the two persons forming the gate or bridge. Then the trapped one gets behind one or the other of the gate people (usually by choosing to be a color, a fruit, or silver or gold), and ultimately a tug-of-war ends the game.

Another game that has been collected widely is *La Rueda de San Miguel* (Wheel of Saint Michael). Aureliano Armendariz, New Mexico folklorist, believes that the rhyme has no real connection with the saint, but the name simply rhymes well:

Rueda, rueda 'e San Miguel, San Miguel,
Todos traen camote y miel.
(Hablado): A lo maduro, a lo maduro
Que se volteé (nombre) de burro.

Wheel, wheel of Saint Michael, Saint Michael,
All carry sweet potatoes and honey.
(Spoken): [roughly, "on your mark, get set..."]
May (someone's name) the donkey turn around.

The game involves any number of children in a circle holding hands, with one child in the center. The circle moves clockwise around the center person, singing the first verse; then the center child shouts the spoken words, naming one of the people in the circle, who must turn around, back to the center. The game goes on, with the circle picking up speed, and the song and action are repeated, until all the children in the circle have their backs to the center. The circle moves faster and faster until it falls apart from its own velocity. After the laughing is over, the game starts again.[16]

Another fun game, especially for rainy days, is *Juan Pirulero.* There are usually two or three children who want to be Juan Pirulero to begin the game; after one is

---

**alante* = *adelante,* forward

chosen, by matching coins or drawing straws, each of the others is assigned a part —playing a musical instrument, washing dishes or ironing, or whatever. Then the children sit down in a circle doing their motions as Juan Pirulero imitates playing a clarinet and singing through twice

Este es el juego de Juan Pirulero
Que cada quien atenda a su juego.

This is the game of John Pirulero
and each must attend to his game.

Suddenly Juan stops playing the clarinet and begins imitating the action assigned to one of the other children—who must then start pretending to play the clarinet. The game goes on, with Juan singing again and changing instruments or actions. Whoever is not fast or alert enough to keep up with the changes has to pay a forfeit —stand on his hands, or howl like a dog, or whatever Juan Pirulero comes up with. Once Juan switches to another action, the first person goes back to his assigned motion and continues to do it without stopping, and on and on.[17] The possibilities for mass confusion and wild hilarity seem endless!

María Blanca is not found in northern New Mexico, according to Dr. Campa, but folklorist Aureliano Armendariz knew it in his native Mexico, and also found it in Mesilla, in southern New Mexico. The children form a ring holding hands with María Blanca inside and another child, sometimes called Fat Man, outside. The group sings the first line:

María Blanca esta encerrada en pilares de oro y plata.
(María Blanca is enclosed by pillars of gold and silver.)
The Fat Man: *Abrirémos un pilar para ver a María Blanca.*
(Let's open a pillar to see María Blanca.)

Then the outsider tries to break through the ring and capture María Blanca, who runs outside the ring and then is allowed to slip back into the ring if she escapes her pursuer. If she doesn't escape, María takes the outside position and another María Blanca is chosen.[18]

In El Paso the outsider is called *El Chicotillo* (the Whip), and a dramatic dialogue takes place between the Ring and the Whip:

Children: Doña Blanca is covered with pillars of gold and silver. Let's break a pillar so we can see Doña Blanca. Who is that whip who is after Doña Blanca?
The Whip: I'm that whip who is after Doña Blanca. Where is Doña Blanca?
Children: She went to mass *(misa)*.
The Whip: Darn her shirt *(camisa)*.
[Then the first speeches are repeated.]

Children: She went to the mountain *(cerro).*
The Whip: Darn her calf *(becerro).*
[Then the first speeches are repeated.]
Children: She's back.
The Whip [pretending to try to break through]: What is this pillar made of?
Children: Of gold.
The Whip: It's hard. [same action] And this one?
Children: Of silver.
The Whip: It's hard. [same action] And this one?
Children: Of marble.
The Whip: It's hard. [same action] And this one?
Children: Of glass.
The Whip: If I break it, I'll cut myself. And this one?
Children: Of paper.
The Whip: This one I can break.
And he does, and runs after Doña Blanca.[19]

One final children's game, which I have chosen to include because of its fascinating history, is *Ambo Gato* (literally, Either Cat[?] but actually nonsense, as will appear). All the players are girls, except for the messenger, who may be male:

Ambo gato, matarili rili rón	Either cat, [nonsense sounds]
¿Qué quiere usted, matarili rili rón?	What do you want?
Quiere un paje, matarili rili rón.	I want a page.
¿Qué paje quiere, matarili ril rón?	Which page do you want?
Quiere a (nombre de niña), matarili rili rón.	I want (name of girl).
¿Qué nombre le pondremos, matarili rili rón?	What name will we give her?
Le pondremos (nombre de flor), matarili rili ron.	We'll call her (name of flower).
Aquí está mi hija, con dolor de corazón.	Here is my daughter, with pain in my heart.
Celebremos, celebremos, todos juntos en la union.	Let's celebrate, let's celebrate, all together in the union.

Ambo Gato is the mother, and the page being asked for is one of her daughters. A *mensajero* (messenger) from the royal court is doing the asking in the odd lines, and the mother answers in the even lines. When one of the girls is finally chosen, the remaining girls form a ring and sing the "Celebremos" line. The whole action is repeated until the messenger has taken all the girls and the game ends.

The curiosity of this game is that it come from a mis-translation of a French song, *"Ah! Mon Beau Chateau,"* (Oh! My Beautiful Castle), which comes out

"Ambo gato," and the nonsense line was originally, *"Ma tante, tire, lire, lire,"* (My aunt, etc.)[20]

Games with Objects

Mexican-American children play marbles *(canicas)* like many other youngsters, but they also have a variation called Oyita (properly *Hoyita,* little hole) that sounds something like horseshoes:

> To play you need marbles and to dig a hole. There can be two or more players. You throw marbles to the hole. If you make more than the others you are the first to shoot the ones that are left out of the hole. If you make [hit?] the ones that are left out you win all the marbles in the hole.[21]

Hide the Thimble or one of the other object-hiding games is present in a number of Mexican-American variants—Hide the Clothespin,[22] Hide the Bone (someone is the dog, and while he covers his eyes, the cat sneaks up and hides the bone), with clues like "You're warm" or "You're cold" to help out.[23] But for some reason, Hide the Belt seems to be most popular—and with some unusual names. In one game, The Beans Are Burning, everyone hides his eyes while someone hides the belt. When it is hidden, the player calls out, "The beans are burning!" and everyone starts hunting. The one who finds the belt gets to hit the others with it.[24] Another version—recalling Drop the Handkerchief—has the players in a circle, hands behind them. "It" walks around outside the circle, finally putting the belt in someone's hands; the one receiving the belt must then chase "it" around the circle. If "it" gets back to the place vacated by the one who gets the belt, then the latter is the new "it" and the game continues.[25]

An adult game that dates from colonial times in New Mexico is *canute,* which means hollow reed or flute. Possibly derived from the Navajo ceremonial game in which something is hidden in one of four moccasins, it resembles the old carnival con man's shell game. As Marc Simmons reports,

> for canute, the Spaniards used four hollow reeds, each with different markings. The object was to hide a splinter of wood or a nail inside one of the reeds and have the opponent—either an individual or a team —guess the whereabouts. Kernels of corn, beans or piñon nuts were used as tokens or chips. These were awarded to the player who selected the right canute on the first or second try. When one team acquired all the tokens it was declared the winner.

Youngsters sometimes got into the action too, although it was a serious gambling game. One little girl who came to New Mexico in 1852 saw the children playing tops and another game—canute. She and her brother soon learned how to play, and they were quite skillful, according to her memoirs:

> I won the Indian children's red beads and then would have to sit on them to keep them from stealing them from me. . . . One day my mother came upon me sitting upon a string of shell beads while in my lap was a heap of piñons; but I was too busy to see her coming. My sole adventure in gambling came to an abrupt halt.[26]

And then there's Spin the Bottle—but this one is obviously for children, not teenagers exploring the delights of social interaction! The children are seated in a circle, and the leader in the center spins a bottle. When it stops, pointing at someone, the leader tells that one what to do—bark like a dog, sing a song, or whatever.[27]

Marc Simmons reports that New Mexican sheepherders in the old days were fond of a game called *pitarilla,* or New Mexican Checkers, although it more nearly resembled Tic-Tac-Toe. "They drew the game board on the ground near the campfire and used pebbles or beans as markers. The aim was to place three of the markers in a line."[28]

The idea of men playing games recalls scenes I have witnessed all my life in various areas of Texas: men playing washers, pitching them at a crack or sometimes a hole in the ground, in a game closely resembling horseshoes. (Of course, I've seen Anglos pitching silver dollars in a similar game, but Mexican-Americans are less likely to have their money out in plain view where the law, which is usually Anglo, might see it and think, quite correctly, that they were gambling.)[29]

The absence of folk toys among Mexican-Americans these days is a curiosity difficult to explain, unless it is a result of advertising and the ready availability of manufactured toys. Whatever the cause, it is not a recent phenomenon: growing up in the Big Bend area of Texas in the 1950s, Joe Graham recalls that his Mexican-American playmates always used manufactured toys, and never played with *trompos* (tops) and other whittled articles, nor even used Mexican toys from just across the Rio Grande. They played "American," and up-to-date as well.[30]

Women play games, too—especially in women-only gatherings such as wedding showers. One game reported from several informants involves a blindfolded woman trying to move cotton balls from one bowl to another, using only a spoon and a certain number of chances—usually three. Sometimes the player feels very confident of her success, only to discover she has missed the bowl completely. Somewhere along the line it is revealed to the prospective bride that the number she placed in the bowl (if any) indicates how many children she will have.[31] Another game involves a small-necked bottle, into which each contestant has thirty seconds to put toothpicks or matches—while reading a book and never taking her eyes off it. The relevance of this game is to see how well different women will be able to juggle the many tasks a wife has to do, often all at once —like diapering the baby while fixing a meal.[32] Sometimes only the bride is involved in a game—such as hanging a laundry basket load of socks on a line in a limited time, while blindfolded. The trick is that as soon as a sock is hung on the line, someone takes it off and returns it to the basket. The bride-to-be is "encouraged" by the group reminding her of the time limit and offering suggestions, all misleading, of course. An added element is that sometimes the bride has to hold a plastic doll in one hand while hanging clothes with the other. One woman laughed so hard that she dropped the "baby."[33] While these games are not culturally significant, they are played by Mexican-American women, and are passed down informally from group to group.

Of course, the ultimate game with an object, already mentioned in Chapter Nine, is the piñata—although it probably wouldn't qualify as a game for Jan Brunvand, since it does not involve competition and has no winner as such. A clay bowl, decorated with crepe paper and filled with candies, is hung up out of reach of the children. One by one they are blindfolded and each takes his turn trying to hit it with a stick—but it is pulled up out of the way, to the amusement of the audience. Finally one child—usually a little one—is allowed to break it, and the goodies spill over the floor,[34] so everybody wins! Maybe it *is* a game, after all.

One final game reported from the Mexican-American community in El Paso is called *La Cabula* (likely a slang term with no equivalent). A small group of close friends who can "take it" sit around drinking beer and one hurls a verbal barb at another, who is expected to come back with a better remark, or one that diverts the point of the comment to someone else, preferably the sender. It is a game of wit, as well as self-control, since nobody is supposed to take offense at the insults.[35] La Cabula does not seem to be widespread, nor especially Mexican-American in its nature, unless one considers it a test of *machismo* (manliness),which is an important part of the Hispanic male's traditional makeup. It resembles the familiar Black game Playing the Dozens, in which the players must endure insults against their mothers without losing their "cool."[36]

Similarities and differences—those cultural items that indicate that we are both alike and different—are certainly present in Mexican-American games!

CHAPTER TWELVE

Folk Architecture

FOLK ARCHITECTURE IS, essentially, that sort of construction that, in style, materials, and methods of construction, follows tradition rather than any formal or learned school of design or building. Vernacular architecture, as it is sometimes called, is most likely to have been the result of techniques and ideas handed down from past generations. In the case of most Mexican-American folk architecture, current practice comes from a blending of two cultures—the Spanish and the Indian.

When Spanish explorers—conquistadores and padres—came into the American Southwest in the 1500s they did not find the Indian living in houses constructed of the adobe building blocks they were familiar with in the Iberian peninsula, and which have since become common in West Texas and New Mexico. Such materials—and even the name, *at tuba*—had come from North Africa and Egypt; early pyramids in Egypt were made of adobe blocks and faced with stone, and buildings in that area are often made of adobe even today.[1]

During the sixteenth century many of the natives in what is now the Southwest were living in multi-story houses, communal-type dwellings that the Spaniards called *pueblos* (as they also named the varied tribes who had settled down and turned to farming instead of hunting and seed-gathering). The homes they lived in, judging by the surviving buildings to be viewed in Mesa Verde, Colorado, and Chaco Canyon, New Mexico, as well as many other Southwestern sites, were made of stone. Such ruins vary in architectural technique, depending upon their ages. These people, whom we consider primitive, learned by doing, often showing considerable skill; the veneer technique found at Chaco Canyon, for instance, uses shaped stones arranged neatly on the outside, with rubble piled within the walls. Other Southwestern tribes built pit houses or free-standing homes with walls or parts of walls made of adobe mud, shaped by hand or even molded with forms of branches and split wood.

In Pueblo building technique, the ceiling of one room supported the floor of the room above—large beams called (by the Spanish) *vigas* had smaller limbs called *latillas,* or even split wood, laid on top and covered with several inches of earth. Beams of large tree branches, five inches or more in diameter, framed the tops of doorways and windows, supporting the rock walls above these openings. In other areas, pit houses were dug into the earth, from a few inches to several feet; then above-ground walls were shaped of mud and allowed to dry. Tree

One of the methods of making roofs is shown here: large peeled logs *(vigas)* support smaller ones *(latillas);* clay tiles complete the job. In a less pretentious form a layer of rushes and another of earth would be laid atop the latillas. Walls have simple adobe plaster, slicked over with a wet tow sack.

branches arched over the structure, and were then covered with smaller branches and, ultimately, a layer of earth. In other areas where there were no stones, grass was set afire and then doused with water, and the resulting mud with grass roots and stems for binder was rolled into balls that were later used in building, using more mud as mortar.[2] These architectural techniques which the New World natives used in pueblos and pit houses were soon joined with Spanish knowledge—essentially the rectangular building block. Indians in Ysleta Pueblo in New Mexico developed a technique called *corte de terrón,* sod cut into blocks about six by eight by twelve inches, allowed to dry thoroughly, and then used to erect homes and outbuildings.[3] Combining Spanish techniques with native skills, the padres used Indian labor to produce a host of missions and churches, as well as family dwellings, in the Southwest.[4]

In 1680 came an upheaval of monumental effect—the revolt by Pueblos of northern New Mexico who resented the padres, feared the supplanting of their own gods, and hated the labor to which the Spanish priests subjected them. Christianized Indians fled with their Spanish leaders, coming to the El Paso del Norte area on the Rio Grande.[5] Construction of houses and places of worship soon followed, utilizing the architectural techniques of northern New Mexico to build missions at Ysleta del Sur (Ysleta of the South, so-called to distinguish it from the New Mexico site) and Socorro, which share the title of oldest missions in Texas. Both missions were constructed combining Pueblo techniques with the molded adobes that had been introduced by the newcomers.

The age-old technique of adobe-making, often handed down even today from one generation to the next through demonstration and hands-on practice, is quite simple. The materials are right at hand: adobe earth, a heavy loam, is mixed sparingly but thoroughly with water; then straw is added to provide binder, helping to hold the bricks together much as reinforcing rods do when imbedded in cement floors and foundations. (The Children of Israel, as punishment from Pharaoh, had to meet their usual quotas of earthen bricks while providing their own straw!)[6] Many a Mexican-American family has built its own home, digging dirt from a hole on the back part of the lot to make adobes to build the house on the front part. The procedure is quite simple, as are the tools: *pico, azadón, y forma* (pick, hoe, and form) are all that is required to transform earth, straw, and water into useful building materials. The forma is like a short section of ladder, about four inches deep, composing two or three box-like areas for shaping the bricks. Earth, dug up with the pick, is mixed with water and chopped with the hoe into a smooth blend, much as a cook cuts shortening into pie dough; then the straw is added and worked in well. Water is added with caution, since too much moisture makes the bricks dry with concave surfaces; too little water, of course, won't allow the mixture to hold together. The combination is then mashed by hand into the form and punched down to make the bricks solid, then slicked off with the hand to make a smooth surface; the mixture is thick enough that the form (inside surfaces slick with water—it is often left in a barrel of water overnight) can be lifted, leaving the moist adobe bricks lying on the ground. There they stay for several days, curing in the sun, and are then turned up on one edge to dry further. Eventually they are stacked edgewise, with air cracks between the blocks, for further drying and baking in the sun until the builder needs them.[7]

The actual building is a simple if back-straining task (the blocks weigh up to sixty pounds each), and again the tools are simple ones: a trowel to handle the mortar, a long string to keep the walls straight, a plumb bob made of a string and a weight (in the absence of a spirit level) for vertical alignment, and the folk builder is in business. Corners are the key to a good house, I have been told, as a weekend architect/laborer/contractor all in one spent what seemed like an enormous amount of time squaring the corner blocks just so. Then, with the strings stretched to keep the wall lined up, the builder dumped a dollop of mortar on the adobes that had been laid previously and spread it out, another block was put on top and aligned, another dollop of mortar, and on and on. The blocks between the corners could be put on with less skill, and for them the man's teenaged son did the work. Frequently the boy learns from the father, who in turn learned from his father—a true process of folk transmission of skills.[8]

Today adobe building blocks are generally about four inches thick, eight to ten

Don Epifanio (he was born on Epiphany, January 6) chops up earth and mixes water in to make *mezcla,* the beginning of adobe bricks. The pile of leaves behind him will be mixed in to provide a binder, since straw is not available.

With his *azadón,* a hoe made out of an old shovel, the worker fills the form that will shape two adobe bricks like those drying on his right. Those in the foreground are becoming paler as they dry.

Don Epifanio uses man's oldest tool—his hand—to press the mud in the form and smooth it out.

The mix was too wet, and the form too dry, so this pair of adobes will be rough and irregular, but mud mortar will be used to smooth it all out.

The adobes in the foreground, stacked *(trinchados)* loosely so air can circulate and dry them, await use in the building behind and to the right. At the rear center is a truckload of dirt to make more adobe bricks.

inches wide, and eighteen or so inches long, although the folk practitioner usually makes his own form to suit himself and in earlier times blocks were often much bigger. They are used with mortar, just as oven-baked bricks are, but folk construction may use lime or cement mortar, or even *zoquete* (adobe mud) to hold them together. After several months of drying for the walls and mortar, the outside is plastered—again with either lime or mud plaster—then smoothed and even painted or whitewashed, both for looks and for protection from the elements. Thousands of buildings in the Southwest have employed these folk techniques from centuries past—homes, especially. Adobe is economical to use, is easy to build with and maintain, and provides excellent insulation against the elements.

Maintenance is necessary, however, if adobe is to endure. Paul Horgan, in his monumental work *Great River,* reports that Spanish padres, with Pueblo converts to do the actual work, would apply fresh mud plaster to mission walls in the spring, using a wet sheepskin—wool side to the wall—to smooth the plaster.[9] Without this care, even the sparse rain of the arid Southwest could wear away the adobe walls in time, although there are existing ruins known to be over two centuries old that still stand, in fairly good repair. Attention to the roof is also vital, since when the roof is gone, or even leaking, the walls are in grave danger. Folk

This building, still in use in Juárez, Chihuahua, is well over a century old. The former doorway, right, has been walled up with adobe. The base of both walls shows the eating away caused by moisture in the soil, carried upward by capillary action. On the left wall, a rough stone foundation did not stop the process.

builders, pragmatic always, have learned that the old techniques can be improved upon. The layer of earth atop the roof of a building has strips of wood laid on top, and then roofing paper is tacked on and tarred down. This is a common practice, making use of both the insulating qualities of the layer of earth and the sealing ability of the tarpaper. If the tarpaper develops leaks, of course, the earth becomes soaked and heavy, adding to the burden of weight supported by the vigas beneath. Before the advent of tarpaper the top of the layer of earth was wet and slicked over to increase its resistance to rainfall; the slope the roof might have was very gradual, achieved by making the higher end of the roof only one adobe thickness above the lower end, to provide for slow runoff and reduce erosion of the roof material—but immediate attention was needed after even a one-inch rain.

A rampaging river in flood can also damage adobe buildings; for example, the Rio Grande washed away the original mission building at Socorro, Texas, in 1740 and again in 1829.[10] Archaeological explorations by crews from the University of Texas at El Paso reveal fascinating clues to the past, including the fact that the adobe blocks used there were huge—four to five feet long and half as wide, making the mission walls eight feet thick, and turning the church building into a veritable fortress, as well as one well-insulated from the elements.[11]

A good roof for an adobe structure is essential, since water leaking into the building or running down the walls can rapidly eat away the adobe. Another source of deterioration is ground water, through capillary action. Just as a cube of sugar placed on a drop of moisture will absorb the wetness and crumble from the bottom up, so does adobe melt away if a good foundation doesn't separate the adobe blocks from moist ground. Many an otherwise sound wall has crumbled away when standing water from a heavy rain or poor drainage has attacked it.[12] Foundations of field stone or of concrete are used to reduce the danger of dampness beneath the walls. With the coming of progress, doorways and windows in adobe houses are now capped with dressed lumber or even structural steel, and dressed lumber beams and rafters have long since replaced the old round vigas in new construction, except when a luxury home is being built with exposed beams. And with the recent concern for saving energy, solar adobe homes have been built throughout much of the Southwest, combining the oldest architecture in the area with the most modern techniques and concepts.[13]

Another asset of building with adobe is its flexibility. If a doorway isn't needed, it can easily be filled up from the bottom, making a window or even an unbroken wall; a new opening can be cut easily; and such modern items as another electrical outlet or space for new plumbing can easily be provided for by punching a hole through an adobe wall. And if there is damage to a wall, a little zoquete soon fills the crack or hole, and a bit of plaster conceals the former blemish. All this and comfort too!

Proportions and orientation of Mexican-American folk housing seem to be free of limitations, other than the length of available logs for vigas or rafters, and the tradition that the outside door never faces the west—probably to keep the evening sun from overheating the dwelling.[14] I have often heard it said that a Mexican home is never finished; as the family grows, more rooms are added (after all, it's just a matter of making a few more adobe bricks) and in many places a long house one room wide is very nearly the standard. Some families, of course, favor the patio—an enclosed combination yard/utility/relaxation area onto which the rooms of the house all open. This style of structure, quite common in Mexico and widely imitated in the Southwest, promotes privacy, since there are usually no windows opening to the outside, and only the central door to the patio faces the street or road. Far from the stylized patio of the luxury home, the Mexican patio is not a decorative enclosed porch, but an extension of the living area.

Windows and doors, particularly in rural areas and in poorer neighborhoods, are custom-made by the local *carpintero* to fit the openings the adobe mason left in the wall, no two exactly alike. Windows are frequently painted turquoise blue, reportedly to keep out evil spirits. Roofs are of two main varieties: essentially flat with a parapet all around, and drainspouts, usually of clay, to carry rainwater away from the walls;[15] and the slightly sloped roof with no parapet. In the El Paso area,

This patio wall (some 75 years old) had four more doors in it, back when it was the exterior of a row of small apartments. The doors have been filled in with adobe—often of very poor, rocky quality—and the top of the wall strengthened and protected by a concrete ledge. Note leaching action that has eaten away the adobe at the base of the wall.

especially since the coming of tarpaper, there is a third kind, with parapet on three sides and a slight slope to the rear. The layer of earth on the roof is largely a matter of history with all three varieties. Joe Graham notes that in much of West Texas, the upwardly mobile Mexican-American is building with cement blocks, despite their lack of adobe's insulating qualities, and gable roofs are sometimes replacing the flat variety.[16]

One curiosity remains—to live in an adobe home, for many Mexican-Americans, has become a symbol of low status.[17] Brick veneer often disguises a more humble dwelling of adobe, just as log cabins in the wooded areas of the United States have been covered with planed lumber to conceal their rustic strength—while the rich and sophisticated build log cabins and adobe ranch-style houses to live in or use as weekend retreats!

The Jacal

While the adobe house is still quite common throughout the arid Southwest, in areas with greater annual rainfall, like South Texas, a folk structure called a *jacal* (originally, hut or shack) was still being used earlier in this century for human habitation as well as farm sheds and shelters for livestock. This type of building came into South Texas with the first non-Indian settlers about 1749; its origin is debated, with the style being called the Spanish version of the log cabin by some, but others cite similarities to the huts of rural Mayans in Mexico that suggest the latter was the more likely source.[18]

The jacal was traditionally built of four forked tree trunks set in the ground to form the four corners of the building. Logs placed in the forks provided the two main roof supports, with smaller limbs or branches laid crossways to the beams supporting the roof. Walls were made of smaller straight sticks, such as ocotillo cactus stalks, daubed with a straw/adobe covering; sometimes walls were formed of a mixture of adobe and rocks—some even with the front exterior white-washed. The roof was made of sticks, thatched or covered with leaves.[19] As with adobe housing built farther west, the materials used were cheap and readily available—although the adobe house's roof held out the rain better; the jacal always leaked.

Some jacales had gabled roofs (requiring two additional forked tree trunks, to support the ridge pole), and one or two windows; the door was usually on the side of the house, and windows or doors were placed on the west side of the house only when that side faced a road or street. As with the adobe structures, the length of available materials was the chief limit on size, with few jacales being longer than thirty feet or wider than ten or twelve; most were smaller, and if there was a pitched roof to allow for rain runoff, the house was reduced to eight or ten feet in width. The side door, under a low overhanging roof, was not a problem for the relatively short people who lived there—although sometimes materials available made the wall so low that a gable-end door was necessary.[20]

As dressed lumber, shingled or tin-covered roofs, and other modernities have become common, a negative social value has been attached to the jacal, and "a cheap wooden building [or] a brick structure in any state of repair is better to the old citizen of the area than a well kept jacal. . . ."[21]

Few jacales still exist in South Texas, and those are in need of preservation, to serve at least as examples of an interesting folk response to the need for housing with limited materials. Conversely, examples of the wide variety of folk architecture using adobe are everywhere in the Southwest, not just as museum pieces but currently used homes, cafes, business establishments, and the like. A brick front or a non-adobe addition may conceal the nature of the original, but adobe folk architecture is alive and well in the Spanish Southwest.

CHAPTER THIRTEEN

Folk Foods

MENTION MEXICAN FOOD to any American and the response will almost certainly include the words "hot," "chile," "tamales," or "tacos." Numerous brands of tamales wrapped in plastic or waxed paper are for sale in cans or quick-frozen —Austex, Wolf Brand, Gebhardt, etc.—as well as the products of less familiar brands and small local firms, especially in the Southwest. But as a radio commercial used to proclaim back in the '50s, "Some tamales are hot, some tamales are not so hot. . . ." I have heard Texans argue about whether *chile con carne* (chile with meat) should have beans in it or not—and some firms can both varieties, to cover all bets. New Mexicans often use cubes of pork in chile con carne, rather than ground meat, and many Southwesterners even argue over whether the word is *chile* or *chili.* Given this division of opinion on such basic matters, it is perhaps needless to point out that the techniques of food preparation described here frequently differ from region to region—and even from family to family.

There's an old Mexican saying I have often heard that, translated, says, "The hundred-percent Mexican lives on corn, rice, beans, and chile." And despite the Anglo influences on the Mexican-American, that saying is not far from the truth for people living north of the border. Time was when the Hispanic family, on either side of the boundary, had a little patch of corn and one of beans, with a few chile and squash plants added for good measure. Barring a crop failure, the family ate and was satisfied—with the combination of corn, *frijole* beans, and squash, through an interchange of amino acids, providing a diet that did not require proteins from meat.[1] And one El Paso dentist swears that the lime used in preparation of Mexican corn foods helps reduce tooth decay![2]

Corn—*maíz* in Spanish—provides the basic food for millions of people. It is a New World food; Aztec, Mayan, and other myths tell varying accounts of how it came to be a food for humans, and virtually every historical record of Spanish colonial times emphasizes the importance of maize to the native cultures of what is now Latin America. Even the words associated with corn in the Spanish borderlands are mostly native American in origin—*tamal* and *comal* (a flat rimless frying pan) are Mexican; *pozole* (softened grains of corn, much like hominy), *pinole* (ground, sweetened toasted corn), and *elote* (from *xilote,* ear of corn) are Nahuatl; *maíz* is Caribe. *Masa* and *tortilla* (from *torta*), however, are Latin in derivation.[3] Traditional stories and the words associated with corn attest to the antiquity of the use of the sacred corn, dating back some 6,000 years. Centeotl was the god in charge of growing things, especially corn;[4] and one of the Mexican gods took the form of an ant and stole grains of corn from the other gods for mankind, much as Prometheus stole fire in the Greek myths.[5]

Corn Foods

The starting point for almost all Mexican-American corn foods is the soaking of shelled dry corn in lime water. A tablespoon or so of unslaked lime added to a gallon of corn, in enough water to cover it all, will soften the husk of the kernel and swell each grain to nearly double its original size. The corn can be soaked overnight, or the mixture can be cooked for thirty minutes. A simple test —mashing the thumbnail into a grain or two—will tell if it is ready for the next step. The softened corn (now called *nixtamal*) is rinsed—usually through three changes of water, and it can then be cooked as pozole with spices and *menudo* (cut-up beef intestines), making a tasty dish that is also a traditional remedy for a hangover. In New Mexico, pork roast, cut into tiny cubes, takes the place of the tripe—although the dish is still called menudo.[6]

Usually, however, the nixtamal is ready to be ground up for other uses. The traditional method of preparation is with a home grinder—a *metate* (a concave grinding stone) and a *mano* (a hand-held piece of stone), both usually made of volcanic rock—that produces *masa,* the ground-up product. One gallon of swollen corn takes about an hour of grinding and regrinding to achieve the degree of fineness needed for making masa to prepare tortillas, *gorditas,* or tamales—and it is hard, tiring work. No wonder that these days most families go to the *molino* (mill) for their masa, specifying *masa para tamales* (masa for tamales) or *masa para tortillas,* which is more finely ground.

Tortillas—pancake-like, but much thinner, about six inches in diameter—can be patted out by hand or mashed in a tortilla press, then toasted lightly on a comal. The uses to which a tortilla may be put are almost endless: A tortilla, especially when it is hot from the *tortillería* (tortilla factory) or the comal, is often salted and/or buttered and eaten as bread. A tortilla may be used as a scoop, to dip up frijoles, in which case the scoop and the beans are eaten together. Many a tale is told of the rich person bragging of his silver tableware or other refinements, to which the poor peon replies proudly that his family is so rich that they use a spoon only one time!

The condiment *salsa casera* (household sauce), made of raw chopped onion, tomato, and chile, is key to the enjoyment of tortillas in their various forms. The more sophisticated variety of salsa found in restaurants has chopped fresh *cilantro* (coriander) added and is often called *pico de gallo* (rooster beak). Another type of salsa contains the same ingredients but cooked and puréed. The degree of "hot" comes from the kind of chile used. Long green chiles are mildest; *jalapeños* are hotter; *güeritos* (little blonde ones) are hotter still; and *chilipi-*

quines require a fire extinguisher on standby. Contrary to some people's automatic response, drinking water to put out a chile fire is not productive of relief; eating a pat of butter or drinking milk is much more helpful.[7]

To make a taco, a tortilla is placed in a frying pan with a little oil to crisp it; then drained; a rounded tablespoon of cooked ground beef or shredded chicken is put on the tortilla, which is then folded over the filling and turned over to cook a bit on the other side. Removed to a paper towel to drain, the taco has shredded lettuce, cut-up tomato, grated cheese, and usually salsa added—making a tasty sandwich. Or the tortilla can be crisped, flat, in hot grease and spread with mashed cooked beans—a launching platform for ground or shredded cooked beef or chicken, cheese, salsa, and whatever the heart desires; this phenomenon is called a *tostada,* a *tapatia,* a *chalupa,* or several other names, depending on the region. If the tortilla is quartered and treated the same way, or baked with grated cheese and strips of green chile on top, it becomes a *nacho.* And restaurants large and small, throughout the Southwest, almost invariably treat the customer to a basket of crisply fried quarters of tortilla (also called tostadas) and a bowl of salsa to dip them in, for munching while waiting to be served.

Quesadillas are a sort of cheese sandwich toasted on a comal; they are made of two tortillas with a layer of melted cheese between, using *Menonita* (Mennonite, a white cheese like Monterey Jack), or even *asadero* (a delightful cheese made by a folk process, to be described later). A *flauta* ("flute-shaped") can be made by rolling a warmed tortilla with shredded cooked beef or chicken inside, and cooking it in hot grease until crisp; then the flauta is eaten plain, or used to scoop up sour cream or *guacamole* (mashed avocado, usually spiced). Slightly older tortillas are still good for cutting into one-inch squares and scrambling into breakfast eggs—*huevos con tortillitas*—with the inevitable salsa. And there's even tortilla soup!

Another basic use of the tortilla is for *enchiladas* (roughly, "chilied"). The traditional ones are made of tortillas softened in hot grease, and dipped into a mixture of dried red chile that has first been boiled and drained, then put through a blender and a strainer or colander to remove skins and seeds. The enchilada may be either sprinkled with grated cheese and baked, or rolled up with cheese and chopped onions inside, then sprinkled with cheese and baked. A stack of flat enchiladas is often served with an over-easy egg on top, especially in New Mexico. Less traditional are the rolled enchiladas made with ground beef or shredded chicken; some people seem to deny their existence, but variety is the spice of life. Anglos are particularly positive in their support of the meat enchilada, but meat is not that regular an item of diet for the poorer Mexican-American, and of course the cheese enchilada is approved eating for Catholics during Lent, while the meat one is less acceptable.[8]

The ground masa that produces the tortilla can also be patted into a fatter but smaller patty—about three inches across—called a *gordita* (little fat one), which is toasted on both sides on a comal, split open, and stuffed with the same variety of ingredients as the taco. The thickness of the masa produces a distinct flavor; food booths at fiestas, church bazaars, and school carnivals usually feature gorditas, although they are also eaten at home. Street vendors on the right bank of the Rio Grande sell *elotes*—young fresh ears of corn, boiled and provided with a stick handle; the delicacy—which serves the shopper as lunch, and keeps the kids occupied—is also found in the United States, particularly at the same special events where gorditas are available.[9]

For the sake of convenience—and for those people with a taste for Mexican food but living far from the sources of supply—commercially manufactured dry masa is available and is quite popular with many people, much as ready-mixed pancake flour has generally taken over the "scratch" production of hotcakes. A small amount of water is added to the dry cornmeal/masa, and the whole is mixed and kneaded into the right consistency. Then tortillas can be pressed or patted out of the mixture, and gorditas are quite easily made on short notice.[10]

A point needs to be made concerning the meat used in making tacos: while many people sauté hamburger meat to stuff taco shells (another commercial horror that is generally too brittle to fill and eat neatly), good traditional taco meat, with tiny diced pieces of boiled potato added as both a meat-stretcher and to help the meat hold together, is boiled in as little liquid (tomatoes, an onion, a clove of garlic, puréed together) as possible; and then cooked nearly dry.[11]

The *tamal,* one of the well-known Mexican-American foods that have been adopted by Anglos throughout the United States, is also made from ground-up masa. The process is time-consuming, and associated with varied traditions—among them, the taboo against anyone's leaving or entering the house while tamales are being prepared, lest the tamales "chill" and not cook properly, and subsequently not come free of the corn shuck they are wrapped in. (In most families, tamales were made only at Christmastime, when the weather is often cold or unpredictable.) Techniques and recipes vary for making tamales, but the method that follows, which I am most familiar with, seems to be fairly typical.

Once the masa is ground to the proper consistency (or brought from the local molino), it has lard creamed into it, as well as the liquid in which the pork (for meat, or "hot" tamales) has been boiled; much arm-power is involved in the creaming, and no electric mixer my family has tried will do the job right. (Of course, there are heavy-duty industrial mixers, such as the kind used in restaurants, that are available.) Then salt and baking powder are added. When the creaming has reached the right point, a small glob of the fluffy mixture will float in a glass of cold water. Meanwhile, three varieties of dry red chile have been cooked, put through a blender, and strained. Broken-up pieces of cooked pork are immersed in this liquid. (The cooked chile can also be ground with mano and metate and then strained—but there's enough work involved without that traditional refinement.)

All night long the *hojas* (corn shucks) have been soaking in a *tina* (washtub), getting ready for their vital part in the action. Rinsed and flattened out, a broad

A standard Mexican-American breakfast in preparation: tortillas, cut into small squares, will be scrambled with the eggs and crumbled bits of *chorizo*—spicy Mexican sausage—to make *huevos con tortillitas y chorizo.*

A rolled enchilada, border style, is made by rolling a tortilla in chile sauce and filling it with grated cheese and chopped onion, then baking it with more cheese sprinkled on top. The Jurado Restaurant in El Paso prepares both the border variety of rolled enchiladas and the flat kind. Both meat and cheese enchiladas are served, although the cheese variety is more traditional.

shuck is held in the palm of one hand while a rounded tablespoon or so of the masa mixture is spread out evenly over most of the hoja; then a smaller scoop of the chile and pork mixture is deposited in the center of the masa and the shuck is rolled up longways, leaving an empty "tail" at one end of the filled shuck, which is somewhat fatter than a man's thumb. The *tamalera* (usually a canning pot, with the rack in place at the bottom) is ready, with an inverted bowl and a pad of shucks at the center of the bottom, onto which one end of the tamal is paced, with the tail extending either toward the outside of the pot or the center. More tamales are made and deposited, like spokes in a wheel, layer upon layer, until the pot is full. Then a double blanket of hojas is spread over the top of the piles of tamales, a quart or so of boiling water is poured in, around the sides of the pot, the cover is put on, and the loaded pot is ready to cook. When the water comes to a boil again, the fire is turned down to a simmer.

After an hour of steaming, the tamales should be ready—and a taste-test is the only way to check. Off comes the top, then the blanket of shucks, and one of the handy tails is pulled out for the test. The tamal is unwrapped, and if it comes free of the hoja, the prognosis is excellent. Then the tasting—and the rolling of eyes, and the pronouncement that these are the best tamales ever made—make it plain that the hours of work have not been in vain!

But the kitchen crew doesn't just sit around reading slim French novels and eating bonbons while the steaming goes on. My family likes sweet tamales too, so more work is under way. The traditional recipe calls for raisins, chopped pecans, cinnamon, sugar, and lime juice to be added to the masa mixture reserved for that purpose. A rounded tablespoonful of the mixture is placed on the center of the shuck, which is rolled up and ready for steaming just as the meat ones were. Because my German father-in-law didn't think sweet tamales prepared the traditional way were too exciting, years ago my mother-in-law began to experiment: she adds fruitcake fruit, bits of candied watermelon rind, and whatever suits her palate to the traditional recipe—and the result is much like fruitcake. It is so rich that one is usually enough, especially after the consumer is stuffed with all the "just one more hot tamal" offerings the hostess has provided. I'll have to admit that some of my Mexican-American students think Madrecita's recipe goes too far—but then I've never served them her sweet tamales, so that judgment can be disallowed. And after all, folklore—and folk recipes—exist in variety. Deep down in Mexico, tamales are often wrapped in banana leaves, for example. And chicken tamales, cheese tamales, and green chile tamales all also exist.

Some uses of corn do not require the grinding of masa. Elotes, which were mentioned earlier, are simply boiled in salted water and buttered. *Chacales,* made of parched, cracked corn that would break the teeth if one munched on it, are cooked with tomatoes, onions, and garlic, to make a traditional dish served during Lent. Pinole is corn toasted and finely ground, but not usually on a metate. *Atole* (a thin watery masa drink) and *champurrado* (a chocolate-flavored beverage sweetened with *piloncillo,* an unrefined brown sugar) can be made from dry commercial masa, although a purist would use the home-ground variety.

Masa de trigo (wheat) can be used to make flour tortillas, usually larger by a couple of inches than those made of corn; warmed on a comal, they can be eaten as bread with the beans, rice, and other items served at a Mexican-American meal. One of the most popular uses for the flour tortilla is to make burritos ("little donkeys"!) by wrapping a warmed flour tortilla around beans, shredded beef or chicken, guacamole, or a combination of ingredients. Burritos are often carried in lunches to work or school, and are for sale from California to South Texas in school cafeterias, restaurants, and rolling lunch wagons that serve factory workers and other working folks; little plastic containers of salsa are a required supplement for the burrito when it is eaten away from home.

Meat Dishes

A current Mexican-American food craze is *fajitas,* strips of marinated skirt steak sautéed with onions (sometimes right at the table in a fancy restaurant, and frequently served in the skillet they are cooked in). The strips of meat are served with flour tortillas for burritos assembled at the table; strips of chicken, sautéed with onions and tomatoes, are also available in many restaurants. The folk have picked up on both kinds of fajitas—another case where a folk food becomes accepted by the elite, and then re-introduced to the folk.[12]

The "skirt" or "belt" of meat comes from the diaphragm muscle that holds in a beef animal's heart and lungs. In early days in Texas, ranch workers were paid in part with the beef skirts and other throwaway parts after a butchering. When a full day of slaughtering was scheduled, workers would gather mesquite wood and start a fire. After tenderizing the meat by beating it on stones, and marinating it with lime juice when it was available, the men placed the belt muscle directly on the mesquite coals after the fire burned down, the coals giving a distinctive flavor to the meat. Cut across the grain for tenderness, the meat was sprinkled with salsa and wrapped in a tortilla.[13]

Back in the 1930s along the border, skirt steak was considered leftover meat, and it sold for a dime a pound. Many a school lunchbox in South Texas in those days had a burrito in it made of this "lowly" meat. Apparently someone from outside the area "discovered" the dish and made a big to-do about it, and its current popularity has driven the price of the meat up to $2.79 a pound, with fancy restaurants charging from $5 to $15 a plate.[14]

In El Paso, where a fajita cookoff was held in September 1984 to benefit the local Lighthouse for the Blind,[15] a restaurant hostess expressed her opinion that fajitas were a Tex-Mex food, not Mexican, since she had never heard of them in her travels in Mexico.[16] Hers is a view borne out by the absence of the dish from the menu of a very popular Mexican food restaurant in Reynosa, across the river from McAllen, Texas.[17] Julio's Corona Restaurant, among the most popular of

Juárez eating places with Anglos and Mexicans alike, now serves fajitas daily—but the item is stamped onto the menu, not printed there, suggesting the newness of the dish in Juárez. UT El Paso folklore student Tisha Workman, noting that it had taken fifty years for this folk food to catch the public fancy, wondered if the dish would still be popular—or even eaten—fifty years hence.[18]

A standard meat dish in the Southwest is *caldillo* (stew), which is made of cut-up pieces of beef and potatoes like the stews of other culture groups, but containing spices that make the dish memorable: *mejorana* (sweet marjoram), garlic, cilantro, onions, and tomatoes. Very similar is *picadillo,* made with the same flavorings, but with the addition of green beans, peas and carrots, and meat that is ground rather than diced, with plenty of juice. *Albóndigas* (meatballs), formed with ground meat and some sort of binder—rice or diced potatoes usually—are cooked and served with the same spices, vegetables, and sauce.[19]

In Richard Bradford's novel *Red Sky at Morning,* Alabama-born Joshua Arnold is transplanted to a small town in New Mexico, Corazón Sagrado (Sacred Heart), where he learns to enjoy the native foods in all their rich variety; his favorite was *carnitas:*

> The little cubes of pork had been baking all morning, and each time I bit into one my eyelids got heavy, as though someone were rubbing warm butter on them. It should be against the law to do anything to a pig but chop him up into cubes for carnitas. No ham, no spareribs, no pork chops, no bacon.[20]

Since Bradford had himself moved from the Deep South to northern New Mexico, perhaps he was expressing through Josh his own reaction to a dish popular among Mexican-Americans.[21] Certainly there are a number of carnitas-lovers around. The dish is usually prepared by parboiling cubes of pork until tender, then roasting them until they are a golden brown.[22] Another method of preparing them, common in the Big Bend area of Texas, is to take thin slices of pork, rolling them in flour and then frying them crisp in lard.[23] Pork skins and fatty pieces of the freshly slaughtered pig are rendered in a big pot, the residual pieces left after the lard is removed being a delicacy called *chicharrones* (cracklings); in northern New Mexico they come in two varieties: *chicharrones de vieja* (roughly, old-style cracklings, served as they come from the rendering pot), and chicharrones that, after having as much of the lard removed as possible, are browned in cream and salt, and eaten with fresh tomatoes, green chile and other spices, and hot tortillas.[24] Graham points out that with increasing urbanization, fewer Mexican-Americans know the luxury of chicharrones and other foods—such as *morcilla* (blood sausage)—associated with the *matanza* (slaughtering) of pigs.[25]

Goats are easily raised in rural areas of the Southwest, Joe Graham points out,

> because of their foraging habits—they'll eat almost anything. As is still

A toothsome delicacy, chicken tacos, awaits a hungry diner. Shredded chicken is folded into the tortilla and fried in hot oil, then stuffed with lettuce, tomato, and shredded cheese. The can of Tecate, a Mexican beer, has segments of lime on top; the traditional way to drink it is with salt and lime juice, like the more potent *margarita,* made of tequila.

> the case along the border, . . . one of the children in a family is given the assignment to take the flock of goats out into the pasture and bring them in at night, often staying the day with them, guarding them.

A favorite method of preparation is barbecuing, traditionally done *en el pozo* (in a pit), a method inherited from the Aztecs. When roasted in an oven it is called *cabrito al horno.*[26] The occasion for such a barbecue, the product of which is called *cabrito* (little goat), lends itself to neighborhood gathering in my experience. But here, too, urbanization has taken its toll of a folk practice.

A meat eaten in many Mexican-American homes is *lengua* (beef tongue), prepared in several different ways. As a salad, it is served chopped, with minced jalapeño chiles, diced tomatoes, chopped celery and hard-boiled eggs, a variety of spices, and ringlets of onion. Tongue can be made into a stew, with onions, potatoes, carrots, several spices, and the usual chile. Shredded, tongue can be served in *mole,* a rich chocolate and chile sauce.[27] Boiled, sliced, and sautéed with tomato sauce and onion rings, it produces *lengua en salsa de tomate.*[28]

Vegetable Dishes

No discussion of Mexican-American folk foods would be complete without mention of frijoles or *pinto* (spotted) beans, just as no meal is considered complete without at least one dish made of beans. Because of the method used in gathering the beans, they come out of the sack with small rocks and clods of dirt; bushes on which they grow are pulled up and threshed, over a blanket or canvas on the ground, which is then emptied into sacks or large containers—along with whatever else falls onto the threshing "floor." Before the beans can be washed and cooked, these tooth-breakers need to be removed. To "pick" the beans, a handful is poured onto a table or kitchen countertop, and spread out so the foreign objects can be seen and removed; then the beans are raked into the *olla* (clay pot) in which they will be cooked. Two or three rinsing waters are used to remove twigs and stems, beans that float, and any that look wrong. Then the beans are put on to cook, usually with several cloves of garlic and an onion—but no salt. Experienced cooks say that adding salt too soon makes the beans tough.

Any number of additives—garlic, baking soda, ginger—are believed in by those who hope to reduce the production of intestinal gas, while some start the beans by soaking them overnight, and discarding the water before filling up the olla for cooking. Some start the beans in cold water, some in hot—each cook believing that his/her method is the best, because that's the way Mamá did it. Once brought to a boil, the beans are allowed to simmer for several hours, with a kettle of near-boiling water handy to add as water is cooked away (adding cold water is believed to chill the beans, and it certainly slows down the cooking). As the beans near doneness they are tasted, and at that point salt is added—but no more water, allowing the liquid to thicken somewhat. As beans are reheated for the next few meals, the liquid becomes even thicker.[29]

Cooked beans can be served in many ways: *graneados* or *enteros* are whole beans, eaten by themselves or with salsa added, eaten either with a spoon or with a folded tortilla as described earlier; whole beans can be added to a mixture of cooked diced or ground meat, onion, and chile to make chile con carne; beans can be mashed to a pulp, with a generous amount of juice, to make a side dish *(frijoles machacados),* or the mixture can be heated in a *sartén* (frying pan) to make *refritos* (refried beans, although they haven't been fried but once). Grated cheese on top of the whole beans makes them into *frijoles con queso; frijoles con chorizo* have added crumbled bits of Mexican sausage, quite spicy; some daring bean-eaters even add cottage cheese for a special tang; the variations are almost endless.[30]

Calabacitas—little squashes, usually zucchini—provide a number of dishes on the Mexican-American table:

> Boiled or steamed and served with butter, it is called *calabaza* (or *calabaza cocida).* With fresh asaderos added, it is known as *asaderos*

> *con calabaza.* Perhaps the favorite squash dish is *calabacita,* or squash boiled, chopped, and fried with onions, tomatoes, and cheese (preferably asadero). When cooked with meat to make sort of a stew, it is called *calabacita con carne.*[31]

Squashes can be stuffed with ground meat or cheese, covered with egg and flour batter, and fried,[32] much like chiles rellenos, our next topic.

Chiles, while forming the base for many kinds of salsa, are often a main or side dish on their own. Making chiles rellenos (stuffed chiles) involves roasting or frying long green chiles briefly, then wrapping them in cold cloth, to loosen the skins for removal. Then the chile is split longways and the seeds and veins inside are removed, and a long strip of cheese is inserted—Monterey Jack, asadero, or cheddar will do. The stuffed chile is rolled in flour and dipped in a stiffly beaten egg, and the whole is fried on both sides in a little oil.[33] Served hot, it can be cut up and eaten; it can be wrapped in a flour tortilla to make a burrito, or eaten with a tomato-onion puréed sauce over it. By holding the stem like a handle, one can nibble on it like a hot *paleta* (a frozen sweet on a stick), but the taste effect is quite different. Most folks say the seeds are what is hot; others say it's the veins. In my experience, eating chiles rellenos is a bit like playing Russian Roulette. Some samples look innocent but are really hot as . . . chile!

Chile con queso (chile with cheese) is a frequent appetizer. It is served in a watery form in restaurants for dipping with tostadas, or making burritos at the table. As a party dip it keeps the guests occupied so the hostess/cook can tend to business in the kitchen; it usually has more cheese and less chile than the restaurant variety, and sturdy potato chips or tostadas dip it up beautifully.

One dish, *carne abobada,* is difficult to categorize; while it is made with meat—two and a half pounds of pork roast, thinly sliced—it requires, according to one recipe, twenty red chile pods. They are cooked, put through a blender, and poured over the meat to marinate for twelve hours, and then the dish is baked.[34]

Sopas are side dishes that accompany many a Mexican-American meal. The word is defined as soup, but there are many sopa dishes that are pasta: *sopa de fideo* has as its base a thin vermicelli, sautéed and usually flavored with tomato sauce and onion. With browned ground meat added, it becomes sopa de fideo con carne, an entree rather than a side dish.[35] *Sopa de arroz* (rice), often called Spanish rice, starts with washed rice sautéed in a cast-iron skillet, constantly being stirred, with very little oil. The sautéeing makes the rice pop, somewhat as popcorn does, and the resulting dish is quite a bit fluffier than if the rice were just boiled. Whole tomatoes are plunged into boiling water to cause the skins to slip off; then the tomatoes, along with chopped onion, and often chicken broth as well, are added to the rice (and sometimes a few peas or chopped carrots) and simmered until done. Traditional cooks do not add chile, but restaurants along the border usually do.[36]

Eggs—besides the huevos con tortillitas already mentioned—are served in several distinctive Mexican-American ways. *Huevos rancheros* (ranch-style eggs) are great waker-uppers: a couple of over-easy eggs are at the heart of things, but they are served on top of a pair of tortillas, softened by warming in a little hot grease, and covered with a lively mixture of salsa that has simmered until it thickens.[37] Eggs are often scrambled with diced left-over boiled potato *(huevos con papa),* usually with a bit of salsa; *huevos con chorizo* are scrambled with fried crumbs of Mexican sausage—but no salsa is needed! Both dishes can be made into burritos by wrapping them in a warmed flour tortilla.[38] *Torta de huevo* is essentially an omelette, but with chopped onion, tomato, and jalapeño peppers added to the cheese, milk, and eggs to make an unusual taste sensation.[39] The Spanish omelette sometimes served for breakfast in non-Mexican restaurants is pale, mild, and colorless beside the true article.

Foods for Special Days

Mexican-Americans have a wide assortment of dishes they use to enliven the limited diet of *Cuaresma* (the Lenten season). Current custom is that during Lent only one large meal is eaten daily, and no meat at all is eaten on Fridays, but the more traditional Mexican-American avoids eating meat for the entire forty days, and usually gives up something dear—like a food or activity—as well.[40] *Torta de camarón* is one quite popular Lenten dish. Peeled shrimp are ground up and added to bread crumbs and beaten eggs to form patties, which are fried in hot lard. Then over them is poured a sauce made of toasted, deveined long green chiles and tomatoes cooked together, with boiled potatoes cut in quarters added into the sauce after it has thickened.[41]

Other torta patties are eaten during Lent as well: tortas de papas are made of boiled, mashed potatoes dipped in beaten egg batter and sprinkled with cheese, then fried.[42] Cooked garbanzo beans are mixed with orange juice, sugar, and beaten eggs, poured over bread crumbs in a greased dish, and baked until a toothpick stuck into it comes out dry. The result is something like a pudding.[43]

A similar pudding is the very traditional and popular Lenten dessert *capirotada,* made of French bread and *piloncillo* (a relatively unrefined brown sugar, loaded with molasses taste, which is sold in cones). The following recipe has been in the same family for three generations:

1 loaf of dry French bread
2 cones of piloncillo
1 stick of cinnamon
3 cloves
4 cups water
½ lb. white Mennonite cheese (sliced)
raisins and peanuts to taste

The piloncillo is cooked over a low flame until it melts, and the water and the cinnamon stick are added. The bread is sliced in one-inch thicknesses, and alternating layers of cheese and bread, raisins and peanuts, are put in a baking dish; then the piloncillo mixture is poured over the layers and the dish is baked until the capirotada dries out.[44]

Lent finds heavy consumption of cooked lentils, a wide variety of fish, and shrimp (which is sometimes added to sopa de arroz for the Lenten season). But the Christmas season is the time when special foods are enjoyed by all concerned.

Buñuelos are plate-sized sweet flour tortillas, deep-fried and sprinkled with cinnamon and sugar—and eaten eagerly. My wife recalls that when she was a child, the buñuelo maker would take a piece of dough about the size of an egg and roll it out to a diameter of about six inches; then she would place a muslin cuptowel over a bent knee, and stretch the dough over the knee, larger and larger, making the center of the buñuelo as thin as possible. Smaller versions are made with soupier batter and a different way of forming the treat; a hot iron mold with a long handle is dipped into the chilled batter, then held steady in hot lard until the *buñuelo de molde* browns. Pried off and left to drain, it is sprinkled with sugar and cinnamon like the bigger ones.[45]

Bizcochos are cookies associated with the Christmas season. Traditionally they are a mixture of flour, wine, anise, and cloves; rolled out and cut into a variety of shapes—circles, diamonds, and triangles especially—they are bite-sized, so one can be put entirely into the mouth, leaving no crumbs. Sprinkled with cinnamon and sugar, they are often served at Christmas Eve parties with hot chocolate, made the Mexican way.[46] The cook starts with solid bars of chocolate in whatever flavor is preferred—vanilla, almond, bitter, semi-sweet, or sweet. The bar is grated and the chocolate is melted in milk. Traditionally it is mixed with a *molinillo* (a wooden mixing tool with a long handle that is twirled between the hands), and flavored with sugar and cinnamon or *nuez moscada* (nutmeg).[47]

On the traditional Mexican Christmas, January 6, the Day of the Magi *(Día de los Reyes Magos),* a traditional dessert is *Rosca de los Reyes* (Three Kings Bread). In addition to the basic bread ingredients, raisins and walnuts, candied cherries, and grated orange and lemon peel are added. The bread is formed into a ring resembling a crown, and baked into it are a tiny doll representing the Baby Jesus, along with whole almonds and coins. Then the bread is decorated with a glaze and bits of candied fruit. Anyone who eats a piece of the bread with a coin or almond in it is assured of good luck for the coming year; the finder of the Baby Jesus is expected to give a party for the group on the Feast of Candelaria, February 2.[48]

Empanadas—sweet fried pies—are made with circles of thin dough with a dollop of fruit preserves or mincemeat in the center. The dough is folded over and crimped around the edges and deep-fried, then sprinkled with powdered sugar.[49] Empanadas are served year-round in some Mexican restaurants, often with a scoop of ice cream on the side.

Christmas foods are not all dessert, of course: Tamales are customary foods for the season, as is menudo,[50] but with modern refrigeration and urbanization, people can buy—rather than make—both dishes at any time of year. Some people serve meat-and-chile balls, deep-fried, as finger foods at Christmastime too.[51] Empanadas filled with picadillo are customary in some families (the turnovers resemble the Russian *pirishki,* Italian *calzone,* Cornish pasty, and Scottish *forfar bridies,* but are distinctively Mexican in their spiciness).[52]

Even if Mexican-Americans were indistinguishable in their use of language, their customs, and other cultural characteristics, the wonders of the kitchen would clearly prove that they exist as a living folk group, one that has influenced other cultures to imitate their tasty foods—although the imitations usually fall far short of the deliciousness of the genuine article.

CHAPTER FOURTEEN

Folk Art and Crafts

FOLK CULTURES EVERYWHERE show an interest in crafts and art. Useful items sometimes cannot be purchased and must be made, often following the techniques learned from the parents or grandparents of the maker. And even common articles made to fill a simple need are decorated with some skill, reflecting a basic desire even among simple folk to improve the looks of the things they live with. The sailor on a whaling ship, whiling away idle hours by creating the art form called scrimshaw, was obeying just such an urge, as were the pioneers who decorated their powderhorns with carved flowers or animal forms. In the Spanish Southwest this urge is also common, visible in a wide variety of areas of life.

As has been suggested, the entrance of the Spanish conquistadores into the Western Hemisphere brought about a significant number of changes in the folkways of both Indians and Spaniards. A mixture of cultures was inevitable over the many years that the two groups lived and worked side by side. Religion, vital as it is to most civilizations worldwide, provided a natural potential for merging of traditions. Both the Aztecs and the invading Spanish Catholics, for instance, used statues and images in their religions. That the Spanish called the natives' images "idols" simply reflected cultural bias—and influenced some of the results. Bernardo de Sahagún, Spanish friar and historian, wrote at length of efforts to replace the "idols" with proper Christian symbols, often with disappointing results.

One case is particularly revealing: the location of the shrine of the cult of Tonantzín, the Mother Goddess of the Aztecs, was the site of the occurrence of a widely accepted miracle. As was described in Chapter Six, atop the hill of Tepeyác outside Mexico City the Virgin of Guadalupe appeared in 1531 and sent word to Bishop Zumárraga to build a shrine in her honor on that spot. The "Dark Virgin" has, over the years, been officially recognized by several popes as the Mother of Mexico; Sahagún, however, noted that Indians frequently confused La Guadalupana and Tonantzín.[1]

Whether in central Mexico or along the Rio Grande, missionary techniques were quite simple:

> To ensure the process of conversion, the missionaries tried to check pagan practices that were in direct conflict with their teachings, but whenever they discovered similarities in deities and ritual, the padres

found it advantageous to substitute the name of a saint or church holiday to implement an already established custom.[2]

That the transfer of loyalties was not always complete is the main theme of Anita Brenner's *Idols Behind Altars.* She cites Spanish colonial writers to the effect that often natives appeared to be worshiping at Christian holy places, when they well knew that images of their "outlawed" gods formed the foundations of many of the newer churches and pedestals for the holy statues forced upon them by the intruders from across the ocean. Thus the Indians' apparent worship of things Catholic was deliberately deceiving.[3] Still, the established use of statues, images, and totemic symbols worked in quite well with the new ways—and such aids to worship are still common throughout the Spanish/Indian/Mexican Southwest.

Grutas

For over two hundred years the Spanish used the Rio Grande as a river highway to upper New Mexico, where conquistadores and padres carried out their efforts at colonizing the Southwest and christianizing the native Americans. Along the entire 2,000-mile length of the river, the Hispanic influence still lingers. The Spanish language, often with local or regional mutations at work, continues to be heard on every hand. The bells in towers or spires of Catholic churches still call the faithful to mass, and from Brownsville, Texas, on the Gulf of Mexico, to the source of the Rio Grande in Colorado, the custom or folk art of having folk shrines—called *grutas* (grottoes) or *nichos* (niches), as well as several other names—still flourishes.[4] As has been suggested, along the lower river, downstream from the El Paso, Texas/Juárez, Chihuahua, area, the influence of the Anglo-American has had more overall influence in things cultural than in the upriver country. Despite being directly on the Mexican border, Texas generally is less Hispanic than is the state of New Mexico. Yet throughout the region many residents speak Spanish as readily as they do English, regardless of their cultural backgrounds; and the pace of life tends to be slower, as is likely true of all small towns—but the Spanish/Mexican atmosphere is definitely at work.

The El Paso/Juárez area, situated roughly in the middle of the length of the Rio Grande's course, holds a unique position both geographically and culturally. Despite the size of the combined population of the two cities—well over a million in the 1980s—the strength of religious customs reminds one of these smaller towns. Since 1598, when Juan de Oñate crossed the Rio Grande and named the area *Paso del Norte* (Pass of the North), the area has been an important crossroads for a blend of cultures. Caravans of merchants, groups of settlers from the Mexican interior, and padres intent upon evangelism came up the desert trail from Parral and Chihuahua and crossed the ford upstream from the settlement at the pass, circling the foot of Mule Driver Mountain on their way north. Paso del

Norte became the capital-in-exile of the New Mexican colonies when the Pueblo revolt of the upper Rio Grande drove out padres and converted Indians of the Tigua and Piros tribes as well. It was here they retreated in 1680, and along the river below the pass they built a succession of missions and settlements—Ysleta del Sur, Senecú, Socorro, San Elizario—to join Nuestra Señora de Guadalupe, which had been founded at the pass in 1659.[5] Descendants of many of these refugees still live in the region; as recently as 1968 the existence of the Tigua tribe at Ysleta was recognized by the United States government, and responsibility for tribal welfare was transferred to the state of Texas.[6]

From El Paso southeastward, the United States is just across the river from Mexico, and the Mexican culture is strong on the left bank, as has been noted. Indeed, Américo Paredes makes a good case for the essential cultural unity of the two sides of the lower river, artificially separated following the Treaty of Guadalupe Hidalgo that ended the Mexican War in 1848.[7] For centuries, from Paso del Norte upriver, throughout the Spanish and Mexican periods of control, caravans of *carretas* (carts) brought settlers, goods, priests, and religious articles up from the interior of Mexico, along with reinforcement of the Hispanic culture.[8] Even following the takeover by the United States, the upper river continued to be closely linked culturally and commercially with the Pass of the North, through which recurrent waves of migrants from Mexico continue to flow to some degree even today, while families cross the border in both directions to keep in touch with kinfolks in the neighboring country. Thus a repeated refreshing of things cultural and religious keeps the old ways alive all along the Rio Grande, but especially at the Pass of the North.

Mule Driver Mountain still looms over the pass, where four centuries of history have left their mark. But it has borne a new name, Mount Cristo Rey, since 1949, and a fifty-three-foot statue of Christ the King looks eastward from its crest toward the settlements founded by missionaries centuries before.[9] It is little wonder that, with such a towering reminder, Southwestern families in the El Paso area keep up the traditions of their heritage even more strongly than in some other settlements along the river. Among the most distinctive of these traditions is the family gruta or nicho. In the area around these river settlements one is struck by the prevalence of these shrines.

The widespread artistry of home shrines or grutas in the Spanish Southwest has a number of explanations, varying greatly in individual cases. Generally, of course, the presence of a gruta says to the passerby, "Christians live here"—especially with grutas located in the front yards of homes and facing the street. Such a situation, on the surface, seems to serve the same purpose as the notice, posted on the front doors of many homes and often adorned with the picture of the Virgin of Guadalupe, saying in both English and Spanish, "This is a Catholic home; we do not want any Protestant propaganda here." Having thus given fair warning to non-Catholics, the family would seem to be unfriendly to them—but such has not been the case in my experience. In well over a hundred homes where I went inquiring about grutas in general or about a specific one seen or reported to be in that family's yard, invariably I pointed out early in the visit that although a Protestant, I was seriously interested in grutas and wanted to learn more about them. Repeatedly I was invited in, offered refreshment, and shown the family album with its pictures of the building or the blessing of the gruta. Frequently I was asked to share a meal, or even to come back and spend the night when a church fiesta would be held. My questions were freely answered, often with quite intimate details of family hopes, trials, and tragedies being shared with me—a stranger as well as one not entirely at home with the Spanish language. Never was I refused permission to photograph a home shrine, indoors or out.

The choice of subject for the gruta often reveals something about the reason a particular family has erected a family shrine. In one case, the memory of a son killed in Vietnam was associated with a front yard gruta containing a large statue —five feet or so in height—of San Martín de Porres. "He was our son's favorite saint," the mother said.[10] Other shrines grew out of memberships in altar societies or confraternities. For many people, devotion to a certain saint or a particular representation of the Virgin Mary seems to demand public acknowledgement in the form of a gruta. Of course, grutas are often erected in hidden spots, too, or in back yards, or in nooks not easily seen from the street. These would seem to be more personal and private—and worn doormats in front of such shrines often bear mute testimony to the fact that these are sacred places, regularly resorted to for kneeling in prayer.

Another motive for the erection of grutas was expressed by an immigrant from Mexico who had lived in a small Texas town for almost a decade. In essence, his view was that Mexico, being a Catholic country with churches on every hand, had repeated reminders of God's presence and importance in people's lives. In the United States, however, he felt it was necessary to put up crosses and shrines and statues of holy figures to remind people about God. The informant, a laborer, was quite articulate, and he was thoroughly convinced of the truth of his statements.[11] In a form of corroboration of what he believed, it is almost impossible to find grutas—or even to find people knowledgeable enough to discuss them—on the right bank of the Rio Grande. The researcher drives or walks through many a Mexican town or village looking in vain for these signs of religious devotion. Even the general shabbiness of homes in these Mexican communities seems to show a lack of concern or self-esteem. By contrast, in the yards of homes on the left bank where there are grutas, things are more often neat and tidy, giving the viewer the impression that those who show religious values also care more about their homes and neighborhoods, however humble the surroundings may be.

Throughout the Spanish Southwest, the reason most frequently given for building grutas is to pay a *manda* (vow) or *promesa* (promise) to a saint or to the Virgin for help received or prayers answered. Not always, of course, is the manda to build a gruta. More often the promise is to visit a saint's shrine, or to say public-

This statue of La Purísima stands in a *gruta* made from an old bathtub.

The Santo Niño de Atocha (the Holy Child of Atocha, a town in Spain) is the center of this homemade *gruta* in Redford, Texas. The symbol IHS is scratched in the cement at the top—IHS being the first three letters of Jesus' name in Greek.

Yard art—an imitation well in Alpine, Texas—holds a *gruta* with the Virgin of Guadalupe in the center, with vases and candles on either side. The pick handle is not a permanent part of the scene.

ly a certain number of prayers of thanksgiving. Saint's corners in Catholic churches are literally overwhelmed with pictures of babies brought into the world through the saint's help, or notes of gratitude, or tiny *milagros* (literally, "miracles") of silver- or gold-colored metal arms, legs, heads—whatever the ailing portion of the anatomy was that needed help and received it. Formally called *ex votos,* these physical evidences of gratitude reflect the same concept that produces the construction of a gruta: public acknowledgement of the generosity of the Virgin or the saint in helping those in need.

On occasion the promesa or vow is not for a specific event but a general feeling of thankfulness. One divorced mother, having raised and educated four children alone, finally was able to buy a home for herself. She pointed out that if she hadn't had the help of St. Jude, often called the Saint of the Impossible, she couldn't have achieved her goals. "I always said, if I ever had a home of my own, then St. Jude would have a home as well." And now he does—a lovely backyard gruta with a trickling water fountain, and an electric pump to keep the water flowing.

Most often found in grutas along the 2,000-mile length of the Rio Grande is the Virgin Mary, in one manifestation or another—especially the Virgin of Guadalupe and La Purísima (Our Lady of the Immaculate Conception). Our Lady of Lourdes,

A stylized Virgin of Guadalupe statue is flanked by San Martín de Porres, a Black saint, on her right, and San Judas, the saint of the impossible, on her left. The gruta was erected as an expression of thanks after the recovery of the father of the family from a serious illness. The three religious figures represent the targets of family prayers for his health.

who appeared to the peasant girl Bernadette in a cave in France in 1858,[12] is frequently found, and less often Our Lady of Fatima, who appeared to three shepherd children in the Portuguese village of Fatima in 1917.[13] Second in frequency to the variety of statues of the Virgin is that of Jesus, in the form of the Sacred Heart, followed by the statue of San Martín de Porres, a saint born of a Spanish grandee and a freed slave woman.[14] Perhaps he is so popular because he was born of mixed ancestry like the Mexican nation itself, and therefore he can best understand the concerns of the people of Mexican origin. Quite naturally, individuals have their special santos who are especially important to them—Saint Anthony, Saint Francis of Assisi, and a host of others.

Materials and artistry may vary with the financial status of the family, but evidence of living tradition and devotion to the Catholic saints and the Virgin shows no class level. Grutas are often adorned with plastic flowers, broken bits of colored glass or tile, seashells, or even kewpie dolls or dime store figures of no particular religious significance, side by side with a string of rosary beads draped about the neck of the statue. Living greenery and flowers are also to be found about the gruta, and sometimes the setting (in more affluent homes) may be a carefully tended arbor or garden. But even a coffee can containing a bedraggled

Part of a formal garden scene, a gruta with the statue of the Virgin in a Socorro, New Mexico, back yard.

geranium reflects the love that finds expression despite limited means. The materials used in this art form are varied indeed—plywood, cement, bricks, sheet metal, or whatever is handy. There is a recurring shape—like that of an inverted letter U—and often a small trough for planting flowers is built in front of the pedestal for the statue. In one of my earliest public presentations of slides of this form of folk art, a lady from upstate New York told me that discarded bathtubs were often half buried—faucet end down—in yards as shelter for a saint's statue. Since then I have found several in mid-state New Mexico.

A study of the indoor shrines found in Hispanic homes, in my experience, reflects the same popularity of La Guadalupana, the Sacred Heart of Jesus, and San Martín de Porres. The indoor shrines are not as visible, of course, as the outdoor ones that appear throughout the Spanish Southwest. Even so, they both speak clearly if silently of the veneration of the saints which conquistadores and padres brought to the Pass of the North over four centuries ago as they explored and settled the region.

Among the art forms incorporated into indoor shrines is the *retablo*—a painted piece of metal, usually, depicting a religious figure or group—that is representative of an almost lost art. During the period of Spanish and Mexican control of the Southwest, itinerant painters supplied the lack of quality religious art caused by the distance from European civilization. A *lamina* (metal sheet), of tin, copper, or even silver, served as the surface for painting, although planed woods or sometimes (in more recent times) plywood was employed. Folk artisans imitated the work of other, more professional artists, and the degree of skill is quite varied. These retablos have become art treasures, with collectors paying enormous prices for them. Apparently the creation of retablos nearly died out about the beginning of the twentieth century; the homes of the more affluent still have the genuine article, but collectors have largely gathered up the majority of them, leaving the poorer folk dependent upon *chromos* (lithographs, or colored prints) from religious articles stores, or even magazine prints pasted onto cardboard or plywood.[15]

A living folk art related in nature to the retablo is the work of the *santero* (saintmaker), who plies his craft in New Mexico. As with the retablo, the hand-carved statues—*santos*—have attracted the eye of the collector, and examples of this folk art, especially older ones, have sold for large sums. But carvers continue to make statues for their original purpose—devotion—and many home altars and indoor shrines, especially in New Mexico, are built with these figures as a focal point. The term santero is also applied to one who paints religious pictures, in a way continuing the retablo tradition of earlier days, as is demonstrated in a recent issue of *New Mexico* magazine, where local santeros are given credit for paintings used as the stations of the cross in a restored mission church, as well as the illustrated *reredos* (altar screen) that adorns many living centers of worship. The altar screen, incidentally, often includes both carving and painting—usually by untrained, i.e, folk, artists.[16] Marc Simmons, the New Mexico historian, notes that

> in colonial times, each household along the Rio Grande had its collections of santos gracing the family altar.
>
> Native woodcarvers, who specialized in religious articles, developed their own distinctive styles, thereby creating a sculptural art form that was unique to New Mexico. . . . On New Mexico's Spanish frontier, the santo was regarded as an intimate member of the family and one who contributed significantly to its survival.[17]

Elizabeth Boyd, long associated with New Mexico museums and folk art, noted that the work of many santeros was destroyed in 1851 when Archbishop John Lamy assumed the leadership of the newly created diocese of New Mexico. To his European taste, adobe churches and hand-carved saint statues were grotesque. He ordered the former covered with facades more like those his background demanded, and had the santos replaced with plaster images and colored lithographs from France—but fortunately some carved statues went "underground." "A few lingered on in lonely chapels and rural homes," Miss Boyd said.[18] Most writers on the santero view the art as a historical oddity or an artistic treasure, not the living tradition that it is today, as a 1979 film made of three actively working New Mexican santeros clearly shows.[19]

A variety of home-made markers appears in this view. In the foreground is a concrete slab/cross combination; on the right a bulky cast cross; between the two, a cast slab/cross imbedded with bits of broken tile to indicate the name of the deceased.

Grave Decoration

In a completely natural tradition, grutas are found frequently in graveyards, adorning graves of the faithful. And as might be expected, the grutas at gravesites follow the same pattern of type frequency as those in home gardens, with the Virgin of Guadalupe most popular of all. Significantly, they are found as often on the Mexican side of the border as on the American side—a situation that recalls official Mexican limitations on public displays of religious forms,[20] which apparently do not prohibit cemetery adornment. One woman interviewed in Ojinaga, Chihuahua (across the river from Presidio, Texas), has a small gruta containing a Sacred Heart in her yard with a candle always lit, day or night, before the statue. Repeatedly, people on both sides of the border nearby urged me to go see "Susana's grutita." Another, larger statue of the Sacred Heart within Susana Fierro's house had been *una herencia de mi mamá* (an inheritance from my mother). She told me that the statue would be incorporated into her own gravestone—thus she would be keeping even after death the beloved statue her mother had left her.

I had seen and photographed gruta gravestones before, but talking with

A tiny Holy Family, probably factory-made, is set into the niche of this home-cast marker. The different coloring at the top indicates that another piece —likely a cross—was part of the original marker. *Nacio* on the left and *fallecio* on the right mean *born* and *died.*

This cast cross with heart-shaped tips shares a plot in Brownsville, Texas, with a standards veterans marker; graves sometimes have three or even more markers, added as family fortunes improve.

Folk art distinguishes this marker in the lonesome *camposanto* in Langtry, Texas. Considerable skill went into its construction.

Susana helped me to understand the personal attachment that many Mexican-American Catholics have for the grutas. Another family I visited in Lajitas, near the Big Bend of the Rio Grande, had a gruta statue in the front yard that the mother intends to have incorporated into her tombstone, as did a lady down in Brownsville. Such discussions gave me a whole new perspective on grutas and grave decoration, and I undertook a serious attempt to study and record this aspect of the culture.

Throughout my wanderings, which ranged from the mouth of the Rio Grande to its source, I found that the gruta headstone is among the forms of grave adornment showing the greatest variety. The Virgin of Guadalupe generally appears in full dress, as it were, with the sun's rays shining forth behind her head, and the star-studded blue cape she usually wears draping her body. Our Lady of Lourdes is second most frequently found, with the Sacred Heart of Jesus close behind. San Martín de Porres, who like the dark-skinned Mexicans knows what it is like to be the target of discrimination, is next in popularity, with the Holy Family and Saint Jude close behind.

As with the yard gruta, gravestone grutas vary considerably in the materials they are constructed of. Native rock and reddish-brown lava are common, but cement is also used, often crudely cast or even apparently hand-shaped by local or family artisans. One of the most memorable I found was in the barren desert cemetery at Limitar, New Mexico, where a manufactured Holy Family grouping

Conch shells, a religious symbol of life since Upper Paleolithic times, adorn the border of this grave in Brownsville, Texas.

In the Cordova, New Mexico, graveyard, several markers like this appear, with the maker, always a person with the same last name, sharing equal billing with the deceased. The marker is of cast concrete, quite artfully molded and inscribed.

A "grave house" shelters this grave in the *camposanto* at Lemitar, New Mexico. Inside, plastic flowers and religious figures adorn the site. A cross-topped gate to the structure stands open for viewing purposes. Similar structures are to be found in East Texas; Africa (whence the custom probably came); and other parts of the world.

with adult figures only four or five inches high was set into an irregular oval opening in a home-cast cement marker less than twenty inches tall. The grave, as is often the case in the Southwest, was outlined with field stones. Both the cement headstone and a wooden cross made of one-by-four boards that stood behind it bore the name of the deceased: the wooden cross had the name painted on it, while the cement marker had the name scratched into it while it was still soft, apparently with a nail or other sharp object. A plastic wreath of roses—called in Spanish a *corona*—encircled the top of the cross, and clusters of yellow, white, and pink plastic flowers surrounded the base of the stone. The simplicity and homemade quality of the whole spoke eloquently of the loving hands that had personally cared for the grave of the departed loved one.

This personal touch (or at least the homemade quality) is sometimes absent from a gruta marker. A skilled artisan has often had a hand in the building and decorating of the gruta, and on occasion a manufactured marble stone is present at the base or beside the rough-hewn gruta. Speculations can sometimes be made about the stages of the family's economic situation: a metal grave-marker supplied by the funeral home is often wired to a hand-carved wooden cross with painted name, with a folk-quality cement marker behind or beside it, and a later

Fifty or more of these grave markers, field stones with a cross or, sometimes, initials, pecked into the surface, are to be found in Limitar, New Mexico. The oldest residents have no explanation, saying simply that the markers have always been there, and perhaps Christianized Indians began the custom.

Even in its broken state, this Langtry, Texas, marker shows the care that went into its construction. Made of sandstone, pinkish in color, it reveals an aesthetic conception that goes beyond the usual skills of the artisan.

factory stone added. But although the family fortunes have improved, the earlier expressions of love and devotion have not been taken away in favor of a more sophisticated marker.

I would not be misunderstood—the homemade marker is not necessarily crude. In the *camposanto* of Los Cordovas, New Mexico, near Taos, a local tradition of skilled artisans has apparently developed over the years. There a dozen or more cast cement markers adorn graves, with the name of the maker—apparently a family member of the deceased—getting equal billing! Several members of the Trujillo family have such markers, made by various members of the family. And judging by dates of death, the Martínez family has adopted the tradition. But from all the markers I observed, it was a family-only practice, since none of the markers seems to have been made for other families. There is a degree of improvement in style evident from year to year, but this is definitely a folk art at work.

Sandstone or other easily-worked materials are frequently found in Mexican-American graveyards. Often there is a clear sense of form present, in borders, corner decorations, traditional crosses, rosettes, doves, and hearts carved into the stone. Names and dates of the deceased are usually framed with one or two lines. Spelling of names and of months of birth and death is frequently phonetic; *fallecío* (died), for example, is regularly spelled with an *s* instead of a *c*. Symbols instead of words are also common—a star for "born," a cross for "died" in the recording of the deceased person's dates. Sometimes the person's name is reduced to mere initials—either scratched into the surface of the marker or made of imbedded rocks or marbles pressed into cement while it was still wet.

Carved wooden crosses are striking in their individuality. A cross frequently will have three tiny crosses "sprouting" from the two arms and the top of the main cross. Some wooden crosses have hearts cut out, through the arms of the cross, and others have inlays of pieces of metal or nails either making designs or spelling out the name of the deceased.[21]

Cast cement crosses also have this inlaid technique on some graves. Pieces of colored tile—square, hexagonal, or irregular broken bits—imbedded in the cement form crosses or decorative lines. Where the arms of a cross intersect, pieces of glass—apparently from the whole bottoms of bottles—often shield a picture of the deceased or of a favorite religious figure, in a technique that manufactured gravestones have utilized; thus folk art imitates sophisticated forms, using, as is common, the materials that are readily available to fulfill a new function.

Descansos

A death-related aspect of folk art exists in many parts of the Southwest in the form of *descansos* (resting places) that relate to ancient custom among Mexican-Americans. In the old days, when a body was carried from the church to the

One historic *camposanto*—where gunfighter John Wesley Hardin and other early El Pasoans lie buried—offers a wide range of grave decoration styles. Clockwise from top left, a pair of mounded graves, with home-made markers at head and foot on one, and on the other a pair of wooden crosses keeping company with a religious statue; a home-cast oval marker, embossed with rocks forming an arch and a cross; a cross with the four arms expanding as they leave the center, studded with rocks; a cast cross, now broken, with insertions including a religious medallion; a wooden cross, ends notched and top broken off; a grave with cement border and cross made of pipe. In the center, a headstone incorporating a *gruta* with the Sacred Heart of Jesus within, and a slab covering the grave with artfully inscribed lettering, and fan- or shell-shaped corner decorations, made by a cement worker who used his ingenuity. (Photographs by Julia D. Clifford)

This roadside *descanso* (resting place) marks the interrupted journey of a man from northern New Mexico. Related to shrines that mark the resting places of pall bearers walking from church to cemetery, it is quite artistically made.

camposanto by the pallbearers, they had to stop and rest from time to time, since the distance was often a mile or so. The places the bearers put down their load were called descansos. Then, in addition, as they entered the graveyard, there was a ritual pausing at the entrance and at each of the four corners of the cemetery. At the entrance, the first decade of the rosary was recited in Latin. Then the procession moved to the right, to the first descanso or shelter, where the next decade of the rosary was recited. The group moved on to the next and the next, repeating the ritual at each stop. Sometimes a requiem prayer was offered instead of the decade. After the fifth stop, the body was then carried to the gravesite for interment. Few cemeteries still have these descanso shelters, and modern ones are not being built—nor are many of the old ones being used.[22]

The descansos along roadsides were hallowed by custom, and small shrines were sometimes built, especially marking the spot where someone died in an automobile or other accident, or just a memorial marker where flowers were brought on Memorial Day. But weather and highway crews and vandals take their tolls on them. Estevan Arrellano, who grew up in Embudo, New Mexico, once counted seventeen of the descanso markers in the twenty-mile stretch between Truchas and Española, a very winding, narrow road—"each the mark of an interrupted journey in the road of life." He tells of his first encounter with a descanso

—a marker for his Tío Julián, who had died young atop a *mesa* (a flat-topped hill) near his home. The uncle had died while hauling firewood from the mesa with a horse-drawn wagon, and now every time Arrellano climbs up the mesa, he straightens up Tío Julián's descanso.[23]

Some of the descansos are ornate, some simple; I recall one, near Pojoaque, New Mexico, which is simply three small crosses, eight or ten inches high, painted on a cement bock wall that a car must have hit, killing three people. There were no names, dates, or other indications of the event—nor did any of the neighbors shed any light. But it was clear to me that the custom of marking the death site was at work there. This one was not fancy, but it is not typical. The form is quite varied; as Arrellano points out,

> descansos are not only reminders of a journey never completed, they are a work of art and perhaps one of the few authentic noncommercial folk arts of New Mexico's Hispanics. They are created out of love in a time of pain and wonderment. These descansos are sculptures, in a sense earthworks, for they occupy a unique relation to the land and the environment. Though most are carved, some are assembled out of parts from the wrecked automobile, built out of rocks or poured cement, and others incorporate photographs. Only out of true love does a work of art evolve.[24]

The enduring nature of the custom and the art that it involves is reflected in the name of the city of Las Cruces (The Crosses), New Mexico, where crosses were erected centuries ago to mark the deaths of people who were killed by Indians there and buried by people who came by the site soon after.[25]

Folk Murals

A living folk art—not too different in some respects from the tendency to write or paint graffiti on any available surface exposed to the public eye—is the folk mural. Sometimes religious, sometimes historical, often Chicano-activist in their motivation, the murals call attention to the Mexicanness of the painter. In fact, one researcher suggests that

> to consider the murals of El Paso's Southside as strictly folk art would be ignoring a Mexican tradition that dates back centuries. Many barrio [ethnic neighborhood] artists are students of Mexico's *tres grandes* [three greats] tradition. Diego Rivera's depiction of the Mexican Indian heritage, José Clemente Orozco's allegories of spirituality, and David Alfaro

Any available space might be a spot for a Mexican-American mural. Here, between the gate and the mailbox, is a stylized version of the so-called Aztec calendar, with flanking symbols of unknown significance.

> Siquieros's metaphors for contemporary subjects all serve as models to barrio wall artists.[26]

And even though officialdom (through city council support in El Paso and elsewhere) finds room—empty walls in housing project areas, and the like—for such folk expressions, they continue to be a reflection of the aims and pains of a subculture long deprived of a voice.

Carol Carlisle, a folklore student at UT El Paso in 1982, found that folk murals in El Paso's Second Ward barrio occupied one or more of three categories:

> The first is social communication, such as political comments. The second is a class of personal or non-objective decorations. The third type is of a historical nature, the roots founded in the Aztec Indians of Mexico. Any one wall painting may be a combination of two or three categories, . . . representative of the people's own stories, history and struggles.
>
> Members of the community, I have found, will often refer to the murals as "ours" rather than the artist's. The murals give the community a sense of belonging and pride. The neighborhood is not artless and the attention given the area [for its murals] by outsiders or local press reinforces this pride.[27]

The Second Ward of El Paso *(Segundo Barrio)* is a place where people take pride in who they are and where they live. The Aztec quality of this mural exhibits pride in Hispanic origins.

Brown Power militancy is the focus of this mural with the face of Che Guevara, coupled with the Thunder Bird symbol—the label of a group beyond gang size that suggests the racial unity of the *barrio.*

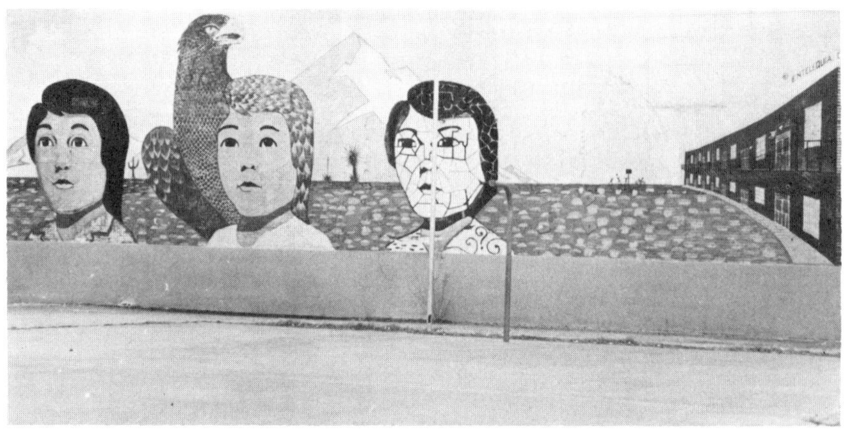

Ethnic pride and roots are merged in this symbolic mural. The cracked face is Spanish, one of the sources of the Chicano's heritage. It is cracked because of its loss of prestige, being merged with the Indian in the center, with the Aztec eagle, to produce the Mexican-American-American face on the left. On the right is a tenement in the area, and in the far rear is a basketball goal and some players. The mural is on the rear wall of the El Paso Boys Club.

The side wall of an El Paso grocery finds room for the religious symbol of the Virgin of Guadalupe, long a special focal point for Hispanics, and the Thunder Birds logo—together with the *caló* name for the city, "El Chuco, TX."

A series of Thunder Birds on a South El Paso sidewalk memorializes dead members of the *barrio,* with a pair of blank birds at the end for others yet to die from turf battles or drug-related confrontations.

The wall of a tenement is beautifully adorned with a montage of Aztec-to-modern ethnic significance. The sleeping princess could have come from a calendar distributed by a South El Paso business, while the group in modern dress suggests that these are the inheritors of the Aztec tradition. Asked about the artists of these murals, a resident said, "Los vatos de aqui" (the guys from around here).

"In memory of the millions of children who will die from malnutrition" —thus reads the inscription on this mural painted on a South El Paso wall by local teenaged artists. The irony depicted, of death from malnutrition in a nation that sends men to the moon, is quite eloquent.

Two churches on El Paso's Southside frame a stylized painting of the Virgin of Guadalupe, suggesting the importance of traditional religion among those who live in the Second Ward. The basketball goal on the right is one of the community efforts to give the children of the *barrio* something to do.

The side wall of a Victory Chapel sports this mural—"Christ Breaks the Chains"—suggesting that drug addicts, drunks, and sinners in general are welcome. The mural tradition takes a variety of directions.

While local artists are sometimes hired by schools, government bodies, or social action organizations, generally the murals are anonymous, or at least no one in the neighborhood knows who painted most of them. Recurring motifs include the Virgin of Guadalupe, for many decades seen by Mexican underdogs as their particular champion; the Chicano Brown Power movement; the return to Aztlan (the legendary home of the Mexican); and the sorrows of the barrio—pollution, poverty, economic enslavement, and similar concerns.[28] Rather than a sterile description of this folk art, I have chosen to let the murals speak for themselves. Done in strong, often primary colors—reds, yellows, and blues especially—the murals are striking even in black-and-white photographs:

Low Riders

Proof that folk expression is alive in the 1980s is offered by a folk art applied to the automobile by Mexican-Americans. In the Dallas/Fort Worth area, in El Paso, and in many other parts of the Spanish Southwest, customized cars occupy the otherwise idle time of hundreds—perhaps even thousands—of car buffs. Usually the subject of this adoration is an older car, often from the 1950s. One man,

Practitioners of the art of low riding have frequent shows to display their art. Cars are restored, artfully painted, reupholstered, and driven slowly in neighborhood parades.

former president of an organization called "Los Bajitos [the little low ones] de Grand Prairie," said that

> he prefers 1950s models because of his nostalgia for what he calls the best decade of his life, his teen-aged years. Others guess that the passion for 1950s models goes hand-in-hand with today's 1950s music and fashion nostalgia craze. Still others suggest that such cars are superior in design and construction and simply look "classier."

And as the researcher points out, such older cars—unless they are in mint condition—are cheaper to buy.[29]

Restoring and dressing up these cars is time-consuming and expensive. If the work of lowering the car's suspension, replacing tires and wheels, painting and reupholstering, and so on is done commercially, the cost may well near $5,000. Of course the average low rider (meaning the devotee, not just the vehicle) does most of his work himself. Some lowered cars barely clear the ground, so traffic bumps and potholes pose a hazard to them, but such cars are usually driven at very low speeds, often in neighborhood parades on Sundays and holidays. Some cars have hydraulic lifts, so they may be raised to drive at normal rates of speed and with less worry abut scraping bottom. Some riders can alternate their lifts so

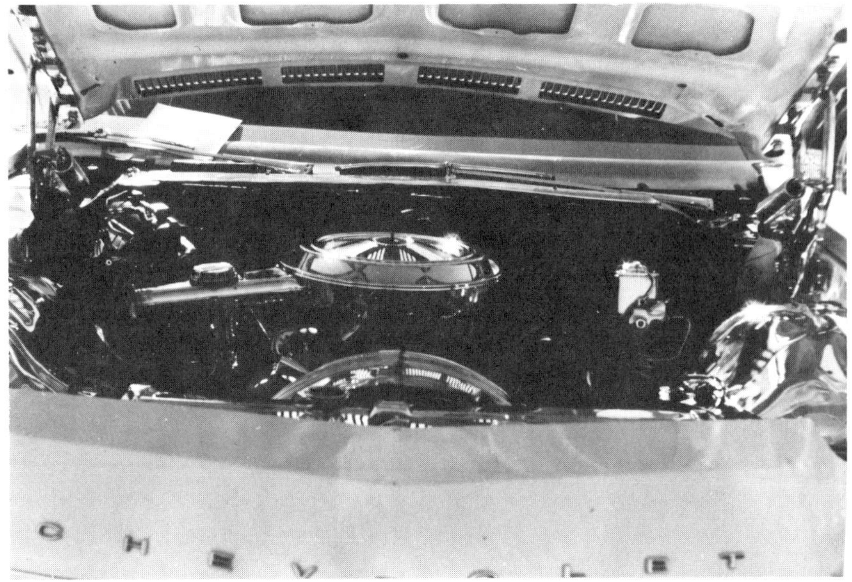

Heat-resistant paint and shiny chrome under the hood demonstrate the extent to which the low rider car buff will go to fancy-up his "ride."

as to make their cars "hop" as they go down the street on parade.[30]

There are over thirty low rider clubs in the Dallas/Fort Worth area alone, and members are proud of their work and love to show it off in car shows as well as driving around slowly:

> To the caravan of cruising low riders, each driver slouching low behind the dashboard into his heavily cushioned seat, the destination is of little importance in comparison with the elaborate and self-consciously staged cultural performance that takes place along the way. Group cruising at excessively low speeds brings the desired result of focusing public attention on the positive aspects of the Mexican community, extolling such values as self and group pride, the virtues of diligence and industry, and the rewards of interpersonal and intra-group cooperation. [One low rider] claims he gets great satisfaction from encounters with inquisitive non-low riders—particularly the Anglo-Americans—as he feels it is one of the very few instances in which he can interact in a positive manner with "white people, because when they see my ride they know I'm a hard worker and a serious and responsible person, because they know I've put a lot of time and money into it."[31]

Mural-like drawings and glass etchings of considerable artistry decorate these

Like father, like son—a low rider bicycle is one of several on display at an El Paso show.

cars, with a variety of themes that echo those of the folk murals described above, as well as typical "low rider" ones—a low rider squatting by his "ride," for instance—as well as Texas themes and abstract designs.[32] At car shows, where these artisans display their work, the atmosphere is almost that of an all-day picnic, with celebrations punctuated by various kinds of Mexican music and other entertainment, in a sort of "new fiesta of the Chicano."[33]

El Paso low riders compete in car shows all over the Southwest, one of the ways they share their artistry; as Art Franco puts it,

> I feel that low riding is a reflection of class of the Chicano and part of the machismo [manliness] a Chicano portrays. I named my car "Street Life" after a song. . . . I used candy apple paint and crushed velour for my interior because that way I could express myself—so the world could see.[34]

Another low rider, Benny Ramos of El Paso, got hooked on low riders seventeen years ago when he saw a dropped '58 "Caddy" cruising by in an East Los Angeles barrio. He grew up there, living just two blocks from what is called locally "Cruising Boulevard," where the low riders do their parading on Sundays, and he now has two "rides" of his own.[35]

Folk art among Mexican-Americans takes a wide variety of forms, as shown in a

1986 exhibit at the San Antonio (Texas) Museum of Art. On display were such art forms as decorative ceramic tiles; yard art imitating tree trunks and animals; religious figures formed of handkerchiefs by prisoners in the Bexar County Jail; and a fascinating assortment of needlework—children's dresses in imitation of the attire of santos, drawnwork, quilts, and embroidered pictures of religious scenes. Materials employed range widely—from ornamental ironwork, gates, fences, even entire car bodies, to crosses made of *palma tejida* (woven palm) for Palm Sunday, and straw figures of saints and peace doves. Traditional Spanish colonial designs find their way into furniture—the exhibition catalog is almost endless in its rich variety, and it attempts to represent only a portion of the state of Texas.[36]

As has been demonstrated here, Mexican-American folk art has a wide range of subjects and materials, with traditions from centuries ago being passed on from father to son, mother to daughter, age to youth. The old ways live on, blending at times with the ultra-modern aspects of life, social turmoil, and self-expression.

CHAPTER FIFTEEN

Popurrí (A Little of Everything)

SOME THINGS JUST don't fit in pigeonholes—and folklore is no exception to that observation. Of course, it is virtually impossible to capture an entire folk group, especially one as rich and varied as the Mexican-American culture. I strongly suspect that as people from Mexico moved north into the United States, even when they have remained close to their folk roots by living in settlements that are mainly Hispanic, or in barrios where the cultural ways and the Spanish language continue to thrive, that the impact of the surrounding Anglo culture waters down the richness that is their heritage.

Such is the case with folk costume. Throughout Mexico there are regional costumes for both men and women; a knowledgeable person can look at the holiday garb of a traditional Mexican and know immediately what state—or portion of a state, in some cases—the person came from. The *China Poblana* costume from the state of Jalisco, for example, with full, colorful skirts and loose-fitting peasant blouses with low neck and puffed sleeves, is truly special. And the male outfit, often seen when folkloric dance groups appear in public—the black, close-fitting trousers and off-white shirt of *manta* (unbleached cotton)—is one of the typical badges of the Mexican. But when one strives to distinguish Mexican-Americans from their neighboring culture by their dress, the task becomes impossible. The schoolboy in Texas or New Mexico or wherever one travels through the Southwest is most likely to be found wearing jeans; the girl might be less likely to dress in jeans than her "American" peers—especially if her parents are conservative—but otherwise little difference can be seen. Perhaps there is a tendency among Mexican-Americans to dress in brighter colors, but even that is largely a matter of individual choice rather than a cultural trait. And Anglos have blurred the original distinctiveness of the *guayabera* shirt—similar to the Philippine wedding shirt—by adopting it for wearing on almost any occasion.

Graffiti has no cultural boundaries that I am aware of. Even the buried city of Pompeii had graffiti. In Scandinavia, I am told, huge billboards are available for the writers of political comments or the expression of feelings, with words or with caricatures. Seemingly everywhere an abandoned building, or an open expanse of wall or fence, invites decoration. New York subways, and subway trains themselves, are a case in point. But there is one cultural brand that is present all along the border, described at some length by Sylvia Grider—the *con safos* mark added to Mexican-American graffiti:

> Throughout the Chicano district of practically any American town, from San Antonio to Los Angeles, one can spot distinctly Spanish surnames, given names, and nicknames written on walls and sidewalks. . . . The problem that such public presentation of names creates for the individual who writes them is the necessity for protecting these inscriptions from defacement and further insult because the graphic depiction of the name is regarded as a tangible extension of the person himself. But, if names are so important and so vulnerable that they require almost ritual and mystic protection, why do the Mexican-Americans write them in public places in the first place?[1]

Dr. Grider goes on to say that such inscriptions are a method of announcing oneself, of claiming the name as something special.[2] (I am reminded of the painted handprint on an Indian cave wall, saying eloquently if silently, "I, too, am a man; I exist!")

> The means by which the Chicano graffitor protects his own name or that of his sweetheart or barrio from erasure or defacement is by writing *con safos* [or more simply, "C/S"] in conjunction with the name. . . . An indication of the linguistic peculiarity and apparent folk origin of the phrase is obvious as soon as one attempts to look it up in a standard Spanish-English dictionary.

She goes on to cite authorities on Mexican-American slang, producing the meaning "the same to you" if one does or writes anything slurring or negative on or near the original inscription.[3] In conversations with my folklore students, I have come to appreciate the power of the "charm" involved in writing "C/S" on walls or beneath bridges. My students affirm the purpose as a protective device, and they agree with Dr. Grider that the charm is powerful only with those who are within the culture, those who understand the meaning. An Anglo might disregard the warning and add insults to someone's writing simply out of ignorance, but where Anglos are aware, as in a school with a mixed student population, they not only respect the taboo, sometimes they even use it themselves.[4]

My students have told me of the richness of another area of Mexican culture that has become severely diminished in the United States—folk gestures. Below the border pulling on an ear or making a certain mouth gesture often has a significance lost on Anglos—and varying from region to region as well. Some gestures have survived the move north, as witnessed by the widespread use of the "horns," the erected forefinger and little finger held up, usually near the forehead, to suggest that someone has been cuckolded, or simply that he's a wimp. Jan Brunvand, curiously, has called the gesture "the Devil's Horns," standing for "baloney," ignoring the rather widespread sexual connotation.[5] A Mexican-American friend

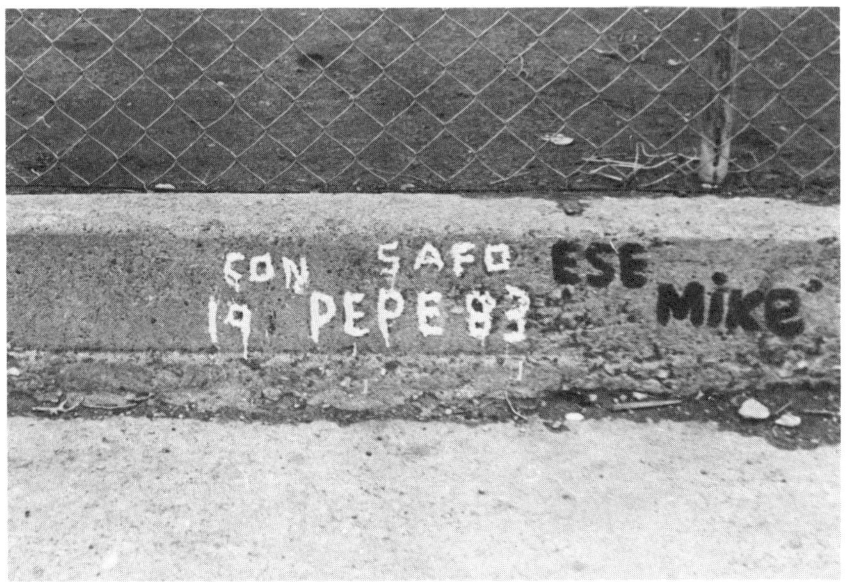

The power of *con safo,* a written charm against defacement of an inscription or gang name, has evidently preserved this curbside grafitti done by Pepe back in 1983. Perhaps Mike has also benefited from the magic of the charm.

says that the act of making this sign is called *echando cometas* (throwing comets) or *echando violines* (throwing violins), and the gesture is used "when someone's wife is being unfaithful."[6]

Another "dirty" gesture that I grew up with, but unknown to my Anglo friends who were raised outside the Southwest, is the *chapulín* (grasshopper), a name suggested by the gesture. Roughly suggesting "to hell with you" but with a sexual slant, the gesture is made by extending the index finger while folding up the fingers on both sides. A bilingual New Mexican friend (whom I won't embarrass by giving her name) recently told me of her bigger brothers thinking it was cute to teach her *"echar chapulines"* when she was five years old. When she innocently asked her mother (in English) why anyone would want to throw grasshoppers, her mother "remonstrated forcibly" with the boys![7]

A gesture with two meanings is made by grasping or slapping the bent elbow, arm held straight up, with the hand. One meaning is quite mild—"He's cheap!" —but the other says graphically "up yours." I suspect that when the sign is made forcefully, the second meaning is more likely to be intended—and understood by the recipient. Again, this gesture, and both of its meanings, I grew up with in the El Paso Valley in the 1930s and '40s. I notice that around El Paso and elsewhere in the Southwest the sign is still current.

Two folk industries that are at work along the border of Texas are the extracting of candelilla wax from desert plants that grow in the Big Bend area, and the burning of limestone to make lime. While both processes are folk in origin and practice, they have apparently been relatively unchanged over the years, nor have they spread nor influenced other Mexican-Americans to imitate them.

Joe Graham, who has filmed the candelilla extraction process in its entirety, as well as describing it in print, notes that it is almost unknown "outside of the trans-Pecos region of West Texas." And it has fallen upon hard times over the years: where there were once hundreds of candelilla camps along the left bank of the Rio Grande, these days there are only a few dozen, not all of them active.[8]

The *candelilla* (little candle) plant, so-called either because it resembles a bunch of slim tapers, or because of the wax it produces, grows freely in the arid Big Bend area. Pulled up by the roots, the plant is immersed in a tank of boiling water, with a little hydrochloric acid added, and the freed wax is skimmed off and put aside to harden. In an interesting example of using everything and wasting nothing, the tank is heated by the dried plants that have had their wax extracted. Candelilla wax is used in making chewing gum and polishing waxes and in a variety of other ways. In the dry Southwest the plant generally grows less than two feet high; elsewhere it grows more luxuriantly because of abundant water, but produces little wax. Speculators who had dreams of making money by irrigating the plant found this out to their regret. In addition, attempts at more efficient gathering methods, using cutters, proved futile because the cut plant "bleeds" to death, while the plant grows back if pulled up. These details suggest that Nature—and folk techniques—are sometimes better than sophisticated folks might think.[9]

Lime burning is another folk process that has apparently changed very little over the years. Limestone is baked in kilns—essentially big holes in the ground—much like the process described briefly in Nathaniel Hawthorne's classic short story "Ethan Brand." Again, Big Bend authority Joe Graham has captured the process in print.[10]

Another industry that was once common in Mexico and the Southwest but has retreated south of the border is the making of *mescal.* The Mescalero Apaches who live in New Mexico once baked for food the heart of the mescal plant (a member of the agave family of cactus), hence their name mescal makers.[11] And mescal, the fiery alcoholic drink made from the mescal or maguey plant, was once made wherever the plant grew. The process, which likely has remained the same over centuries, begins with the removal of the center part—the heart—of the plant, leaving a hollow. Juice called *agua miel* (literally, honey water) is dipped out with a gourd and poured into *bejiagas* (pigskin bags) to ferment. For family use, it is still done that way, I am told, but commercial producers use wooden barrels. The liquid ferments naturally; after twelve hours it is ready to drink—and after thirty-six hours (two days at the most), it must be discarded. Again, folk limitations make sense. When people have tried to can or bottle the drink, the containers blew up. The plant dies within about ninety days after its heart is cut out; when dried, it is used for fuel.[12]

A food mentioned several times in the preceding chapter is *asadero* cheese, a delicacy loved by most Southwesterners and pretty certainly by all Mexican-Americans. Although modern health regulations have altered the process of making asaderos, individual families still use the same technique.[13] To a couple of liters of cow's or goat's milk, a mixture of sweet and sour, the folk asadero maker adds the juice of six or eight crushed berries (or one cup to ten gallons) of the *trompillo* plant—a "weed" that grows wild in the arid Southwest. The berries look like tiny yellow tomatoes, but they are far more deadly. A member of the nightshade family, the plant is *Solanum eleagnifolium,* and although not all parts of the plant are toxic,[14] I have been told that women once used doses of the berry juice to produce abortions. In forty-five minutes to an hour and a half, the milk has begun to curdle. When the milk has been heated, the curds can be separated from the whey. The curds are spread by hand in thin tortilla shapes, and are about that size, six inches in diameter. By the time they are cooled the curds have solidified and are ready to be used in any number of ways.[15] For my money, the best use is eating them folded up in tortillas still warm from the comal. I can't imagine nectar and ambrosia tasting any better!

Mexican-American folklore covers the whole range of life, from before the cradle to after the grave. While this glimpse is by its very nature limited, I hope that at least it has shown the many areas of culture that exist among other people that are also found among Mexican-Americans. We all do some things differently, do the same things in different ways and even for different reasons—that is one of the chief lessons taught by a study of folklore. Yet we all have dreams, we all express ourselves traditionally in tales and songs, and we all strive to pass the valuable qualities of our world on to our children. So if a child should sit at your feet and beg for a story, remember—a rooster goes *qui-qui-ri-qui-qui;* a dog says *guau guau;* and when the story comes to an end, don't forget to pronounce the magic phrase *"Colorín colorado, este cuento se ha acabado"* (Colorín colorado, this story has ended).

Notes

PTFS — Publications of the Texas Folklore Society

Chapter 1. The World of the Mexican-Americans

[1]C.L. Sonnichsen, *Pass of the North: Four Centuries on the Rio Grande,* 2 vols. (El Paso: Texas Western Press, 1968, 1980), vol. 1, pp. 26-72; Katherine H. White, *The Pueblo de Socorro Grant* (El Paso: The Katherine Hope White Memorial Foundation, 1987), pp. 29-37.

[2]Cleofas Calleros, *El Paso's Missions and Indians* (El Paso: McMath, 1953), pp. 17-19.

[3]Sonnichsen, vol. 1, p. 15.

[4]Elizabeth Aeby, "Española to El Paso: Folk Cures of the Spanish in America," August 1985. Unpublished manuscript in the University of Texas Folklore Archive.

[5]Richard M. Dorson, *American Folklore* (Chicago: University of Chicago Press, 1959), pp. 101-2.

[6]Marc Simmons, *People of the Sun* (Albuquerque: University of New Mexico Press, 1979), p. 52.

[7]Jan Harold Brunvand, *The Study of American Folklore,* 3rd ed. (New York: Norton, 1987).

Chapter 2. Folk Speech and Naming

[1]See Ramon W. Adams, *Western Words* (Norman: Oklahoma University Press, 1944); Haldeen Braddy, *Mexico and the Old Southwest* (Port Washington, N.Y.: Kennikat Press, 1971), pp. 88-94. Julian Mason ("The Etymology of 'Buckaroo,'" *American Speech* 35.1 [Feb. 1960]: 51-55) disputes the *vaquero* source of "buckaroo," claiming the African word *bucra* (white man) is the true origin; his argument is scholarly but unconvincing.

[2]Collected by Jorge Serrano on August 1, 1976, from Frank Garay, 22, born in Zacatecas, México, and raised in South El Paso.

[3]Marcela Conde, a Juárez student at UT El Paso in the fall of 1986, greeted me with this expression in class one day. The study of fiction was put on hold while the entire group—over 50 percent Mexican-American—discussed such current expressions. The professor learned as much as the class that day!

[4]Richard Bradford, *Red Sky at Morning* (New York: Pocket Books, 1969), p. 23.

[5]Robert H. Fuson, "The Origin of the Word *Gringo,*" and Américo Paredes, "On *Gringo, Greaser,* and Other Neighborly Names," *Singers and Storytellers* (Dallas: Southern Methodist University Press, 1961), *PTFS* 30: 282-84, 285-90.

[6]John O. West, "The Historian, the Folklorist, and Juan Diego," *Southwest Folklore* 4.1 (Winter 1980): 38.

[7]Personal observations over a lifetime in various parts of Texas. The "Black Anglo" attended Canutillo (Texas) High School during the 1963-64 school year.

[8]In El Paso in April 1971, Manuel Bañales interviewed a number of local Hispanics, many of whom objected to the term *Chicano.* Included were LULAC member M.J. Romero and physician Francisco Licón. Dr. Licón said he reacted to being called Chicano just as a Black would to being called "nigger."

[9]Collected by Jorge Serrano from Gregorio Martínez, 23, born in Riverside, California, but raised in El Paso. See also Lurline H. Coltharp, *The Tongue of the Tirilones*

(University, Ala.: University of Alabama Press, 1965), pp. 32-33.

[10]Lucy Fischer West, personal interview, El Paso, Texas, June 12, 1987; Martin Kasindorf, "'Hey Haole, Wassamattayou?'," *Newsweek* (March 14, 1983): 49.

[11]See Coltharp, pp. 78-85. Jorge Serrano's survey in 1976 confirmed the continued currency of the caló expressions in South El Paso and elsewhere, and added several new ones to Dr. Coltharp's listings.

[12]In the 1960s Ted Baker collected these ethnic bias terms from Lily Avila, in her forties. A native El Pasoan, "by tradition Mexican but very Americanized," she worked in the library at Texas Western College (now UTEP) at the time and is still employed there.

[13]Lucy Fischer West, interview.

[14]Collected in 1970 by Ted Baker from an unnamed informant. I have used this story repeatedly in speeches about the folklore of the El Paso Southwest.

[15]Collected in 1971 by René J. Cantú from Elco Lozano, a UTEP student. Beatrice F. Buehler collected a similar "sunny beaches" story about California in August 1971 from Joy Rohmer, nineteen, of El Paso.

[16]Collected by Beatrice F. Buehler, August 1971, from Ignacio Ortega, 65, formerly a rancher in the state of Chihuahua, México, now living in El Paso.

[17]Collected by Beatrice F. Buehler, August 1971, from her mother, Mary H. Buehler, 73, a German-Mexican of El Paso.

[18]Collected in 1971 by René J. Cantú from María de los Angeles Delgado, a UTEP student.

[19]Collected by Beatrice F. Buehler, August 1971, from Nena Martínez, eighteen, raised in Clint, Texas. Her mother spoke only Spanish, and never attended school.

[20]Collected by Beatrice F. Buehler, August 1971, from Henrietta Martínez, 60, El Paso hairdresser, "who loves telling stories."

[21]I first heard this expression around 1970 from Margarita Corral, 20, raised in Canutillo, Texas. Jorge Serrano also collected it in 1976 from Salvador Garay, 22, El Paso resident born in Zacatecas, México.

Chapter 3. Proverbs

[1]King James version of the Bible. Worth comparing with the sense of the last is "It is ill with the roost when the hens crow and the cock must remain silent," which was reported found on the Mexican border from an unnamed source by Mrs. Morgan Smith and A.W. Eddins, "Wise Saws from Texas," *Straight Texas* (Dallas: Southern Methodist University Press, 1937), PTFS 13:240. Archer Taylor (*The Proverb* [1931; rpt. Hatboro, Pa.: Folklore Associates, 1962], p. 190) says "to rule the roost" is really "to rule the roast," but the Texas citation suggests otherwise.

[2]Brunvand, p. 74.

[3]Aurelio M. Espinosa, *The Folklore of Spain in the American Southwest,* ed. J. Manuel Espinosa (Norman: University of Oklahoma Press, 1985), p. 161. His collection includes 40 proverbs in Spanish, 22 with rhymes and 18 without (pp. 161-64). In an interesting contradiction to Espinosa's stand on the use of the word *proverbios,* a textbook widely used in Mexico does indeed use the word, with three examples: *Más vale un pájaro en mano que cien volando* (see note 8); *Muchos pocos hacen un mucho* (Many littles make a much); and *Cuando el rio suena, agua lleva* (When the river sounds, it is carrying water). Carmen Norman, *Mi libro de sexto ano* (México, DF: Secretaría de Educación Pública, 1968), p. 165.

[4]Taylor, p. 211.

[5]Stanley L. Robe, *Antología del Saber Popular* (Los Angeles: University of California Press, 1971), p. 71.

[6]Brunvand, p. 77.

[7]Collected by Robert Seltzer from Luz Hernández, 59, who was born in Chihuahua, México, and now lives in El Paso; 15 November 1974.

[8]Collected by Robert Seltzer from an anonymous informant, 22 November 1974. She was introduced to proverbs in Chihuahua, México, and brought them with her to El Paso in 1950. She has passed the wisdom of proverbs on to her four children. The "All that glitters" dicho was collected in South Texas: see Mark Glazer, ed., *Flour from Another Sack* (Edinburg, Texas: Pan American University Press, 1982), p. 59; three variations, including *No todo que tiene pelo es cepillo* (Not everything with hair is a brush) are found in Ruben Cobos, *Refránes: Southwestern Spanish Proverbs* (Santa Fe: Museum of New Mexico Press, 1985), #1203, p. 108; #1288 and #1289, p. 116. Cobos says his materials were collected ranging from Colorado to El Paso and San Antonio, Texas, and California, but provides us no further details. The "bird in the hand" dicho is found literally everywhere Spanish is spoken (with sometimes 10, sometimes 100 in the bush); an interesting variation, *Más vale pájaro en mano que buitre volando* (A bird in hand is worth more than a buzzard flying), is found in Cobos, *Refránes,* #1090, p. 98. For confirmation of the "circumstances" idea, see Rosan A. Jordan, "Five Proverbs in Context," *Midwestern Journal of Language and Folklore* 8 (1982): 109-15.

[9]Collected by Robert Seltzer from his mother, Amada Muro, 56, 18 November 1974. She was born in Chihuahua, México, and immigrated to El Paso during the Mexican Revolution. Héctor R. Venegas collected the same frequently heard dicho in 1970 from his mother, Esther Meraz Venegas, 60, "a storehouse of dichos." This philosophical dicho is also very popular, as are wry twists: *El que nace para guaje nunca llega a ser jícara* (He who is born to be a gourd [also meaning "foolish"] will never be a *jicara* [a polished cup made from a calabash]), from the lower Rio Grande Valley (Howard D. Wesley, "Ranchero Sayings of the Border," *Puro Mexicano* [Dallas: Southern Methodist Press, 1935], PTFS 12: 217); and *El que nace para buey, del cielo le caen los cuernos* (He who is born to be an ox [a cuckold also] will have his horns fall from heaven), Cobos, *Refránes,* #600, p. 52.

[10]Jovita González, "Folk-Lore of the Texas-Mexican Vaquero," *Texas and Southwestern Lore* (Austin: The Texas Folklore Society, 1927), PTFS 6:7. *Matrimonio y mortaja del cielo bajan* (Marriage and the shroud come down from heaven) is reported by Cobos, *Refránes,* #1118, p. 100.

[11]Collected by Ignacio Escandón from Carmen Blancas de Quiñones, 60, at an unknown date. Also reported by Cobos, *Refránes,* #1465, pp. 133-34, and a variation, *El que siembra cadillos recoge espinas* (He who sows burrs will reap thorns), #652, p. 57.

[12]Collected by Robert Seltzer from Guadalupe Silva, 43, 1 December 1974. She was born in El Paso; in a lengthy childhood visit to Cienegas, Coahuila, she reinforced her knowledge of proverbial wisdom. See also Cobos, *Refránes,* #1022, p. 91, and a variation, *Como siembras, segarás* (As you sow, so shall you harvest), #212, p. 18.

[13]Collected by Héctor R. Venegas from his mother, Esther Meraz Venegas, in 1970.

[14]Collected by Ramona Sosa from Juliana Aguilar, 82, 7 November 1963. Born in Camargo, Chihuahua, she came to El Paso in 1915. See also Robe, p. 72; Joseph Raymond, "Mexican Proverbs," *Western Folklore* 12 (1953): 249, collected from his Mexican maid; and George M. Foster, collecting near Pátzcuaro, México, who found a longer version: *Para gato viejo, ratón tierno, para macho viejo, aparejo nuevo* (For an old cat, a tender mouse; for an old mule, a new harness), "Character and Personal Relationships Seen Through Proverbs in Tzintzuntzán, México," *Journal of American Folklore* 83 (1970): 314.

[15]Collected by Ramona Sosa from Merced Sosa, aged 68, 28 November 1963.

[16]Collected by Linda Hulse from Robert J. Salazar, in his late thirties, 16 February 1970; he learned many proverbs from his mother. See also Robe, p. 69; Cobos, *Refránes,* #1429, p. 131; and Jordan, p. 110, who reports a dicho with similar import: *El*

que no oye consejo, no llega a viejo (He who doesn't listen to advice never reaches old age). On p. 114 Jordan cites Robe, p. 66, *El que no no toma consejo, nunca llegará a viejo . . . porque más sabe el diablo por viejo que por diablo* (the ending adding, "because the devil knows more because he's old than because he's the devil.") Glazer reports both *El que no oye consejos* sayings (p. 46) and the commentary on the devil (p. 47).

[17]Collected by Ignacio Escandón from Carmen Blancas de Quiñones. Virtually universal, the idea of the dicho is found in varying forms as well: from Cobos, *Refránes*, #468, p. 41, *El hijo del asno dos veces rebuzna al día* (The son of the ass brays twice a day—which Cobos translates as "Like father, like son"); Rubén Cobos, "New Mexican Spanish Proverbs," *New Mexico Folklore Record* 12 (1969-70): 7, provides *Cada cosa se parece a su dueño* (Everything resembles its owner—a chip off the old block); Foster, p. 209, to the *Tal palo* dicho adds *y de la flor, la semilla* (and from the flower, the seed), as well as providing a contrasting dicho, *No hay astilla tan mala como la del proprio palo* (There's no splinter as bad as that from one's own stick—meaning that a good father can have a bad son or one who will betray or reject him).

[18]Collected by Gwen Claybaker from Blanche Ludwig, July 1965, a Spanish teacher in the El Paso public schools. Taylor has an English equivalent, "What's yours is mine and what's mine is my own" (p. 130).

[19]Collected by Gwen Claybaker from Blanche Ludwig, July 1965. See also Cobos, *Refránes*, #182, p. 16. Soledad Pérez ("Mexican Folklore from Austin, Texas," *The Healer of Los Olmos and Other Mexican Lore* [Dallas: Southern Methodist University Press, 1951], PTFS 24:119) also provides *Al que le apriete el zapato, que se lo afloje* (He whose shoe pinches him should loosen it). Taylor (p. 5) reports from Plutarch via St. Jerome, "The wearer best knows where the shoe wrings him."

[20]Collected by Héctor R. Venegas from his mother, Esther Meraz Venegas, in 1970.

[21]Recalled by Héctor R. Venegas, 29, from his own childhood in a Mexican-American culture area in El Paso. See also Cobos, *Refránes*, #122, p. 10; Raymond, p. 256; Glazer, p. 54; and Espinosa, p. 162.

[22]Collected by Héctor R. Venegas from Raquel Ramírez, 48, in 1970. The collector's mother-in-law, she was born in Chihuahua, México, and learned most of her dichos from mother and grandmother. Cobos (*Refránes*, #343, p. 31) has a variant, *Despacio se llega a tiempo* (Slowly, one arrives on time).

[23]Collected by Robert Seltzer from Luz Hernández, 19 November 1974. A common dicho, it is reported by Wesley, p. 218; Foster, p. 307; and Cobos, *Refránes*, #310, p. 28. Cobos also provides a variant, *Gota a gota el balde se llena* (Drop by drop the bucket is filled), #777, p. 68.

[24]Collected by Héctor R. Venegas from his mother, Esther Meraz Venegas, in 1970. See Cobos, *Refránes*, #1082, p. 97. Raymond (p. 255) found an interesting—if obvious—dicho: *Más vale llegar horas antes que minutos después* (It is better to arrive hours early than minutes late).

[25]Collected by Héctor R. Venegas from his mother, Esther Meraz Venegas, in 1970. Taylor has an English variant, "Money makes the mare go" (p. 12), which is echoed in *Con dinero baila el chango* (roughly, "For money, the monkey dances") (Robe, p. 67).

[26]Collected by Héctor R. Venegas from his mother, Esther Meraz Venegas, in 1970. Wesley reports (p. 212) *Trae el rancho encima y no puede negar el rancho* (He has the ranch all over him, and he can't deny the ranch), and a comparable idea (p. 213), *No puede negar la cruz de su parroquia* (He can't deny the cross [the influence] of his parish).

[27]Collected by Héctor R. Venegas from his mother, Esther Meraz Venegas, in 1970. Often heard among Spanish speakers, this dicho is reported by Cobos, *Refránes*, #713, p. 62, and Robe, p. 67.

[28]Collected by Héctor R. Venegas from his mother, Esther Meraz Venegas, in 1970. Very common; Perez's version (p. 124) uses the verb *chiflar,* also meaning "to whistle."

[29]Collected by Robert Seltzer from Guadalupe Silva, 1 December 1974. Also found in Cobos, *Refránes,* p. viii, and Glazer, p. 42.

[30]Collected by Ignacio Escandón from Rosa Socorro Escandón de Yáñez, 26, date unknown. See Cobos, "New Mexican Proverbs," p. 9; Pérez, p. 124; Wesley, p. 216, and Glazer, p. 57.

[31]Collected by Robert Seltzer from Luz Hernández, 19 November 1974, and Héctor R. Venegas from his mother, Esther Meraz Venegas, in 1970. See also Cobos, *Refránes,* #131, p. 11.

[32]Collected by Robert Seltzer from his mother, Amada Muro, 18 November 1974. See Glazer, p. 51; Cobos, "New Mexican Proverbs," p. 7; Cobos, *Refránes,* #2, p. 1; Pérez, p. 118. Robe, provides four variants with the same sense (p. 64); Raymond reports *A buen sueño no hay mal cama* (For a good sleep there's no bad bed) (p. 249).

[33]Collected by Robert Seltzer from Luz Hernández, 19 November 1974. Cobos, *Refránes,* #565, p. 49, substitutes "tortillas" for "bread."

[34]Collected by Héctor R. Venegas from Raymond Cordero, 45, in 1970. Raised in a Mexican-American home, he absorbed many dichos from his mother and other relatives. Espinosa (p. 162) reports *Los duelos con pan son buenos* (Sorrows with bread are good).

[35]Collected by Robert Seltzer from Luz Hernández, 19 November 1974. Cobos (*Refránes,* #1033, p. 92) reports *Los duelos con pan son menos* (Sorrows with bread are less), but Raymond takes it a step further, with *Si los duelos con pan son menos, con dinero no son duelos* (If sorrows with bread are less, with money they aren't sorrows), p. 253.

[36]Collected by Héctor R. Venegas from Raymond Cordero, in 1970. Cobos reports the same dicho (*Refránes,* #703, p. 61) as well as a rhyming variant (#407, p. 35), *Donde no hay harina, todo se vuelve remolina* (Where there's no flour, everything whirls like a whirlwind).

[37]Collected by Héctor R. Venegas from Raquel Ramírez, in 1970; also found in Cobos, *Refránes,* #109, p. 9.

[38]Collected by Héctor R. Venegas from his mother, Esther Meraz Venegas, in 1970, and by Ignacio Escandón from Guadalupe González de Yáñez, 55, at an unknown date. Born in Mexico City, she has lived in the El Paso area for well over ten years. Cobos (*Refránes,* #531, p. 46) has the identical dicho.

[39]Collected by Héctor R. Venegas from his wife, Raquel Olivas Venegas, 26, in 1970. She was born in Chihuahua, México, and lived there until the age of twelve. She learned most of her dichos from her mother and grandmother. Cobos has two variants: *Refránes,* #1314, p. 118, *Otra vez la burra al trigo y por la misma veredita* (The burro's in the wheat again, and by the same path), and #1315, p. 118, *Otra vez la burra al trigo y el burrito al alberjón* (The burro's in the wheat again, and the little one is in the peas).

[40]Collected by Héctor R. Venegas from his mother, Esther Meraz Venegas, in 1970. This very popular commentary is reported by Pérez, p. 119; Robe, p. 68; and Cobos, *Refránes,* #163, p. 15. Cobos adds *—y yo con mi terquedad,* which he translates, "— and I with my stubbornness, said when everyone is busy doing some particular task."

[41]Heard repeatedly by the author from Martin Frank Fischer, in his eighties, during the 1970s. Born in Hamburg, Germany, he married into the Mexican culture after World War II and enjoyed the rich interchange between his own culture and that of his wife. This was one of his favorite sayings—and he always added *"con una prieta"* (with a brunette) to flatter his dark-haired wife. In my experience the dicho is more commonly heard without his addition, but I did not find it in the collections I sampled.

[42]Collected by Ignacio Escandón from Rosa Socorro Escandón de Yáñez, date unknown.

[43]Collected by Héctor R. Venegas from his mother, Esther Meraz Venegas, in 1970. Also found in Cobos, *Refránes,* #428, p. 37, in a different form: *El amor y el melón no pueden ser ocultados* (Love and a cantaloupe cannot be hidden).

[44]Collected by Ramona Sosa from Manuela viuda de Almeida, 30 October 1963.

[45]Collected by Ramona Sosa from Juliana Aguilar, 18 November 1963.

[46]Collected by Robert Seltzer from his mother, Amada Muro, 18 November 1974. Also found in Cobos, *Refránes,* #223, p. 19.

[47]Collected by Ramona Sosa from Merced Sosa, 58, fall 1963; Raymond (p. 250) reports the same dicho.

[48]Collected by Ramona Sosa from Merced Sosa, fall 1963, who heard it from her mother in 1940. Also found in Glazer, p. 42, Robe, p. 63, and Cobos, *Refránes,* #82, p. 7, and #425, p. 37.

[49]Collected by Ramona Sosa from Juliana Aguilar, 1 November 1963.

[50]Collected by Ramona Sosa from Francisco Rodrígues, 72, summer 1962. Born in Mexico City, he came to the United States in 1918.

[51]Collected by Ramona Sosa from Merced Sosa, fall 1963.

[52]Collected by Ramona Sosa from Francisco Rodrígues, summer 1962.

[53]Collected by Ramona Sosa from Manuela viuda de Almeida, 21 November 1963.

[54]Collected by Ramona Sosa from Merced Sosa, date unknown, and by Raymond, p. 251.

[55]Collected by Héctor R. Venegas from Raymond Cordero in 1970; Cobos (*Refránes,* #963, p. 86) reports a related item, *La viuda llora y otros cantan en la boda* (The widow weeps and others sing at a wedding).

[56]Collected by Ramona Sosa from Juan Ontiveros, 64, date unknown. Born in Camargo, Chihuahua, he came to the United States in 1921.

[57]Collected by Ramona Sosa from Juan Ontiveros, date unknown.

[58]Collected by Ramona Sosa from Angela B. de Yáñez, 62, of Juárez, Chihuahua [5 November 1963]; Robe, p. 65, reports a slightly different form: *La que viste de amarillo, de su hermosura se atiene* (She who dresses in yellow relies on her beauty).

[59]Collected by Ramona Sosa from Margarita Vásquez, 30 September 1963.

[60]Collected by Ramona Sosa from Manuela viuda de Almeida, 15 December 1963; Raymond (p. 251) reports the same.

[61]Collected by Ramona Sosa from Francisco Rodrígues, summer 1962.

[62]Collected by Ramona Sosa from Francisco Yáñez, 72, of Juárez, Chihuahua, 5 November 1963. Taylor (p. 217) has an interesting variation in English: "'Give her her will or she will burst,' quoth the good man, when his wife was dinging him."

[63]Collected by Ramona Sosa from Juan Ontiveros, date unknown.

[64]Collected by Ramona Sosa from Juliana Aguilar, 29 November 1963.

[65]Collected by Ramona Sosa from Angela B. de Yáñez, 5 November 1963.

[66]Collected by Ramona Sosa from Francisco Yáñez, 5 November 1963. Taylor (pp. 73-74) provides a similarly ungallant saying in English: "A woman, a dog, and a walnut tree, the more they are beaten the better they be"; he notes a similar saying in Spanish with an almond tree instead of the walnut, but I have not heard it.

[67]Collected by Ramona Sosa from Merced Sosa, date unknown; Raymond (p. 254) reports the same. Taylor (p. 162) reports a similar English saying from A.D. 1577: "Three things a man lendeth rife,/His horse, his fighting sword, his wife."

[68]Collected by Ramona Sosa from Francisco Yáñez, 5 November 1963; Cobos (*Refránes,* #1219, p. 110) explains it as meaning to use common sense in choosing a wife. Variants also have been collected: Cobos (*Refránes,* #859, p. 78) has *La cara guarda la honra* (The face saves the honor), and Raymond (p. 250) wrily reports *No*

hay quince años feos, ni viuda rica despreciable (There's no ugly fifteen-year-old, nor a rich widow worth scorning).

[69]Collected by Ramona Sosa from Guadalupe Sosa, 65, in 1956. Born in Torreón, Durango, he was reared in El Paso, where he died in 1959. He first heard this dicho from his great-uncle. Raymond (p. 250) and Cobos (*Refránes,* #218, p. 19) report the same dicho.

[70]Cobos, *Refránes,* #762, p. 67.

[71]Collected by Ignacio Escandón from Carmen Blancas de Quiñonez, in 1970; Cobos (*Refránes,* #1059, p. 95) reports the same.

[72]Collected by Ramona Sosa from Refugio Beard, 19 November 1963. The same sense is reported by Cobos (*Refránes,* #631, p. 55) with *El que quiere bailar, que pague al musico* (He who wants to dance must pay the musician).

[73]Collected by Ramona Sosa from Merced Sosa, September 1963. Robe (p. 72) reports a curious dicho of some kinship: *Debo no niego, pago no puedo* (I don't deny the debt, but I can't pay).

[74]Collected by Ramona Sosa from Juan Ontiveros, summer 1963; Cobos (*Refránes,* #1404, p. 127) reports the same.

[75]Collected by Ramona Sosa from Merced Sosa, date unknown.

[76]Collected by Ramona Sosa from Juan Ontiveros, summer 1963. Cobos (*Refránes,* #7, p. 1) reports a related item, *Acabándose el dinero se termina la amistad* (When the money runs out, the friendship ends); Raymond (p. 252) provides a humorous parallel: *Cuando yo tenía dinero me llamaban Dón Tómas, y ahora que no tengo nada me llaman Tomás nomás* (When I had money I was called Mr. Thomas, and now I have none, I'm called Thomas and that's all).

[77]Collected by Ramona Sosa from Dolores Ontiveros, 64, before 1947, when she died.

[78]Collected by Héctor R. Venegas from his mother, Esther Meraz Venegas, in 1970.

[79]Collected by Ramona Sosa from Luisa Gutiérrez, 61, date unknown; Cobos (*Refránes,* #454, p. 40) reports the same.

[80]Collected by Ramona Sosa from Manuela Carrasco in Camargo, Chihuahua, about 1951; Robe (p. 69) has a related item: *Donde hay higos hay amigos* (Where there are figs, there are friends). Taylor, however, notes the opposite in a common saying in English (p. 142): "Misery loves company." Whether misery *gets* friends is doubtful, however.

[81]Collected by Héctor R. Venegas from his mother, Esther Meraz Venegas, in 1970. Cobos (*Refránes,* #422, p. 37) has the similar *El amigo del rico es un peso en la bolsa* (The friend of the rich man is a peso in his pocket)—obviously prior to the devaluation of the peso in recent years; a peso in mid-1987 was worth less than one-tenth of a cent.

[82]Collected by Héctor R. Venegas from his mother, Esther Meraz Venegas, in 1970. Robe (p. 69) reports the same dicho, as does Cobos (*Refránes,* #711, p. 62).

[83]Collected by Ramona Sosa from Refugio Beard, 19 November 1963, and by Linda Hulse from Ruperto Santana, 45, 17 February 1970. He was then Director of Inter-American Studies at UT El Paso. Cobos (*Refránes,* #79, p. 7) reports the same.

[84]Collected by Linda Hulse from Ruperto Santana, 17 February 1970. Cobos (*Refránes,* #414, p. 36) reports the same dicho (though with a regional mispronunciation, *abujas*); his translation is curious: "Equal forces can't overpower each other."

[85]Collected by Linda Hulse from Ruperto Santana, 17 February 1970. Cobos (*Refránes,* #1625, p. 152) has the variant *Un lobo no muerde a otro* (One wolf doesn't bite another).

[86]Collected by Linda Hulse from Ruperto Santana, 17 February 1970; by Robert Seltzer from Luz Hernández, 30 November 1974; and by Héctor R. Venegas from his mother, Esther Meraz Venegas, in 1970. Glazer (p. 48), Espinosa (p. 163), Pérez

(p. 120), and Cobos (*Refránes,* #369, p. 33) all report the dicho. In the author's experience, it is probably the most commonly heard dicho in the area. Cobos (*Refránes,* #1183, p. 107) gives an interesting variant: *No con quién naces sino con quien paces* (Not with whom you are born but with whom you pasture).

[87]Collected by Robert Seltzer from Luz Hernández, 30 November 1974. Cobos ("New Mexican Proverbs," p. 7) reports the same; he also (*Refránes,* #1337, p. 121) gives the dicho with Clemente as the popular lad, and (#23, p. 2) reverses matters with Vicente tagging along after others: *Adonde va la gente, va Vicente* (Where people go, Vicente goes).

[88]Collected by Héctor R. Venegas from Raymond Cordero in 1970. This dicho is quite popular, but Pérez (p. 123), after reporting the same dicho from Austin, Texas, provides a contrast: *Más vale pobre que solo* (Better poor than alone); and Raymond (p. 251) has a similarly patterned *Más vale bien quedada que mal casada* (Better left single than badly married).

[89]Collected by Ignacio Escandón from Guadalupe González de Yáñez in 1970. Cobos reports the same dicho (*Refránes,* #1450, p. 132) and a variant (#576, p. 50): *El que mal anda, bien no espere* (He who goes wrong can't expect good). A parallel to this dicho has also been collected: *Quien con los lobos anda a aúllar aprende* (He who walks [runs around] with wolves learns to howl) is found in Robe, p. 70; Foster, p. 309; Cobos, *Refránes,* #517, p. 45; and Glazer, p. 52.

[90]Collected by Ignacio Escandón from Carmen Blancas de Quiñonez in 1970; also found in Cobos, *Refránes,* #1031, p. 91.

[91]Collected by Héctor R. Venegas from his mother, Esther Meraz Venegas, in 1970. Cobos (*Refránes,* #677, p. 59) has a shorter version: *El tiempo da consejos* (Time gives advice), as well as other variants—"Time causes forgetfulness," "Time removes doubt," "Time is a great healer," etc.—#675, #678, and #679, p. 59.

[92]Collected by Héctor R. Venegas from Raquel Ramírez in 1970; the same is reported by Robe, p. 66; Glazer, p. 50; and Cobos, *Refránes,* #185, p. 16.

[93]Collected by Héctor R. Venegas from Raymond Cordero in 1970; also in Cobos, *Refránes,* #1253, p. 113.

[94]Collected by Héctor R. Venegas from Raymond Cordero in 1970; also in Cobos, *Refránes,* #487, p. 42. Two other rhyming variants have been collected: Pérez (p. 123) and Glazer (p. 55) report *Los muertos al pozo y los visos al negocio* (The dead to the pit and the living to business), and Robe (p. 68) provides *El muerto al hoyo,al vivo el pollo* (The dead to the grave, to the living, the chicken).

[95]Collected by Héctor R. Venegas from Raymond Cordero in 1970. Taylor (p. 16) has a pair of sayings in English that reverse the commentary: "Young saint, old devil," and "Young angel, old devil." He also reports (p. 17) from German a rhyming saying more like the Spanish dicho: *Jung gefreut, alt gerault* (Rejoiced in youth, repented in age).

[96]Recalled by Héctor R. Venegas from his childhood in El Paso's Southside.

[97]Collected by Ignacio Escandón from Rosa Socorro Escandón de Yáñez in 1970. Glazer (p. 48), Espinosa (p. 162), and Robe (p. 64) also report the dicho; Cobos (*Refránes,* #300, p. 27) offers the variant *De decir y hacer hay mucho que ver* (There's much to see between saying and doing), and in #135, p. 12, a parallel, *Bien reza pero mal ofrece* (He prays well but offers poorly).

[98]Collected by Robert Seltzer from an anonymous informant, 6 December 1974. Also found in English in Taylor, p. 19.

[99]Collected by Linda Hulse from Robert J. Salazar, 16 February 1970. Also found in Espinosa, p. 164; Glazer, p. 53; Pérez, p. 124; and Cobos, *Refránes,* #1234, p. 111.

[100]Recalled by Héctor R. Venegas from his childhood. Reported also in Foster, p. 312, Glazer, p. 58, and Cobos, *Refránes,* #666, p. 58.

[101]Collected by Ignacio Escandón from Carmen Blancas de Quiñonez in 1970, and

recalled by Héctor R. Venegas from his childhood. Glazer (p. 59), Robe (p. 69), and Cobos (*Refránes,* #674, p. 59) have the same dicho.

[102]Collected by Héctor R. Venegas from his wife, Raquel Olivia Venegas, in 1970. See Glazer, p. 57. This common dicho is also found in variants: Robe (p. 71) offers *Ése es como el perro del rancho; ladra pero no muerde* (This one is like the ranch dog, he barks but doesn't bite); Cobos *(Refránes)* in addition to the "standard" form (#1365, p. 124), also has *Perro ladrador, poco mordedor* (roughly, Dog with big bark, little bite) (#1363, p. 124) and the curious *Víbora que chilla no pica* (The snake that hisses doesn't sting) (#1683, p. 158).

[103]Collected by Héctor R. Venegas from his wife, Raquel Olivia Venegas, in 1970. Glazer (p. 60) reports the dicho; Cobos (*Refránes,* #1281, p. 115) has the variant *No se ve la cola la zorra pero sí la ajena* (The fox doesn't see her own tail, but that of another); Jordan (p. 115) notes that Foster (p. 308) has a fuller version and an explanation: *La zorra no se ve su cola, ni el zorrillo su fundillo* (The female fox doesn't see its own tail, nor the skunk its ass). "Usually the first part only is quoted, as a gentle reminder to someone who criticizes, to remember that he too may have faults. . . . The second part is added in anger and is highly offensive, a deadly insult."

[104]Collected by Linda Hulse from Robert J. Salazar, 16 February 1970. Cobos (*Refránes,* #381, p. 33) has the same dicho, and also provides one with a reverse sentiment (#111, p. 9): *A quien no habla, Dios no oye* (God doesn't hear him who doesn't speak), which is echoed by Glazer (p. 50).

[105]Collected by Linda Hulse from Robert J. Salazar, 16 February 1970. Cobos (*Refránes,* #1574 and #1580, p. 147) has the pitcher falling in or breaking. In the movie *Man of La Mancha,* Sancho Panza, who has a belly full of proverbs, notes that it matters little if the rock hits the pitcher or the pitcher hits the rock—it's bad for the pitcher either way.

[106]Collected by Héctor R. Venegas from his mother, Esther Meraz Venegas, in 1970.

[107]Collected by Linda Hulse from Ruperto Santana, 17 February 1970. Cobos (*Refránes,* #477, p. 41) has the dicho, and offers the parallel English saying "The leopard can't change his spots."

[108]A favorite dicho of Lucina Lara Rey de Fischer, the author's mother-in-law, born in Chihuahua, México. See also Robe, p. 72. Pérez (p. 122) also has the saying, but with the word *elotes* (ears of corn), as do Cobos (*Refránes,* #736, p. 64) and Glazer (p. 43).

[109]Smith and Eddins (p. 240) and Cobos (*Refránes,* #695, p. 60) report this dicho.

[110]Collected by Linda Hulse from Ruperto Santana, 17 February 1970. This is another dicho which is heard everywhere in the Southwest. It has been reported in Robe, p. 66; Glazer, p. 43; Wesley, p. 215; Pérez, p. 118; Espinosa, p. 163; and Cobos, *Refránes,* #689, p. 60.

[111]Brunvand, pp. 8-9, 40-41.

Chapter 4. Riddles

[1]Mark Twain, *The Adventures of Huckleberry Finn* (New York: Charles L. Webster, 1885), Chapter 17.

[2]Jan Harold Brunvand, *The Study of American Folklore,* 3rd ed. (New York: Norton, 1987), p. 89.

[3]Brunvand, p. 94.

[4]J.A. Rickard, "Riddles of Texas Mexican Children," *Backwoods to Border* (Dallas: Southern Methodist University Press, 1943), PTFS 18:187. Stanley L. Robe (*Antología del Saber Popular* [Los Angeles: University of California Press, 1971], p. 59) has an interesting variant: *Entre abril y mayo un árbol floreció; abril le pregunta a mayo: ¿duras? y mayo le contesta:—nó* (Between April and May a tree flowered. April asked

May "Will you last?" and May answered her, "No.")

[5]Mark Glazer, ed., *Flour from Another Sack* (Edinburg, Texas: Pan American University Press, 1982). The collection comes from dozens of lower Rio Grande towns, especially Edinburg, Mission, McAllen, Pharr, and Weslaco, Texas. Another interpretation of the dicho might be "A horse of a different color."

[6]Archer Taylor, "The Riddle," *California Folklore Quarterly* 2 (1943): 187.

[7]Glazer, p. 91. Glazer's source for this riddle reads as follows: "A.P., 86, male, retired, Mexican American, speaks Spanish. Riddle was first heard around 1905. Collected by C.S. in Escobares, Texas, 2-29-79." Analytical indexes in *Flour from Another Sack* provide a great deal of comparative information relative to the sources (interviewees) of the lore, the places where most of the lore was collected, and the like, but no fuller information is given as to who collected the individual items nor from whom. I shall therefore cite the age and description of the informant, the place and date of the interview, and the page in Glazer's work where it may be found. For my purposes, speaking to a general audience, this information seems sufficient. Obvious errors have been corrected silently, and my translation sometimes differs from that of the source. This riddle is also found in Soledad Pérez, "Mexican Folklore from Austin, Texas," *The Healer of Los Olmos* (Dallas: Southern Methodist University Press, 1951) PTFS 24:126, in a different form: *Blanca como la nieve, prieta como el carbón, anda y no tiene pies, habla y no tiene boca* (White as snow, black as coal, she walks and has no feet, she speaks and has no mouth).

[8]Glazer, pp. 91-92; from a 47-year-old Mexican housewife, first heard around 1946, collected in Edinburg, 2-19-79.

[9]Glazer, p. 91; from a 21-year-old Mexican female student, first heard three years before, collected in Edinburg, 2-19-79. Frances Alexander and others (*Mother Goose on the Rio Grande* [Dallas: Banks Upshaw, 1944], pp. 64-65) have the same adivinanza, but translate the second detail as "runs fast with its hands" rather than "gives without hands."

[10]Glazer, pp. 93-94; from a 29-year-old Mexican-American female teacher, collected in McAllen, 2-6-79.

[11]Glazer, p. 94; from a male Mexican-American school bus driver, collected 1-30-79. Rickard (p. 184) has another riddle about the air or the wind: *Paso contra ti, y no ves, juego con tu ropa, y no ves* (I push against you, and you don't see me; I play with your clothes and you don't see me).

[12]Glazer, p. 95; from a 61-year-old Mexican-American laborer, first heard around January 1962; collected in Rio Grande City.

[13]Glazer, p. 95; from a 25-year-old Mexican-American secretary, first heard about ten years before; collected in Harlingen, 2-10-79. Alexander, pp. 62-63, has a shorter version: *Si los amarras, se van; y si los sueltas, se quedan* (Tie them, and they will go away; loosen them and they will stay).

[14]Glazer, p. 96; from a 20-year-old Mexican-American police dispatcher, first heard about three or four years before [1975 or 1976].

[15]Glazer, pp. 96-97; from a female Mexican-American mother, first heard several years before; collected in La Joya, 2-18-79. Rickard (p. 181) and Alexander (pp. 70-71) report the same; Pérez (p. 127) has a variant: *Una vieja larga que se le escurre la manteca. ¿Qué es?* (Who is the tall old woman whose garments drip fat?)

[16]Glazer, p. 97; from a 40-year-old Mexican bracero, first heard around 1920; collected in La Joya in the 1960s.

[17]Glazer, p. 97; from a Mexican-American bilingual housewife, first heard around 1932; collected in McAllen, 1-25-79.

[18]Glazer, pp. 98-99; from a male Mexican-American retired cook; collected in La Joya, 2-9-79. Alexander (pp. 68-69) has a much more detailed version: *Un árbol con doce*

ramas, cada una tiena su nido, cada nido tiene siete pájaros, y cada cual su apellido (A tree has twelve branches each with four nests. Each nest has seven birds, and each bird has a name). *El año, los meses, los días de la semana* (The year, the months, the seven days of the week).

[19]Glazer, p. 99; from a 65-year-old female Mexican-American. Variants of this riddle are found in Alexander, pp. 70-71; Aurelio M. Espinosa, *The Folklore of Spain in the American Southwest* (Norman: University of Oklahoma Press, 1985), p. 166; and Charles Aranda, *Dichos: Proverbs and Sayings from the Spanish,* rev. ed. (Santa Fe: Sunstone Press, 1977), p. 29.

[20]Glazer, p. 99; from an 18-year-old bilingual Mexican-American student; collected in Weslaco, 2-7-70.

[21]Glazer, p. 100; from a 52-year-old bilingual Mexican-American female store manager, first heard around 1960; collected 1-26-79.

[22]Glazer, p. 101; from a 51-year-old Mexican housewife, first heard around 1940; collected in Rio Grande City, 2-11-79. Rosalinda González, "Work and Play on a Border Ranch," *The Golden Log* (Dallas: Southern Methodist University Press, 1962), PTFS 31:152, has a variant reading *Retorción, retorción, cuida la casa como un león* (A turn, a turn, guards the house like a lion) and the answer is "The key to a house."

[23]Glazer, pp. 102-3; from a 62-year-old male Mexican farmer, first heard around 1928 in Mexico; collected 2-20-79. Alexander (pp. 68-69), Rickard (p. 182), and Robe (p. 61) report the same riddle—but Robe's answer is *el repollo* (the cabbage).

[24]Glazer, p. 103; from a 49-year-old bilingual Mexican-American housewife, first heard from her mother around 1947; collected in Elsa, 1-30-79. Aranda (p. 28), Espinosa (p. 165), Rickard (p. 184), and Robe (p. 60) all have variations on this riddle.

[25]Glazer, p. 104; from a male bilingual Mexican-American student, first heard around 1978, from a friend with whom he likes to exchange riddles; collected in Mission, 2-15-79.

[26]Glazer, p. 105; from a 19-year-old male Mexican-American student; collected 2-16-79.

[27]Glazer, p. 105; from a male Mexican-American welfare technician, first heard ten years before at a family party; collected in Alamo, 2-16-79.

[28]Glazer, p. 106; from a 30-year-old Spanish-speaking Mexican disc jockey and teacher, first heard around 1975 from one of his students; collected 1-27-79. González (p. 152) has different beginning lines. The birds are sitting on a branch, and the hunters are shooting, but the outcome is the same.

[29]Glazer, p. 107; from a 53-year-old female Mexican-American housekeeper, first heard around 1920; collected in Brownsville, 1-13-79. Also found in Rickard, p. 181.

[30]Glazer, p. 107; from a 45-year-old Mexican-American housewife, first heard when she was about six, from her mother; collected 1-23-79. Pérez (p. 127) has the same, as does Rickard, p. 181—but his answer is *La nuez* (The nut), which makes less sense, and is not embedded in the riddle as obviously as the word *platano.*

[31]Glazer, p. 109; from a fifteen-year-old Spanish-speaking Mexican babysitter, who learned it from a teacher who was interested in riddles; collected in Edinburg, 11-8-78. The collector was told that the teacher used proverbs and riddles "from the text" as well as some that were not in the text. It is highly possible that the text was one provided by the Secretaría de Educación Pública in Mexico, which combines things cultural, folk, and patriotic from the primer grade up. *Español: Segundo Grado* (México, D.F.: 1972), for example, has eight adivinanzas, including the broom riddle cited in note 10. Such reinforcement, from a respected and liked teacher, would do much to assure the continuation of such folklore.

[32]Glazer, pp. 109-10; from a 36-year-old Mexican-American housewife, first heard around ten years before; collected in Roma, 1-27-79.

[33]Glazer, p. 110; from a 65 year-old female Mexican-American.

[34]Glazer, pp. 110-11; from a 27-year-old female Mexican-American teacher.

[35]Heard repeatedly over the years around El Paso by the author, probably first from Mrs. Lucina Lara Rey de Fischer, his mother-in-law—and used repeatedly in folklore classes to typify the conundrum type of riddle.

[36]Glazer, pp. 111-12; from a 71-year-old Spanish-speaking Mexican-American housewife; collected in Edinburg, 2-27-79.

[37]Glazer, p. 113; from a 21-year-old housewife; collected in Mission, 12-6-77.

[38]Américo Paredes, "Mexican Riddling Wellerisms," *Western Folklore* 19 (1960): 200. Paredes goes on to date the riddle as belonging to the period immediately following Mexican expropriation of oil in 1938, when Mexicans were being urged to switch from charcoal to kerosene for cooking. About the same time, the author remembers a popular Mexican song—*"Tu ya no soplas"*—which means "You don't rate any more."

[39]Glazer, p. 110; from a 32-year-old female Mexican-American teacher, who heard it from a seventh-grade student; collected 1-31-79.

[40]Glazer, p. 111; from a 23-year-old female Mexican-American teacher, first heard around 1960 while making tortillas; collected in Edinburg, 2-1-79.

Chapter 5. Rhymes and Folk Poetry

[1]Frances Alexander and others, *Mother Goose on the Rio Grande* (Dallas: Banks Upshaw, 1944), pp. 22-23. The translations in this delightful book are rather freely done, so that the English version also rhymes.

[2]Alexander, pp. 16-17.

[3]Aurelio M. Espinosa, *The Folklore of Spain in the American Southwest* (Norman: University of Oklahoma Press, 1985), pp. 169-70; also collected by María Elena Hernández from Mrs. Apodaca, 29-year-old Ft. Hancock housewife, and eight-year-old Rosie Peña, an El Paso third-grader, in August 1973.

[4]Alexander, pp. 16-17. Espinosa (p. 169) has a New Mexican version only slightly different.

[5]Collected by María Elena Hernández from Mrs. Apodaca, 29-year-old Ft. Hancock housewife, in August 1973.

[6]Stanley L. Robe, *Antología del saber popular* (Los Angeles: University of California Press, 1971), collected by Frank Aguilar. It should be noted that *pescuezo* is a term ordinarily used with animals, not humans; perhaps it is used in fun with children. Also collected by María Elena Hernández from Mrs. Apodaca, 29-year-old Ft. Hancock housewife, in August 1973.

[7]Robe, p. 54.

[8]Alexander, pp. 20-21.

[9]Alexander, pp. 22-23.

[10]Recalled by Martha Margarita Domínguez from her childhood in El Paso, and by Ramona Salazar, who grew up in El Paso's Smeltertown.

[11]Robe, p. 55, collected by Frank Aguilar. The "Engine, engine" rhyme was collected by María Elena Hernández in 1973 from two El Pasoans, eighteen-year-old Alicia Hernández and ten-year-old Susana Martínez. The author served as volunteer school photographer in the 1960s, following all the sports activities involving such boys as "Engine, engine," who was a powerhouse weighing about 125 pounds, but playing as though he weighed half again as much.

[12]John O. West, "Cultural Confusion on the Playground," *Journal of American Folklore* 84 (July-September, 1971): 342. This was my first use of student-collected material for publication, and I neglected to include the name of the collector, Richard A. Southern, who was—and is—a good friend despite my goof. He collected it during his

practice-teaching days at Beall School in 1965.

[13]Recalled from childhood by Ramona Salazar. Miss Salazar's comment recalls the view expressed by William W. Newell, early American folklorist and first editor of the *Journal of American Folklore,* who said, "There is no transference from one tongue to another, unless in a few cases, when the barrier of rhyme does not exist. The English-speaking population, which imposes on all new-comers its language, imposes also its traditions, even the traditions of children." *Games and Songs of American Children* (1883, 1903, rpt. New York: Dover Books, 1963), p. 2.

[14]West, p. 342, again using materials from the collection of Richard Southern. Roger D. Abrahams, *Jump-Rope Rhymes: A Dictionary* (Austin: The American Folklore Society, 1969), has over 600 standard jump-rope rhymes and variants, including such as these.

[15]F.S. Curtis, Jr., "Spanish Folk Songs of New Mexico," *Happy Hunting Ground* (Austin: Texas Folklore Society, 1925), PTFS 4:22, 25-26.

[16]Collected by Etta G. Kern in April 1970 from Carolina Meléndez, eight, of Hawkins Elementary School in the San Juan area of El Paso, a predominantly Spanish-speaking neighborhood and one of the oldest sections of the city.

[17]Collected by Etta G. Kern in April 1970 from Julián Cervantes, nine, Norma Menchaca, twelve, and Oscar Reyes, ten, students at Hawkins Elementary.

[18]Collected by María Elena Hernández in August 1973 from Mrs. Angela Hernández, 49-year-old El Paso native housewife. Etta Kern collected a similar verse in April 1970 from Isidro Mireles, ten, of Hawkins Elementary: after the fall in the mud it is a *panadero* (bread man) who can't help Juana up.

[19]Collected by Etta Kern in April 1970 from Alejandro Ramírez, ten, of Hawkins Elementary.

[20]Collected by Etta Kern in April 1970 from Annette Villareal, thirteen, of Hawkins Elementary.

[21]Collected by María Elena Hernández in August 1973 from Mrs. Concepción Rodríguez, 51-year-old native El Paso housewife.

[22]Collected by Etta Kern in April 1970 from Elia Valenzuela, nine, of Hawkins Elementary; she attended schools in Juárez, Chihuahua, for three years.

[23]Collected by Ignacio Escandón in 1970 from Rosa Socorro Escandón de Yáñez, 26-year-old El Paso housewife.

[24]Charles Aranda, *Dichos, Proverbs and Sayings from the Spanish* (Santa Fe: Sunstone Press, 1977), p. 27.

[25]Collected in March 1978 by Gloria D. Martínez from Rita M. Bentley, El Paso office worker raised in Santa Fe.

[26]Collected by Gloria D. Martínez from W.O. Tovar, 60-year-old native El Pasoan and inveterate girl-watcher. When he reminisces about his own days of "throwing flowers," his wife "sizzles with jealousy."

[27]Collected by Gloria D. Martínez from W.O. Tovar.

[28]Collected by Gloria D. Martínez from Ed Day, 23-year-old university student, "another one of the specialists of the piropo."

[29]Collected by Gloria D. Martínez from W.O. Tovar.

[30]Collected by Gloria D. Martínez from Ed Day.

[31]From a delightful interview with my mother-in-law, who was raised in northern Mexico and enjoyed the custom of hechando flores for many years. A public school teacher who married in her thirties, she had ample opportunity to receive such compliments during her single days; she is still beautiful and vivacious at 78.

[32]Collected by Gloria D. Martínez from Fred Márquez, student at the University of Texas at El Paso—and another girl-watcher.

[33]Reported by Gloria D. Martínez from an unnamed source.

[34]From a December 30, 1977, letter to Gloria D. Martínez from her aunt, Josefina F.

Martini of Buena, Italy; she has been married three times and says "home is where the good men are."

[35]Collected by Etta G. Kern from Velia Armenta, eleven, at Hawkins Elementary.

[36]Collected by Etta G. Kern from Patricia Sandoval, eleven, at Hawkins Elementary.

[37]Collected by Etta G. Kern from Susana Ramírez, ten, at Hawkins Elementary; until the preceding year (1969) she went to school in Juárez.

[38]Collected by Etta G. Kern from Norma Ortiz, nine, at Hawkins Elementary.

[39]Recalled by Ramona Salazar from her childhood in El Paso's Smeltertown; also collected by her from Blanca Urías, sixteen-year-old Juárez student at Loretto Academy.

[40]*Espanol: Segundo Grado* (México, D.F.: Secretaría de Educación Pública, 1972), p. 106.

[41]Alexander, pp. 56-57.

[42]Collected by Ramona Salazar from Graciela Gómes, fourteen-year-old Juárez student at Loretto Academy.

[43]Collected by María Elena Hernández from Mrs. Angela Hernández, 49-year-old El Paso housewife.

[44]Recalled by Ramona Salazar from her childhood in El Paso's Smeltertown; also collected by Martha Margarita Domínguez in 1977 from five El Pasoans, ranging in ages from 11 to 49.

[45]*Espanol: Primer Grado* (México, D.F.: Secretaría de Educación Pública, 1972), pp. 112-13.

[46]Collected by Ignacio Escandón in 1970 from Rosa Socorro Escandón de Yáñez, 26-year-old El Paso housewife. Robe (p. 52) reports what might be a fuller version, collected by Manuel H. Rodríguez in Los Angeles: *Allá esta la luna, comiendo su tuna,/ tirando las cascaras para su laguna./Allá esta la estrella, comiendo salea,/tirando pedazos para la azotea.* (There is the moon, eating her prickly pear, throwing the peelings in her lake. There is the star, eating pieces of salted animal hide, throwing pieces on the roof.—Since neither of my Spanish dictionaries was any help on *salea,* I had to rely on my mother-in-law's translation. In this context it sounds like *chicharrones* (pork skins), eaten as a snack, as Southerners eat "cracklins.")

[47]Collected by Ignacio Escandón from Rosa Socorro Escandón de Yáñez.

[48]Collected by the author from an unknown student, who remembered the verse as a jump-rope rhyme from the 1950s in the El Paso Lower Valley. Technically it should be "mató *a* su tía," but the *a* gets swallowed in practice.

[49]Collected by Etta G. Kern in 1970 from Raul Castro, nine, and Gilbert Marrufo, ten, of Hawkins Elementary.

[50]Collected by Etta G. Kern in 1970 from Erminda Torres, nine, of Hawkins Elementary.

[51]Jan Harold Brunvand, *The Study of American Folklore,* 3rd ed. (New York: Norton, 1987), p. 121.

[52]John G. Bourke, "The Folk Foods of the Rio Grande Valley and of Northern Mexico," *Southwestern Lore* (Dallas: Southern Methodist University Press, 1931), PTFS 9:108.

Chapter 6. Prose Narratives

[1]*Español: Segundo Grado* (México, D.F.: Secretaría de Educación Pública, 1972), pp. 177-79, 182-83, 159-60.

[2]Jan Harold Brunvand, *The Study of American Folklore,* 3rd ed. (New York: Norton, 1987), pp. 136-42, 148-49.

[3]Bernardo de Sahagún, *Historia general de las cosas de Nueva España,* ed. Miguel Acosta Saignes (México: 1946), vol. 2, p. 481. Elsewhere Sahagún, who was present in

Mexico during its colonization, noted that the Indian population was not universally converted to Christianity—but the "Brown Virgin," who looks Indian, apparently helped in the conversion process, even though the Indians often confused her with Tonantzín.

[4]A number of sensationalist newspapers, published in Mexico, have reprinted enlarged pictures of the Virgin's downcast eyes, and have convinced many that Juan Diego's image—or at least the shape of a man—does indeed appear reflected in the eyes. A scientific study, undertaken reluctantly (because he did not want to disappoint the faithful, if his findings were negative) by an ophthalmologist, Dr. Enrique Graue y Díaz González, convinced him that not only was there such an image, but it obeyed all the physical laws of what would have been reflected in the eye if a photograph of the face had been taken from the position of the kneeling Juan Diego. "La Tilma de Juan Diego," *Álbum Conmemorative del 450 aniversario de las apariciones de Nuestra Señora de Guadalupe* (México, D.F.: Ediciones Buena Nueva, 1981), pp. 117-20. Incidentally, Dr. Graue also noted that the red and yellow dyes in the picture on the cape had been analyzed chemically, and found to be not of animal, vegetable, nor mineral origin.

[5]Marta Weigle, ed., *Two Guadalupes* (Santa Fe: Ancient City Press, 1987), pp. 31-32. Collector Lorin W. Brown, speaking of village customs in northern New Mexico, is quoted thus: "All santos within the church are common property and an individual or group can carry a santo home for the night returning it the next morning."

[6]The Ruvalcaba home is of four or five rooms, adobe, with two or three bedrooms, a kitchen-dining area, and the sala. Water for bathing is hauled from a well and heated on a curious stove—half wood-burning, half kerosene (which side is used depends, I suppose, on family finances at the time); an outhouse provides the other necessity. Light and airy, the house is open practically all the time for visitors. Returning to El Paso from a trip, one Sunday just before New Year's, I made a detour by the house when the decorations were still up, and at least 20 family friends and relatives were there, enjoying companionship. I showed the slides I had made previously of the rock and the "altar"—shining my projector on a whitewashed adobe wall—and I thought I would never be able to leave. My respect for Our Lady and their village treasure—even though I am a Protestant—made me part of the family.

[7]Weigle, pp. 4-5.

[8]Stephen F. Borhegyi, *El Santuario de Chimayó* (Santa Fe: Ancient City Press for the Spanish Colonial Arts Society, 1956), pp. 20-21. A visit to the little church is a moving experience, and the sincerity of the pilgrims is quite obvious. Conversely, as the tale of the Santo Niño roaming the valley was told to me, it seemed to be almost a local joke, but Borhegyi (pp. 20-22) reports that there is (or has been) serious rivalry between the supporters of the pozo and its powers and the supporters of the Santo Niño's chapel. Perhaps my source was among the anti-chapel group.

[9]Accounts of the mysterious carpenter and the miraculous staircase are available for purchase in the Loretto Chapel gift shop, but no actual claims are made in the leaflets; I recall phrases like "it is said" and "the people believe" throughout. There are also donation boxes here and there for the support of the Sisters of Loretto, a practice that is customary in many churches and historic museums, of course, since they depend upon popular support for their maintenance.

[10]Collected by Irma Sánchez in December 1964 from residents of Socorro. One of the two oldest residents told Miss Sánchez that the miracle took place in 1838, and that it was Indians who were escorting the statue to New Mexico. When they had to leave it behind they cried, feeling that they were leaving part of themselves behind. Historical leaflets published in the area also contribute to the life of the legends of San Miguel. One such is Cleofas Calleros, *El Paso's Missions and Indians* (El Paso: McMath Printing

Co., 1951), which notes (p.35) that some people call the mission San Miguel instead of La Purísima. It is a matter of record that the statue of San Miguel was "solemnly transferred to the new church" on October 29, 1845; the old mission had been destroyed by a flood in 1829. Ernest J. Burrus, S.J., "Outstanding historical dates and events of the towns, missions and churches in the El Paso Valley," (El Paso: The Historical Cultural Commission of the Catholic Diocese of El Paso, Texas, 1981), unnumbered p. 4. A *Foxfire* spinoff, *Sombras del Pasado* (Shadows of the Past), published by Socorro High School students and edited by Julia Kumor, had several locally collected San Miguel stories in the first issue (Spring, 1979).

[11]The frequently heard legend of San Miguel and his apparent battle with the Indians (I have been told the story at least a dozen times) fits in quite well with the tradition of him as a warrior, following the statement in Revelation 12:7 that he was the leader of the heavenly host fighting the dragon.

[12]The representation of the Virgin as the Immaculate Conception *(La Purísima)* shows Her standing atop a snake, symbolizing Her victory in Revelation 12:5-9 over the powers of evil. Marc Simmons, eminent New Mexican historian, does not believe the story to be historically valid (letter to the author, 29 July 1987). However, in an interview on 13 October 1987 with Father Ernest J. Burrus, S.J., I learned that in Sonora, México, a common story circulates about La Flechada (the arrow-pierced woman), describing exactly this motif: La Purísima is shot with many arrows, since she represents a threat to the sacred snake symbol of the Yaqui Indians. Apparently my informant had heard an account that mistakenly blended the two different areas, some four hundred miles apart—although such enmity by all snake-revering Indians toward the usurping Virgin is readily understandable.

[13]Collected by Robert A. Salome in May 1969 from residents of Silver City of assorted cultures—Mexican-American, Anglo, and undetermined.

[14]The Devil at the dance has been reported to me by at least ten student collectors over the years, often with specific dens of iniquity as the "actual place" where this happened—a feature pretty well standard in the traveling legend. It has also been reported from Balmorhea, Texas, in Artell Dorman, "Speak of the Devil," *And Horns on the Toads* (Dallas: Southern Methodist University Press, 1959), PTFS 24:142-44; from Austin, in Soledad Pérez, "Mexican Folklore from Austin, Texas," *The Healer of Los Olmos and Other Mexican Lore* (Dallas: Southern Methodist University Press, 1951), PTFS 29:86-87; and from La Junta, where the Río Conchos from Mexico flows into the Río Grande, Elton R. Miles, "The Devil in the Big Bend," *Folk Travelers: Ballads, Tales and Talk* (Dallas: Southern Methodist University Press, 1953), PTFS 25:207. There is also a Black version, in which the Devil's victim is a "dancin' woman" who dances down every partner, until the Devil beats her. He vanishes in a flash of fire and smoke but leaves his cloven hoof mark burned on the floor (Charles F. Arrowood, "Well Done, Liar," *Backwoods to Border* [Dallas: Southern Methodist University Press, 1943], PTFS 17:81-82). The list of such reportings is almost endless. Several are to be found in W.K. McNeil's *Ghost Stories from the American South* (Little Rock: August House Publishers, 1985), pp. 121-23 and note, pp. 160-61.

[15]Collected in 1975 by Regina Holmes from Chuy (Jesús) Téllez, a sixth-grader at Ysleta Elementary.

[16]Collected by Susanne J. Fitzgerald in 1970 from Isabel González, 42, who grew up in Roswell, New Mexico.

[17]Ruth Laughlin Barker, "New Mexico Witch Tales," *Tone the Bell Easy* (Dallas: Southern Methodist University Press, 1932), PTFS 10:69-70.

[18]Humberto Garza, "Owl Bewitchment in the Lower Rio Grande Valley," *Singers and Storytellers* (Dallas: Southern Methodist 1961), PTFS 30:223-24.

[19]Bacil Kirtley, in "'La Llorona' and Related Themes," *Western Folklore* 19.3 (July

1960), presents international variations of the theme commonly found in La Llorona tales. For a factual account of Cortés and La Malinche, see Jon Manchip White, *Cortés and the Downfall of the Aztec Empire* (New York: St. Martin's Press, 1971), pp. 173-76. The Chicano use of the Llorona story was reported frequently by folklore students at UTEP during the Brown Power movement of the 1960s. In 1970 Ralph Montelongo, a graduate student at UTEP, surveyed Mexican-Americans in El Paso, finding that many elementary school students had lost their fear of the Weeping Woman, and that college-age students saw her primarily as a traitor figure.

[20]Soledad Pérez, "Mexican Folklore from Austin, Texas," in *The Healer of Los Olmos* (Dallas: Southern Methodist University Press, 1951), PTFS 24:73-76, provides a wide variety of La Llorona stories; the account given here is a synthesis combining the most common motifs collected over more than 20 years by folklore students at UTEP. A related story, collected by an unknown student from María Chávez of El Paso—but not including the returned spirit motif—tells how a deserted girlfriend took her new baby to the church, after having stabbed it to death and wrapped it in a towel. She laid the bundle on the bride's bosom and ran, while the blood covered the wedding dress.

[21]Collected in 1963 by a UTEP folklore student whose name I have forgotten. She said that the experience happened to her uncle.

[22]See John O. West, "The Weeping Woman: La Llorona," in *The Legendary Ladies of Texas* (Dallas: E-Heart Press, 1981), PTFS 43:31-36.

[23]Richard L. Hayden, Radioman 3/c, was stationed at the U.S. Navy Communications Station, some 40 miles north of Subic Bay in the Philippines, during 1968 and 1969. Because the 3,000 men stationed there had three trucks a week delivering San Miguel beer, the locals called the base "San Miguel." He heard this account from a houseboy from San Antonio, a little village nearby. La Llorona tales are known quite widely. Besides those reported herein, La Llorona tales are found in *Arizona* (*AFFWord* 1 [April 1971]: 1) and Thomas A. Janvier, *Legends of the City of México* (New York: Harper and Brothers, 1910), pp. 134-38 and note, pp. 162-65. Kirtley (pp. 155-68), arguing for a European origin for La Llorona, finds the legend in Texas, New Mexico, Costa Rica, Guatemala, Germany, and several countries in Europe.

[24]Everardo Gamiz, "Legends from Durango," *Puro Mexicano* (Dallas: Southern Methodist University Press, 1935), PTFS 12:170-73.

[25]*Encyclopaedia Britannica* (1960) 1:887, 991; 2:127; 6:262; 16:49a.

[26]Jan Harold Brunvand, *The Study of American Folklore,* 3rd ed. (New York: Norton, 1987), p. 163.

[27]Collected in 1963 by Jacqueline Miller from an unnamed informant. This story is reported in McNeil, pp. 34-35 and note, p. 138.

[28]Collected in 1974 from Beatrice C. Campos from Juanita Colomo Trujillo, "about 90," of Clint.

[29]L.C. (Elsie) Hayden, "A Haunting in Chamberino," *New Mexico Folklore Record* 12 (1973-74): 19-21.

[30]Collected in 1970 by Richard M. Thomas from Sylvia Ramírez of El Paso.

[31]Collected by Richard L. Hayden in 1968 or 1969 from an unnamed jitney driver, while on duty in the U.S. Navy in the Philippines.

[32]Baldemar A. Jiménez, "Cuentos de Susto," *The Golden Log* (Dallas: Southern Methodist University Press), *PTFS* 31:163-64.

[33]C.L. Sonnichsen, "Mexican Spooks from El Paso," *Straight Texas* (Dallas: Southern Methodist University Press, 1937), PTFS 13:128-29.

[34]W.H. Timmons, Lucy F. West, and Mary Sarber, eds., *Census of 1841 for Ysleta, Socorro, and San Elizario* (El Paso: El Paso County Historical Commission, 1988), p. 116.

[35]Collected by Nancy Poe from Teresa Bermea, seventeen years old, raised in Chi-

huahua, México. For comparison, see Jan Harold Brunvand, *The Vanishing Hitchhiker: American Urban Legends and Their Meanings* (New York: Norton, 1981).

[36]Collected by Jean Roser in 1975 from sixteen-year-old Ernie Aguilar of El Paso.

[37]Collected by Regina Holmes in April 1965 from sixth-graders at Ysleta Elementary School. Aged eleven to thirteen, the youngsters were bilingual, but with strong Mexican backgrounds. Ysleta is on the Rio Grande, the oldest settlement in Texas. Ruth Dodson ("The Ghost Nun," *Backwoods to Border* [Dallas: Southern Methodist University Press, 1943], PTFS 18:137-39) reported several such tales; Anne Clark ("The Ghost of White Rock" in the same volume, pp. 146-47) tells another.

[38]Collected by Regina Holmes in April 1965 from her sixth-graders. The eloquent tale-teller was Ricky González. I wonder what kind of tales he's telling now, 23 years later!

[39]Américo Paredes, *"With His Pistol in His Hand"* (Austin: University of Texas Press, 1958), p. 29.

[40]Paredes, pp. 33-54.

[41]This is a reaction that my Mexican-American students often give voice to, when the police seem to have ganged up on a teenager on El Paso's South Side.

[42]Yellow Bird [John Rollin Ridge], *The Life and Adventures of Joaquín Murieta, the Celebrated California Bandit* (San Francisco, 1854), reprinted in "Western Frontier Library" (Norman: University of Oklahoma Press, 1955).

[43]John O. West, "To Die Like a Man: The 'Good Outlaw' Tradition in the American Southwest," Ph.D. dissertation (The University of Texas at Austin, 1964), pp. 138-40.

[44]Murieta was given to cutting off ears (especially of Chinese), and other niceties. West, "To Die Like a Man," pp. 155-57.

[45]Collected by Rubén Norte from an unnamed source in 1970. See also Haldeen Braddy, *Cock of the Walk: The Legend of Pancho Villa* (1955; reprint Port Washington, N.Y.: Kennikat Press, 1970), which merges the history and the legend of Pancho Villa.

[46]Collected in 1970 by Rubén Norte from Danny Quintana, 25-year-old El Pasoan.

[47]Collected by Rudy Norte in 1980 from Raul Norte.

[48]Collected by Nancy Poe at an unknown date from Héctor Acevedo, fourteen, born in Juárez, Chihuahua, but now living in El Paso. His Mexican grandfather told him the story.

[49]Collected by Nancy Poe at an unknown date from Teresa Bermea, seventeen, born in Durango, and now living in El Paso.

[50]Rubén Norte collected the story in 1970 from Guadalupe Norte of El Paso; ten years later Rudy Norte collected the same story from the same source, apparently their mother.

[51]Collected by Barry Diamond from Cleofas Calleros, El Paso historian who was born a few kilometers from Villa, near Durango.

[52]Collected by Barry Diamond from Mrs. Maud Bently, born and raised in the Mormon colony of San José, Chihuahua.

[53]Collected by Nancy Poe from Arturo González, fourteen, raised in Juárez, Chihuahua, and now living in El Paso. Susanne J. Fitzgerald collected a story in 1970 from Al Martínez, who grew up in Toyah, Texas, of Villa slaughtering cattle so that the poor people could have food. His grandmother told him, "Although Pancho Villa was considered a bad man by many, he did take from those who were rich and gave it to the poor."

[54]Collected by Barry Diamond from Cleofas Calleros; Braddy, pp. 109-10, tells only part of the story, but tells it well.

[55]Collected by Rubén Norte in 1970 from Tinan Windsor of El Paso.

[56]Collected by Rubén Norte in 1970 from Ricardo Vega, born in Chihuahua but now living in El Paso.

[57]Collected in 1971 by Patrick Lowe from an unnamed source.

[58]The decapitation of Villa is quite popular. Rubén Norte collected the story in 1970 from Irene Kosturakis; Patrick Lowe got it from Cleofas Calleros; Nancy Poe collected it from Lucía Alfaro, fourteen, and Rubén Castañeda, sixteen, of El Paso; and Braddy, pp. 161-62, also recounts the event.

[59]Braddy, p. 168.

[60]Aída Siqueiros collected this story in 1974 from Eloisa Chavíra of El Paso, who heard it from her mother, a native of Mexico.

[61]Collected in 1970 by Rubén Norte from Roberto Siqueiros, student from Chihuahua. The "Los Muertos No Hablan" motto served J. Frank Dobie for a chapter title in his *Coronado's Children* (New York: Grossett and Dunlap, 1930), pp. 189-203.

[62]These three stories were collected in 1967 by Louis Belmont from a lady who would not give her name, but she lived all her life in the Southwest, and heard the stories from her treasure-hunting father.

[63]In addition to *Coronado's Children,* Dobie also published *Apache Gold and Yaqui Silver* (Boston: Little, Brown, 1939).

[64]Collected by Susanne J. Fitzgerald in 1970 from 95-year-old Francisco Montoya, life-long sheepherder in New Mexico.

[65]Collected in 1967 by Louis Belmont from Harvey T. Maddox of El Paso, who heard it from a Mexican yard man.

[66]Collected in 1970 by Susanne J. Fitzgerald from Mary Bautista, who grew up in Ysleta.

[67]Collected by an unnamed collector from an unnamed informant.

[68]This is a composite of dozens of Padre Mine stories collected over the years. Among the accounts is one collected in 1971 by Betty B. Whatley from Héctor Venegas, who swears that there is a mine shaft on Mount Franklin, filled up with twenty feet of red river soil. The soil in the Rio Grande, incidentally, is desert-brown for miles in both directions from El Paso. Downriver from El Paso in the village of San Vicente, a similar story is told of a lost mine in the Chisos Mountains, the mouth of which can be seen on Easter morning by standing in the mission doorway and looking toward the mountain just as the sun rises. Collected by Robert Sholly in 1970 from residents of Alpine, Texas.

[69]Dobie, *Coronado's Children,* pp. 185-88, includes the Cheetwah story. Leon Denny Moses, "Five Legends of the Southwest," *Tone the Bell Easy* (Dallas: Southern Methodist University Press, 1932), PTFS 10:70-75, reported stories that it was indeed a mine, and that an Apache raid caused it to be covered up; the miners chiseled two arrows in the rock near their camp, pointing toward the hidden mine. An informant found the arrows, as well as holes in nearby rock, used by the miners' women to grind corn to make tortillas—but not the mine. In 1969 Margaret Sanger collected several "Padre Mine" stories—from New Mexico, Arizona, and Old Mexico—with similar details. The Arizona story, told to her by Ross Martínez of Española, New Mexico, has Jesuit priests owning the mine; isolated from "Mother Church," they became greedy, and didn't even pay a tithe of their gold and silver. The bishop excommunicated them, and they hid the mine, expecting to return when the matter blew over, but it never did.

[70]Riley Aiken, "A Pack Load of Folk Tales," *Texas Folk and Folklore* (Dallas: Southern Methodist University Press, 1954), PTFS 26:30-36; see also Stanley L. Robe, *Hispanic Folktales from New Mexico* (Los Angeles: University of California at Los Angeles Press, 1977), pp. 51-54.

[71]Dan Storm, "The Little Animals of Mexico," *Coyote Wisdom* (Dallas: Southern Methodist University Press, 1938), PTFS 24:24-26. Other articles in this volume have a number of good coyote stories.

[72]Pérez, pp. 80-84.

[73]Rudolfo A. Anaya, *Cuentos: Tales from the Hispanic Southwest* (Santa Fe: Museum of New Mexico Press, 1980), pp. 111-13.

[74]José Limón shared this story via a handout (undated) with people attending the American Folklore Society meeting several years ago. It was collected in Austin, mostly in Spanish, from a waitress. The gringa in the story spoke English.

[75]José Limón handout.

[76]T.M. Pearce and Catherine Delgado Espinosa, *Stories of the Spanish Southwest* (Albuquerque: Pearce, 1973), pp. 9-13. The story was collected by Lou Sage Batchen for the New Mexico Writers Project, and was also published in *Western Folklore* 15 (April 1956): 89-92.

[77]Anaya, pp. 25-27.

[78]Anaya, pp. 63-75.

[79]Anaya, pp. 15-21; see also Riley Aiken's "La Madrina Muerte" from another "Pack Load of Mexican Tales" in *Puro Mexicano* (Dallas: Southern Methodist University Press, 1935), PTFS 12: 76-77.

[80]Anaya, pp. 115-17.

[81]Collected in July 1970 by Sebastian T. Martínez from Javier Hernández Barraza.

[82]Collected in July 1970 by Sebastian T. Martínez from Javier Hernández Barraza.

[83]Aiken, *Puro Mexicano,* pp. 29-36.

[84]Aiken, *Puro Mexicano,* pp. 41-44.

[85]Anaya, pp. 97-109. While this story resembles "The kind and the unkind girls" (AT 408), with the series of encounters present, there is no attempt by the disobedient sons to gain the same reward as the faithful son; he, however, does ask for them to be rewarded, and is refused. The story is a folk commonplace, dealing with three brothers, only the youngest of whom is obedient and worthy of emulation.

[86]Aiken, *Texas Folk and Folklore,* pp. 24-27. See also Anaya, pp. 87-91.

[87]Weigle, pp. 97-101.

[88]See Frederick Klaeber, *Beowulf and the Fight at Finnsburg,* 3rd ed. (New York: D.C. Heath, 1950).

[89]Robert A. Barakat, "The Bear's Son Tale in Northern Mexico" (El Paso: M.A. thesis, Texas Western College, August 1964), pp. 31-38. Barakat's work was also published in shortened form under the same title in *Journal of American Folklore* 78 (October 1965): 330-36.

[90]Weigle, pp. 60-66. See also Aiken, *Puro Mexicano,* for an abbreviated version which has Juan Oso mainly fighting and doing wild things; the Type 301 story is essentially omitted.

[91]J. Frank Dobie, "Catorce," *Puro Mexicano,* pp. 194-200.

[92]Aiken, *Puro Mexicano,* pp. 79-86. See also Elizabeth Willis DeHuff, "The Metamorphosis of a Folk Tale" in *Puro Mexicano,* pp. 122-34, for an interesting comparative study.

[93]José Limón handout. Collected in an Austin restaurant, with the teller switching from Spanish to English for appropriate parts of the story.

[94]José Limón handout. Collected in Austin and South Texas; Limón wondered if the seller was a deliberate trickster, telling the truth but deliberately fooling the buyer.

[95]I first heard this tale about 50 years ago, and have told it innumerable times. Its widespread existence is suggested by the fact that repeatedly over the years I have heard the punchline on national television, including the Johnny Carson Show. "Wait I get my hat, I go with you" is certainly well known. In many of the tellings of this story (and the way I heard it first) the third item Pablo carries is a "poosy weelow." The response, of course, is the same. I suspect that the "horse fly" is a sanitized version of

what is probably the original.

[96]Collected by Carol Anne Strohmeyer in 1969 from Mrs. Julia P. Ramírez, 68 years old.

[97]Aiken, *Puro Mexicano,* pp. 45-55.

[98]I have had this story told to me many times over the past 20 years. It is also reported from Los Angeles by Stanley Robe, *Antología del saber popular* (Los Angeles: University of California at Los Angeles Press, 1971), pp. 19-20.

[99]Collected by Norma Morales from Julieta Nevarez in October 1975.

[100]Collected by Norma Morales from Julieta Nevarez in October 1975.

[101]Robe, *Antología,* p. 19. This is probably the best pun I have ever heard in Spanish.

[102]Frequently told in the El Paso area; see also Robe, *Antología,* p. 21.

[103]Recalled in 1965 by Juan Armendáriz from his life in El Paso's Southside.

[104]Collected in 1965 by Juan Armendáriz from Robert González of Smeltertown (a slum-like suburb of El Paso).

[105]Collected by Juan Armendáriz in 1965 from an anonymous informant.

[106]Collected by Conchita Pytcher from 62-year-old Mrs. Reyes of Ysleta, Texas.

[107]Collected in 1965 by Juan Armendáriz from an anonymous informant.

[108]Collected by René J. Cantú in 1971 from Eduardo Liano, a student from Juárez. Over half a century ago I heard this as an ethnic joke, in which the people all go into the basement, one at a time, and come out holding their noses—until the last one, a Negro, takes off his shoes and goes in, with the same result, the skunk exiting holding *his* nose.

[109]Collected by René J. Cantú in 1971 from Enrique Alvarez, UTEP student from Juárez. The story is also told with no national rivalry involved.

[110]Recalled by René J. Cantú from his youth (he was then 23). He also collected a variant in 1971 from Eduardo Liano, in which the Mexican says he eats *"con sus ojos"* (with his eyes), with the same final response.

[111]Robe, *Hispanic Folktales,* p. 206; the story was collected in Artesia, in an area deprecatingly referred to as "Little Texas."

[112]Collected in 1971 by René J. Cantú from Eduardo Liano. The story recalls the oft-repeated anecdote that General Sherman, after a tour of duty in the Lone Star State, said that if he owned Hell and Texas, he'd live in Hell and rent out Texas.

[113]Stanley L. Robe, *Amapa Storytellers* (Los Angeles: University of California at Los Angeles Press, 1972), pp. 94-95. See also his *Index of Mexican Folktales* (Los Angeles: University of California at Los Angeles Press, 1973), and *Hispanic Folktales from New Mexico.*

[114]Riley Aiken, "Fifteen Mexican Tales," *A Good Tale and a Bonny Tune* (Dallas: Southern Methodist University Press, 1964), PTFS 32:54-55. Don Burgess, a linguist and Bible translator working with Mexico's Tarahumara Indians, recently collected a Mexican version of the lightning-struck horse story, published in *Chistes de la Sierra Tarahumara* (Chihuahua: Don Burgess, 1987), p. 9.

[115]Robe, *Amapa Storytellers,* pp. 82-90. Although this variant is from Mexico, its parallel to the Mexican-American version makes it appropriate here.

[116]J. Frank Dobie, "Tales of the Two Companions," *From Hell to Breakfast* (Dallas: Southern Methodist University Press, 1944), PTFS 19:36-41.

[117]Aiken, *Puro Mexicano,* p. 57; Robe, *Hispanic Folktales,* pp. 212-13. Robe also reports a big eagle story as well as a shirt with three sleeves, both told under similar circumstances.

[118]Robe, *Amapa Storytellers,* pp. 93-95; a similar tale collected from Mexicans in Tarahumara country is found in Burgess, p. 23; the third story is from Aiken, *Puro Mexicano,* pp. 55-57.

[119]Robe, *Hispanic Folktales,* pp. 216-17. I couldn't resist the opportunity for the pun!

[120]W.A. Whatley, "Mexican Munchausen," *From Hell to Breakfast,* pp. 45-49.

Chapter 7. Ballads and Folksongs

[1]John D. Robb, *Hispanic Folk Music of New Mexico and the Southwest: A Self-Portrait of a People* (Norman: University of Oklahoma Press, 1980), pp. 3-4. This book is the best single source I have discovered on the subject, with literally hundreds of songs with translations and music. Robb has devoted a lifetime to this work. Incidentally, throughout this chapter I have silently amended translations into English where I thought necessary—especially where the source seemed to depart markedly from the actual sense of the Spanish.

[2]William J. Entwistle, *European Balladry* (Oxford Clarendon Press, 1931, rpt. 1951).

[3]Aurelio M. Espinosa, *The Folklore of Spain in the American Southwest* (Norman: University of Oklahoma Press, 1985), pp. 83, 84.

[4]Américo Paredes, *"With His Pistol in His Hand": A Border Ballad and Its Hero* (Austin: University of Texas Press, 1958).

[5][Norman] "Brownie" McNeil, "Corridos of the Mexican Border," *Mexican Border Ballads* (Dallas: Southern Methodist University Press, 1946), PTFS 21:4.

[6]F.S. Curtis, Jr., "Spanish Songs of New Mexico," *Happy Hunting Ground* (Austin: Texas Folk-Lore Society, 1925), PTFS 4:19. The falsetto style is still common along the Mexican border, as are voice breaks and a descending scale of "Ah hah hah hah hah" or an "Ah hoo ah" with rising and falling pitch, interjected between lines or verses—a feature which perhaps was adopted by Bob Wills and his Texas Playboys in their freewheeling style of singing, with such exclamations as "Ah hah, San Antone" in "San Antonio Rose."

[7]Curtis, p. 21.

[8]In addition to Robb, see Américo Paredes, *A Texas-Mexican Cancionero* (Urbana: University of Illinois Press, 1976) (hereafter cited as *Cancionero).* Aurora Lucero-White Lea, *Literary Folklore of the Hispanic Southwest* (San Antonio: The Naylor Co., 1953), is also valuable.

[9]*Cancionero,* pp. 9-11.

[10]*Cancionero,* pp. 14-16.

[11]"Brownie" McNeil, p. 7. W.A. Whatley, "A Mexican Popular Ballad" in *Happy Hunting Ground,* pp. 12-17, has a longer variant; J. Frank Dobie, who edited the volume, appended an interesting ending to the Bernal corrido: "Oh, but Bernal was handsome on his cream-colored horse! He did not rob the poor but rather gave them money./Fly away, fly away, little dove, fly away, fly away to the walnut tree, for now the roads are solitary since they have killed Bernal./Oh, but Bernal was handsome on his horse of black, with his pistol in his hand fighting with thirty-and-five!/Fly away, fly away, little dove, fly away, fly away to the olive tree, for Don Porfirio Díaz was wanting to know Bernal alive." (pp. 16-17).The "fly away, little dove" ending is one of many traditional closings for the corrido, somewhat similar to Kentucky ballad endings such as "There's a little bit of honey up on the shelf,/if you want any more you can sing it yourself!"

[12]Jovita González, "Tales and Songs of the Texas-Mexicans," *Man, Bird, and Beast* (Dallas: Southern Methodist University Press, 1930), PTFS 8:110-11.

[13]Américo Paredes, "Folklore and History," *Singers and Storytellers* (Dallas: Southern Methodist University Press, 1961), PTFS 30:63-68.

[14]Américo Paredes, "The Mexican Corrido: Its Rise and Fall," *Madstones and Twisters* (Dallas: Southern Methodist University Press, 1958), PTFS 28:100.

[15]Curtis, pp. 22, 25-26.

[16]Curtis, pp. 28-29; the variant of the last cited verse that I have heard most often around El Paso uses the simple future tense *fuera* instead of the subjunctive *fuere,* and goes thus: *Si Adelita se fuera con otro, la seguiría por tierra y por mar;/Si por mar en un buque de guerra, si por tierra en un tren militar.* (If Adelita goes away with another, I'll follow her by land and by sea;/If by sea on a warship, if by land on a military train.)

Such is also the way professional and folk singers along the border sing the verse.

[17]*Cancionero*, pp. 113-14.

[18]Jovita González, "Folklore of the Texas-Mexican Vaquero," *Texas and Southwestern Lore* (Austin: Texas Folklore Society, 1927), PTFS 6:20.

[19]Interview with Lucina Lara Rey de Fischer, 15 September 1987, in El Paso. The Coral Mexicano de Bellas Artes, famed Mexican singing group, sings it thus also.

[20]Robb, p. 271.

[21]*Cancionero,* pp. 117-18.

[22]*Cancionero,* pp. 118-19. *De los* (of them) is not as idiomatic as *denos* (give us), and makes less sense in the song's first and last verses.

[23]*Cancionero,* pp. 113-14, 119-20. My mother-in-law, Lucina Lara Rey de Fischer, uses the same terms of loving care for our son—*mi sol* (my sun), and *mi corazón* (my heart)—in a lovely family and cultural tradition.

[24]Américo Paredes, "The Love Tragedy in Texas-Mexican Balladry," *Folk Travelers* (Dallas: Southern Methodist University Press, 1953), PTFS 25:110-14.

[25]Curtis, pp. 19-20.

[26]González, "Tales and Songs," pp. 113-14.

[27]J. Frank Dobie, "Versos of the Texas Vaqueros," *Happy Hunting Ground,* pp. 41-43.

[28]González, "Tales and Songs," p. 114. The trousers the ranch girl is going to make the singer, begun with wool and finished with leather, sound like the leather-seated riding britches worn by the charro, the fancily dressed Mexican horseman taking part in parades or *charreadas* (Mexican-style rodeos). See Chapter Nine herein. It is interesting to observe that while *"(Alla En) El Rancho Grande"* (Yonder in my Big Ranch) was copyrighted in 1934, with English words by Bartley Costello, Spanish words by J. Del Moral, and music by Silvano R. Ramos, and new English lyrics were added in 1958 for "El Rancho Rock," Jovita González had published this version in 1930, and Joaquín Moro published another, shorter and slightly different, in "Songs the Vaqueros Sing," *Southwestern Lore* (Dallas: Southern Methodist University Press, 1931), PTFS 9:119. It is apparent that this is a folk song that was copyrighted several years after its life among the folk was established.

[29]Robb, pp. 353-54.

[30]Robb, pp. 355-56.

[31]*Cancionero,* pp. 149-150.

[32]*Cancionero,* pp. 153-61.

[33]*Cancionero,* pp. 161-62.

[34]"Brownie" McNeil, pp. 10-12, and note p. 33.

[35]"Brownie" McNeil, pp. 29-32.

[36]"Brownie" McNeil, p. 3.

[37]Folklore student Lucía Servín bought the corrido from a street vendor in Juárez, and inquired to no avail about the author and the tune to which the song would be sung. The "broadside" has eighteen four-line stanzas and is printed in two columns on one side of a sheet of typing-quality paper, in bold-face capital letters, with a printer's border around the song. At the bottom is the statement PROHIBIDA LA REIMPRESIÓN SIN PERMISO DE SU AUTOR, FELIPE MARTÍNEZ SANDOVAL (Reprinting prohibited without permission of the author. . .).

[38]As further evidence of the continuing tradition of corrido production, consider the following article by Peter Applebome, "Outrages and Brave Deeds Live On in South Texas Ballads," *The New York Times,* 19 December 1986, which reports that when "a notorious drug dealer escaped from a Texas prison one evening in August 1974," singer Salomé Gutiérrez wrote a corrido that same night, "recorded it after midnight, and it was played on KEDA by six o'clock the next morning."

Chapter 8. Beliefs and Superstitions

[1]Joe S. Graham, "The Role of the Curandero in the Mexican-American System in West Texas," *American Folk Medicine: A Symposium,* ed. Wayland D. Hand (Berkeley: UCLA Press, 1976), pp. 175-76.

[2]Cervando Martínez and Harry W. Martin, "Folk Diseases among Urban Mexican-Americans: Etiology, Symptoms, and Treatment," *Journal of the American Medical Association* 196.2 (April 11, 1966): 161-62; Graham, p. 172.

[3]Literally dozens of my students have collected the basic information on mal ojo; see also Linda Griego, "The 'Ojo,'" *Southwest Folklore* 1.4 (Fall 1977): 35. Perhaps it need not be pointed out that an egg sitting in the open air overnight would tend to dry, leaving a series of concentric circles that resemble the pupil of an eye.

[4]Martínez and Martin, p. 162. Joe Graedon, "The People's Pharmacy," a syndicated column appearing in the El Paso *Times,* 20 May 1979, notes that chamomile tea can bring on symptoms of a severe allergic attack in sufferers from hay fever and ragweed allergy.

[5]Martínez and Martin, pp. 148-49. Again, dozens of my students have reported this ailment.

[6]David Werner, *Donde no hay doctor* (Palo Alto, California: The Hesperian Foundation, 1973), p. 9. The handbook is also available in English as *Where There Is No Doctor.*

[7]Martínez and Martin, p. 163.

[8]Several years ago, a professor at UTEP who was experiencing a series of falls and other mishaps was advised by many of her students to have a *limpia* (cleansing); she had one, involving a sweeping ritual, and seemed to have better luck from then on. Student Belinda Sanchez in 1982 also collected a number of accounts of limpias for houses, involving the use of holy water, burning herbs, and smoking charcoal to dispel evil spirits. See also Eliseo Torres, *The Folk Healer: The Mexican-American Tradition of Curanderismo* (Kingsville, Texas: Nieves Press [1983], p. 23.

[9]Martínez and Martin, p. 149.

[10]Torres, p. 18. While the brujo and the curandero both have the reputation of calling on supernatural powers and both can heal, the brujo(a) is generally associated with diabolic forces or black magic, and the curandero(a) with heavenly forces or white magic.

[11]Torres, pp. 41-44.

[12]William C. Holden, *Teresita* (Owings Mills, Maryland: Stemmer House, 1978), pp. xi-xii.

[13]Ruth Dodson, "Folk-Curing among the Mexicans," *Tone the Bell Easy* (Dallas: Southern Methodist University Press, 1932), PTFS 10:91 ff.

[14]Ruth Dodson, "Don Pedrito Jaramillo: The Curandero of Los Olmos," *The Healer of Los Olmos* (Austin: The Texas Folklore Society, 1951), PTFS 24:56.

[15]Dodson, "Folk-Curing," pp. 91-92.

[16]Dodson, "Don Pedrito Jaramillo," 48-49.

[17][Norman] "Brownie" McNeil, "Curanderos of South Texas," *And Horns on the Toads* (Dallas: Southern Methodist University Press, 1959), PTFS 29:35-36. See also Ari Kiev, *Curanderismo: Mexican-American Folk Psychiatry* (New York: The Free Press, 1968), pp. 31-32.

[18]"Brownie" McNeil, pp. 36-37.

[19]"Brownie" McNeil, pp. 40-41.

[20]Ernest Herrerra, Jr., "Healing Herbs of Northern New Mexico" (August 1967), unpublished manuscript in the University of Texas at El Paso Folklore Archive.

[21]L.C. [Elsie] Hayden, "This Plant Is a 'Medicine Cabinet,'" *Rio Grande Gazette* (March 1979), p. 4. Note should also be taken of the long line of commercial products, ranging from wrinkle reducer to sunburn gel, made commercially from this folk resource.

[22]Collected by Geraldine Orr about 1975 from Bonifacia and Roberto Chuka of Fabens, Texas.

[23]Collected by Geraldine Orr about 1975 from Margarita Lara and Ramona Almengor of the Tortuga barrio of Fabens. Ramona noted that the cottonwood tree will give headaches to those who sleep beneath it.

[24]Collected by Geraldine Orr about 1975 from Angelita and Elpidio Contreras of Fabens, who also noted that alfalfa has the same effect; without such protection, Elpidio said, *"el sol lo vuelve loco"* (the sun will drive you crazy).

[25]Collected by Geraldine Orr about 1975 from Paula Domínguez of the Tortuga barrio of Fabens.

[26]Collected by Geraldine Orr about 1975 from Guadalupe Luna of the Tortuga barrio of Fabens.

[27]Collected by Geraldine Orr about 1975 from Ramona Almengor.

[28]Collected by Geraldine Orr about 1975 from Margarita Lara. Josefina Alvarádo, who is partially paralyzed, told Mrs. Orr that a neighbor once offered to bring her clothes in off the line after nightfall; the neighbor was "hot from the stove" when she went out, and an *aire* (chilling blast of air) hit her and twisted up her mouth "in a terrible way and it stayed that way." Señora Alvarádo lives in the Papalote barrio of Fabens.

[29]This very commonly reported belief was collected in August 1965 by Juan Armendáriz from Mrs. V.P. Portugal; in August 1985 by Irene Acosta from Irma Acosta; and in August 1985 by Irene Acosta from 70-year-old María Salgado.

[30]Collected in July 1967 by Ed Hickerson from Gus Hickerson, raised in Coahuila, México, but living in El Paso since 1925.

[31]Collected in August 1985 by Irene Acosta from Guillermo González. María Salgado told Ms. Acosta that the first twelve days of January predict the weather for the coming twelve months—followed by a complicated *caniculas al derecho y al revez* (predictions forward and backward) running throughout January—but city living and modern technology have diminished the use of such methods.

[32]Collected in August 1965 by Juan Armendáriz from Mrs. R.K. Foust, who heard it from an old Mexican laundress, "many years ago."

[33]Collected by Julieta Macías several years ago from a group of women now living in Juárez, but coming there from Albuquerque, New Mexico, and Parral and San Francisco del Oro, Chihuahua.

[34]Collected by Julieta Macías from Senora Victoria Prieto, who did not bathe for forty days after the birth of her first child, although she was not so careful after later births. My wife, Lucy Fischer West, has often expressed her disapproval on seeing a woman out of the house with a baby only ten or fifteen days old: such actions violate the traditions she grew up with.

[35]Collected about 1975 by Geraldine Orr from Josefina Alvarádo and Guadalupe Luna.

[36]Collected several years ago by Nancy Poe from Raul Santana of El Paso, who was raised in Parral, Chihuahua.

[37]Collected in August 1965 by Juan Armendáriz from Mrs. R.K. Foust.

[38]Collected in August 1985 by Elizabeth Aeby from Orlene Roybal of El Rancho, New Mexico, who has used the remedy on her two children.

[39]Collected in August 1985 by Elizabeth Aeby from Trinie Esquibel of Española, New Mexico; her mother had this remedy tried on herself, but there was no improvement noticed.

[40]Collected in August 1985 by Elizabeth Aeby from Francis Lopez of Española. Next to youngest in a family of seventeen children, she reports that her mother used this remedy on the children when aspirin was too expensive—and it also was effective in reducing fever.

[41]Collected in August 1985 by Elizabeth Aeby from Mary Martínez of Española. My students have noted that even if the remedy doesn't fix the cough, it makes you feel better—especially if you drink enough of it. I prefer to use tequila instead of whiskey, myself.

[42]Collected in July 1967 by Ed Hickerson from Gus Hickerson.

[43]Collected in August 1985 by Yolanda Martínez from Ana Sophia García and Enrique de Santiago of El Paso.

[44]Collected in August 1985 by Yolanda Martínez from Ana Sophia García.

[45]Collected in August 1985 by Yolanda Martínez from Ana Sophia García.

[46]Collected in August 1985 by Yolanda Martínez from Roger Johnson of El Paso.

[47]Collected in August 1985 by Yolanda Martínez from Martha Cordero, whose mother regularly keeps a pail of water outside the door.

[48]Collected in August 1985 by Yolanda Martínez from Martha Cordero and Enrique de Santiago.

[49]Oran Warder Nolen, "Some Odd Mexican Customs," *From Hell to Breakfast* (Dallas: Southern Methodist University Press, 1944), TFSP 19:58.

[50]Collected about 1970 by Terry Acosta from Pepe Peria, who heard the story in Durango, México. The nino is reputed to be poisonous, and to cause the earth to open up and "eat up" a person who bothers it. Ms. Acosta noted that "similarities between the baroque design and the cuento are too relative to be scratched off as mere coincidence" ("Ninos de la Tierra," unpublished, undated manuscript in the University of Texas at El Paso Archive). Perhaps it is worth pointing out that the old movie *The Little Shop of Horrors,* produced in 1960 by Roger Corman and recently remade, features a plant that produces not only flowers with faces, but hungry ones that cry, "Feed me!"

Chapter 9. Customs and Festivals

[1]Jan Harold Brunvand, *The Study of American Folklore,* 3rd ed. (New York: Norton, 1987), p. 329.

[2]"Manners and Customs," *The International Folklore Bibliography* (1975).

[3]Collected in the 1970s by Lidia Ruiz from Isabel Rey of Midland.

[4]Collected in the 1970s by Lidia Ruiz from Alfredo Curtis of El Paso.

[5]Florence Johnson Scott, "Customs and Superstitions Among Texas Mexicans on the Rio Grande Border," *Coffee in the Gourd* (Austin: Texas Folklore Society, 1923), PTFS 2:77-80. According to Socorro G. Santiesteban, who was interviewed in 1986 by Alma Santiesteban, baptizing a child during a wedding is supposed to bring luck to the couple—and perhaps to the baby.

[6]Collected by Alma Santiesteban in 1986 from Inocencia G. Santiesteban, her 81-year-old grandmother. Writing before the turn of the century, John G. Bourke disputed the idea that the thirteen coins of the arras symbolize the twelve Apostles and their Master, as he was told in Saltillo, Mexico. He said the custom, called in Arabic *jarras,* came into Spain with the Moors and is still practiced in Algeria and Morocco. "The Folk Foods of the Rio Grande Valley and of Northern Mexico," *Southwestern Lore* (Dallas: Southern Methodist University Press, 1931) PTFS 9:116. The article was a reprint from the *Journal of American Folklore* 8 (1895).

[7]Collected by Alma Santiesteban in 1986 from Socorro G. Santiesteban, her mother.

[8]Collected by Alma Santiesteban in 1986 from Sylvia S. Haynes, her sister.

[9]Scott, pp. 79-80. In my experience, people attending such a dance often spent a considerable time arguing over whether or not the custom is traditional! An unpublished paper by Phyllis Lee Thompson in the UT El Paso Folklore Archive, "Mexican Wedding Customs" (1979), presents an excellent survey of the subject.

[10]Personal interview with Connie Hulbert, who grew up in Ysleta and attended the Ysleta Mission in her youth; 13 October 1987.

[11]In May of each year, says Mrs. Hulbert, young girls also bring flowers from home

which they present to the Virgin, reciting, *"En este día, Madre querida, yo te doy mi corazón"* (On this day, dearest Mother, I give you my heart).

[12]Scott, pp. 76-77.

[13]Collected by Saleh Azzam in the summer of 1986 from David González, who was born in Mexico but has lived in El Paso for over 30 years. He was quoting a friend of his on keeping alive the old tradition on naming.

[14]Aurelio M. Espinosa, *The Folklore of Spain in the American Southwest,* ed. J. Manuel Espinosa (Norman: University of Oklahoma Press, 1985), p. 73.

[15]Collected by Pat Henry in 1983 from Father Ramon Durán of La Purísima Church in Socorro, Texas.

[16]Collected by Pat Henry in 1983 from Patti Steinman, bridal consultant in a large El Paso department store.

[17]Collected by Pat Henry in 1983 from Nora Armendáriz, secretary at La Purísima Church.

[18]Collected by Pat Henry in 1983 from Monica Robertson and her father, Barry Robertson; published in the *El Paso Times,* 14 August 1983.

[19]Scott, p. 80.

[20]Personal observations and collection in the El Paso/Juárez area, 1970 to the present.

[21]*El Paso Times,* 31 October 1974.

[22]"All Souls' Day," *New Catholic Encyclopedia* (1967); William S. Walsh, *Curiosities and Popular Customs* (Philadelphia: Lippincott, 1898), p. 29. Locally the two days tend to blend, with the weekend attracting the majority of those who do their duty to the family dead, especially when everybody works and can't get off on the "right" day.

[23]"Halloween," *Encyclopaedia Britannica* (1973); "Halloween," *The American Book of Days,* 3rd ed., ed. June M. Hatch (New York: H.W. Wilson, 1978).

[24]Ensho Ashikaga, "The Festival for the Spirits of the Dead in Japan," *Western Folklore* 9 (1950): 217-28.

[25]"All Saints, Festival of," *Encyclopaedia Britannica* (1973).

[26]"Halloween," *American Book of Days.*

[27]"All Souls' Day," *New Catholic Encyclopedia.*

[28]Recollections of Felix Rubert-Negron, a folklore student at UTEP who lived in Puerto Rico until the age of 25. Patzcuaro, west of Mexico City, according to Guadalupe Silva, is the only place where "the velación de muertos is still a ritual. Natives pay homage to their dead in the plazas and the streets by recreating their graves decorated with flowers, foods and tall lighted candles." "Cities Are Filled with History, Culture and Celebrations," *El Paso Times,* 13 July 1987, p. 2D.

[29]Frances Toor, *A Treasury of Mexican Folkways* (1947; reprinted New York: Bonanza Books, 1985), pp. 236-37; Rudolph Brasch, *How Did It Begin?* (New York: David McKay, 1967), pp. 60-61. *Posada's Mexico,* ed. Ron Tyler (Washington: Library of Congress, 1979), shows that the work of José Guadalupe Posada, Mexican artist and political cartoonist of great influence, was strongly shaped by the spirit of the calavera. See especially the section "Eternity: The Calaveras," pp. 260-72.

[30]"All Souls' Day," *American Book of Days;* Toor, pp. 136-37; Christine Hole, *British Folk Customs* (London: Hutchinson, 1976), pp. 187-88. When I made a presentation of Día de los Muertos at the annual meeting of the American Folklore Society which preceded the proper date that year by over a week, I had to bribe an El Paso baker to prepare some pan de muertos early—and I'm sure he felt quite uncomfortable breaking a tradition by so doing. A booklet by Robert V. Childs and Patricia B. Altman, *Vive tu Recuerdo: Living Traditions in the Mexican Days of the Dead* (Los Angeles: University of California at Los Angeles Museum of Cultural History, 1982) provides a beautifully written and illustrated description of the Mexican custom and its roots, in both Spanish and English. Spanish-language newspapers on both sides of the border regularly de-

vote a full page or even more to the custom on the appropriate dates.

[31]Toor, pp. 237-38; Rudolph Brasch, *Mexico: A Country of Contrasts* (New York: David McKay, 1967), p. 124; Brasch's book was actually a guidebook for visitors to the 19th Olympics held in Mexico City in 1968.

[32]See Guy Kirtley, "'Hopin' Out' in East Texas: The Wake," *Texian Stomping Grounds* (Dallas: Southern Methodist University Press, 1941), PTFS 17:31-32; Robert Cowser, "Community Memorial Day Observances in Northeast Texas," *Western Folklore* 31 (1972): 120-21; and Florence Johnson Scott, "Customs and Superstitions among Texas Mexicans on the Rio Grande Border," *Coffee in the Gourd* (Dallas: Southern Methodist University Press, 1923) PTFS 2:81-82.

[33]Personal observations, 1970 to the present. An outsider would be puzzled by the absence of priests in clerical garb on these important days, but since 14 June 1926 the Ley Calles (Law of President Plutarco Elias Calles), Article 18, prescribes a fine of 500 pesos or fifteen days in jail for a priest wearing even the clerical collar in public! Joseph H.L. Schlarman, *Mexico: A Land of Volcanoes* (Milwaukee: Bruce Publishing Co., 1950), pp. 501-2.

[34]Sara Clark, "Decoration of Graves in Central Texas with Seashells," *Diamond Bessie and the Shepherds* (Austin: Encino, 1972), PTFS 36:33-43. More of this custom will be found in my chapter on folk art.

[35]Scott (pp. 77-80), as well as conversations with my folklore students over the years.

[36]John E. Englekirk, "The Source and Dating of New Mexican Spanish Folk Plays," *Western Folklore* 16.4 (October 1957): 233, note 6.

[37]The play was directed by John Phelan Quarm, associate professor of English at UT El Paso and drama director for several little theater groups in the area. Raised in the British Isles, she had a great admiration for the medieval drama, and had lived in or near Latin America for a score of years, so she was at home in all the traditions concerned.

[38]Honora DeBusk Smith, "Mexican Plazas along the River of Souls," *Southwestern Lore* (Dallas: Southern Methodist University Press, 1931), PTFS 9:76-77.

[39]John Donald Robb, "The Music of Los Pastores," *Western Folklore* 16.4 (October, 1957): 275. The first word in the second song, *entre,* would logically be *entren,* since it should be the plural command form.

MUSICAL SELECTIONS

1158. EN EL NOMBRE DEL CIELO (LAS POSADAS)
1.
EN EL NOM-BRE DEL CIE-LO OS PI-DO PO-SA-DA
PUES NO PUE-DE AN-DAR MI E-SPO-SA A-MA-DA.
1159. ENTRE SANTO PEREGRINOS
2.
EN-TRE SAN-TOS PE-RE-GRI - NOS. RE- CI-BAN E-STE RIN- CON.

QUE AUN-QUE ES MO-RA- DA OS LA DOY DE CO-RA-ZON
PO-BRE LA
1160 CUANDO POR EL ORIENTE
3.
CUAN- DO POR EL O- RIEN- TE SA- LE LA AU-
RO- RA ¿ CA- MI- NA- BA LA VIR- GEN NUE-
STRA SE- ÑO- RA. ¡AY QUE
GU- STO, AY, QUE A- LE- GRI-
A DEL AL- MA MI- A! LO QUE GRAN-GE-
AS O, REI-NA DE LOS CIE-LOS BEN-DI-TA SE- AS.

[40]Nancy Hamilton, "The Lights of Christmas," *Texas and Christmas,* ed. Judy Alter and Joyce Gibson Roach (Forth Worth: Texas Christian University Press, 1983). Churches along the border also employ the luminaria tradition. See Carol Dean and Nancy Bagby, "We Saw the Lights," *Presbyterian Survey* (November 1980), pp. 26-28. Strings of electric imitation luminarias, with plastic look-alike sacks in a variety of colors, are for sale in Southwestern specialty shops. See advertising in *New Mexico* (October 1987), p. 13, for sets of ten for $19.95 plus shipping. An equivalent number of the real thing might possibly cost as much as 75 cents, sand, candles, sacks and all.

[41]Toor, pp. 148-49. The account of the posadas is charmingly told in Spanish and English by Lila Perl in *Piñatas and Paper Flowers,* tr. Alma Flor Ada (New York: Clarion Books, 1983).

[42]Ramon Villalobos, "Mexican Yuletide Rich in Tradition," *El Paso Times,* 24 December 1978.

[43]Many of my UT El Paso students as well as Jewish friends of my daughter in El Paso High School in the 1960s confessed to such successful wheedling. But Mexico tends to hold on to old traditions; witness this account from Juárez, Chihuahua: "For the first time since 1934, the Juárez Fire Department did not distribute refurbished toys to the city's poor children Christmas Day. Acting Mayor Alfredo Urías Cantú ordered the firefighters to conduct their annual toy distribution Tuesday, the Latin holiday Día de los Santos Reyes, or Three Kings Day," in an effort to combat growing Americanization of the season. David Hancock, "Mexican Tradition Revived in Juárez," *El Paso Times,* 7 January 1987, pp. 1-2B.

[44]Rosalinda González, "Work and Play on a Border Ranch," *The Golden Log* (Dallas: Southern Methodist University Press, 1962), PTFS 31:144-45.

[45]Interview by the author with Father Ernest J. Burrus, SJ, in December 1981.

[46]Pat Henry, "Faithful Honor San Lorenzo," *El Paso Times,* 12 August 1983, p. 1C.

[47]A variety of people attending the fiesta gave me some of these details on 27 September 1987; Ann Enríquez, a member of a San Elizario family that has lived there for several generations, shared her own memories with me, and lent me family pictures of the festival dating back at least to the time of World War I.

[48]Marc Simmons, "Irrigation Traditions Still Hold Water," *El Paso Times,* 24 February 1985, pp. 8-9B. Arthur L.Campa (*Hispanic Culture in the Southwest* [Norman: University of Oklahoma Press, 1979], pp. 189-90) describes the Southwestern system for administering the precious water resources—a system growing out of the "Tribunal de las Aguas, which has been meeting regularly on the steps of the Cathedral of Valencia since the Middle Ages."

[49]Thomas F. Glick, *The Old World Background of the Irrigation System of San Antonio, Texas* (El Paso: Texas Western Press, 1972), pp. 3-6.

[50]Glick, p. 6.

[51]Matt Mygatt, "Spring Ritual: Acequias Bind Towns Together," *El Paso Times,* 23 March 1986, p. 10B.

[52]Doug McClellan, "Traditional Spring Rite Draws 80 To Clean Important 'Mother Ditch,'" *El Paso Times,* 7 April 1987, and Simmons, p. 8B.

[53]C.L. Sonnichsen, *Pass of the North: Four Centuries on the Rio Grande* (El Paso: Texas Western Press, 1968), vol. 1, pp. 384-85.

[54]John Nichols, *The Milagro Beanfield War* (New York: Holt, Winston, and Rinehart, 1974).

[55]Glick, p. 51.

[56]The author, living in El Paso's Lower Valley on land with water rights, from 1932 to 1947 was involved in work parties to keep up the ditches and, from 1969 to 1975 was a voting member of the local water district. I have seen members of the water district snubbed on the street for not having attended the annual meeting!

[57]Reported to me by Marta Weigle, folklorist of the Albuquerque and Santa Fe, New Mexico, areas.

[58]Marc Simmons, "Unsavory Side of History Included 'Rooster Pull,' " *El Paso Times,* 31 March 1985. Recent reports from my students are that a milder form of the sport has evolved, in which a cloth bag, corners tied with red cloth and designated as head and feet, is pulled by riders from a hole in the dirt and fought over. Then parts are thrown over a certain boundary line, with separate points scored for head, feet, and body—if there's one left after all the tug-of-war action!

[59]"The Charreada," *Sombras del Pasado* 3 (Spring 1981): 13.

[60]Julia A. Kumor, "La Charreada—The Mexican Rodeo," May 1981, unpublished paper in the University of Texas at El Paso Folklore Archive, p. 13, reporting an interview with charro Juan Rodríguez, 12 April 1981.

[61]Kumor, p. 15, reporting an interview with charro José Quiñónez, spring 1981.

[62]Kumor, p. 15.

[63]Rob McCorkle, "Charros Ride for the Glory of It," *El Paso Times,* 27 September 1987, p. 2E.

[64]Kumor, p. 17, citing H.D. Foster, "Audacious Horsemen," *Holiday* (October 1962): 133-35.

[65]McCorkle, p. 2E.

[66]Kumor, p. 18, citing Scottie King, "Los Charros de Santa Fe," *New Mexico* (May 1981): 23-27.

[67]González, p. 150; see also Ida B. Hall, "Pioneer Children's Games," *Texian Stomp-*

ing Grounds (Dallas: Southern Methodist University Press, 1941), PTFS 17:145.

[68]From the reminiscences of Frank Moore, quoted by Marc Simmons, "Lawyer from Kansas City Found New Mexico Territory Had Strange Customs," *El Paso Times,* 3 August 1986. The invitation to the hanging took place in Albuquerque in 1900; the sheepherder/patrón scene in Bernalillo, New Mexico, a few years later.

[69]I have been told a number of stories about these marks of respect over the years. My mother, Bertha West, taught in El Paso's predominantly Mexican schools for about 30 years. I have also been told of families in recent times who feel a great deal of shame, even to the point of disowning the person, when a son or daughter breaks the law—a far cry from more affluent Anglo families who spend large sums and use all their influence to get their "kids out of trouble." Such is another demonstrable cultural difference exhibited by Mexican-Americans.

[70]Scott, p. 79. In neighborhood stores and all along the border the custom of giving pilón is still common.

Chapter 10. Folk Drama and Dance

[1]Joel Romero Salinas, *Diciembre en la tradicion popular: La Pastorela Mexicana, origen y evolucion* (México, D.F.: Fonart, 1984), pp. 7, 9. Salinas provides a history of the pastorela form in Mexico, as well as texts and illustrations of a variety of such plays that have been interpreted by modern authors—for example, *"Pastorela de siete vicios"* (Pastorela of the seven vices or sins) by corrido scholar Vicente T. Mendoza.

[2]Aurora Lucero-White Lea (*Literary Folklore of the Hispanic Southwest* [San Antonio: The Naylor Company, 1953], pp. 3-5) describes a variety of folk plays found in New Mexico, with emphasis on *Los Pastores.* For an excellent version of *El Niño Perdido* (The Lost Child), see "Canto del Niño Perdido," ed. Mary R. Van Stone and E.R. Sims, *Spur of the Cock* (Dallas: Southern Methodist University Press, 1933), PTFS 11:48-89. Arthur L. Campa (*Hispanic Culture in the Southwest* [Norman: University of Oklahoma Press, 1979], p. 230), says *El Niño Perdido* is essentially a retelling of the story of the young Jesus confounding the elders in the temple.

[3]Campa, pp. 139, 149, 230-33; Honora DeBusk Smith ("Mexican Plazas along the River of Souls," *Southwestern Lore* [Dallas: Southern Methodist University Press, 1931], PTFS 9:71-72) reports both *Los Comanches* and a religious form, *Las Comanchitas,* which she calls basically a pageant dedicated to the Christ Child (who, in a comic element, is kidnapped by the Indians).

[4]John E. Englekirk, "The Source and Dating of New Mexico Spanish Folk Plays," *Western Folklore* 16:4 (October 1957): 245-46. He has seen 63 manuscripts and knows of 56 others—all of *Los Pastores.* He knows of only about 30 play manuscripts on all other subjects. Campa (pp. 50-51) says that some plays were adapted by the folk from the performances of traveling players who came up the Camino Real from Mexico in Viceregal days. These players often acted in exchange for food, since money was usually scarce.

[5]M.R. Cole, *Los Pastores: A Mexican Play of the Nativity* (Boston: Houghton-Mifflin Co. for the American Folklore Society, 1907).

[6]John G. Bourke, "The Miracle Play of the Rio Grande," *Journal of American Folklore* 6 (April-June, 1893): 89-90. The Cole publication (above) employs the manuscript Captain Bourke provided, and gives evidence of a considerable amount of scholarly research.

[7]Quoted in Cole, pp. xxviii-xxx; Miss DeBusk's text is reproduced on pp. 211-34. Cole says that the use of a swing to lower Saint Michael was a feature of Spanish plays of the Middle Ages as well, p. xxx.

[8]Richard M. Dorson, *Buying the Wind* (Chicago: University of Chicago Press, 1964), pp. 266-79.

[9]Cf *The Norton Anthology of English Literature,* rev. ed. M.H. Abrams, (New York: Norton, 1968), pp. 291-92.

[10]John Igo, "Julia Mott Waugh on Los Pastores," *Diamond Bessie and the Shepherds* (Austin: Encino Press, 1972), PTFS 36:15-25.

[11]Nancy Mae Wilkes, "Religious Folkdrama in the Southwest," unpublished manuscript in the University of Texas at El Paso Folklore Archive, dated about 1969. Other details come from a telephone interview with Bobbie Provencio, current member of the group, 5 November 1987.

[12]Wilkes, pp. 4-5.

[13]Campa, p. 229; in some of the New Mexican villages, he says, a live baby was used when available. In others, people "boast lifelike Christ dolls that were imported from Germany and have been continuously used in the Nativity play for over 150 years."

[14]Taken from a series of interviews by UT El Paso folklore students. In 1978 Mary Helen Nuñez interviewed the priest, Father Joseph Eslava, of an El Paso Catholic church, as well as a number of local parishioners. In 1985 María Elena Flores interviewed a number of El Pasoans who continue the piñata tradition they learned as children as a natural termination for the posadas.

[15]A brief but clear description of the teatro campesino is presented in "Valdez, Luis Miguel," *Chicano Literature: A Reference Guide,* ed. Julian A. Martínez and Francisco A. Lomeli (Westport, Conn.: Greenwood Press, 1985).

[16]"Valdez, Luis Miguel," p. 399. *Soldado Razo* was first performed, according to the typed playscript in my files, on 3 April 1971, in Fresno, California, at the Chicano Moratorium on the War in Vietnam.

[17]Hector Serrano, founder and for many years leader of Chicano little theater activities in El Paso, sees these *actos* (as the shorter plays of Valdez and others are called) as true heirs of the Hispanic folk drama tradition. Interview by the author, 9 November 1987. For an excellent bibliography of the campesino theater see Betty Ann Diamond's *Brown Eyed Children of the Sun: The Cultural Politics of El Teatro Campesino* (Ph.D. dissertation, University of Wisconsin, 1977). Worth noting is the fact that the 1987 hit movie *La Bamba* dealing with the struggles of a Mexican-American singer, Ritchie Valens, was written by Valdez; the movie scene in the campesino camp, according to Serrano, comes straight out of Valdez's own experience as a farmworker.

[18]Lorin W. Brown with Charles L. Briggs and Marta Weigle, *Hispano Folklore of New Mexico* (Albuquerque: University of New Mexico Press, 1978), pp. 175-78.

[19]Peggy V. Beck, "Abuelos y Abuelas," *New Mexico* (December 1987): 32-37. An interesting parallel in German Christmas practices exists in the visit of St. Nikolaus and Knecht Rupprecht, the latter being, like the abuelo, an interrogator of bad children. From her father, raised in Landsberg, Germany, Erika Aigner obtained reminiscences of how the Knecht Rupprecht would "knock on the door with his rods, and the children would cry, they were so scared. He would growl ominously and then call out, 'Where are all the bad children?'. . . Naturally the parents had already informed him of all the sins committed in the past year, so to prove that they could be good children, each had to recite a prayer or poem without making any mistakes. If you stumbled through, you got the rod right there." After Knecht Rupprecht was satisfied, St. Nikolaus would reward the children. Miss Aigner, whose mother is Mexican-American, collected this from Erich Aigner in December, 1987. Erika E. Aigner, "A Melted Christmas," unpublished manuscript in the UTEP Folklore Archive, December 1987. Cf Rachel Davis-Dubois, *The Germans in American Life* (New York: Thomas Nelson and Sons, 1936), p. 71.

[20]Campa, p. 231.

[21]Honora DeBusk, "Los Matachines," *Hispanic Colorado,* ed. Evelio Echevarría and José Otero (Ft. Collins, Col.: Centennial Publications, 1976), pp. 193-95. Miss DeBusk

collected folklore and wrote over half a century ago, but this reprinting gives no indication of when this piece was written nor where it was earlier published. One wonders if La Vieja and El Viejo with his whip were reflected in the abuelos. Aurelio M. Espinosa (*The Folklore of Spain in the American Southwest,* ed. J. Manuel Espinosa [Norman: University of Oklahoma Press, 1985], pp. 224-25) discusses the Spanish roots of Los Matachines, and suggests that the mock battle between the bull and the abuelo is an imitation of the Spanish bullfight. A beautiful publication with a rich assortment of color pictures is Flavia Waters Champa, *The Matachines Dance of the Upper Rio Grande: History, Music, and Choreography* (Lincoln: University of Nebraska Press, 1983).

[22]Anita Gonzáles Thomas, "Traditional Folk Dances of New Mexico," a speech given before the 1971 meeting of the New Mexico Folklore Society, reprinted in *Folk-Dances of the Spanish-Colonials of New Mexico,* 2nd ed., comp. and ed. by Aurora Lucero-White and Helen Mareau (Santa Fe: International Folk Art Foundation, 1978), p. 109. In her presentation Mrs. Thomas quoted a long train of visitors to colonial and territorial New Mexico—Zebulon M. Pike, George C. Sibley, Josiah Gregg, et al.—who all commented on the frequency of bailes in the nineteenth century, often describing the action in great detail in their journals. Brown (p. 122) reports how the musicians walked around town playing their instruments in an invitation to the dance called *sacando el gallo* (literally, pulling out the rooster) in the 1930s.

[23]Telephone interview with Rosa Guerrero, 12 November 1987. Her 28-minute 16mm sound film *Tapestry,* produced by the El Paso Public Schools in 1972, gives an impressive overview of Mexican folk dance and its worldwide roots.

[24]Brown, p. 187.

[25]Brown, p. 104.

[26]Richard B. Stark, Anita Gonzáles Thomas, and Reed Cooper, comp. and ed., *Music of the Bailes in New Mexico,* reprinted in *Folk Dances of the Spanish-Colonials of New Mexico,* p. 102

[27]Stark, Thomas, and Cooper, p. 88.

[28]Stark, Thomas, and Cooper, p. 86.

[29]Stark, Thomas, and Cooper, p. 84.

[30]Campa, p. 96.

[31]Espinosa, p. 71.

[32]Florence Johnson Scott, "Customs and Superstitions Among Texas Mexicans on the Rio Grande Border," *Coffee in the Gourd* (Austin: Texas Folklore Society, 1923), PTFS 2:77-78.

[33]Américo Paredes, "The Love Tragedy in Texas-Mexican Balladry," *Folk Travelers* (Dallas: Southern Methodist University Press, 1953), PTFS 25:110-12.

[34]Personal interview with Ruth Elaine Vise, 5 December 1987.

[35]Personal interview with Margarita B. Kanavy, 31 December 1987.

[36]Personal interviews with Lucy Fischer West and Margarita B. Kanavy, 31 December 1987.

[37]Personal interview with Margarita B. Kanavy, 31 December 1987.

Chapter 11. Folk Games

[1]Brian Sutton-Smith, *The Folkgames of Children* (Austin: University of Texas Press for the American Folklore Society, 1972), p. xiv.

[2]Jan Harold Brunvand, *The Study of American Folklore,* 3rd ed. (New York: Norton, 1986), p. 380.

[3]Brunvand, pp. 384-86.

[4]Aurelio M. Espinosa, *The Folklore of Spain in the American Southwest,* ed. J. Manuel Espinosa (Norman: University of Oklahoma Press, 1985), pp. 170-75.

[5]Collected by Lucy Jones from R.M., eleven years old, at Ascarate School, El Paso, in 1970. He learned the game from his brothers and friends.

[6]Collected by Lucy Jones in 1970 from members of a fifth-grade class at Ascarate School. The Blind Chicken came from A.F., eleven years old; I.S., eleven years old, learned Blindfolded from her family and friends; Sit on the Pillow came from A.P., who learned it from her friends.

[7]Lucy Jones collected this in 1970 from S.T., fifth-grader at Ascarate; she learned it from her sister and friends.

[8]Lucy Jones collected this in 1970 from R.M., fifth-grader at Ascarate; she learned it from family and friends.

[9]Collected by Ramona Salazar in 1971 from Laura Valencia, fourteen, who attended Loretto Academy in El Paso. She learned it in Juárez.

[10]Collected by Lucy Jones in 1970 from M.P., fourth-grader at Ascarate, who learned it from his brother and friends.

[11]Ramona Salazar remembered Las Escondidas and La Patada del Bote from her childhood in El Paso's Smeltertown; Lucy Jones collected the Kissing Tag Game in 1970 from eleven-year-old H.D., fifth-grader at Ascarate, who says he learned it from his friends and that it was played only at friends' houses, never at school.

[12]Lucy Jones collected Touch Ball in 1970 from nine-year-old E.R., who learned it from his friends at Ascarate School.

[13]Ramona Salazar remembers playing this in Smeltertown as a child; Lucy Jones collected a similar game, Fire Ball, in 1970 from J.L., fifth-grader at Ascarate. Each time the person throwing the ball doesn't hit anyone, the leader puts a rock in that person's hole; if he gets five rocks he has to stand against a wall and let three boys throw the ball at him. If he is hit three times, he's out of the game.

[14]Lucy Jones collected Firing Squad from F., a fourth-grader at Ascarate, in 1970; he plays this with his friends, from whom he learned the game.

[15]A.L. Campa is quoted in *Juegos Infantiles Cantados en Nuevo México,* Richard B. Stark, comp. (Santa Fe: Museum of New Mexico Press, 1973), pp. 15-16 and notes, pp. 35-36. Ramona Salazar played this game in Smeltertown as a child. Her husband, Luis, recalled in 1971 having mis-heard London Bridge as a child, and played it with his friends with the rhyme *"Loren dichen, Lorinda, Lorinda, Lorinda. Lorin dichen, Lorinda mm, mm, mmmm."*

[16]Stark, pp. 11-12 and note, p. 33. Frances Alexander, *Mother Goose on the Rio Grande* (Dallas: Banks Upshaw and Company, 1944), pp. 92-93, has a similar version; Ramona Salazar played the game in Smeltertown as a child, and Martha Margarita Domínguez collected it in 1977 from Hortencia Marquez, 25, of El Paso.

[17]Stark, pp. 7-8; in a note (p. 33) he says that "Juan Molinero" is sometimes substituted for the name Juan Pirulero, an observation borne out by the report I have heard that Juan's motion is the grinding of a *molino* (mill); *molinero* means "miller." Martha Margarita Domínguez also collected it in 1977 from Alicia Marquez, 49-year-old El Paso housewife.

[18]Stark, pp. 9-10 and note, p. 34. Alexander (pp. 94-95) names the outsider (ungrammatically) *El Vieja* (male definite article + "old woman"!), but translates it into English as Old Fat Man.

[19]Doña Blanca is obviously a variant of María Blanca. Collected by Ramona Salazar in 1971 from Altagracia Yapor, fourteen, a student at Loretto Academy who was born in Chihuahua. The puns—*misa/camisa,* and *cerro/becerro*—are lost in English, of course. The game was collected in Spanish, but I gave only the English translation because of its length and its repetitiveness.

[20]Stark, pp. 41-49; Dr. Campa says the game is usually known as "Matariliriliron" or "Ambo a dos," and explains the confusion with the French song. Alexander (pp. 98-

101) calls it "Mata-li-ri-li," with dramatic additions that suggest a kinship to *Hilitos de Oro* (Threads or Ribbons of Gold), found in Stark (pp. 25-28), but Campa, in a note on p. 40, calls the latter game a part of "the old ballad 'Hilo de Oro'" popular throughout Spanish America. Ramona Salazar recalls playing the game as a child in Smeltertown, with the messenger, mother and daughters, and so forth; in her version, as well as Alexander's, the daughters play hard to get until the messenger makes the right offer. The game deserves further study.

[21]Collected in 1970 by Lucy Jones from F.V., a ten-year-old fifth-grader at Ascarate; he learned the game by watching his big brothers play.

[22]Collected in 1970 by Lucy Jones from R.C., a fifth-grader at Ascarate; she learned the game from her cousins.

[23]Collected in 1970 by Lucy Jones from L.C., a fifth-grader at Ascarate; she isn't sure where she learned the game.

[24]Collected in 1970 by Lucy Jones from B.Z., an eleven-year-old fifth-grader at Ascarate; she plays this game at home. Ramona Salazar played the same game (without the beans) as a child in Smeltertown, as well as collecting it from several of her students at Loretto Academy in 1971.

[25]Ramona Salazar recalls the game from her childhood in Smeltertown; one of her students at Loretto Academy in 1971, Aida Maldonado, learned the game as *"Ojos a la Vela ye Manos Atras"* (Eyes to the Candle and Hands Behind), but no candle was involved as she learned to play it.

[26]Marc Simmons, "Games Have Filled Many Leisure Hours," *El Paso Times,* 13 July 1986: 8-B. The memoirs he quoted are those of Marian Russell, who came to New Mexico at the age of seven.

[27]Collected in 1970 by Lucy Jones from N.C., a twelve-year-old fifth-grader at Cedar Grove School in El Paso; she learned the game from friends.

[28]Simmons, p. 8-B.

[29]Among my earliest recollections from the 1930s in El Paso, when I visited with the stevedores who worked on the Southern Pacific Railroad freight dock, was seeing the men play washers after they had eaten their lunches of beans and tortillas and drunk their sweetened coffee and milk, carried from home in pint whiskey bottles and left in the sun to stay warm. They let me play too, but not for money. I have seen the same game played—often by men waiting outside labor hiring offices—in Lubbock, Austin, and Odessa. An interesting article is Robert Cochran's "The Interlude of Game: A Study of Washers," *Western Folklore* 38 (1979): 71-82.

[30]Telephone interview with Joe S. Graham of the Conner Museum, Kingsville, Texas, 9 January 1988.

[31]Collected by Patricia Gallardo in 1976 from Rose Marie Bechtel, Juan Alonzo, and Alice Jaquez, all Mexican-American students at the University of Texas at El Paso.

[32]Collected by Patricia Gallardo in 1976 from Clara Lozoya, raised in Chihuahua but a resident of El Paso for several years.

[33]Collected by Patricia Gallardo in 1976 from Rose Marie Bechtel.

[34]The piñata "game" is played everywhere the Mexican culture lingers. Ramona Salazar recalls piñata-breaking, especially at birthday parties, from her childhood in Smeltertown; Lucy Jones collected a similar description in 1970 from Y.R., a nine-year-old fourth-grader at Ascarate, who learned about the practice from her family.

[35]Collected by Richard Talavera in the 1970s from the South El Paso group he hung around with in those days. The term *cabuliar* (to make fun of) is apparently caló, as are some of the other terms he supplied that are related to the game: *aguante* (level of tolerance), *aguante callado* (suffer in silence), *no sea mamón* (don't be a baby), and *¡aguante!* (take it!). Talavera stresses that la cabula is not a "cut-down" session but "a binding exercise of friendship."

[36]See Roger D. Abrahams, *Deep Down in the Jungle* (Hatboro, Penn.: Folklore Associates, 1964).

Chapter 12. Folk Architecture

[1]"Adobe," and "Pyramid," *Encyclopaedia Britannica* (1960); G.E. Middleton, *Build Your House of Earth: A Manual of Pise and Adobe Construction* (Sidney: Angus Robertson, 1953), pp. 8-9; Arthur Oden, "Mud, Sticks, and Stones," unpublished master's thesis, Texas Western College (now UT El Paso), 1951, pp. 1-13.

[2]In 1540, Spanish explorer Pedro de Castañeda saw this technique being used at the Hopi and Acoma Pueblos; see Roland Dickey, *New Mexico Village Arts* (Albuquerque: University of New Mexico Press, 1970), pp. 32-38.

[3]Interview with Carlos Chávez, assistant superintendent of the Chamizal National Memorial in El Paso, September 1974. Mr. Chávez was raised in the corte de terrón area; I have visited the San Agustín Mission there, and saw stacks of such building blocks as well as unplastered buildings made from them. In some of the buildings the grass within the blocks started growing again, making the buildings look as if they needed a haircut!

[4]Paul Horgan, *Great River* (New York: Rinehart, 1954), vol. 1, 48-51, 222-23; Dickey, p. 40.

[5]C.L. Sonnichsen, *Pass of the North* (El Paso: Texas Western Press, 1968), vol. 1, pp. 26-37.

[6]Exodus 5.

[7]John O. West and Roberto González, "Adobe: Earth, Straw, and Water," *Built in Texas* (Waco: E-Heart Press, 1979), PTFS 61:60-72.

[8]Interview in 1978 with a man who didn't give his name, in Fabens, Texas, where I watched for several hours while he worked building his house.

[9]Horgan, vol. 1, pp. 222-24.

[10]Ernest J. Burrus, S.J., "Outstanding Historical Dates and Events of the Towns, Missions, and Churches in the El Paso Valley" (El Paso: The Historical Cultural Commission of the Catholic Diocese of El Paso, n.d.), unnumbered p. 5.

[11]Interview with archaeologist Rex Gerald, summer 1985, at the Socorro dig.

[12]Interview with architect Pat Rand, August 1987. Mr. Rand is the architect in charge of restoration at the present Socorro Mission, where ground water has recently been a problem.

[13]"Adobe," *Sombras del Pasado* 2 (Spring 1980): 1-10.

[14]Joe Graham, "Folk Housing in South and West Texas: Some Comparisons," *An Exploration of a Common Legacy: A Conference on Border Architecture,* ed. Marlene Heck (Austin: Texas Historical Commission, 1979), p. 44. The avoidance of doors on the west side of the house has frequently been explained to me by rural people in New Mexico as well as West Texas.

[15]Graham, "Folk Housing," pp. 440-45. The third variety, parapet on three sides, is about as popular in the El Paso and New Mexico areas I have visited as the type with four-sided parapet and clay drains—but the latter tend to be older construction, in my observations.

[16]Graham, "Folk Housing," p. 44.

[17]The trend to avoid the use of adobe, or at least to cover it up, is quite prevalent in West Texas. Many of my students who were raised in adobe homes report that the family ambition is to get a brick one. I would love to have an adobe house, even to build it myself!

[18]Graham ("Folk Housing, p. 39) supports convincingly the native origin of the jacal; however, he quotes Ada Louise Newton's master's thesis, "The History of Architecture along the Rio Grande as Reflected in the Buildings Around Rio Grande City 1749-1920," Texas A&I University, 1964, as maintaining the Spanish origin (p. 11). Another work by

Graham, "The Jacal in the Big Bend," *Occasional Papers of the Chihuahuan Desert Research Institute,* ed. Robert Mallouf (Alpine, Texas: in press), presents fuller documentation and proof of the native origin of the jacal.

[19]Trent E. Sanford, *The Story of Architecture in Mexico* (New York: Norton, 1948), pp. 253-54, quoted in Graham, "Folk Housing," p. 39.

[20]Graham, "Folk Housing," pp. 39-40.

[21]Newton, "The History of Architecture," pp. 14-15, quoted in Graham, "Folk Housing," p. 41.

Chapter 13. Folk Foods

[1]Joe S. Graham, "Mexican-American Traditional Foodways: Sources and Prospects," *American Frontiers: Past, Present, and Future,* ed. Mildred J. Schoenecke. Proceedings of the Fourth Annual Meeting of Southwestern and Texas Popular Culture Associations (Oklahoma City: Oklahoma Historical Society, 1984), p. 432.

[2]Interview with Dr. Truett Maddox, DDS, of El Paso, in 1965.

[3]Vicente García de Diego, *Diccionario Etimologico: Español e Hispánico* (Madrid: Editorial S.A.E.T.A., n.d.).

[4]Lewis Spence, *The Myths of Mexico and Peru* (Boston: Longwood Press, 1977 [1913], pp. 90-91.

[5]Edgar L. Hewett, *Ancient Life in Mexico and Central America* (New York: Tudor Publishing Co., 1936), pp. 232-33. Hewett also discusses the various botanical speculations about the source of corn, pp. 228-34.

[6]Interview with Ruth E. Vise in El Paso, 11 January 1988.

[7]My wife, Lucy Fischer West, an excellent cook of Mexican-American foods, provided this analysis of the kinds of salsa. I have learned most of what I know (and love) about Mexican food from her and her mother, Lucina Lara Rey de Fischer, over the past 18 years. Curiously, neither of the Spanish dictionaries from my own library had menudo, pozole, nor most of the other corn-food words cited above; and chilipiquin was listed in one as *chiltipiquin.*

[8]Joe S. Graham, "Mexican-American Traditional Foodways at La Junta," *Occasional Papers of the Chihuahuan Desert Research Institute.* Graham grew up on the Mexican border, acquired traditional notions of what good Mexican food ought to be, and although he may eat an occasional meat enchilada in a restaurant, he does not have them at home—only the cheese variety.

[9][Norman] "Brownie" McNeil ("Haymarket Plaza," *The Sky Is My Tipi* [Dallas: Southern Methodist University Press, 1949], PTFS 22:168-72) describes the San Antonio market plaza where he ate from booths where a variety of Mexican foods was for sale. Elizabeth Hurley ("Come Buy, Come Buy," *Folk Travelers* [Dallas: Southern Methodist University Press, 1953], PTFS 25:117-21) tells of street peddlers in South Texas who sold tamales, tacos, enchiladas, barbecue, and fresh bread from pushcarts.

[10]Two very popular brands along the border are *Maseca* (dry masa) and *Masa Harina* (masa flour), the latter manufactured by the Quaker Oats Company, which also makes *Masa Trigo* for making wheat flour tortillas. One of my students, María Bertha Gutiérrez, collected a recipe in 1985 from an El Paso Mexican-American, Haydee Saenz, that begins, "3 cups Masa Harina. . . ." One would think that if a cook were going to the trouble to make tamales, at the very least real masa from a molino would be used. Some fifty years ago an El Paso firm, Ashley's, developed a procedure for canning a variety of Mexican foods, including tortillas, which they shipped all over the world to Mexican food-lovers who were away from the border. California-born Max Montoya, right guard for the Cincinnati Bengals, has taken Mexican-American food to Kentucky, where he opened a restaurant "introducing Kentuckians to the Mexican food that most of us in the Southwest are used to. The response has been great." Sabrina Nelson, "From Grid-

iron to Grill: The Unlikely Hobby of Max Montoya," *El Paso Times,* 2 January 1988, Vista section, p. 16.

[11]This belief is common in Mexico, where my mother-in-law was raised. And, considering that many Mexican homes are small and lack central heating, opening a door to the frigid outside air can indeed chill tamales and slow the cooking process. In December 1987, Texas was hit by an unusual cold spell; El Paso had over 22 inches of snow within 24 hours—in the midst of which our annual tamal-making had been scheduled, with a dinner party already set for two days later. The tamales were steamed about three hours—and neither of the cooks said, "These are the best tamales we've ever made!" But they were consumed, anyway—and the guests were too polite to complain.

[12]In a survey on folk foods common in the Big Bend of Texas in 1980, Joe Graham didn't even include fajitas among the foods he was inquiring about, although he had been familiar with the dish in his childhood. "They just didn't call it anything special," he told me. Personal interview in El Paso, 30 November 1987. My wife Lucy says the dish, familiar to her all her life, is "what you cook in a hurry, when you're too tired to come up with anything else!"

[13]Trisha L. Workman, "Fajitas: The Folk Food Phenomenon," August 1986, unpublished manuscript in the University of Texas at El Paso Folklore Archive. Julia Catalano ("Fajita Madness," *El Paso Times,* 6 December 1986, Vista section, p. 23) says that when skirt steak is in short supply, flank steak serves the purpose.

[14]Catalano, p. 23.

[15]Pat Henry, "Translated into 'Little Belts,' Entree Can Tighten Budget," *El Paso Times* (September 1984), cited by Workman, p. 6. Jack Maguire ("The Melting Pot Ethnic Cuisine in Texas" [San Antonio: Institute of Texas Cultures, 1977], p. 2) reports such fajita cookoffs all across the state of Texas.

[16]Workman, p. 2, reporting an interview with Emma Carrasco, for 25 years a waitress and hostess with Leo's Restaurants in El Paso, August 1986.

[17]Catalano, p. 23.

[18]Workman, p. 6.

[19]Robert Harris interviewed Mrs. Elizabeth Durán, then owner of Tony's Cafe in El Paso, about 1975, for her caldillo recipe, handed down in the family for many years. The picadillo recipe is from my wife, Lucy Fischer West; her mother, Lucina Lara Rey de Fischer, makes albondigas with spaghetti, "because Lucy likes them that way." Dieticians Carolyn Jackson Gleason and Judi Jaquez, in *Handbook of Mexican American Foods: Recipes, Nutritional Analysis, Diabetic Exchanges, and Common Practices* (San Antonio: Intercultural Development Research Association, 1982), p. 17, define albondigas as "meatball soup," with a description that sounds very much like the almost-picadillo dish I described.

[20]Richard Bradford, *Red Sky at Morning* (New York: Pocket Books, 1969), p. 116.

[21]"Bradford, Richard Roark," *Who's Who in America* (1970-71 ed.).

[22]David Gómez (*Traditional and Contemporary New Mexican Recipes* [np., nd.], p.21) gives a recipe starting with pork steaks, fried and then covered with green chile sauce. Ella T. López and José A. López, in *Make Mine Menudo: Chicano Cook Book* (La Puente, Cal.: Sunburst Enterprises, 1976), do not give a recipe, but define carnitas simply as "small pieces of pork or meat chunks" (p. 74).

[23]Graham, "Foodways: La Junta." Huntley Dent (*The Feast of Santa Fe: Cooking of the American Southwest* [New York: Simon and Schuster, 1985], p. 100) describes carnitas as "braised pork that is salted,roasted in the oven, and shredded," to be used wherever shredded pork is called for in a recipe.

[24]A.L. Campa, *Hispanic Culture in the Southwest* (Norman: Oklahoma University Press, 1979), p. 278; Robert Harris, interview with Mrs. J.C. Griggs, about 1975. A member of a New Mexican family involved in the restaurant business for several gen-

erations, she uses family recipes.

[25]Graham, "Foodways: La Junta."

[26]Graham, "Foodways: La Junta," citing A. Farga, *Historia de la comida en México,* 2nd ed. (México, D.F.: Litografia México, 1980), p. 21. See also Campa, p. 279.

[27]López and López, pp. 9, 11, 18.

[28]Gleason and Jaquez, p. 35.

[29]Lucy Fischer West cooks her beans this way. I have "picked" beans myself for nearly 60 years; in the Southwest, this is one of the earliest chores a child is taught to do.

[30]Graham, "Foodways: La Junta."

[31]Graham, "Foodways: La Junta."

[32]Lucy Fischer West. See Gómez, p. 21, for a recipe for sausage-stuffed squash that is baked.

[33]I learned to prepare chiles rellenos this way in 1964 from a Mexican who worked for me as a domestic.

[34]Gómez, p. 21.

[35]Gleason and Jaquez, p. 40.

[36]Gleason and Jaquez, p. 39. My basic method of preparing sopa de arroz comes from my wife and her mother.

[37]López and López (p. 40) say that huevos rancheros can also be made with scrambled eggs, but I have never seen the dish prepared that way.

[38]Gleason and Jaquez, p. 34.

[39]Gleason and Jaquez, p. 43.

[40]Carlita Carpio, "Panza Llena, Corazon Contento," unpublished manuscript in the University of Texas at El Paso Folklore Archive, 1974, p. 2, citing an interview with her father, Héctor Carpio. My wife knows a number of older Mexicans and Mexican-Americans who insist that Lent is a time for sacrifice, and they live up to their beliefs.

[41]Carlita Carpio interviewed Mrs. José Silva in 1974; her recipes came down from her great-grandmother in Mexico.

[42]Carlita Carpio, interview with Mrs. José Silva.

[43]Carlita Carpio, interview with Mrs. José Silva.

[44]Carlita Carpio, interviews with Señora Isaura Pérez and Mrs. Luz Carpio in 1974. Almost every Mexican cookbook I have examined has a similar recipe.

[45]Carlita Carpio, interview with Mrs. Jacinta Morales in 1974; María Berta Gutiérrez interviewed her mother (but did not give her name) as well as Haydee Saenz in 1985.

[46]Carlita Carpio, interview with Mrs. Alma Morales in 1974; my wife recalls a neighbor, Mrs. Consuelo Reyna, who for many years sent over several dozen bizcochos made with wine and heavily sprinkled with cinnamon and sugar, in time for any Christmas party that might occur.

[47]Carlita Carpio, interviews with her father, Héctor Carpio, and Mrs. Alma Ornelas, in 1974; their recipes simply had the chocolate being melted, but my wife insists that the grating does something special to the flavor—so I get drafted to grate the chocolate. It is worth the work.

[48]Carlita Carpio, interview with her mother, Mrs. Luz Carpio; Guadalupe Silva ("In Mexico, Christmas Isn't the Only Day for Giving," *El Paso Times,* 1 January 1988) describes the January 6 custom and the tradition of the person selected by chance to give the Candelaria party. See also Lila Perl, *Piñatas and Paper Flowers: Holidays of the American in English and Spanish* (New York: Clarion Books, 1983), pp. 14-21.

[49]Robert Harris, interview with Mrs. J.C. Griggs, about 1975.

[50]Carlita Carpio, in an interview with Mrs. Virginia Montoya in 1974, received an interesting recipe for "Monticello Pozole," a kind of menudo, that Mrs. Montoya learned in Monticello, New Mexico. Instead of tripe, the meat used was pork and beef neck bones, as well as pig's feet. The recipe reminds me of Joe Graham's comment that when

Mexicans slaughter an animal, every part is used in some way; interview in El Paso, 30 November 1987.

[51]Carlita Carpio, interview with Mrs. Virginia Montoya in 1974. The recipe was called chiles rellenos, but there was no stuffing—just the same ingredients as the well-known dish by that name.

[52]Carlita Carpio, interview with Mrs. Luz Carpio in 1974. My wife's grandmother made such meat empanadas; and one of the appetizers at a luxurious restaurant in Juárez is made from a raw corn tortilla, filled with spiced ground meat, crimped around the edges, and deep-fried. Mrs. Phyllis Strauss pointed out for me, from her childhood memories, the similarities between empanadas and the Cornish and Scottish items.

Chapter 14. Folk Art and Crafts

[1]Bernardo de Sahagún, *Historia generál de las cosas de Nueva España,* ed. Miguel Acosta Saignes (México, 1946), vol. 2, p. 481.

[2]Arthur L. Campa, *Hispanic Culture in the Southwest* (Norman: University of Oklahoma Press, 1979), p. 37.

[3]Anita Brenner, *Idols behind Altars* (New York: Harcourt Brace, 1929), pp. 137-47, 149-53. Aurelio M. Espinosa (*The Folklore of Spain in the American Southwest,* ed. J. Manuel Espinosa [Norman: University of Oklahoma Press, 1985], pp. 244-46) comments on the incomplete fusion of native and Catholic religions in New Mexico.

[4]I published a version of the following portion on grutas as "Grutas at the Crossroads of the Spanish Southwest" in *Password* 32.1 (Spring 1987): 3-12. Reproduced here with the permission of the editor, Mary Lillian Collingwood.

[5]Bud Newman, "Fray García de San Francisco," *Password* 29.4 (Winter 1984): 179-86. See also C.L. Sonnichsen, *Pass of the North: Four Centuries on the Rio Grande* (El Paso: Texas Western Press, 1980), vol. 1, pp. 19-23; Cleofas Calleros, *El Paso's Missions and Indians* (El Paso: McMath, 1953), pp. 17-19. Paso del Norte (present-day Juárez, Chihuahua) had its name changed in 1888 to honor revolutionary leader Benito Juárez. Present-day El Paso was initially a cluster of settlements including Magoffinsville, Franklin, Concordia, and Hart's Mill.

[6]Joséph Leach, "Of Time and the Tiguas," *Password* 30.4 (Winter 1985): 174.

[7]Americo Paredes, *"With His Pistol in His Hand"* (Austin: University of Texas Press, 1958), pp. 9-15.

[8]Campa, pp. 49-51.

[9]Sonnichsen, vol. 2, p. 74.

[10]The writer has traveled the entire length of the Rio Grande, from Colorado to where the river empties into the Gulf of Mexico at Boca Chica, photographing substantially over 400 grutas and grave markers, as well as talking with (interviewing is too formal a word) scores of residents, many of whom owned or had built grutas, or who had grown up in families where the tradition was strong. This particular gruta is in the front yard of an El Paso home in a Hispanic neighborhood.

[11]From casual conversation that developed into much more, with a filling station attendant in Rio Grande City, Texas, during the summer of 1982.

[12]Donald Attwater, *The Avenel Dictionary of Saints* (New York: Avenel Books, 1979), pp. 65-66.

[13]Keith Crim, ed., *Abingdon Dictionary of Living Religions* (Nashville: Abingdon, 1981), p. 254.

[14]Richard Cardinal Cushing, *San Martín de Porres* (Boston: Daughters of St. Paul, 1962), pp. 14-15, 56-61.

[15]Gloria K. Giffords, *Mexican Folk Retablos* (Tucson: University of Arizona Press, 1971); Sue Olson, "Mexican Retablos," unpublished manuscript in the University of Texas at El Paso Folklore Archive, May 1978; R.L. Tolland, "Retablos: Mexican Icon-

ographic Folk Art," unpublished manuscript in the University of Texas at El Paso Folklore Archive [1972?].

[16]Johnnie Martínez, "El Rito Church: Where People Make the Difference," and Michael Miller, "Churches of Earth: A Heritage of Faith," *New Mexico* (February 1986): 18-25, 26-33.

[17]Marc Simmons, "Santos Remain Rich Part of Down-Home Culture," *El Paso Times,* 30 June 1985.

[18]E[lizabeth] Boyd, *Saints and Saint Makers of New Mexico* (Santa Fe: Laboratory of Anthropology, 1946), pp. 3-7; see also E[lizabeth] Boyd, *Popular Arts of Colonial New Mexico* (Santa Fe: Museum of International Folk Art, 1955) and E[lizabeth] Boyd, *The New Mexico Santero* (Santa Fe: Museum of New Mexico Press, 1969).

[19]Michael Earney and Jack Parsons, *Los Santeros,* 16mm sound and color film (Santa Fe: Blue Sky Productions, 1979). José E. Espinosa (*Saints in the Valleys* [Albuquerque: University of New Mexico Press, 1960]) discusses in detail retablos, santos, and the colonial art form of religious pictures painted on dried cowhides.

[20]Henry S. Parkes *(A History of Mexico,* 3rd. ed. [Boston: Houghton Mifflin, 1960], p. 363) notes that the Constitution of 1917 outlawed the holding of religious ceremonies outside of churches, a reflection of the anticlerical spirit of the Mexican Revolution. But the monuments themselves, whether on church or municipal property, apparently are permissible. I published a version of this section on grave art as "Folk Grave Decoration along the Rio Grande," in *Folk Art in Texas* (Dallas: Southern Methodist University Press, 1985), PTFS 45:46-51. Reproduced here with the permission of the editor, Francis E. Abernethy.

[21]For a striking graveyard collection especially of wooden crosses, see *Camposantos* (Fort Worth: Amon Carter Museum of Western Art, 1966), with photos by Dorothy Benrimo, commentary by Rebecca Salsbury James, and historical notes by E[lizabeth] Boyd.

[22]From a letter of Cleofas Calleros, Catholic historian of El Paso, to Miss Kay Harris, dated 11 October 1970, in the El Paso Public Library.

[23]Estevan Arrellano, "Descansos," *New Mexico* (February 1986): 42.

[24]Arrellano, p. 42.

[25]"Las Cruces," *New Mexico Place Names: A Geographical Dictionary,* comp. and ed. T.M. Pearce, Ina Sizer Cassidy, and Helen S. Pearce (Albuquerque: University of New Mexico Press, 1965), pp. 84-85.

[26]Jacquelyn Spier, "El Paso Murals," *Folk Art in Texas* (Dallas: Southern Methodist University Press, 1985), PTFS 45:65.

[27]Carol Carlisle, "Murals of South El Paso," unpublished manuscript in the University of Texas at El Paso Folklore Archive, May 1982, p. 3.

[28]Luis E. Guzmán, "Chicano Muralism in El Paso," unpublished manuscript in the UTEP Folklore Archive, August 1984.

[29]Bill Gradante, "Art Among the Low Riders," *Folk Art in Texas,* p. 73.

[30]Eduardo Ray Rodríguez, "Lowriders—Folk Art," unpublished manuscript in the UTEP Folklore Archive, August 1985, p. 5.

[31]Gradante, pp. 75-76.

[32]Gradante, pp. 76-77.

[33]Rodríguez, p. 6.

[34]Interview with Art Franco by Eduardo Ray Rodríguez, 12 August 1985. Franco has been low riding for fourteen years.

[35]Interview with Benny Ramos by Eduardo Ray Rodríguez, 13 August 1985.

[36]Pat Jasper and Kay Turner, *Art Among Us/Arte Entre Nosotros: Mexican American Folk Art of San Antonio* (San Antonio: San Antonio Museum Association, 1986).

Chapter 15. Popurrí (A Little of Everything)

[1]Sylvia Ann Grider, "Con Safos: Mexican-Americans, Names and Graffiti," *Journal of American Folklore* 88.348 (April-June 1975): 133.

[2]Grider (p. 133), citing Herbert Kohl and James Hinton, "Names, Graffiti and Culture," *Rappin' and Stylin' Out,* ed. Thomas Kochman (Urbana: University of Illinois Press, 1972), pp. 109-33.

[3]Grider, pp. 133-35, citing Haldeen Braddy, "The Pachucos and Their Argot," *Southern Folklore Quarterly* 24 (1960): 255-71, and Lurline Coltharp, *The Tongue of the Tirilones: A Linguistic Study of Criminal Argot* (University, Ala.: University of Alabama Press, 1965).

[4]Grider, pp. 136-37.

[5]Jan Harold Brunvand, *The Study of American Folklore,* 3rd ed. (New York: Norton, 1986), pp. 368, 371, 376, citing an item from the Korean War in Captain Harold E. Fischer, Jr.'s "My Case as a Prisoner Was Different," *Life* (27 June 1955), pp. 147-60.

[6]Interview with a friend who wished to remain anonymous, 16 January 1988.

[7]Interview with an anonymous lady, 5 December 1987.

[8]Joe S. Graham, "Tradition and the Candelilla Wax Industry," *Some Still Do: Essays on Texas Customs* (Austin: Encino Press, 1975), PTFS 39:39.

[9]Graham, p. 39.

[10]Joe S. Graham, "Mexican-American Lime Kilns in West Texas: The Limits of Folk Technology," *Hoein' the Short Rows* (Dallas: Southern Methodist University Press, 1987), PTFS 47:72-91, presents both the history and the process of lime-making, as well as describing its many uses.

[11]C.L. Sonnichsen, *The Mescalero Apaches* (Norman: University of Oklahoma Press, 1958), pp. 16-19. Dr. Sonnichsen says (pp. 17-18) that the Mescaleros roasted the heart of the maguey for food. Mexicans have done so for many decades; see Frances Toor, *A Treasury of Mexican Folkways* (New York: Crown, 1947; rpt. New York: Bonanza Books, 1985), pp. 14-18.

[12]Interview with Carlos Sarmiento Luna, a knowledgeable tour bus driver for Golden Lines, in Socorro, Texas, October 1987.

[13]In a telephone interview on 16 December 1988, Joe S. Graham told me that health authorities now require that asadero be prepared with rennet to curdle the milk.

[14]Interview with bio-scientist Charles Edward Freeman of the UT El Paso faculty, September 1987.

[15]Telephone interview with a Mr. Licón, the son of the founder of the Licón Dairy of Socorro, Texas, in September 1987. The dairy began making asaderos with the folk process, using trompillo, over 30 years ago, but has had to switch to rennet; their asadero is such a popular item with their customers that they usually run out of stock shortly after noon each day. Some commercial producers of asadero cheese make it in "wheels" about fifteen inches in diameter and four inches deep — but the folk usually make (and prefer) the smaller variety.

Motif and Tale Type Index

Motif Numbers in the following list are taken from Stith Thompson, *Motif Index of Folk Literature,* 6 vols., revised (Bloomington: Indiana University Press, 1955). Tale Type Numbers are taken from Stith Thompson, *The Types of the Folktale* (Helsinki: Suomalainen Tiedeakatemia Academia Scientiarum Fennica, 1961).

The Indexes were prepared by Jacquée Keller.

Motif Index

Motif No.		Page No.
J426.2.	Snake wants to eat frog (rabbit) friend	91
J512.	Animal cannot change his nature	91
J1050.	Attention to warnings	99
J1116.	Foolish person becomes clever	99
J1750.	One thing mistaken for another	106
J1786.	Man thought to be the devil	73, 74
J1791.3	Diving for cheese	90
J1800.	One thing mistaken for another — misc.	106
J1802.	Words in foreign language thought to be insults	105
J1802ff.	Words misunderstood	105-6
J1805.	Other misunderstandings of words	105-6
J1810.	Physical phenomena misunderstood	106
J1813.4.	Boiling pot on floor thought to be self-cooking	107
J1820.	Inappropriate action from misunderstanding	105-6
J1902.	Absurd ignorance concerning the hatching of eggs	106
J1930.	Absurd disregard for natural facts	106
J1937.	Absurd ideas about the dead	106
J2022.	Numbskull cannot find ass he's sitting on	110
	K. Deceptions	
K131.1.	Rabbit sold as letter carrier	95-96
K249.3	Pseudo-magic money-dropping ass	112
K710.	Victim enticed into voluntary captivity or helplessness	108, 112
K815.6	Snake promises to do no harm to frog (rabbit)	91
K1932.	Imposters claim reward earned by hero	103
K2010ff.	Attack on hare by hypocrite who pretends friendship	91
	L. Reversal of Fortune	
L210.	Modest choice best	100
	M. Ordaining the Future	
M101.3	Death as penalty for broken oath	94
M201.1.	Covenant of blood	98
M210.	Bargain with the devil	102-3
	N. Chance and Fate	
N135.2.1.	Discovery of treasure brings good luck	78
N576.	Ghosts prevent men from raising treasure	87
	P. Society	
P251.	Brothers	97, 106
	Q. Rewards and Punishments	
Q10.	Deeds rewarded	98, 100, 103, 104, 105

Motif No.		Page No.
Q40.	Kindness rewarded	
Q140.	Miraculous/magic rewards	98, 100, 103
Q411ff.	Death as penalty or punishment	94
Q503.	Wandering after death as punishment	76, 77
	S. Unnatural Cruelty	
S100	Revolting murders or mutilations	84, 85
S160.	Mutilations	84
S180.	Wounding or torturing	84
S300.	Abandoned or murdered children	75, 76, 77
S330.	Circumstances of murder or exposure of children	75, 76, 77
	T. Sex	
T81.2.1.	Scorned lover kills self	76
T89.	Tragic love — miscellaneous motifs	75, 76, 79
T91.7.2.	Falling in love with someone of a different caste	75
T93.3.	Disappointed lover kills self	75, 76
T102.	Returning hero marries first love	100
	V. Religion	
V67.3.	Treasure buried with dead	78, 87
V111.3.	Place where church must be built miraculously indicated	68, 71
V113.	Shrines	71
V127.	Image of deity in wood	68-69
V134.	Sacred wells	70
V134.2.	Offerings to holy wells	70
V141.	Possession of relic brings prosperity, its loss, sickness	69
V144.	Belief in miraculous powers of sacred relics	69
V143.2.	Images (relics) carried away return to their original church	69, 71
V263.	Portrait of Virgin appears to devotee	68
V265.	Virgin miraculously prevents nun from leaving church	73
V410ff.	Charity rewarded	101
V433.	Charity of the saints	71
	W. Traits of Character	
W11.14.	Youngest brother shares wealth with older ones	99
	X. Humor	
X910.	Lie: the remarkable man	113
	Z. Miscellaneous Groups of Motifs	
Z32.3.	Little ant finds a penny	91
Z47.	Series of trick exchanges	95-96, 96-97

Index of Tale Types

Type No.		Page No.
316	Eagle's feather transforms man	104
465	Hero accomplishes task with help of the devil	102-3
471	Hills (mountains) strike one another, red river, youths refuse to cross river of blood, moment is actually 100 years, advice rather than money taken as reward	97-99
480	Kind and unkind girls (boys)	
506	Dead man demands half of child	100
612	Pact with Death	94
650	Catorce	103-4
653A	Magic conveyance takes brother to princess	100
670	A man learns animal languages. His wife wants to learn his secret. The advice of the cock	93
	(Religious Tales)	
828	Man and animals readjust life span	93
	(Romantic Tales)	
938	Wife of officer killed by ship captain	76-77
980	Boy wants to cut blanket in half to cover his father and grandfather	95
910B	Counsels profit man	99
	(Tales of the Stupid Ogre)	
1004	Tails (ears) cut from hogs and stuck in mud	107
1013	Bathing or warming grandmother	106
1062	In a contest in throwing, the ogre (giant) throws a stone, the hero a bird	108
1085	Pushing a hole into a tree	107
	III. JOKES AND ANECDOTES	
	(Numbskull Stories)	
1218	Numbskull sits on eggs to finish hatching them	106
	(Stories About a Man)	
1535	Rich and poor peasant	95-96
1539A	Rabbit sold as letter carrier	95
1539B	Cap that pays all	96-97
1539C	Tree (bush) that produces money	107
1539D	The self-cooking pot	107
1539E	The gold-dropping ass	92, 112
1587	Man allowed to pick out tree to hang from, chooses tree with weak trunk	108
1699	Misunderstanding because of ignorance of foreign language	105

Ballad Index

The standard references on American folk balladry are primarily oriented towards Anglo-American songs and have little to do with Mexican-American items. For that reason the following references are used here: Arthur L. Campa, *Spanish Folk-Poetry in New Mexico* (Albuquerque: University of New Mexico Press, 1946); Américo Paredes, *A Texas-Mexican Cancionero: Folk-songs of the Lower Border* (Urbana: University of Illinois Press, 1976); and John Donald Robb, *Hispanic Folk Music of New Mexico and the Southwest: A Self-Portrait of a People* (Norman: University of Oklahoma Press, 1980).

This Index was prepared by W.K. McNeil.

"La Ciudad de Jauja"
Campa, 49-50
Paredes 2, 9-11
Robb D-14, 337-38

"Delgadina"
Campa, 30-33
Paredes 5, 14-16
Robb A2a-j, 31-43

"Corrido de Heraclio Bernal"

"Tragedia de Remigio Treviño"

"La Cucaracha"
Robb, 6, 200 (mentioned only)

"Adelita"

"Las Mañanitas de San Juan"
Robb C61, 271 ("Las Mañanitas" only)

"Las Posadas"
Paredes 42, 118-19

"Los Aguinaldos"
Paredes 42, 118-19

"Señora Santa Ana"
Paredes 43, 119-20

"Rosita Alvírez"
Robb B-19, 125-28

"Coplas del Payo"

"El Abandonado"
Robb C22, 225-26

"El Rancho Grande"
Robb X51, 818

"Dos Reales"
Robb D27, 353-54

"Los Diez Perritos"
Robb, 14 (mentioned only)

"El Crudo"
Paredes 59, 149-50

"Bonita Está Tierra"
Paredes 60, 161-62

"El Corrido de Kansas"

"Corrido a Sierra Blanca"

General Index

JOHN O. WEST, born in El Paso in 1925, received his B.A. from Mississippi College, his M.A. from Texas Tech, and his Ph.D. from the University of Texas. He is currently professor of English at the University of Texas at El Paso. The founder and first editor of the American Folklore Society's *American Folklore Newsletter,* he is the author of *Tom Lea: Artist in Two Mediums* as well as numerous articles on other aspects of the culture of the American Southwest.

W.K. McNEIL, General Editor of the American Folklore Series, is the folklorist at the Ozark Folk Center at Mountain View, Arkansas. He has written many studies in American folklore and has edited two anthologies. McNeil holds a Ph.D. in Folklore from Indiana University.